CANON LAW SOCIETY
OF AMERICA

PROCEEDINGS OF THE FORTY-NINTH ANNUAL CONVENTION

NASHVILLE, TENNESSEE
OCTOBER 12-15, 1987

Canon Law Society of America
Washington, DC 20064

© Copyright 1988 by Canon Law Society of America

ISBN 0-943616-39-5

SAN 237-6296

TABLE OF CONTENTS

ADDRESSES

Diocesan Synods
    Ann Rehrauer 1
The Personal Power of Governance of the Diocesan Bishop
    Julian Herranz 16

SEMINARS

Instituted Lay Ministries: the History and Future of Canon 230
    Thomas Richstatter 35
Ecumenical Questions in the New Code
    Royce R. Thomas 45
NCCB Implementation of the Code
    Donald E. Heintschel 61
Lay Persons in the Diocesan Curia: Legal Structures and Practical Issues
    Rosemary Smith 67
The Permanent Diaconate: A Commentary on Its Development from the End of the Second Vatican Council to the 1983 *Codex Iuris Canonici*
    Richard J. Lyons 77
CLSA Scholarship Fund: A Hearing 101
Deference or Neutral Principles: The Dual Approach by Civil Courts to Ecclesiastical Disputes
    Peter M. Shannon 105
Canon 1098 of the Revised Code of Canon Law: Key Points and Questions in Its Historical Development and Interpretation
    Kevin W. Vann 115
Secular Institutes: Can They be Both Clerical and Lay?
    Sharon Holland 135
Issues in Sacred Orders
    David M. Hynous 145
Religious Issues of Dissolutions, Mergers, Aggregation
    Ellen O'Hara 155
Canonical and Civil Liability for Lay Ministries
    Melanie DiPietro 169
The Economic Pastoral: Foundation in the Church's Mission; Challenge for the Church's Life
    John J. Myers 187

Presbyteral Councils and Colleges of Consultors: Current Law
and Some Diocesan Statutes
  James H. Provost 194
Synodal Governance in Eastern Catholic Churches
  John D. Faris 212
Clerical Misconduct: Canonical and Practical Consequences
  John G. Proctor, Jr. 227

Officers' Report

President
  Richard G. Cunningham 245
Treasurer
  Royce R. Thomas 255
Executive Coordinator
  Edward G. Pfnausch 260

Committee Reports

Membership and Nominations 264
Professional Responsibility 265
Research and Discussion 266
Resolutions 267
Advisory Opinions 268
Eastern Canon Law and Interritual Matters 269
Religious Affairs 270
Roman Replies 270
Women in the Church 271
Apostolic Visitation and the Limitation of Powers of a
 Diocesan Bishop 272
Civil and Canon Law 273
Continuation of *Canon Law Digest* 273
Joint Committee on "Doctrinal Responsibilities" 274
Joint Committee on the *Imprimatur* 275
On Liturgies 275
Marriage Research 275
Permanent Seminar: Protection of Rights in the Church 280
CLSA Scholarship Criteria 280
Selection of Bishops 282
Study of Procedures for the Protection of Rights of Persons
 in the Church 282
Symposium on Lay Ministry 283

Task Force to Study the Procedures of the Congregation of
    the Doctrine of Faith 288
Task Force on the Scholarship Fund 289
Task Force to Survey Due Process Experience 291
Tribunal Statistics 1986 297
Canonical Standards in Labor-Management Relations:
    A Report 311
Observations on the 1986 *Schema Codicis Iuris
    Canonici Orientalis* 336

BUSINESS MEETING

Minutes 360

MISCELLANEA

Citation for the Role of Law Award
    Richard G. Cunningham 375
Response to the Role of Law Award
    James A. Coriden 377
Homily, October 14, 1987
    Richard G. Cunningham 382
Contributors to *Proceedings* 384

THE DIOCESAN SYNOD

Ann F. Rehrauer, OSF

"We the People of the United States, in order to form a more perfect union, establish justice, insure domestic tranquility, provide for the common defense, promote the general welfare, and secure the blessing of liberty to ourselves and our posterity, do ordain and establish this Constitution for the United States of America." This year we celebrate the 200th anniversary of the drafting and ratification of the fundamental legislative document for our nation. As Americans we have been called to reflect upon the freedoms we enjoy because of the vision of the drafters of that document. I would propose that the process of drafting the Constitution is both similar to and different from the diocesan synod.

The United States Constitution is the result of previous legislation which failed to meet the needs of the 13 colonies. In light of the experience of powerlessness and poor organization under the Articles of Confederation, the early leaders of our country sought to create something better. On the journey from 13 colonies to a nation and then to the status of a world power, our forebearers needed to assess where they had been and where they wanted to be. Then they designed a document and procedures that would, they hoped, enable them to travel toward that desired future. In that design, Benjamin Franklin and the representatives drew on the experience of the Iroquois nation as well as the history of British legal practice to develop a system that protected the values they espoused.

The Constitution was a compromise document—balancing the creative tension between central authority and local autonomy; a document that attempted to meet the needs of the individual states—large and small—and yet preserve a vital relationship with the central or more universal structure of the composite. In the formulation of the Constitution those early patriots attempted to define and celebrate the basic reality that we call the United States of America.

As a legislative document, the Constitution is the result of a consultative and a representative process. It was achieved only after months of work, consultation, discussion, the sharing of lived experience, revisions, and the attempt of good people to provide a vision and a structure to meet the needs of a developing nation. And part of the document's genius was the process of amendment and expansion, providing the ability to grow as the nation grew.

The Constitutional Congress was called and the members attending received a mandate from their respective states. As the work of the Congress progressed, the positions of individual states and regional polarities yielded to the broader vision achieved by consensus, sacrifice, and compromise. The Constitutional Congress was more than an academic exercise, for the members had committed themselves to create a document by which they would live and govern their lives.

Canon 462 describes the diocesan synod as a representative gathering of the laity, clergy, and religious with the diocesan bishop. Such a gathering is consultative rather than legislative, and the law is very clear that the sole legislator in the synod is the diocesan bishop.

The diocesan synod will gather members from various parishes and areas of the diocese. The needs of many may be similar, but there will be differences and members will come with a special parochial sensitivity. These must give way to the common good if the synod body is to fashion a vision and pastoral plan reflective of the diversity and the unity of the local Church. There is the commitment of synod members to create pastoral priorities and legislative documents by which they will govern their life as a local Church.

The documents of a diocesan synod will result from an analysis of previous policies and legislation that need revision, particularly in light of the new Code of Canon Law. The synod assembly will consider the universal law (or central authority, if you will) and particularize it for the local Church, looking to the needs of God's people in the present and as they walk to the future. The preparation, the process, and the synod assembly will be opportunities to express and celebrate the identity and nature of the local Church and the gifts of the members who create that faith community. As the Code of Canon Law envisions the diocesan synod, it is a body that is representative and a process that is consultative.

We know only too well and have been reminded recently that the Catholic Church is not a democracy. That is both a blessing and a difficulty for members of the Church in America. The gift of a hierarchical structure that does not depend upon the will the majority can insure that the prophetic message of the Gospel will not be subjected to the interpretation and the whim of popular morality or the comfort level of the mediocre. However, as Americans we are steeped in a tradition that believes that the power to rule derives from the consent of the governed. While this may be true in the political arena, it is not the case in the Roman Catholic Church or its entities.

The power to govern in the Church derives from the legitimate holding of office. Authority in the Church is designated as well as charismatic. The power of the Spirit—the power of wisdom and insight, the power of knowledge and understanding, the power of courage, of holiness, and of reverence for God—comes as gift, not only to those who hold office but in virtue of baptism, to other members of the people of God.

The final legislative determination in the diocesan synod rests with the legislator—the diocesan bishop. The parameters of the proposed legislation from the synod assembly are the provisions of universal law. Unlike the Constitutional Convention, the diocesan synod works within the limitations of another and higher law.

The term synod comes from two Greek words *(syn hodos)* that mean "with (someone) and road." A synod as an assembly and as a process reflects the life of a community traveling together upon the same road. Because of shared interests and a similar vision of a future destination, members of a local church take the time to pause and view their past progress, their future goals, and the vehicles they are utilizing to achieve those goals. This experience of church is consonant with one of the images of church from the Second Vatican Council. The Church is indeed a sheepfold, a tract of land to be cultivated, an edifice of God. But it is, as well, a pilgrim people, journeying in a foreign land. (LG 6) As pilgrims, we travel, conscious that we have no lasting city here and no security save in the Lord who walks with us. And in the face of such a task, we do not fear, for "the People of God believes that it is led by the Spirit of the Lord who fills the earth. Motivated by this faith it labors to decipher authentic signs of God's presence and purpose in the happenings, needs, and desires in which this People has a part along with others of our age." (GS 11)

It is not my purpose to provide you with an extensive historical survey of the diocesan synod. Father James Coriden has already done that in an admirable piece of research in the 1974 *Jurist*.[1] I would direct your attention to that article for further reference and insights. I will merely highlight some of the aspects of the history that can, I believe, provide some insight into the nature and purpose of the synod.

Father Coriden begins his survey of the history by stating that the practice of the diocesan synod is probably rooted in two ancient practices—the gathering of the presbyterium with the bishop to share in the governance of the diocese, and the gathering of bishops of an area to address issues of common concern—the meeting of the provincial council. When every town had its bishop, the local clergy were naturally in close contact with the bishop and with each other. As the Christian community grew, particularly in the rural areas, clergy meetings were called to facilitate that sense of the unity of ministry and to communicate necessary changes and legislation.

In each case the gathering was that of the clergy—the priests with their bishop or the bishops, called together by the metropolitan. The agenda for these meetings seem to have been issues of concern in the local church and the fostering of good governance.

While there is some indication of the occurrence of a diocesan synod in Rome in the fourth century, we find the more reliable evidence from sixth century Europe in Auxerre, France, between 561 and 605.[2]

One of the provisions of that synod prescribed that all priests were to attend the synod in mid-May and all abbots were to convene for a council on November 1st, indicating the frequency of meeting and the existence of a regular gathering.

From that period on we find evidence of synodal legislation during the Carolingian period (8th to 10th century) and the Gregorian Reform (11-12th century). In some cases the synod meeting was an occasion for the bishop to give a financial accounting of his administration. For many it was the official occasion for the provincial council decrees to be promulgated.

The first formal universal legislation concerning a diocesan synod was enacted

---

[1] Cf. James A. Coriden, "The Diocesan Synod. An Instrument of Renewal for the Local Church" in *The Jurist* 34 (1974): 68-93.
[2] *Ibid.*, 71.

by the Fourth Lateran Council (1215). The Council mandated that a diocesan synod be celebrated every year to facilitate the publication and observance of the disciplinary actions of the annual provincial councils. The Fifth Lateran Council (1515) reiterated the previous legislation.

During the 24th and 25th sessions of the Council of Trent, there was discussion about the diocesan synod and its special function. The Council restated the traditional practice of the annual meeting and designated specific functions to that gathering: the review and acceptance of the statutes of the Council, the profession of obedience to the Pope, the appointment of synodal judges and examiners, and the adjustment of Mass stipends as needed.[3]

In 1748 Pope Benedict XIV completed his work on the diocesan synod *(De Synodo Dioecesana)*. In that work he described the synod as

> a legitimate gathering convoked by the bishop of priests and clergy of the diocese and others who must attend in which those matters relative to pastoral care were to be discussed and acted upon.

He also listed possible topics for discussion:

> public prayers, allocutions, sermons, decrees to be read and profession of faith, the election of synodal judges and examiners and the appointment of diocesan officials, the review of cases reserved for atrocius crimes, discussion of the cathedraticum, stole fees, and taxes to be determined, aims for Mass stipends and abuses about stipends, the time for rendering an account of the seminary.[4]

At least in Benedict's mind, the synod was not merely meant to repeat the general law of the Church or to communicate the decisions of other gatherings, but it was also an occasion to develop the law and apply it to local circumstances.

In the 1917 Code of Canon Law, canons 356-362 deal with the diocesan synod. The interval between synodal sessions was lengthened from 1 to 10 years; the synod's purpose was broadened to include action on matters that were useful and necessary for the diocese. The bishop was to convoke and preside over the synod. The vicar general could preside at a session, but only by mandate of the bishop. There were requirements for those who were obliged to be called and to attend, and there was the option for the bishop to call others as well. All the members of the synod had a right to a consultative vote (unless the invitation specified otherwise), but it was clear that the bishop was the sole legislator.

In Canon 360 of the 1917 Code, preparatory commissions for the synod were recommended but not mandated. Schemata were to be sent to the members before the sessions (presumably for study), and free discussion was to occur at the preparatory sessions and the final assembly (CIC 361).

As to the time and place, the Code only prescribed that the assembly meeting

---

[3] Sess. XXIV, de reformatione, c. 18 in *Conciliorum Oecumenicorum Decreta*, ed. Alberigo, Dossetti, Joannou, Leonardi, et Prodi. Bologna: Instituto per le Scienze Religiose, 1973. cf. pp. 746-7; Sess. XXV, de reformatione, cc. 2, 10, 18 in *COD:* 761-767.

[4] Charles Augustine, *A Commentary on Canon Law*. St. Louis: B. Herder Book Co, 1923. Vol. II: 386.

be in the cathedral unless there was good reason to hold the sessions elsewhere (CIC 357). If members were not able to attend the sessions, they could not send a proxy, but they were to inform the bishop of the reasons for their absence (CIC 359).

Canon 385 of the 1917 Code enumerated the specific people who were to be called to the synod:

> the vicar general, the canons of cathedral or consultors, the rector of major seminary, the deans of vicars forane, one deputy from each collegiate church chosen by the chapter, the pastors of city where the synod is held, one pastor from each deanery elected by those with pastoral care, abbots who were actual superiors of abbeys, and one superior of each clerical religious organization.

From the promulgation of the 1917 Code until Vatican II, diocesan synods were held throughout the Church, but sporadically. Some dioceses followed the law consistently and held them every ten years. Others held them infrequently. Some bishops found that other vehicles, such as diocesan statutes, better met their purposes.

In 1959, Pope John XXIII issued a pastoral letter to the faithful of Rome, calling them to a diocesan synod. In that letter he stated: "The synod is a reunion of the bishop with his priests to study the problems and the spiritual life of the faithful, to give a new vigor to ecclesiastical laws, correct abuses, promote the Christian life, stimulate divine worship and the practice of religion."[5]

During the Council there was some discussion of various consultative bodies and gatherings, but the only mention we find of the diocesan synod in the Council documents is the provision in chapter II of *Christus Dominus*.

Article #36 referred to synods, provincial councils, and plenary councils, describing them as occasions when bishops legislated a common program to be followed for teaching truths of the faith and for ordering ecclesiastical discipline. It was the earnest desire of the Council that synods and councils "flourish with vigor." In that case, "faith will be spread and discipline preserved more fittingly and effectively in the various churches as the circumstances of the times require."[6]

The *Directory of the Pastoral Ministry of Bishops*, issued by the Congregation for Bishops on May 31, 1973, discussed the nature of the bishop's exercise of episcopal authority. In article #34 the bishop was admonished to be careful to respect the legitimate liberty of the faithful to think differently. In various questions he is to do his best to consult everyone concerned; and as far as charity and justice permit, not withhold full and accurate information from those who ask for it. He is to foster discussions among faithful of different conditions and of different ages; but the principle is to be kept clear: "When determining pro-

---

[5] John XXIII, "Lettre de Sa Saintete au people romain." *La Documentation Catholique* 56 (15 mars 1959): 329-332.

[6] *Christus Dominus*, #36 in *The Documents of Vatican II*, ed. Walter M. Abbott, S.J. New York: America Press, 1966: 424.

grams of pastoral action and ways to accomplish them, the decision—after suggestions have been heard and examined—belongs to the bishop who, according to the seriousness of the matter and his own prudent judgment, will make the decision either alone or collegially."[7]

Chapter VI of the *Directory* deals specifically with the bishop and the diocesan synod. Article 162 considers synods and pastoral visitation to be matters of extraordinary importance in the ministry of the bishop. "It will cost the bishop long hours of careful labor to prepare for, organize and accomplish these two charges of his ministry using the methods which the new needs of today's Church demands."[8] I would suggest that more than the bishop will be asked to devote long hours to the process.

Article 163 describes the nature of the diocesan synod:
> it is convoked and moderated by bishop, clergy, religious, and laity are summoned, it is an assembly in which the bishop, with the help of experts in theology, pastoral and law, drawing upon the advice of the diocesan community's various associations, officially fulfills his function and ministry of feeding the flock entrusted to him by adapting the laws and norms of the universal church to local conditions, by pointing out the policy and program of apostolic work in the diocese, by resolving problems encountered in the apostolate and administration, by giving impetus to projects and undertakings and by correcting errors in doctrine and morals if any have crept in.

The synod also offers an occasion for some sacred celebrations which do very much to arouse or renew faith, piety, and aposolic zeal throughout the diocese.[9]

The issue of preparation was addressed in article #164:
> The synod needs careful preparation, an organizing of the topics to be treated, the arousing of public opinion and consciences, preparatory commissions comprised of clergy, religious, and laity who meet to study the questions;
>
> Considerations from the standpoint of theology, canon law, liturgy, social charitable action, the spiritual life;
>
> The bishop considers all items with the priest's council and (if he wishes, with the diocesan pastoral council) and "sifts it all out for presentation to the entire synod.[10]
>
> Everywhere in diocese, there should be communication and abundant exchange, sermons on the synod and its importance as well as the questions that will be handled by the synod.
>
> During entire preparatory period, the bishop is to call the entire

---

[7] The Sacred Congregation for Bishops, *Directory on the Pastoral Ministry of Bishops*. English translation prepared by the Benedictine monks of the Seminary of Christ the King, Mission, B.C. Ottawa: Publications Service of the Canadian Catholic Conference, 1974: 22-23.

[8] *Ibid.*, 83.

[9] *Ibid.*, 82-83.

[10] *Ibid.*, 83.

diocese to earnest prayer to God.

Article #165 deals with the centrality of the Eucharist, discussion and study, the work of the members, and full freedom to express their opinions.

The bishop draws up the conclusions of the synod from the combined opinions of the commissions and assembly sessions. It is he who defines the juridical force of the orders and decrees and he promulgates and sets the time for them to take effect.

The schemata for the Revised Code included provisions for the addition of laity as members. The ten-year interval between synods was kept but there was also the allowance of greater discretion for the bishop—allowing for a longer interval but not beyond 20 years.

The proposed legislation broadened the scope of the synod to give it a more positive pastoral character and make it a more representative structure of the people of God in advising the bishop.

The key differences between the legislation of the 1917 Code and that of the 1983 Code seems to lie in the membership and the method for proceeding:

WHAT IS IT:

Canon 460 of the 1983 Code provides a general definition and description of the diocesan synod:
>A synod is a group of selected priests and other Christian faithful of a particular church
>—which offers assistance to the diocesan bishop
>—for the good of the entire diocesan community
>—according to the norm of the following canons.

WHO CONVOKES IT:

Before a bishop calls a diocesan synod (in this day and age) he is to consult with the presbyteral council. At the time of the 1917 Code there was no such body. Now the role of the presbyteral council in the consultative process and the areas of diocesan governance is evident.

The consultors or the chapter of canons did not fulfill the same kind of role, and there was no suggestion in the 1917 Code that the bishop consult those bodies.

The bishop is not bound to follow the advice of the council, but if there were consensus he would be remiss if he failed to follow it unless there were prevailing reasons. Besides respecting the wisdom of the presbyterate and its relationship to him, the bishop will probably follow the advice because he needs the cooperation and enthusiasm of the presbyterate to insure an effective celebration.

(c. 462, §1) With the new Code, ONLY the diocesan bishop has the right to convoke the synod and - only after he takes canonical possession of the diocese.

TIME AND FREQUENCY:

The 1917 Code directed that a synod be held every 10 years. The schemata stated it be held every 10 years but allowed up to a 20 year interval. There is no suggested or mandated time frame in the new law. It is celebrated when the bishop judges that the circumstances warrant it and after having consulted with the presbyteral council.

PLACE:

CIC 357, §2 provided that the synod be held in the cathedral church unless there was good reason to hold it elsewhere.

In the 1983 Code there is no mention of place. However, the new ceremonial of bishops presumes that the cathedral is the usual place.

MEMBERSHIP:

Before 1917 there were no distinctions among the clerics who were to attend. Every priest within the jurisdiction was bound to come if he had the care of souls. (Religious were an exception.)

With the 1917 Code there was a change: Now there were representative groupings of clergy and representatives were called to the synod. The 1983 Code broadens that representation to include laity and even permits non-Catholic observers.

In both the 1917 and the 1983 Codes there is a list of those obliged to be called, to attend, and with the right to vote.
- —Coadjutor and auxiliary bishops—new in the 1983 Code by their status
- —vicar general - 1917 and the 1983 Code
- —episcopal vicars - didn't exist before 1983 Code
- —judicial vicar - 1983 Code, not in the 1917 Code

These additions to the various vicars came because the vicars share extensively in the power of the bishop.
- —the chapter of canons - 1917 Code, or if there were no canons, the consultors were called (CIC 358, §1,2)
- —consultors - in the 1983 Code because of their role on the presbyteral council. If you have both canons and consultors, the 1983 Code says both may attend
- —other collegiate chapters had delegates in the 1917 Code—no longer
- —members of the presbyteral council
- —lay members of the faithful

—members of religious institutes

The pastoral council selects the religious and laity in a manner and number determined by the diocesan bishop.

- —rector of the major seminary
- —the vicars forane
- —one presbyter from each vicariate forane (chosen by all who have pastoral care)—and an alternate is chosen
- —others can be called (religious, clerics, lay)
- —if bishop judges opportune he can also call observers from other churches and communities

LEGISLATOR:

Canon 465 states that the bishop is the sole legislator; remaining members possess only a consultative vote. He alone signs the synodal declarations and decrees and they are published only through his authority. There is no change in this aspect.

In common parlance, the diocesan synod has come to mean a time and process of *walking together*. Both elements are important. It is a *time* and it is a *process*.

We have to give time and attention to the process nature of preparation, and consultation, but there must also be some concrete results of that consultative process. The education about the issues and the experience of discussion and working together is a valuable tool for understanding the meaning of community and hierarchy. Beyond the educational value, there is the concrete result that people expect. Will anything be different when all is said and done—or will more be said than is done?

A synod takes place in time and space. Each of us has a history and together we have a shared history. In the United States we are composed of various cultures and ideologies—not only the American democratic model, but with European and Asian, African and Latin American backgrounds that espouse other models of leadership and governance. We are also a Roman Catholic Church with a hierarchical form of governing. As we gather today and as a diocesan synod gathers, it will be comprised of people who are the product of the changes and renewal, the pain and the struggle, the movement and the resistance generated by the Second Vatican Council; We live in a time of instant communication and of authors with the power to sway the multitudes. This age places us at the mercy of and gives us the power of the mass media. Through the media an idea is broadcast before the sentence is entirely out of the person's mouth—and there is no time or occasion for revision. In the synod process we need to help people understand that "preliminary conclusions" or "drafts" of papers are just that—and that the major work of discussion and consensus is yet to come.

Synod as a process is messy. There is no clear blueprint to follow other than the broad outlines provided by the Code. It is the task of the bishop, the council, the coordinating committee, and anyone else involved to envision the final product and then design a process or processes that will bring about the desired end.

Synod as a process and as an event takes longer than we imagine because more folks are constantly coming on board—and our work spirals rather than proceeds in linear fashion.

There are several elements that the *Pastoral Manual for Bishops* and the experience of those who have participated in synods in the past few years would consider important:

PRAYER: The first is the importance of prayer, for in a diocesan synod the work must be God's work or it will remain much ado about nothing. It must be the basis for all the work, gatherings, planning, and activity. And the prayer must be integral to the process and integral to the lives of the participants. I speak of the difference between prayer and prayers. Otherwise it functions in the same manner as the logo or the directional signs. It is easy to get caught in the details of the process and the numbers and the work to be accomplished and difficult to remember that the work is not the result of our efforts alone.

OWNERSHIP: The building of ownership from the onset is critical. I noted earlier that the support of the presbyteral council and I would add of the clergy and laity, are vital. A synod is a representative gathering. It will reflect and hopefully give impetus to the life of the local church. I cannot represent your ideas unless you tell me what you think. A synod assembly cannot represent a local church and speak with the broadness of vision for that church unless the church shares its wisdom. In an era when priests in parishes, chanceries, tribunals, hospitals, and Newman Centers have more than enough to do, we must mobilize their interest and energy for "one more meeting"—one that will be far more demanding than others they attend. But one with the potential for much greater benefit. But unless we can convince them—the process doesn't have a chance.

It is also important to gain ownership from your diocesan agency personnel. They have worked consistently with people in parishes and have assessed needs and designed programs. If they believe that they know what the needs are—and that others really don't, there will be a problem of credibility with the synod's work.

We need to mobilize the laity as well. Their questions are similar and yet different. They too are asking "is it worth my time and energy?" But they add, "Will you really listen?" "Will what I say change things—or do you already have your mind made up?" But they are also saying, "Thank you for giving me an opportunity to shape the future of my church." If there is no commitment to the process and the product of the synod, then the results will remain published documents that sit on a shelf and never take on flesh.

REPRESENTATION AND AVOIDING POLARITIES: The training of synod delegates who are representatives is critical for the process. Unlike political candidates who run for a particular office and who woo the voters with promises and platforms, synod delegates are called to represent the local church. They may be drawn from a geographic area or a parish or a body, but they are called to represent the good of the local church. In discussion they are called to listen and to speak for the good of the church of Northeast Wisconsin or Western Montana, or the church of Harrisburg—rather than for the good of the presbyteral or pastoral council of a diocese. They need to believe that only when we provide for the good of the local church will the good of a particular group also be accomplished. Recently a midwestern Archbishop called on the synod delegates at the opening session of the synod to be the voice of those who have no voice—to speak and to listen with a concern broader than that with which they came.

In order to vision for a community, the synod delegates must surface and address two kinds of needs—what I would call the felt needs (at which we are particularly adept) and the learned needs. When we gather a body for consultation, we are as rich as the expertise and holiness of that group—and as poor as the narrowness of vision and the selfishness of that group. The protection of the bishop's right as sole legislator is not a medievel carryover to limit the base of power—it is the safeguard that enables the leader of the community (who may be a few steps ahead of the vision of the total body) to continue the challenge. It is the safeguard that enables him, who may have information (some of which cannot be shared) to challenge a decision of the group.

There is a risk in asking the people of God what their needs are. The needs they express and perceive may be very different from our perceptions and from the needs we may *want* to address. The process of education demands that we listen to the people's perceived needs and that we lead them to another level of understanding about needs as well. The same is true when we ask *whether* to address those needs and *how* to do this. They may come up with a different answer than we would give. And sometimes their touchstone for decision-making may be a dollar sign or the aversion to adding one more member to the diocesan bureaucracy. How do we deal with all of this—the rich diversity, the hours of education, the differences of opinion, and the frustration of a lack of consensus—respecting the integrity of the process, listening, and together making the best decision.

In drafting the documents and working with study commissions it is important to have a mixture of persons on the committee, and to provide access to information within the diocesan structure. If you have all diocesan personnel, there is a danger that the recommendations will merely guard the status quo. If you have no diocesan personnel on the commissions, the commissions may recommend what is already being accomplished, or fail to take cognizance of the important achievements and assessments that have already occurred.

PASTORAL AND LEGAL: One of the key questions as we begin the synod process is "what is the agenda?" What can and should the synod consider? "The joys and the hopes, the griefs and the anxieties of the people of this age, especially those who are poor or in any way afflicted, these too are the joys and hopes, the griefs and anxieties of the followers of Christ. Indeed nothing genuinely human fails to raise an echo in their hearts." (GS 1) Just as the principles for the revision of the Code called canonists to blend the pastoral and the juridic elements, so must there be the blending of the pastoral and vision elements with the legislative and the procedural. Often the lack of clarity about the latter is the source of strife at the parish or diocesan level. As we undertake a diocesan synod, will our agenda really address the pastoral needs, the personal faith struggles, and the pain of the people of God in our midst? If the occasion is merely a time to collect our policies and procedures—I suggest that there are more efficient ways to do that. If we seek to address the faith life of our local church includings its legislative needs—I would suggest that the synod is a primary opportunity.

SETTING THE AGENDA: Agenda items for the synod meeting can be determined in a variety of ways. A number of dioceses engaged in the synod process have begun with a survey to test the concerns and issues of interest for the "average Catholic." Others have used existing structures or divisions including the curial departments or the books of the Code. Others have used evaluation instruments already in use for pastoral planning in the diocese. Some have hired consultants to help plan the process. Others have drawn on their own personnel.

Dioceses have begun with preparatory commissions to provide background information and then allowed the process to move from parish, to the regional level and then to the diocesan wide discussions. Others have begun with issues that were raised and turned the organization of the material and the formulation of action statements over the preparatory commissions.

Again, as personnel who may be working in a directive or administrative capacity with the synod, it is important to note that specific agenda items may not surface automatically. If there is an issue that you or the bishop or a body considers of critical importance, there must be a vehicle for placing that on the agenda for study, discussion, or action. A certain amount of control of the agenda is needed to avoid unrealistic expectations or the embarrassment of the bishop and the disillusionment of the synod members. (Note, I emphasize CERTAIN AMOUNT of control.)

HONESTY AND PARAMETERS: Since many members of the church have never participated in a synod process (ourselves included) we need to educate the church about what the synod can and cannot do. It will be important as we move through the process to tell all the people and especially the synod delegates what the limits are. If things are off limits for discussion (women's ordination, clerical celibacy, the cathedraticum) we must say so up front and not raise unfounded hopes. People can deal with limits if we tell them the right way. They cannot deal with the promise of wide horizons and then the stifling of their most creative conclusions.

COST—PERSONAL AND MONETARY: There is cost involved in a diocesan synod. It is both personal and monetary. It is the first that we tend to underestimate and the first that is the most difficult to provide. Much of someone's time will be needed to provide advice, to listen to frustrations, sometimes to run interference, to clarify the task (whenever you have some clarity), to energize, to thank, to motivate, to monitor. This is a new endeavor—even if we have done it within the last 30 years. These folks have never done it—and they want answers we don't have and they need answers before we can give them. Our task is to help them learn to deal with the frustrations of the process, the ambiguity of their product, and the nature of the consultative process.

Somewhere in the process we need to address the meaning of "consultative" and at the same time to avoid the undue emphasis on the *merely consultative* nature of the synod. For some – "giving advice" means a mandate that is accomplished by casting a ballot. For others, "merely consultative" indicates that people speak and the legislator does whatever he pleases—and in fact, what he had decided to do before we ever had this listening session. The truth lies somewhere between the two. The nature of consultation protects both the rights of the local bishop and the wisdom shared by the people of God.

Having the freedom to legislate for the good of all allows the bishop to challenge the local church to the full meaning of the Gospel, to address the prejudices and narrow vision, to call forth a community hampered by the predominant philosphies of the time (such as materialism and individualism).

The participation of the group symbolizes the reality that the Spirit speaks through the community as well and gives gifts as God wills. Many times 500 heads are better than 1 committee.

The costs are not only time and energy—but money to do a diocesan synod. The finished product should reflect what we have invested. And Murphy's Law has a definite application here. It takes more time, more money, more paper, more research for fewer results than we had planned.

Things to consider: Someone who *directs the work* as his or her primary job;
Support staff to type, mail, duplicate, research, analyze;
Staff to *monitor the work* and catch problems before they multiply;
Planning time and lead time—to develop the process to organize the work; to analyze the data, to get materials, to research your issues.

ROLE OF CLERGY: If the priests of your diocese are like those in a number of places in the country, they have no time for another job or committee meeting; no interest in something from the 1930's; and the constant question is—how will this makes a difference? How do we model that we do in fact believe that the Spirit of God rests in the community, and not only those marked by orders or who work in diocesan offices? How will the synod process foster their own ministries and help them to order the ministries in the community? How do we model a church as servant, as community, as proclaimer, as community of disciples, as sacrament as well as an institution? It takes more time and energy to do it this way—involving the community, than it does to handle it alone. And sometimes we have to make decisions and carry them out without consultation. But the synod deals with issues where consultation is needed.

IMPLEMENTATION: When the process and the gathering is finished, how will we give life to the words we have spoken? Papers don't move people. Goals, plans, timelines, assigned responsibilities, objectives, and processes can—if those to whom they are directed buy into the results and the process by which the results were achieved. We need to translate from idea to reality and let people know WHO, BY WHEN, HOW and WHO checks up on it. Often our previous planning institutes failed at the implementation stage—because there was no formal design for this. And we need that—and we need it soon. If the structure of plan for implementation can be designed even before the session ends (knowing that things will be modified), people can have a deeper sense of commitment because they see the possibilities.

REALISM: We are often tempted in our planning to design the ideal. However, with a synod in the real church, we will be designing not the ideal but what I would call "the optimum." Given the limits of time, energy, money—what are the best possible solutions, programs, goals, we can devise for the next X number of years. And yet we need to allow the dream—to allow us to consider what we would do if things were different—if we had the money we needed—if people were ready. Meanwhile we live with "the best we can do for now." And this will not be the last synod we have, or the last consultative session, or the last word on the limited issues we treat. It is the best "for now."

As a methodology, however, I would suggest that we BEGIN WITH THE DREAM and then pare down to address the real: It is more effective to brainstorm and choose among the options, rather than designing one option based on restraints.

MIX AND MATCH: The synod discussion will be *easier* if we have people with the same vision of church and the same basic ideologies. BUT it will not necessarily be better. With a basic ecclesiology that is shared, a plurality of ideologies has to be present if the discussion, the needs assessment, and the proposed solutions are to represent the real church—rather than the one we wished were there.

SHARE WHAT WE HAVE LEARNED: In working on our own diocesan synod, I have found that anyone who has gone through the experience or is now going through it is most willing to share ideas, and experiences. There is no need to re-invent the wheel. Each of us will do it a little differently, but there are things we have all learned along the way that could help someone else, especially if we are humble enough and objective enough to share the missteps as well as the success stories.

BLUEPRINT: Earlier I mentioned that dioceses are using a variety of processes. No one is the best one. We need to decide on the kind of building we want, and then design the blueprint. Decide on the kind of meeting and documents we want—and then design the process to achieve it.

MAINTENANCE: In the dreaming stage, people tend to look at new possibilities and unmet needs and forget that the good things that have occurred must also be maintained. Also—and it is part of any bureaucracy—there must be sunset clauses. Is there any program, department, agency, body that has outlived its usefulness—or should be working itself into obsolescence? Only an outside yet knowledgeable enough body can help make that determination. Recommendations and goals need to affirm what has been good and what must be kept as well as addressing what is not yet accomplished.

PUBLICITY: We need to tell our story—and we need to tell it in a variety of ways. One of the opportunities that the synod offers is the occasion to speak about the structure of the diocese and to do so with the folks in the pew. It is also necessary since people can't even spell synod, much less envision what it is, to communicate constantly and in a developmental fashion—to use every occasion, to say and say again what it is we are about, and what our hopes are for the synod and the church. Use of bulletin inserts, the diocesan paper, video presentations, personal ambassadors, TV and radio spots all help to get the message across.

The diocesan synod is a time of possibility. It enables us to gather as a community and to share in its wisdom. It is a call to be church in dialogue, in planning, in prayer, and in celebration. It is an opportunity to respond to Christ's plea spoken through St. Paul,

"If our life in Christ means anything to you, if love can persuade at all, or the Spirit that we have in common, or any tenderness and sympathy.

Then be united in your convictions and united in your love, with a common purpose and a common mind . . . there must be no competition among you, no conceit: But everyone is to be self-efacing. Always consider the other person to be better than yourself, so that none thinks of his or her own interests first but everyone thinks of other people's interests instead. In your minds you must be the same as Christ Jesus." (Phil 2:1-5)

THE PERSONAL POWER OF GOVERNANCE OF THE DIOCESAN BISHOP

JULIAN HERRANZ

Before beginning allow me to express my thanks in a special way to Father Richard Cunningham, the esteemed president of your Society, for inviting me to meet you and to address a few words to you. But I would also like to thank all of you for your courtesy and for being so friendly to me and for everything that I have learned from you in these days of studying in common and of being together. I already had many friends among you, some even from the time of the revision of the Code. Now, however, I have many more. Thank you!

One of the members of your Society, whom I have known for some time now, Msgr. John A. Alessandro, wrote an interesting paper last year entitled "Implementing Church Law. A Theological Specialty." With a very fine sense of humor, he drew upon the speculative and pragmatic qualities of the detective Sherlock Holmes to give the canonist some good advice: that one should not fall prey to the pragmatism of an excessively technical specialization, without maintaining a necessary breadth of outlook. The reason for this is that the one who administers the law must never separate its implementation from an understanding of its doctrinal implications and meanings.

Leaving Sherlock Holmes aside, I am in complete agreement with Msgr. Alessandro on this point. I think this kind of prudence is particularly necessary now in addressing the issue which we are considering: the diocesan bishop's personal power of governance. This theme involves questions of a very practical nature, for example: the organization of the diocesan curia; the ordinary ministry of diocesan officials exercising general or special vicarious power; the extent of the faculty to dispense from universal laws; the nature and specific functions of various structures which help the diocesan bishop in fulfilling his pastoral ministry; the ways the diocesan bishop can delegate his executive power and so on. But it would be difficult to approach these and other practical questions in this field correctly without prior careful consideration of some important doctrinal postulates or theological-canonical principles which the legislator of the new Code of Canon Law took into account.[1]

These principles are in fact the consitutional foundation of the diocesan bishop's power of governance. They determine the broad directive lines within which this power ought to be exercised as a service both to his own particular church and to the universal Church. These principles furnish the light that is necessary for an adequate understanding of the norms by which the practical questions I just

---

[1] I intend to refer only to those doctrinal principles of a juridical-constitutional nature which delineate the power of the diocesan bishop as teacher of Christian doctrine, priest of divine worship and minister of governance. These principles will refer to the diocesan bishop's power of governance *(potestas regiminis)*, which is the only concern here.

indicated are regulated. In my opinion this body of norms regarding diocesan government is one of the parts of the Code in which appears most evidently the delicate work of the doctrinal and technical-juridical synthesis accomplished by the legislator.

Keeping all this in mind, I would like to develop the theme of this conference along the following lines:

> 1.) to put in a nutshell the three fundamental theological-canonical characteristics of the diocesan bishop's power of governance;
>
> 2.) to see how the legislator harmonized these characteristics with the technical juridical principle of the threefold division of functions (legislative, executive, and judicial) in the exercise of the power of governance by the diocesan bishop;
>
> 3.) to examine briefly some problematic questions which arise in the ordinary exercise of executive power.

I. Constitutional Principles of the Diocesan Bishop's Power of Governance

1. It seems to me that the first principle that ought to be put into relief, following the teaching of the Second Vatican Council and the norms of the Code, is the *sacred and personal character* of the diocesan bishop's power of governance. In fact, canon 375, §1 says: *"Through the Holy Spirit who has been given to them,* bishops are the successors of the apostles by divine institution; they are constituted pastors within the Church so that they are . . . ministers of governance.*"* In civil and democratic societies it is the citizens and their representatives who themselves establish in their constitutions what the offices and structures of government, and the powers surrendered and entrusted to them, ought to be. In the Church, on the contrary, it was the divine Founder himself who established what are the two principal offices and ministries that have a constitutional character (namely, the primacy of Peter and the episcopacy). He also determined at the same time the fundamental rights and duties of their respective missions and power.

In any natural society which has jurisdiction, power is conferred on those who govern through an act which is *exclusively juridical* in nature. While in the Church, the bishop's power of governance, like that of teaching and sanctifying, is conferred ontologically on sacred pastors through an act which is of a *sacramental nature:* episcopal consecration.[2] In a purely natural society the person or persons invested with jurisdiction (head of State or government, representatives, senators, governors, etc.) receive their respective powers without any particular spiritual

---

[2]Cfr. *Lumen gentium,* 21. With respect to patristic and magisterial sources about the sacramentality of the episcopate, see esp.: G. Philips, *L'Eglise et son mystere au deuxieme Concile du Vatican,* Paris, 1967, Vol. I, 246-269; J. Lecuyer, "Il triplice ufficio del Vescovo" in *La Collegialita per il futuro della Chiesa,* Florence, 1966, 851-871.

or supernatural gift being added to their human qualities. In the best of situations only an awareness of a greater responsibility is added to their presumed intelligence and experience. Whereas in the Church, bishops receive a stable gift or charism of the Holy Spirit with episcopal consecration, which elevates their natural and spiritual faculties. This enables them to fulfill their demanding task of sustaining the people of God in the name of God. The bishops in fact "fulfill in an eminent and visible manner the role of Christ himself, the Teacher, the Shepherd and the Pontiff and acts in his name."[3]

More concretely the diocesan bishops govern their communities of the faithful not only by reason of their natural authority, which their qualities of heart and intellect, prudence in giving counsel and example might confer upon them, but also and primarily by reason of an authority which they receive directly from God: therefore, with a power which is sacred. They govern the particular churches entrusted to them as vicars and legates of Christ, with counsel, persuasion, example, but also with the authority and sacred power" [as stated in a well known text of *Lumen gentium*].[4] Moreover, along with this *sacred* character (by reason of its origin, content and finality as well as the manner in which it is conferred) this power has the characteristic of being *personal*. In fact the office of governing *(munus regendi)* that the bishop receives ontologically by consecreation becomes a juridical power *"ad actum expeditum"* by means of the mission or canonical determination from superior authority.[5] But both the consecration through which he is incorporated in the episcopal college and the canonical mission received for governing a particular diocese are conferred on the person of the bishop. That is to say consecration and canonical mission form a power of governance of a personal nature, whose complete entitlement and juridical and moral responsibility effects only the conscience of the diocesan pastor in an immediate and non-transferable way.

Certainly we cannot and should not see the figure of the bishop as "an isolated monarch out of touch with the dynamics of the particular community entrusted to him."[6] Nor can we think that the sacred and personal character of his power makes the freedom and action of the bishop safe from every human weakness or arbitrariness, including the lack of due respect for the subjective rights and

---

[3]*Lumen gentium*, 21. All the members of Christ's Body, each in his own measure, participates in the kingship, the priesthood and the prophetic spirit of their Head. This *co-responsibility* is a constant in the Magisterium of the Council and in the new Code (cfr. can. 204 and 208). But only the bishops (and, in their own measure, the clergy) represent the Head and act in his name; and so, through their priestly ministry, it is still Christ who here on earth teaches, sanctifies and guides his people.

[4]*Lumen gentium*, 27.

[5]Cfr. *Lumen gentium*, 22, 24, and the *nota praevia*, 2; can. 379, 380, 382. Since there are still questions of a doctrinal nature to resolve, it is only fair to note that the Code did not explicitly and unitarily qualify "potestas regiminis seu iurisdictionis" as "sacra potestas." However in the Code itself, the sacred character of the power of the Roman Pontiff (cfr. can. 331-333), of the college of bishops (cfr. can. 336-337), and of the diocesan bishop (cfr. can. 375 and 381) appears quite clearly.

[6]Cfr. Thomas J. Green, "The Diocesan Bishop in the Revised Code: Some Introductory Reflections" in *The Jurist* 42 (1982) 326.

legitimate interests of the faithful that have been entrusted to them.[7] It would be erroneous and naive to think that. Therefore, the legislator has made better provisions than in the preceding Code for the recognition and protection of such rights and interests.[8] But neither can we apply to the diocesan bishop's power of governance the same ideological and juridical patterns according to which the nature of public authority is understood and by which its legitimate exercise is regulated in a democratic society.[9]

2.) The second theological-canonical principle regarding the power of the diocesan bishop is that it concerns a power that is complete *(potestas plena)*. The Council says: "This power, that they (the bishops) exercise personally in the name of Christ, is proper, ordinary and immediate."[10] Therefore it was reaffirmed in the Code in canon 381, §1: "A diocesan bishop in the diocese committed to him possesses all the ordinary, proper and immediate power which is required for the exercise of his pastoral office . . ."

As is well known, the power of the bishop is said to be *ordinary* because it belongs to his office by law. It is not concerned with a simple power which has been delegated by a higher human authority.[11] Episcopal power is therefore a stable power, as the office attached to it is stable. And it is a complete power, i.e. it extends to all the realms of competence in which the diocesan pastor is required to be active—the mission as a teacher of the faith, as a dispenser of the sacraments and as a protector of a correct social order.

The power of the bishop is also said to be *proper* because it is exercised in his own name and not in the name of another. This means, as has been affirmed by the Magisterium many times even before the Second Vatican Council,[12] that

---

[7]John J. Folmer, "Promoting and Protecting Rights in the Church: An Introduction" in *The Jurist* 46 (1986) 1-13, esp. 5-7.

[8]The 1983 CIC sanctions, for all the faithful, the principle of the protection of rights *"in foro competenti ecclesiastico ad normam iuris"* (can. 221, §1) and establishes in Part V of Book II the norms concerning administrative recourse (can. 1732-1739). For an overall evaluation of the innovations concerning this question, notwithstanding the suppression in the *Schema novissimum* of the CIC (can. 1736-1752) of the administrative tribunals inferior to the *Sectio altera* of the Apostolic Signatura, cfr. Z. Grocholewski, "Giustizia amministrativa nel nuovo Codice di Diritto Canonico" in *Angelicum* 63 (1986) 333-335. Cfr. also J. Herranz, "La triplice articolazione della potesta di governo," a paper delivered at the 13th annual meeting of the "Gruppo Italiano di Docenti Diritto Canonico," La Mendola, July, 1986, 29-30.

[9]Concerning the divine-constitutional *uniqueness* of the government of the Church, the Pope who promulgated the dogmatic constitution *Lumen gentium* said the following: "But let it be very clear with respect to this question that the government of the Church should not take on the appearances and the norms of temporal regimes, today guided on the one hand by democratic institutions which are at times excessive, or on the other by totalitarian forms which are contrary to the dignity of the persons subject to them. The government of the Church has its own unique form which seeks to reflect in its outward expressions the wisdom and the will of her divine Founder." (Paul VI, Allocution to the Synod of Bishops, October 11, 1969 in AAS 61 [1969] 720).

[10]*Lumen gentium*, 27: "Haec potestas qua, nomine Christi personaliter funguntur, est propria, ordinaria et immediata . . ." Cfr. *Christus Dominus*, 8, a.

[11]Cfr. Pius IX, Apostolic Letter to the Bishops of Germany, March 12, 1875 and his Allocution to the Consistory of March 15, 1875 (DS 3112-3117).

[12]Cfr., in addition to the documents cited in the previous note, Leo XIII, Encyclical *Satis cognitum*, June 29, 1896 (AAS 28 [1895-1896] 732); Letter *Officio Sanctissimo*, December 22, 1887 (AAS [1887] 264).

in their dioceses they are not vicars of the Roman Pontiff.[13] In fact their power is not a participation in the power granted by God to Peter and his successors. It is instead a participation in the power that Christ conferred directly on the apostolic college and that is transmitted to the episcopal college. This power is exercised by bishops, as the Apostles already had done, "together and under the authority" of Peter, whose successor "retains supreme ordinary power over the whole Church."[14]

Finally the fullness of the diocesan bishop's power is configured also by the fact that it is an *immediate* power. That is, that it can be exercised directly over the people and things which have been made subject to his jurisdiction. In other words, the power of the bishop can be activated at any moment and in any matter without the necessity of any intermediary. However, this *non necessity* is not to be identified with *non convenience*. Therefore besides the pastors who make the bishop present in the parochial communities,[15] there are a series of persons and structures that help the bishop in the exercise of his ministry. They have also been foreseen by ecclesiastical law: the vicar general and episcopal vicars, the diocesan curia, the presbyteral council, the college of consultors, etc. Later we will return to this issue.

3.) The third and last theological-canonical principle which shapes the power of the diocesan bishop is the principle of communion *(communio)*. This principle means above all that the functions *(munera)* conferred on all bishops by consecration "by their very nature, however, can be exercised only when they are in hierarchical communion with the head of the college and its members" (can. 375, §2). As this principle refers concretely to the diocesan bishops, it means that their power cannot be exercised in an entirely autonomous or independent manner. Rather they must act in accord with the *communio*[16] structures given by Christ to the Church: that is, in communion with the whole of the episcopal body, and in submission to the one who is its head. The Constitution *Lumen gentium* also reminds us that the exercise of episcopal power "is ultimately regulated by the supreme authority of the Church," and can be circumscribed "within certain limits, in view of advantages to the Church or to the faithful."[17]

---

[13]They are in fact Christ's vicars. In this sense, even when the vicars apostolic and prefects apostolic are bishops, their situation, like that of the prelates to whom an apostolic administration is entrusted, differs from that of a diocesan bishop, since these others rule their respective ecclesiastical circumscriptions *nomine Summi Pontificis* (cfr. can. 371).

[14]*Christus Dominus*, 2. Cfr. CIC, can. 331 and 333.

[15]"The pastor is the proper shepherd of the parish entrusted to him . . . under the authority of the diocesan bishop in whose ministry of Christ he has been called to share . . ." (can. 519).

[16]Among the many works concerning this question, cfr. H.M. Legrand, "Nature de l'Eglise particuliere et role de l'eveque dans l'Eglise" in *La charge pastorale des eveques*, Paris, 1969, 106-111; J. Hamer, "Dix Theses sur l'Eglise comme *communio*" in *Nova et Vetera* 59 [1984] 161-180; R.J. Castillo Lara, "La communion ecclesiale dans le nouveau Code de Droit Canonique" in *Communicationes* 15 [1984] 242-266; J. Ratzinger, *Chiesa, ecumenismo, politica*, Roma, 1987, 9-48.

[17]*Lumen gentium*, 27.

The ministry of Peter, or the primatial function, is concerned not only with the possibility of *coordinating* the various authorities and lesser ecclesiastical powers, or of acting as a last *court of appeal* in the case of conflicts of rights or interests. That would be a reductive vision of the *manus petrinum,* of the Primacy.[18] The supreme authority (Pope, college of bishops) can also *limit* the power of the diocesan bishop with universal or particular norms, and he can *structure (ordinare)* the manner in which it ought to be exercised. In the first case we have those matters which traditionally are known in canon law as *"causae maiores,"* that is, cases "which the law or a decree of the Supreme Pontiff reserves to the supreme or to some other ecclesiastical authority" (can. 381, §1). Following the principle of a *hierarchy of norms* the second group comprises all the superior dispositions of a universal or particular character which the diocesan bishop ought to keep in mind in the government of his own diocese. We cannot forget that it includes government *"ad normam iuris,"* according, that is, to the ways of exercising power, within the limits and the conditions fixed by the legislator in view of the common welfare of the universal Church.[19]

---

[18]Some advocates of a false *decentralization,* theologically uncritical, tend to conceive the Primacy of Peter and the central structures of the ecclesiastical government as instruments of *uniformity,* and therefore as obstacles to the just autonomy and the specific identity of every particular Church (cfr., for example, H. Stehle, "Le centralisme romain est-il un avantage dans l'Europe de l'Est?" in *Concilium* 147 [1979] 91-96; J. Dammert Bellido, "Les Eglises locales et leur communication avec la Curia Romain," *ibid.,* 97-101). In fact, these authors confuse the necessary unity of the universal Church with a *uniformity* in which there would be no room for the charisms and the cultural pecularities of particular churches. But this seems to me to be a false contraposition. In fact, true pluralism and the just autonomy of particular churches presupposes the existence of a visible principle of catholic unity for the Church. This principle is certainly operative in the particular church which is presided over by its diocesan bishop, but in the *munus petrinum,* in the primatial ministry of the Roman Pontiff, it finds its fundamental point of reference. "The Roman Pontiff, as the successor of Peter, is the perpetual and visible source and foundation of the unity both of the bishops and of the whole company of the faithful. The individual bishops are the visible source and foundation of unity in their own particular churches . . ." (*Lumen gentium,* 23). We also read in *Lumen gentium,* 13: ". . . within the Church, particular churches hold a rightful place; these churches retain their own traditions, without in any way opposing the primacy of the Chair of Peter, which presides over the whole assembly of charity and protects legitimate differences, while at the same time assuring that such differences do not hinder unity but rather contribute to it." John Paul II has said the following with respect to this question: "In fact, there is among the individual particular Churches an ontological relationship of mutual inclusion: each particular Church, as a realization of the one Church of Christ, is in some way present in all the particular Churches 'in which and from which the one and unique Catholic Church exists' (*Lumen gentium,* n. 23). . . . A particular task of the Apostolic See consists precisely in *serving this universal unity. Rather, it is in this that the specific office and, we can say, the charism of Peter of his successors lie. . . . Indeed, he is the "rock" on which Christ willed to build his Church (cf. Mt. 16: 18); and it is precisely from the foundation that the compact firmness of the entire edifice expected."* (*Allocution to the Roman Curia, December 21, 1984 in AAS 77 [1985] 505-506; English trans, from L'Osservatore Romano,* English edition, 21 January 1985, 7). And: "In this perspective too, we must see the ministry of the Successor of Peter, not only as a "global" service, reaching each particular Church from "outside" as it were, but *as belonging already to the essence of each particular Church from "within."* Allocution to the Bishops of the United States, September 16, 1987, Los Angeles, text as found in *L'Osservatore Romano,* September 18, 1987, xxxv.)

[19]Cfr. can. 391. Paul VI had already reminded the Fathers of the Second Vatican Council, "Praeterea si apostolicus munus a Nobis requirit ut, an potestatis episcopalis perfunctionem quoad obtinet, aliquid Nobis reservemus, limites praefiniamus, formas statuamus, agendi rationes ordinemus: haec omnia, ut probe nostis, ipsum Ecclesiae universae bonum postulat, postulat unitas Ecclesiae." (Allocution to the Council Fathers at the beginning of the Third Session of the Second Vatican Council, September 14, 1964, in AAS 56 [1964] 810).

We can conclude the first part of this exposition in the following way. The three theological-canonical principles briefly examined present the diocesan bishop's power as: having a *sacred and personal* character; it is *complete* in the threefold dimension of ordinary, proper and immediate power; and it ought to be exercised *in communion*. Now we can pass to the other parts of this paper which pose these two questions: what concrete practical significance do these three characteristics have in the threefold functions (legislative, executive and judicial) of the diocesan bishop's power? and, what practical criteria can be deduced for the orientation and solution of some problems posed concerning the correct exercise of executive power, which is the power more frequently activated in the ordinary government of the diocese?

II. The Threefold Division of the Diocesan Bishop's Power of Governance

Notwithstanding the personal title of the diocesan bishop to sacred power *(sacra potestas)*, the Code Commission and the legislator judged it appropriate from the very beginning[20] to sanction expressly a technical-juridical principle in the new Code that has been accepted in almost all civil societies having jurisdiction. It is concerned with the distinction of functions in the exercise of the power of governance. Canon 391, with few modifications of the first text (1968) says:

"§1. The diocesan bishop is to rule the particular church committed to him with legislative, executive and judicial power in accord with the norm of law.

"§2. The bishop personally exercises legislative power; he exercises executive power either personally or through vicars general or episcopal vicars in accord with the norm of law; he exercises judicial power either personally or through a judicial vicar and judges in accord with the norm of law."

This norm has been understood by canonists in very different ways. After pointing to the theories of Locke and Montesquieu, one author commented that this canon and canon 135 had introduced into the Code "the threefold division of legislative, executive and judicial powers that is familiar to liberal political doctrine."[21] It seems to me that this affirmation is a bit exaggerated. On the one hand, because this threefold distinction of the power of governance is not new in the law of the Church: it was already, even if in a less pure form, in the 1917

---

[20]The study group "Questiones speciales Libri II," first reviewed Title V "De potestate ordinaria et delegata" of the CIC 1917 during the session of November 9-13, 1970. In that session, among other things, the transfer of the above-mentioned title to Book I of the new Code (Title VIII: "De potestate regiminis") and the introduction of a new canon (the present can. 135) in which the threefold distinction of functions in the exercise of the power of government was explicitly formulated, were approved.

[21]J. Gaudemet, "Reflexions sue le Livre I 'De normis generalibus' du Code de Droit canonique de 1983" in *Revue de Droit Canonique* 34 (1984) 112. Cfr. also E. Corecco, "I laici nel nuovo Codice di diritto canonico" in *La Scuola Cattolica* 112 (1984) 216.

CIC and also before.[22] On the other hand, because canon law succeeded in achieving an effective independence of the various judges in its procedural system centuries before Illuminist philsophy began to propose the division of powers in the constitution of the State.

Other authors [23] have correctly pointed out that the definitive application of the distinction of functions in the new Code happened through the influence of a series of factors that were technical and pastoral at the same time. Among the most important was the existence in the Church of the frequent situation of a juridical uncertainty at the level of both universal and diocesan government. This was so for three principal reasons: 1) the lack of a clear technical application of the principle of the *hierarchy of norms;* 2) the lack of judicial control of individual administrative acts and consequently the lack of protection of the subjective rights of the faithful;[24] 3) the lack of an adequate distinction and practical delimitation between legislative acts and general administrative acts of a regulatory character.[25]

These juridical imperfections made the range of the bishop's discretion in exercising his power excessively broad with the consequent danger of arbitrary decisions. So, already in the directive principles for the new codification the following were affirmed: 1) the constitutional unity of ecclesiastical power and its primary personal entitlement: this however could not legitimate the arbitrary use of such power;[26] 2) the appropriateness that "the diverse functions of ecclesiastical power, namely legislative, administrative and judicial, be clearly distinguished and that the structures be appropriately defined which would exercise the individual functions."[27] This was how the new Code had been drafted, out of respect also for the principle of legality[28] which the Second Vatican Council itself has recommended with regard to governmental legislation.[29]

It would be interesting to ask at this point what had been the exact meaning

---

[22] Concerning the notion and the divisions of jurisdiction in the law of the Church considered both from a historical perspective and in the 1917 CIC, cfr. V. Tirado, *De hurisdictionis acceptione in jure ecclesiastico*, Rome, 1940. For a study of the more recent aspects, see P.G. Marcuzzi, "Distinzione della 'potestas regiminis' in legislativa, esecutiva e giudiziaria" in *Salesianum* 43 (1981) 275-304.

[23] Cfr., for example, P. Lombardia, *Lecciones de Derecho Canonico*, Madrid, 1984, 117-120.

[24] At the highest level of government in the Church, this situation was remedied by the Apostolic Constitution *Regimini Ecclesiae universae*, 106 (August 15, 1967), concerning the "Sectio altera" of the Apostoloic Signatura. This introduced the possibility of judicial review of individual administrative acts. It seems that similar norms are foreseen in the new Apostolic Constitution concerning the Roman Curia, as well as others, to safeguard the principal of the hierarchy of laws expressed at the end of canon 135, §2 in the 1983 CIC.

[25] In fact, neither the Apostolic Constitution *Sapientii consilio*, June 29, 1908, in which Pius X reorganized the Roman Curia, nor the 1917 CIC furnished the technical elements necessary to remedy these situations. Canonical study has been concerned with them for some years. For a basic bibliography concerning this question, see: J.A. Souto, "Sugerencias para una vision actual del Derecho Administrativo Canonico" in *Ius Canonicum* 5 (1965) 111 ff.

[26] Cfr. "Principia quae Codicis Iuris Canonici recognitionem dirigant," 6, Typis Polyglottis Vaticanis, 1967, 12-23, published subsequently in *Communicationes* 1 (1969) 78-85.

[27] *Ibid.*, 7.

[28] Cfr. J. Herranz, "De principio legalitatis in exercitio potestatis ecclesiasticae" in *Acta Conventus Internationalis Canonistorum*, Rome, May 20-25, 1968, Typis Polyglottis Vaticanis, 1970, 221-238.

[29] Cfr. *Gaudium et spes*, 75.

attributed to the word "organa," which appears in the text of the directive principles cited above ("that the *structures (organa)* be appropriately defined . . ."). If one would have thought of a simple transposition to canon law of the juridical patterns of the State proffered by liberal philosophy, this word would certainly be interpreted in the work of the new Code as "collegial structures" or "social bodies." But it is enough to read canon 391 and parallel places in the Code to see that the word "organa" has a primary and generic reference to persons and to ecclesiastical offices: concretely, at the diocesan level, the diocesan bishop, vicar general and episcopal and judicial vicars, and judges.[30]

In the democratic state, the *threefold division of power* is understood as mutual control and balance of social forces. The Houses (Parliament, Senate) exercise legislative power in a collegial way, inasmuch as they represent the people the primary holders of such power. Executive power resides in the administrative branch, while the court is the holder, at various levels, of judicial power. Both administrative branch and the court act according to the norms and power that the people themselves have entrusted to them. It is obvious that in the Church, where power comes not from the people but from God and is structured by him on the constitutional level, that things are understood differently. This is also the case with the *distinction of functions* in the exercise of the power of governance. Lets look at it briefly:

a.) In the diocese *legislative power* belongs solely to the person of the bishop, nor can it be validly delegated by him to another, *"unless the law expressly provides otherwise"* as is stated in canon 135, §2. Certainly he should exercise his function as legislator *"ad normam iuris"* (can. 391, §2). Therefore he is required among other things, to listen to advice or to ask the opinions of the competent diocesan structures (especially the college of consultors and the presbyteral council[31]), whenever this is required by universal law. And he can listen to the opinion of the episcopal council (if it exists cfr. can. 473, §4) in questions of governance, of the pastoral council in questions about pastoral and apostolic activities in the diocese (cfr. can. 511). But the bishop cannot attribute to any of these consultative structures for helping in governing a deliberative or decision-making power for the making of laws, general decrees or other acts of a legislative character.[32] Nor can the bishop attribute a legislative power to the diocesan Synod or to individuals of the diocesan Synod that have a deliberative vote, since the principle *"the bishop is the only legislator"* (cfr. can. 466) is valid also for the

---

[30]The phrase "primary and generic reference" is used because secondarily, as a consequence of the corresponding ecclesiastical offices, there are also organizational structures, such as the Roman Curia and the diocesan curias, the Congregations, the tribunals, etc.

[31]To these two obligatory councils is entrusted in a specific way the mission of helping the bishop "in regimine dioecesis" (cfr. can. 495, §1 and 502, §2), unless the conference of bishops applies the provisions of can. 502, §3 concerning the college of consultors.

[32]For example, the approval of statutes which are subject to the norms of the law (cfr. can. 94, §3), the approval or reprobation of a custom *contra ius* or *praeter ius* (cfr. can. 23 and 26); granting a privilege by a particular act of the legislator (cfr. can. 76, §1).

diocesan Synod.[33]

Certainly it is very appropriate that the bishop ensure that the various diocesan structures which help him in governing be adequate instruments for fostering exchange of insights, for gathering broad information, for articulating policy options and diocesan goals, for judging which option is advisable in a given set of circumstances, and even for forming a prudent personal judgment about eventual norms of a legislative character. However, his personal legislative power always remains juridically free, because these matters which require the "consent" of a given collegial body for the validity of the act *("ad validitatem actus")* (cfr. can. 127, §2, 1°), do not concern acts of a legislative character but rather administrative acts.[34] On the other hand the bishop cannot issue norms contrary to those of higher authority, that is those coming from supreme power or from structures which share in it.[35] In fact to do that would be contrary to the doctrinal principle of *"communio."* according to which the juridical principle of a hierarchy of norms, was sanctioned in canon 135, §2 for avoiding situations of juridical uncertainty which I pointed out above.

The sacred personal character of the diocesan bishop's power of governance (though, I repeat, it is not absolute or arbitrary) has been carefully safeguarded by the codified norms. At the same time they harmonize two other necessities: the fullness with which legislative power is exercised by the bishop in his own particular church and the necessary communion of every single particular church with the universal Church. Even in the law it appears so clear, that given the sociological and organizational variety of particular churches, none of them are autonomous or self-sufficient.[36] While it is a pastoral reality that in each and every

---

[33]In the first draft of the present can. 391, §2 (March, 1968), we read the following: "Potestatem legislativam exercent (Episcopi) sive in Synodo diocesana sive extra eandem . . ." However, one consultor called attention to the fact this this expression could be understood to mean that the Synod has a collegial character. For this reason, the text was amended in the following way: "Potestatem legislativam exercet ipse Episcopus sive in Synodo diocesana sive extra eandem . . ." (cfr. *Communicationes* 18 [1986] 146-147, 165).

[34]Cfr. can. 272; 515, §2; 1018, §1; 1263; 1277' 1742; 1750.

[35]Cfr. can 135, §2. For the entire question, see J.L. Gutierrez, "La potesta legislativa del Vescovo diocesano" in *Raccolta di scritti in onore di Pio Fedele,* Perugia, 1984, 471-489.

[36]A selective emphasis of certain Council texts has led some authors to affirm the complete self-sufficiency and self-realization of particular churches without the mediation of the universal Church (cfr., for example, G. Alberigo, "Servir la communion des Eglises" in *Concilium* 147 [1979] 45). This is clearly an uncritical affirmation. Among other considerations, the diocesan bishop, who has the role of *"visible principium et fundamentum unitatis"* in the particular Church *(Lumen gentium,* 23, a) does not possess, as *"Singulus praesul"* the charism of infallibility *(Ibid.,* 25, b). This means that the bishops taken individually, cannot guarantee the unity of the Catholic faith within their particular churches; nor can all of them together, without the Bishop of Rome, do so for the universal Church. For this reason, the particular church, as such, does not have all the elements of consistency and unity necessary to ensure *communio.* These elements are found only in the universal Church. Precisely for this reason, the particular church cannot be *simpliciter* the *Ecclesia Christi,* but only *imago Ecclesiae universalis (Ibid.,* 23, a; cfr. *Ad gentes,* 20, a). And this is also the reason that communion within the *unity of the Churches* is not sufficient; what is needed is communion within the *unity of the universal Church.* "The 'vertical dimension' of the ecclesial communion is of profound significance in understanding *the relationship of the particular Churches to the universal Church.* It is important to avoid a merely sociological view of this relationship. 'In and from such individual Churches there come into being the one and only Catholic Church' *(Lumen Gentium,* 23), but this universal Church cannot be conceived as the sum of the particular Churches, or as a federation of particular Churches." (John Paul II, Allocution to the Bishops of the United States, September 16, 1987, *cit.).*

one of them *"the one, holy, catholic and apostolic Church of Christ is present and active."*[37]

b.) Regarding *executive* and *judicial* power it is evident from canon 391, §2 that the primary and personal entitlement of such power is the diocesan bishop himself. He can exercise these other two functions of government either directly or through his vicars. In the latter case they act in the name of the only Pastor of the diocese, who coordinates their activities (cfr. can. 473), and whose mind and intentions they always should respect (cfr. can. 480). However, the possibility of hierarchical recourse to the bishop against the decrees of authorities that are subject to him has been provided for (cfr. can. 1734, §3, 1°); something which was not present in the preceding Code.

Respect for canonical tradition, as well as pastoral and technical reasons, make the principle of the distinction of functions advisable. The established approach is that *ordinarily* the diocesan bishop exercises executive and judicial power through the previously mentioned vicars and the corresponding administrative and judicial structures of the diocesan curia and tribunal (cfr. can. 472). Therefore, in the new Code norms concerning the ordinary ministry of diocesan officials who exercise vicarious power have been perfected.[38] There is no doubt that these norms, together with those concerning the structure and competence of the various consultative bodies,[39] will have much to do with both the correct exercise of diocesan government and the apostolic dynamism of the diocesan community. In fact, the experience of these years demonstrates that all these norms, if well applied, are also very useful in helping all the faithful of the diocese to participate actively in the mission of the Church *"each one according to his own condition."*[40] This should not however be confused with the much more limited concept of the participation of the laity in the organizational structures of diocesan government.[41] The personal and complete character of the bishop's power does not constitute, not even at the level of executive functioning, an impediment or a limitation to the legitimate exercise of the personal charisms of the faithful. If this were possible it would be a contradiction in the constitutional norms themselves of the divine law of the Church. On the contrary, the bishop and with him his vicars are required to stimulate the exercise of such charisms and to respect and foster all

---

[37]*Christus Dominus*, 11. "The Catholic Church herself subsists in each particular Church, which can be truly complete only through effective communion in faith, sacraments and unity with the whole Body of Christ." (John Paul II, Allocution to the Bishops of the United States, September 16, 1987, *cit.*).

[38]Cfr., for example, W.C. Paguio, "On the Vicar General and the Episcopal Vicar" in *Philippiniana Sacra*, 2 (1985) 192-224.

[39]For a detailed examiniation of these structures, see F. Daneels, O.Praem., "De dioecesanis corresponsabilitatis organis" in *Periodica* 74 (1985) 301-324.

[40]Can. 204, §1 and 208.

[41]There are persons for whom the "advancement of the laity" in the Church would consist above all in the presence of lay persons (that is, of non-ordained faithful) in the ecclesiastical organizational structures. Such persons are very interested in official ecclesiastical involvement in making decisions in "big issues." As a result, they forget the primary apostolic importance of lay persons who carry out the work of redemption in the ordinary circumstances of daily life: in their families, in their professional work, in their cultural and social activities, and so forth (cfr. *Lumen gentium*, 31; and can. 225).

the various forms of the apostolate that would legitimately be present in the diocese (cfr. can. 394). In fact all are necessary or useful, each according to its specificity, to carry the message of Christ to a society inclined to be agnostic and pagan.

However we are now in the realm of the exercise of executive power where there are more practical problems regarding the correct understanding and application of the law. I would like to explore briefly two concrete issues: dispensation from universal laws and delegation of the faculty to dispense. I realize that these questions have generated some doubts among bishops and some of you have already given attention to them as scholars and as persons actively engaged in legal concerns.

III. Two Problematic Questions

A. The legitimate use of the faculty to dispense

Out of respect for the theological-canonical character of the fullness of the diocesan bishop's power, the decree *Christus Dominus,* n. 8, b and consequently canon 87, §1 grant the diocesan bishop a wide faculty of dispensing from the disciplinary laws enacted by supreme authority, "both universal and particular for his own territory." As we all know, the proper finality for every dispensation is that of mitigating the rigor of the law in a particular case. Therefore, it is expressly foreseen that the bishop can exercise this faculty at any moment, but it always includes his own judgment[42] that the dispensation would be *"for the spiritual welfare of the faithful."* The extraordinary circumstances mentioned in §2 of canon 87 are no longer required, as in the former law:[43] namely, the difficulty of having recourse to the Holy See and the danger of serious damage while awaiting a reponse.

But we could ask: wouldn't such a broad faculty to dispense result in arbitrary decisions and abuses? Wouldn't universal law and the whole canonical system be undermined? Without a doubt there is danger. But I think that it will not become real if the doctrinal principles recalled at the beginning of this presentation are respected regarding the diocesan bishop's power of governance.

A correct interpretation and application of the faculty to dispense requires that

---

[42]With the expression *"conferre iudicet"* in can. 87, §1, the legislator has entrusted to the *personal judgment* of the bishop the authority to dispense from universal law in ordinary circumstances. During the work of revising the 1980 Schema CIC, a member of the Commission requested the substitution of *"Ordinarius loci"* for *"Episcopus dioecesanus"* in the canon. He received the following reply, subsequently confirmed at the Plenary Session: "Non expedit. Agitur de amplissima potestate et in Decreto *Christus Dominus,* n. 8 haec potestas datur 'Episcopus dioecesanis' tantum" ("Relatio complectens synthesim animadversionum" in *Communicationes* 14 [1982] 137). For this reason, these dispensations cannot be conceded by the general or episcopal Vicars, except when they have received a "special mandate from the bishop" (cfr. can. 134, §3). For the same reason (namely, the prudence of good government), the Code notes that this power to dispense, even in extraordinary circumstances, is not given to pastors of parishes nor to other priests or deacons "nisi haec potestas ipsis expresse concessa sit" (can. 89).

[43]Cfr. 1917 CIC, can. 81.

the theological-canonical principle of *"ecclesiastical communion"* also be taken into consideration in the exercise of this episcopal power. In virtue of this principle:

1) Certain laws promulgated by supreme authority are excluded from the power of dispensation. They are not only divine laws (which is obvious), constitutive (can. 86), procedural and penal laws (can. 87, §1) but also disciplinary laws *"whose dispensation is especially reserved to the Apostolic See or to another authority"* (can. 87, §1).[44]

2) The Code, being faithful to the doctrinal tradition in this matter,[45] recalls the extraordinary character, i.e. of its being an exception, which always attends the juridical act of dispensation no matter who the authority is who grants it: *"A dispensation from an ecclesiastical law may not be granted without a just and reasonable cause"* (can. 90, §1). This primarily obliges the diocesan bishop, since he is expressly advised by the legislator: "Since he must protect the unity of the universal Church, the bishop is bound to promote the common *discipline* of the whole Church and therefore to urge the observance of all ecclesiastical laws." (can. 392, §1.)[46]

3) Finally, it should be noted that the bishop ought to ponder attentively in the individual cases the concrete circumstances and the seriousness of the law from which he is dispensing, especially as it concerns a higher law (cfr. can. 90, §1). That is, the purpose for the dispensation ought to be harmonized with the purpose of the law. Otherwise it would effectively be an arbitrary use of the faculty of dispensing which would injure not only the stability of the whole canonical system, but also the common good of the faithful of the diocese. They would, in fact, be placed partially at the edge of the necessary "communio in regimine" (can. 205), that is one of their fundamental duty-rights (cfr. 209).

Concerning this I think it is opportune to indicate, out of respect for the inter-

---

[44]It should be noted that the word "especially" *(specialiter)* of can. 87, §1, does not mean "expressly" *(expresse)*. Thus the reservation may be either *explicit* (as for example in can. 242, §1; 290, 3; 1014, 1031, §4; 1047; etc.), or *implicit* (for example, the dispensation from form for the marriage of two Catholics: cfr. can. 1117 in relation with can. 1079; 1027, §2; and 1165, §2; likewise the authentic interpretation of July 5, 1987, III (cfr. AAS 77 [1985] 771).

[45]Cfr. 1917 CIC, can. 84, §1. In Book VI of Boniface VIII, a reasonable motive is required for a dispensation (cfr. C. 14, I, 6 in VI). Saint Thomas Aquinas describes the person who arbitrarily grants a dispensation or who does so without cause as unfaithful and imprudent (cfr. *S.Th.* I-II, q. 97, a. 4). Suarez uses similar language (cfr. *De leg.*, 1.6, c. 18). The Council of Trent warns that being overly indulgent with those who request a dispensation "would be nothing other than opening the way so that all might transgress the laws" (Sess. 25, "De reform.", c. 18). Among the *Fontes* of the above-mentioned can. 84 of the 1917 CIC (cfr. vol. I, n. 339), Card. Gasparri included the following judgment of Benedict XIV regarding dispensations without a just cause: "non dispensationes sed dissipationes essent, a quibus fidelis prudensque minister Christi omnino se abstinere tenetur." (Ep. encycl. "Inter omnigenas," 2 Feb. 1744).

[46]The Pope himself had addressed the bishops concerning this particular duty, just before the new Code became effective (cfr. Allocution "Ad Italiae episcopos occasione oblata XXII coetus generalis extraordinarii," September 21, 1983, AAS 75 [1983] 112-113).

pretative criteria of canon 17, that the *mens* either of the Council or of the legislator of the new Code, has been to fix as the only legitimate reason for a dispensation "the spiritual welfare of the faithful."[47] Therefore, besides the disciplinary laws whose dispensation has been reserved to the Holy See, in an explicit or implicit form, are also excluded those other laws that are likewise disciplinary but whose dispensation would not bring about any spiritual benefit to the faithful. I think that this *mens* of the legislator obeys the evident reason of prudence, while keeping in mind that the concept of *disciplinary law* is very broad in canonical teaching. It comprises, in fact, all the laws which concern the juridical order of the Church as opposed to laws regarding faith and morals.[48] There are therefore many disciplinary laws (besides constitutive, procedural and penal), which according to their nature and finality cannot be dispensed: since such a dispensation would not be to the spiritual benefit of the faithful. In fact we can ask: outside of some rare exception,[49] what spiritual benefit would dispensations bring about for the faithful, for example, from the laws regarding the rights and duties of sacred ministers, their adequate and complete formation, or the correct exercise of their ministry; or else from universal laws regulating the dignity and unity of Catholic worship, the protection and good administration of ecclesiastical patrimony, and so forth?

I do not intend these remarks to indicate that the diocesan bishop's power of dispensation, which does not enter in the legislative proposition of canon 92, ought to be interpreted strictly. I am of the opinion that to do so would be contrary to canon 138 which deals with the interpretation of ordinary executive power, which bishops have: in fact, it "ought to be broadly interpreted." But canonical doctrine teaches[50] that one should not confuse a *broad* interpretation with an *extensive* interpretation. The first happens when one chooses the most favorable of a variety of possible meanings of the normative text. The other supposes that the law, or a concession made by the law, can be enlarged to such a degree that it can include cases, matters of circumstances that are not contained in the text or context of the law. And this *extensive* interpretation, to be authentic, or at least legitimate, always requires the intervention of the legislator.[51] This concerns a *technical juridical* necessity (because an *extensive* or *restrictive* interpreta-

---

[47]*Christus Dominus*, 8, b; can. 87, §1.

[48]Cfr., for example, A. Vermeersh—I. Creusen, *Epitome Iuris Canonici,* Tom. I. Brussels—Rome, 1963, 8th ed., 96.

[49]For example, granting permission, outside the limits set by can. 905, §2, to celebrate the Eucharist more than once on the same day, "si sacerdotum penuria habeatur."

[50]Cfr., for example, H.J. Cicognani—D. Stafa, *Commentarium ad Librum Primum Codicis Iuris Canonici,* Rome, 1939, Vol. I, 258-260 and Vol. II, 628-629.

[51]Cfr. can. 17, §§1-2. If there were a true "dubium" concerning the reservation of a law or the sufficiency of the motive, the reservation of the dispensation would cease. But it would always be a moral obligation for the bishop to ask the competent authority to clarify the doubt by an official reply. He should not allow himself to be satisfied with the simple personal opinion of one or of several private authors writing according to their own insights. It should also be kept in mind that a dispensation is often equivalent to a privilege, which should not be given an extensive interpretation (cfr. cann. 77 and 36, §2).

tion is factually equivalent to a new law) and simultaneously a doctrinal necessity of *ecclesiastical communion.*

B. Delegation of the power of governance[52]

As you know, there is a greater terminological precision in the new Code about specific ecclesiastical authorities (the *diocesan bishop,* the *local ordinary,* or the *ordinary*) who are regarded as having the juridical capacity for carrying out single acts of governance. That is, an attempt was made to avoid as far as possible the generic expressions ("auctoritas competens," "Superior," etc.), that in the previous law created situations of ambiguity or judicial uncertainty. This task of technical perfection[53] is at the foundation of the norm contained in canon 134, §3, that seems very important for illuminating the complex field of dispensations, delegations, and delegations of the faculty to dispense. The Code says: "Whatever things in the canons in the realm of executive power which are attributed by name to the diocesan bishop, are understood to pertain only to the diocesan bishop . . . excluding the vicar general and the episcopal vicar unless they have received a special mandate."

The legislator, respecting the personal character of the diocesan bishop's power of governance, intended to affirm with these norms that:

1.) There are acts of governance of an executive character that, given their particular importance, are reserved to the personal decision and responsibility of the *diocesan bishop.* These acts are therefore excluded from the ordinary executive power of other local ordinaries in the diocese (vicars general and episcopal vicars). For example, the provision of all ecclesiastical offices of the diocese, incardination and excardination of clergy, the approval of the statutes of the seminary, the erection of institutes of consecrated life, etc.

2.) Given some precise exceptions[54] and only in extraordinary circumstances,[55] the diocesan bishop could delegate some of these ex-

---

[52]In reality, in the new Code (cfr. can. 135, §4, and 137-142), the possibility of delegation appears to be limited to executive power alone. We have in fact briefly referred earlier to the non-delegability of power which legislators have "infra auctoritatem supremam," "nisi aliud iure explicite caveatur" (can. 135, §2). But neither can judicial power given to judges and tribunals be delegated "except for the preparatory acts leading to a decree or a sentence" (can. 135, §3).

[53]This not only serves to indicate clearly the areas of competence, and for that reason the legitimacy and validity of the acts of government, but it also helps to identify the nature of these acts. For example, a general decree proceeding from a vicar general or an episcopal vicar (from the local Ordinary) will always be an *executive* decree. It cannot be a legislative decree (cfr. can. 30), because instances of delegated legislative powers are not provided for at the diocesan level.

[54]The exceptions to the faculty to delegate are either expressly stated in the law ("Nisi aliud iure expresse caveatur"—can. 137, §1), or else they are based on the very nature of things ("ex ipsa rei natura;" for example, acts which require the episcopal character, when the vicar general or episcopal vicar is not a bishop).

[55]This means, in fact, transferring to another person a judgment or an action of government which the supreme authority wanted to entrust expressly to the personal and direct responsibility of the *Pastor proprius* of the diocese.

clusive features of his power to other local ordinaries collaborating with him. In this case, the vicar general or episcopal vicar can posit acts of governance with *delegated power,* based, that is, on a "special mandate" with precise provisions, which lie outside of the competence of their office.

3.) On the other hand, there are other acts of executive power that the legislator entrusts in a generic way to the *local ordinary,* i.e. either to the diocesan bishop or, under his control, to vicars general and episcopal vicars (cfr. can. 134, §2; 479). For example, the dispensation from universal disciplinary laws in extraordinary circumstances (cfr. can. 87, §2); or from diocesan laws in ordinary circumstances (cfr. can. 88); the nomination or approval of religion professors (cfr. can. 805); the dispensation from canonical form in mixed marriages (cfr. can. 1127, §2); the dispensation of matrimonial impediments that are not reserved to the Holy See (cfr. can. 1078, §1), etc. In this way a broad participation in the executive power of the diocesan Pastor is effected by using the normal course of *vicarious* power, rather than the exceptional route of delegated power.

4.) Precisely to facilitate the good government of the diocese, the legislator has introduced in the new Code the new juridical figure of the episcopal vicar. This figure reduces the need for the bishop to delegate his executive power. Applying almost verbatim a decision of the Council,[56] it has been established that the diocesan bishop can name one or more episcopal vicars: "for a determinate part of the diocese, or to a specific type of activity, or to the faithful of a particular rite or to certain groups of people" (can. 476). So there is nothing unusual about the pastoral organization of a diocese, especially the larger and more complex ones, which would include several episcopal vicars. Often they are named for specific territorial zones or groups of people. But they can also be named to accomplish in the whole diocese certain executive acts that have been entrusted by the legislator to the *local ordinary*.

Delegated power, as you know, is a delicate juridic instrument decentralizing power. At times it can be useful and even necessary. But in my humble opinion, adopting this special governmental instrument requires a keen sense of pastoral responsibility. It is clear that the diocesan bishop and, in the limits of their respective competence, the vicar general and episcopal vicars, can delegate to other persons, "ad actum" or "ad universitatem casuum," some faculties of their ordinary executive power (cfr. can. 137, §1). They can do it, i.e. whenever such

---

[56]Cfr. *Christus Dominus,* 27. Those commenting on the Code have understandably highlighted the importance of these new immediate collaborators of the bishop in the exercise of his executive power; see, for example, F.J. Urrutia, "Delegation of the Executive Power of Governance" in *Studia Canonica* 19 (1985) 340-355, esp. 348-349. Few, though, have called attention to the fact that the phrase "or of a determinate group of persons" had been added by the legislator to the Council text. This addition will serve to facilitate further the possibility of decentralizing the executive power of the bishop by ordinary vicarious power, rather than by delegated power.

delegations are not expressly prohibited by law or by the very nature of what is delegated.[57] But precisely for the reasons presented in the last two points, I think that these delegations ought to be exceptional, corresponding, that is, to extraordinary pastoral necessity, and should be done with the greatest prudence.

This appeal for prudence in delegating, seems particularly necessary in the case of *dispensations* from the universal laws that the supreme authority has expressly entrusted to the ordinary executive power of the bishop or of his vicars. For example, dispensations from matrimonial impediments of ecclesiastical law which are not reserved to the Holy See (cfr. can. 1078, §1); or, under certain conditions, dispensations from canonical form in mixed marriages (cfr. can. 1127, §2), etc. Certainly also the faculty of dispensing from these laws can be delegated by the diocesan bishop and by his vicar general and episcopal vicars, within the limits of their respective realms of power and competence (cfr. can. 85 and 90, §1). But we cannot forget that the legislator wanted to entrust the individual decisions of governance in these matters to the immediate and personal judgment of the diocesan ordinaries. Renouncing this personal responsibility without a just and serious reason, would not, in my opinion, be in accordance with the mind of the supreme authority.

Probably someone might ask: so what should the diocesan bishop do when the growing number of requests for matrimonial dispensations creates an exceptional situation of extraordinary pastoral necessity?

One thing is certain: the legislator has not prohibited delegating the faculty of dispensing in these cases: otherwise he would have explicitly said so (cfr. can. 137, §1). But neither did he want an indiscriminate application of the well known *regula iuris:* "Potest quis per alium, quod potest facere per se ipsum" [One can do through another, what he can do on his own].[58] We must remember that these words "per alium" ("through another") are valid when applied not only to the person *delegated* but also to the *vicar.* So, I think, it would be more in keeping with the mind of the legislator for the bishop to have recourse to the possibility offered him by can. 476. Thus he could name an episcopal vicar "for a certain type of business" (specifically for matrimonial dispensations).

On the other hand, it would be less appropriate to make use of the diocesan chancellor, as used to be done in some countries in the past, when the figure of the episcopal vicar "for a certain type of business" did not exist in the law.

---

[57]Cfr. above, note 54.
[58]Reg. 68, R.J. in VI.

In fact the chancellor, whether or not a cleric,[59] does not share in the power of governance "vi officii:" his functions are fundamentally those of a notary or secretary of the curia (cfr. can. 482). And particular law could not change the nature of such an ecclesiastical office. Consequently the faculty of dispensing must be granted to him by the bishop by way of delegation ("vi delegationis"). Now: why is it necessary to have recourse to this extraordinary means of extending the power of dispensing from certain universal laws, when this could be done through an episcipal vicar, who is an ordinary and a *local ordinary?* (cfr. can. 134, §§1-2).[60]

Conclusion

We are finishing. We first tried to put into a nutshell three theological-canonical principles which represent the constitutional bases for the diocesan bishop's power of governance. Then we saw what influence these doctrinal principles have had in the manner of technically applying the threefold distinction of legislative, executive and judicial functions to the unique and personal power of the bishop. Finally, taking into consideration the first two points, we synthetically examined two particular major questions regarding the correct exercise of executive power, especially in the area of dispensation and delegation. Allow me to conclude with two brief general considerations, one of a scientific character and the other of a pastoral nature.

In the history of every society having jurisdiction, and therefore also of the Church, the promulgation of a new body of legislation has always brought a development of juridical science. The progressive study and application of the new Code offers scholars of canon law a great opportunity for scientific creativi-

---

[59]Concerning the possibility or impossibility that a chancellor who is a *lay person* might exercise *vi delegationis* the faculty to dispense from matrimonial impediments, cfr. F.J. Urrutia, "Delegation of the Executive Power of Governance," *op. cit.*, 341-355; J.H. Provost and J.J. Cuneo, "The Power of Lay Chancellors to Dispense" in *Roman Replies and the CLSA Advisory Opinions 1986*, 56-64. I personally think that the Bishop *should not* concede such delegated power to the lay chancellor as long as the underlying doctrinal doubt remains. This doubt, however, does not seem to me to be resolved by appealing to the sense of the expression "cooperari possunt" of can. 129, §2, because the word "cooperare" is too generic and polyvalent. Rather it is necessary to go deeper, from a theological-canonical perspective, into a different question: is the dispensation from matrimonial impediments of this kind principally a technical function, an application of the law—as in the case of the lay person who is a judge: cfr. can. 1421, §2—or does it rather have a pastoral effect which requires and *intrinsically* hierarchical discretionary power? (With respect to the functions and the offices which are "intrinsically hierarchical," cfr. for example, V. Betti, "In margine al nuovo Codice di Diritto Canonico" in *Antonianum* 58 [1983] 641, note 36; A. Cattaneo, *Questioni fondamentali della canonistica nel pensiero di Klaus Morsdorf*, Pamplona, 1986, 227-233 and 408-413.)

[60]If there were really to be a coincidence of *two extraordinary circumstances,* i.e. the continuous accumulation of requests and the impossibility of constituting an *ad hoc* episcopal vicar, even in the eventuality of having a cleric as chancellor, it seems to me that a different solution could be sought. One could choose as passive subject of this delegation, those who have the faculty of assisting at marriages "vi officii," that is, in virtue of their pastoral office. But even in this eventuality, it should be a question of delegations with very exact and restrictive clauses, not granted in a broad or generalized way. Otherwise, the very aim of the relevant laws would be impeded, with evident violence to the *mens Legislatoris.*

ty. I think that we could adequately respond to this historic challenge if we develop our research in fidelity to the delicate theological and technical-juridical synthesis used by the legislator. In fact he restrained, it seems to me, the excesses of the two opposing doctrinal polarizations that were strongly manifested in the period immediately following the Council. On the one side, there was the *ecclesiologism* of those, who rightly wishing to avoid a divorce between theology and law, attributed to canon law the sole function of being a juridical safeguard for Word and Sacraments. On the other side, there was the *secularism* of those who thought that canon law owed its juridical nature and scientific weight only to a transplanting of civil patterns preferentially characterized by the defense of subjective rights of citizens.

The consideration of a pastoral nature that I would like to make is this. Today there exists in the Church, even following the promulgation of the new Code, a renewed awareness of the diaconal dimension, of service, which the *sacra potestas* has.[61] The bishops know well that in the Church the greatest dignity of power is because *salus animarum* is its supreme goal and because it is conferred and exercised in *nomine Christi Capitis*. From this comes the profound theological and pastoral necessity that they feel of exercising their personal power as pastors justly and prudently, not in an arbitrary manner or in a way which would be a renunciation of their proper rights and duties. Precisely because their power has this function of service, bishops are more conscious than ever of the truth of the words of the Bishop of Hippo: "We should make an account to God first of all for our lives as Christians, but then we ought to reply in a special way about the exercise of our ministry as pastors."[62]

Let us thank God for this praiseworthy pastoral and scientific concern of bishops and of canon lawyers and let us ask that it be further developed with the help of the Mother of the Redeemer, *Speculum iustitiae*.

---

[61]Cfr. *Lumen gentium*, 27; *Christus Dominus*, 23; *Gaudium et spes*, 23 and *passim*. This is one of the most significant aspects of the new legislation found in the Code, as John Paul II underlined in the Apostolic Constitution *Sacrae Disciplinae Leges:* "Among the elements which characterize the true and genuine image of the Church, we ought to bring into relief above all the following: the doctrine according to which the Church is presented as the People of God (cfr. *Lumen Gentium* 2) and the hierarchical authority as service (cfr. *ibid.*, 3) . . ." (AAS 75 [1983] xii).

[62]*Nos autem, excepto quod christiani sumus, unde rationem reddemus Deo de vita Nostra, sumus etiam praepositi, unde retionem reddemus Deo de dispensatione nostra:* Saint Augustine, "Sermo de Pastoribus" (Sermo 46, 2: CCL 41, 530).

INSTITUTED LAY MINISTRY: THE HISTORY AND FUTURE OF CANON 230

Thomas Richstatter, O.F.M.

Canon 230 §1. Lay men *[Viri laici]* who possess the age and qualifications determined by decree of the conference of bishops can be installed *[assumi possunt]* on a stable basis in the ministries *[ad ministeria]* of lector and acolyte in accord with the prescribed liturgical rite; the conferral *[collatio]* of these ministries, however, does not confer on these lay men a right to obtain support or remuneration from the Church.

§2. Lay persons *[Laici]* can fulfill the function of lector during liturgical actions by temporary deputation *[deputatione]*; likewise all lay persons can fulfill the functions *[muneribus]* of commentator or cantor or other functions, in accord with the norm of law.

§3. When the necessity of Church warrants it and when ministers *[ministris]* are lacking, lay prsons *[laici]*, even if they are not lectors or acolytes, can also supply for certain of their offices *[officia]*, namely, to exercise the ministry *[ministerium]* of the word, to preside over *[praeesse]* liturgical prayers, to confer baptism, and to distribute Holy Communion in accord with the prescriptions of law.[1]

Introduction

The first words of this cannon, *viri laici*, are the point of interest for many canonists. As a liturgist, I would approach the canon from a different perspective. This canon is proof of the wisdom of canon 2: "For the most part the Code does not define the rites which are to be observed in celebrating liturgical actions." A code of law by definition requires a certain systematic arrangement and logical ordering. Liturgical rites, on the other hand, require a certain unlogical disordering; we liturgists call this chaos "celebration."

The liturgical origins of this canon are the reason not only for the *viri laici* but also for the introduction of the vocabulary of "ministry" into that part of the code (Title II of Book II) treating "The Obligations and Rights of the *Lay Christian Faithful*." Canons 230 and 231 become the final two canons of Title II and immediately precede the canons of Title III "Sacred Ministers or Clerics."

---

[1] All citations of the current Code are taken from Canon Law Society of America, *Code of Canon Law: A Text and Commentary*, ed. James A. Coriden and others (New York/Mahwah: Paulist Pressm 1985), (= Commentary). All citations of the 1917 Code are taken from Stanislaus Woywod *A Practical Commentary on the Code of Canon Law* revised by Callistus Smith, (New York: Joseph Wagner, 1962), (= Woywod).

Once removed from the clerical context of incardination and seminaries, canons 230 and 231 must say something about money and formation.

> Canon 231 §1. Lay persons *(Laici)* who devote themselves permanently or temporarily to some special service *(servitio)* of the Church are obliged to acquire the appropriate formation which is required to fulfill their function *(munus)* properly and carry it out conscientiously, zealously, and diligently.
>
> §2. With due regard for can. 230, §1, they have a right to a decent remuneration suited to their condition; by such remuneration they should be able to provide decently for their own needs and for those of their family with due regard for the prescriptions of civil law; they likewise have a right that their pension, social security and health benefits be duly provided.

In one sense, things were more logical in the former code when "Those who have been assigned to divine ministry at least by the first tonsure are called clerics"[2] and questions of incardination, remuneration, benefices were treated together in the second book of the 1917 Code "Persons," Part one "Laws Concerning the Clergy." Formation for ministry was treated in Part IV of Book III (Things) of the former Code "Of the Teaching Authority of the Church," Title XXI "Of Seminaries."

> Canon 1352. It is the proper and exclusive right of the Church to educate the men who desire to devote their lives to the ecclesiastical ministry.
>
> Canon 1353. All priests, especially pastors, shall see that boys who show signs of ecclesiastical vocation, are carefully preserved from the contamination of the world. They shall train such youths in piety, give them elementary instruction in the study of letters, and foster in them the seed of the divine vocation.[3]

The seeds of the divine vocation would then grow in the Church's nursery (seminarium).

The ministries of lector and acolyte were treated together with all other liturgical ministries in Title VI "Of Holy Orders" for "[t]he Sacrament of Holy Orders by Christ's institution distinguishes in the Church the clergy from the laity for the government of the faithful and the ministry of divine worship." (canon 984)[4] Canon 974 demanded the reception of the "inferior orders" as requisite for licit ordination; and canon 973 restricted their conferral to those "who have the intention of advancing to the priesthood and who one may reasonably expect will be worthy priests."[5]

Note that in the present code canon 231 states that lay persons who devote

---

[2]Woywod, I, page 63.
[3]Woywod, II, page 131.
[4]Woywod, II, page 619.
[5]Woywod, II, page 651.

themselves permanently or temporarily to some special service of the Church are obliged to acquire the appropriate formation which is required to fulfill their function properly, whereas the following canon 232 (which is the first of the canons which treat of clerics) states that the Church assumes the responsibility for the formation of those who are commissioned for the sacred ministries.

The placing of canon 230, that is the removal of certain liturgical ministries from the title on clerics and placing them in the title on the laity is more than a liturgical change, it implies a change in ecclesiology.

THE HISTORICAL CONTEXT OF CANON 230

Pope Paul VI begins the motu proprio *Ministeria quaedam* by stating:
> Certain ministries were established by the Church even in the most ancient times for the purpose of suitably giving worship to God and for offering service to the people of God according to their needs. By these ministries, the offices to be carried out in the liturgy and the practice of charity, deemed suitable to varying circumstances, were entrusted to the faithful. The conferring of these functions often took place by a special rite, in which, after God's blessing had been implored, a Christian was established in a special class or rank for the fulfillment of some ecclesiastical function.[6]

At the time of Cyprian we find the term "cleric" being used in opposition to "people." In the fourth century the ministries of porter, lector, exorcist, acolyte, and subdeacon are in use in the Western church and the clerical state became a privilege given to these ministers. A cleric was no longer under the civil authority but under the authority of the church. For example, he was no longer bound by obligations of military service. With the introduction of the tonsure, one could be a cleric independent of exercising a ministry. As late as the eighteenth century tonsure could be given to children as young as eight or twelve (thus removing them from the authority of the state). "Cleric" denoted a state independent of ministry or function.[7]

During the Middle Ages in Rome the candidate for orders would have exercised at least one of the minor orders, that of lector or subdeacon. The rule that one would first receive tonsure and then each of the minor orders before diaconate is of Gallican origin; it found its way to Germany but did not become the rule in Rome before the eleventh or twelfth century. By the time of the Council of Trent, the minor orders had lost their independent meaning and were seen *only* as steps to the priesthood; indeed, the Council of Trent stated that no one should

---

[6]Paul VI, Motu proprio *Ministeria quaedam*, on first tonsure, minor orders, and the subdiaconate, August 15, 1972. AAS 64 (1972) 529-534; Notitiae 9 (1973) 4-8. International Commission on English in the Liturgy, *Documents on the Liturgy* (Collegeville: The Liturgical Press, 1982), (= DOL) number 340, par. 2922.

[7]Pierre Jounel, "Les Ministeres non Ordonnes dans l'eglise," *La Maison-Dieu* 149 (1982) 96.

receive the minor orders unless he seemed qualified to be raised in due time to higher orders.[8]

The distinction between "ordination" and "institution" is found already in the *Apostolic Tradition* of Hippolytus. Jounel says: "The root of the term "institution" means "to be charged with a task." It was used at the time of Hippolytus to indicate the entrance into responsibility for a certain function."[9] The principle ritual distinction between ordination and institution is that ordination is accomplished by the "imposition of hands" and institution is not. However, in the 1917 Code the term ordination was applied to episcopal consecration, the three major orders, the four minor orders and also to first tonsure.[10]

The former Code did not speak of liturgical roles or ministries of the laity because the liturgy was a clerical function: a service performed by the clergy for the laity. In the first article of the 1958 *Instruction on Sacred Music and the Liturgy* (which summarizes the liturgical legacy and reforms of Pius XII and is one of the principle pre-Conciliar liturgical documents) we read:

> The sacred liturgy consists in the totality of the public worship of the Mystical Body of Jesus Christ, that is of the Head and his members. Therefore, "liturgical actions" are those sacred actions which, whether instituted by Jesus Christ or instituted by the Church, are performed in their name according to the liturgical books approved by the Holy See, *by persons legitimately deputed for this* . . .[11]

It was not baptism that designated one for liturgy but a further deputation by the Church, e.g. sacred ordination or in some cases religious profession. (Thus, if in 1958 my mother and I recited the Breviary together I would have been performing a liturgical act but she would not, for she was not legitimately deputed for worship.) It was with great hesitancy and even reluctance that the Congregation of Rites permitted the "Dialogue Mass." The prayers belonged to the minister, not to the faithful. (A response from the congregation on August 4, 1922, allows the bishop to permit a dialogue Mass, but the Congregation does not hide its fears that all this noise of people talking out loud will be a distraction to the other priests saying Mass at the side altars of the church!).[12]

It is the rediscovery of a more complete understanding and appreciation of baptism that has opened the door to a renewed understanding of liturgy and liturgical ministry. As we read in canon 204, the opening canon of Book II, The People of God,

---

[8] Session XIII, cap. 11. See Woywod, II, page 651.
[9] Jounel art. cit. 97.
[10] Canon 950. In iure verba: *ordinate, ordo, ordinatio, sacra ordinatio,* comprehendunt, praeter consecrationem episcopalem, ordines enumeratos in can. 949 et ipsam tonsuram, nini aliud ex nature rei vel ex contextu verborum eruatur.
[11] AAS 50 (1958) 630-663, emphasis added.
[12] Martimort, A. G., and Picard, F. *Liturgie et Musique,* Lex Ordandi number 28, (Paris, Cerf, 1959) 91.

The Christian faithful are those who, inasmuch as they have been incorporated in Christ through baptism, have been constituted as the people of God; for this reason, since they have become sharers in Christ's priestly, prophetic and royal office in their own manner, they are called to exercise the mission which God has entrusted to the Church to fulfill in the world, in accord with the condition proper to each one.

PROXIMATE ORIGINS OF CANON 230

In 1963 Pope John XXIII established the Pontifical Commission for the Revision of Code. The commission began its formal work in 1965. The work of the study group which revised the law on the sacrament of Orders can be found in the 1978 edition of *Communicationes*.[13] However, as Edward Gilbert has indicated in his commentary on Title VI Orders, "The law on orders—probably more than any other sacrament—had already been significantly changed due to legislation promulgated by Pope Paul VI. In part, the work of the Commission was to incorporate this material into the revised law in the form of canons."[14] Consequently we will turn our attention to this legislation of Pope Paul VI and the revision of the liturgical rites of ordination.

The grandparents of canon 230 are found in the *motu proprio* of Pope Paul VI *Sacram liturgiam* of January 25, 1964.[15] The Introduction to this document stated that a special commission was being established to revise the liturgical rites and to prepare the new liturgical books. This is the origin of the "Commission for the implementation of the *Constitution on the Sacred Liturgy*" which we refer to as the *"Consilium."*[16] The Consilium quickly divided the tasks of preparing the new liturgical books and formed about thirty working groups. One of these, under the leadership of Dom Bernard Botte, O.S.B., undertook the revision of the first book of the Roman Pontifical: Ordinations and Solemn Blessings and Consecration of Persons.[17] The work of revising the minor orders fell to this working group also; however, at that time, the issue was not the abolition of the minor orders.

Toward the end of 1966, the secretariat of the Consilium formulated a proposal to present to Paul VI:

1. The pope would be asked to suppress the four minor orders.

---

[13] Communicationes 10 (1978), 178-208.
[14] Edward J. Gilbert, Commentary 716.
[15] For the emended text see: AAS 56 (1964) 139-144.
[16] Further information on this *motu proprio* can be found in my book *Liturgical Law Today: New Style, New Spirit* (Chicago: Franciscan Herald Press, 1977) 89-91.
[17] I am dependent for much of the history of the formation of those documents on the information given in class by Monsignor Pierre Jounel, professor at the Institut Superieur de Liturgie de l'Institut Catholique de Paris and upon his articles in *Notitiae* (March 1982) and "Les Ministeres non Ordonnes dans l'eglise," *La Maison-Dieu* 149 (1982) 91-105.

2. The subdiaconate would become the only remaining minor order and it would be open not only to candidates for the diaconate, but to others as well; indeed the subdiaconate would no longer be an obligatory step before being ordained deacon.

3. That the rite of entrance into the clerical state would be separate from ordinations.

4. A special blessing would be established to dedicate lay persons to permanent liturgical service as lectors, acolytes, or special ministers of Communion, or to dedicate them to non-liturgical ministries, for example, catechist.[18]

The curia learned of this proposal even before it was presented to the pope. The proposal met with much criticism; so much criticism that it had to be abandoned.

Meanwhile, the working group which was revising the rites of ordination completed their task and the revised rites, introduced by the Apostolic constitution *Pontificalis Romani recognitio* (June 18, 1968) were approved by decree of the Sacred Congregation of Rites on August 15, 1968.[19]

One of the general liturgical principles operative in the revision of the Ordination rites was the principle of "authenticity:" things should be what they seem. For example, a night watch (vigil, Easter vigil) should be at night; morning prayer (laudes) should be in the morning, etc. Ministries or orders that will never be used (e.g. exorcist) should not be given, etc. The rites of ordination were to be revised so that "they express more clearly the holy things they signify and that the Christian people, as far as possible, are able to understand them with ease and to take part in the rites fully, actively, and as befits a community."[20]

Apart from, but not unrelated to the liturgical issue of the role of readers and acolytes in the revision of the ordination rites was the pastoral issue of the growing need for readers and ministries of Holy Communion. At this same time we were witnessing a great increase in the number of communicants. The shorter formula "The Body of Christ" was introduced in 1964.[21] Already in 1965 certain women religious are authorized to give communion in Brazil.[22] This authorization was extended to certain situations in Canada (1966)[23] and West Germany (1968).[24] The Sacred Congregation for the Discipline of the Sacraments greatly extended this authorization for lay ministers of the eucharist with the instruction *Fidei custos,* April 30, 1969.[25] The following month, May 29, 1969, the Sacred Congregation for Divine Worship published the instruction *Morale Domini,* on

---

[18]Jounel art. cit. 92.

[19]*Pontificale romanum . . . De ordinatione diaconi, presbyeri, et episcopi.* Editio Typica, Typis Polyglottis Vaticanis, 1968.

[20]Constitution on the Liturgy, 21.

[21]Sacred Congregation of Rites, Decree *Qua actuosius* April 25, 1964. DOL 252. AAS 56 (1964) 335-338.

[22]SC Extraordinary Affairs. Rescript (Brazil) of April 24, 1965. DOL 253.

[23]DOL 255.

[24]DOL 257.

[25]DOL 260. AAS 61 (1969) 541-545. Notitiae 5 (1969) 347-351.

the manner of giving communion.[26] (Within a week, Belgium, France and Germany had received authorization for receiving communion in the hand.)[27] Note that these changes with regard to the minister and rites for communion are several years prior to the Instruction of the Sacred Congregation for the Discipline of the Sacraments *Immensae caritatis* of January 29, 1973, which treated in a broader way special ministers for distributing communion; a broader faculty to receive communion twice in a day; mitigation of the eucharistic fast; and the reverence required when communion is received in the hand.[28]

Following upon the publication of the new rites for ordinations in 1969, the French and German bishops (each independently) asked the Holy see for permission to suppress tonsure, the four minor orders, and the subdiaconate and to replace them by a rite of admission to candidacy for diaconate or presbyterate, two blessings for lectors and acolytes, and a formula for the promise of celibacy in the ordination of unmarried deacons.[29]

Towards the end of 1970 the Sacred Congregation for Divine Worship itself presented a similar proposal which called for the suppression of tonsure, porter, exorcist and the subdiaconate but preserved the minor orders of lector and acolyte as necessary steps to the reception of the diaconate. Before the reception of the diaconate there was to be a rite of admission to the clerical state.

The careful historian can see the great differences between these two similar proposals. The remarks of Monsignor Jounel are pertinent here:

> Despite the similarity with the project of the transalpine bishops, the project of the Congregation evidences a totally different mentality. The Congregation for Divine Worship had to ratify the remarks of the Congregation for the Discipline of the Sacraments which considered it essential to retain the two minor orders as well as the notion of the clerical state.[30]

Meeting in plenary session, the members of the Congregation for Divine Worship rejected the project and sent the following project to the Pope:

1. The word "cleric" would be preserved only for those in sacred orders; and the notion of "privilege" that had become attached to the word is no longer appropriate after the Council. Orders are a ministry within the church and a service to the people of God.

2. Incardination would be operative with the reception of the diaconate.

3. The word "ordination" would be reserved for sacred orders, those conferred by imposition of hands.

4. The rite of admission to candidacy for orders should have a spiritual rather than a juridic thrust. Such a rite would be superfluous for religious.

---

[26]DOL 260. AAS 61 (1969) 541-545. Notitiae 5 (1969) 347-351.
[27]See *Liturgical Law Today* 124.
[28]DOL 264. AAS 65 (1973) 264-271. Notitiae 9 (1973) 157-164.
[29]Jounel 93.
[30]Jounel 93.

5. Faculties would be given to the various episcopal conferences for determining and arranging rites which would sanctify other liturgical and non liturgical ministries.

The details for this proposal were to be worked out by representatives of the various Congregations concerned: Sacraments, Divine Worship and Catholic Education (Seminaries).

Pope Paul VI took these proposals and thought about them for over a year. His response is the motu proprio *Ministeria quaedam,* August 15, 1972, "By which the Discipline of First Tonsure, Minor Orders, and Subdiaconate in the Latin Church is Reformed."[31] It is this *motu proprio* which is parent of the legislation in the current code.

The *motu proprio* and consequently the code both reflect the two theologies that were operative in the project presented to the Pope: one sees the ministries of lector and acolyte as lay ministries (this accounts for the location of canon 230 in the present code) and the other theology sees lector and acolyte as minor orders, restricted to males (as are all orders) and a necessary prerequisite to ordination. It is actually this theology which is operative in the church today.

In the United States the ministry which Catholics see and experience is not the instituted ministries of canon 230, §1 but non-instituted ministries of readers and special ministers of the eucharist which are not restricted to males.[32]

On the other hand, the ministries envisioned in canon 230, §1 are still experienced (nearly exclusively) in a seminary context as they were before the new Code. Canon 1035 states that "Before anyone is promoted to either the permanent or the transitional diaconate he is required to have received the ministries of lector and acolyte and to have exercised them for a suitable period of time." The canon repeats article XI of *Ministeria quaedam* which added the reason for this: "in order to be better disposed for the future service of the word and of the altar."[33] Consequently, despite the fact that these two ministries have been moved in the new code to the canons treating "The Obligations and Rights of the *Lay* Christian Faithful" in the United States, in most dioceses they are exercised *only* by men preparing for the diaconate or presbyterate. And I would add as one who has been charged with the preparation of candidates for these ministries, a special difficulty is presented by the fact that those preparing for these ministries have almost always been exercising these ministries in large part before being installed in them liturgically because most candidates for ordination serve as readers

---

[31] DOL 340.

[32] With regard to the viri laici and the liturgical ministries of women in the United States see *General Instruction of the Roman Missal: Liturgy Documentary Series 2,* (Washington: Office of Publishing Services, United States Catholic Conference, 1982), p. 92. On the ministry of the altar being restricted to males (1917 Code, canon 813) see the James Provost's commentary on canon 230, and John Huels' commentary on canon 906, in James A. Coriden et. al., eds, *The Code of Canon Law: A Text and Commentary* (New York/Mahwah: Paulist, 1985).

[33] DOL par 2936.

and special ministers of the eucharist both in their parishes of origin and in ministry assignments. I have often had to try to prepare the candidates to receive something they feel they already have. (In contrast to my own experience: I was ordained lector and acolyte but never read until I was a Subdeacon or touched a host until I was ordained Deacon!)

William James said that the best way to understand what something means is to see what difference it makes. The idea to put these ministries in the context of the laity has not made much difference except that seminarians today only receive two minor orders rather than four. This was certainly not the idea beind the revision.

The Future of Canon 230

There is little possibility that canon 230 will be changed. I have recently had the opportunity to discuss this issue with a number of European Catholic and non-Catholic sacramental theologians at the meeting of the Societas Liturgica in Brixen during August 1987. The role of women in ministry is viewed by the European Church as a specifically American problem resulting not from our experience of "all being created equal" but from our refusal to accept the implications of being a member of the Body of Christ. An eye is not a hand; an ear is not a foot. European theologians feel that it is American individualism,[34] not insight into the Gospel, that leads us to the erroneous opinion that anyone can be anything. (For example, I have been born in a country where anyone, including me, can [at least theoretically] become president. But try as I might, I could never become Queen of England. European theologians would respond to this analogy with a simple: "Of course; that's the nature of things").

In any case "ministry" (and especially the ministry of the presbyterate) is not a fruitful starting point for dialogue on the "viri laici" of canon 230. The issue is baptism. How can the same univocal baptism render some human natures so conformed to Christ that they are capable of receiving all the other sacraments and the same baptism make other human natures conformed to Christ in such a way that they are capable of receiving only certain of the other sacraments? It has been insight into the meaning of baptism that gave birth to an ecclesiology which enables lay ministry at all. As we read in the opening canon of Book II "The People of God:" The Christian faithful are those who, inasmuch as they have been incorporated in Christ *through baptism* . . . (Can. 204, §1).

Liturgists have always trusted the axium *Lex orandi lex credendi*. This principle would seem to imply that the problem will not be solved until a person's baptismal day is more important that that person's ordination day. When the rites of ordination become more elaborate and take precedence over rites in initiation,

---

[34]For a popular treatment of American individualism see Robert N. Bellah and others, *Habits of the Heart; Individualism and Commitment in American Life* (New York: Harper and Row, 1985).

the principle of *Lex orandi lex credendi* assures us that the resulting defective ecclesiology will inevitably birth a deformed theology of ministry. As Thomas O'Meara concludes in his *Theology of Ministry:*

> The church is ministerial. Ministry is not a rare vocation or a privileged office but belongs to the nature of the new covenant; God's religious destiny happens in community but is intended for the entire human race. As with its universal source, baptism, ministry exists in the churches as an apect of every Christian's life.[35]

Ministry is not a rare vocation but a necessary consequence of Christian Initiation. We have always taught that the sacraments are efficacious signs but I wonder if we really trust the power of the sacraments.

I once heard of a catechumen, a young man about 27 years old, who was a participant in an RCIA program in a midwest diocese. The catechist had told the catechumens that ministry was a consequence of initiation, and after the sacraments of initiation, during the mystagogical period, there would be a special commissioning ceremony in the parish at which each of the neophytes would be asked to fulfill a certain ministry in the Church. This young man was wondering what he might be asked to do. Several weeks later a missionary spoke to the catechumens one evening about the missionary activity of the Church in general and in particular about a new mission in Guatemala that the Diocese was sponsoring. That night the catechumen couldn't sleep; he wondered if the parish might ask him to go as a missionary to Guatemala. For quite some time before his baptism, he struggled with this idea: What if the commitment to baptism involved leaving his job and home town? What if the Church would ask that of him? But finally he resolved the issue for himself and decided that if that's what baptism, confirmation, and eucharist demanded, then he was ready for the challenge. I remember the disappointment in his voice when he told how, after his baptism at the parish commissioning ceremony, he was asked, not to go to Guatemala, but to take up the collection at the 11:30 Mass on the second Sunday of each month!

The Church is structured liturgically: sacraments make Church. The sacraments are powerful, efficacious signs. It is time to trust the efficacy of the sacraments and to courageously face the implications of baptism. "For as many of you as were baptized into Christ have put on Christ. There is neither Jew nor Greek, there is neither slave nor free, there is neither male nor female; for you are all one in Christ Jesus." (Gal 3:27-28 RSV)

---

[35] Thomas Franklin O'Meara, O.P. *Theology of Ministry,* New York: Paulist Press, 1983. p. 209.

ECUMENICAL ISSUES IN THE REVISED CODE OF CANON LAW

Royce R. Thomas

I think it is appropriate that we talk about ecumenism here in Nashville.[1] At the end of the Second Vatican Council the bishop of Nashville, Bishop Durick stated that ecumenism and better relations with other faiths was to be a high priority. It was and continues to be the same under the leadership of our host bishop, Bishop Niedergeses. For example, there is a Roman Catholic presence on the faculty and in the student body at the school of Divinity at Vanderbilt—formerly a Methodist school and now nondenominational; and, in the school of Theology at the University of the South, Sewanee—an Episcopal school. It is interesting to note that "Monk" Malloy the new president of Notre Dame received his Ph.D. in theology from Vanderbilt and Sewanee gave Fr. Hesburg the former president of Notre Dame an honorary degree in theology.

The Diocese has a common marriage policy with the Episcopalians and the Catholic Hospitals in the diocese have ecumenical pastoral care teams.

What many of us may not realize is Nashville is the "Vatican" for the Southern Baptists. Their convention headquarters is here; their Sunday School Board is here; and, their Sunday School publishing house is here. It is interesting to note the difference between them and us in the matter of religious education. We have one magisterium but many publishers of books and aids. They on the other hand believe in the autonomy of the local congregation and yet have only one publisher of Sunday School materials. As decentralized as they are, I understand that the Vatican employs about 3500 people and the Southern Baptist Convention employs over 15,000. Our host bishop is the NCCB liaison to the Southern Baptists and Nashville is the host for the Scholars Dialogue where three or four times a year scholars representing the NCCB and the Southern Baptists meet to discuss substantive issues dealing with ministry, authority and orders. So, I do feel it is appropriate to be discussing ecumenical issues here in Music City.

The issues that I would like to discuss here today will pertain mainly to the non-Catholic ecclesial bodies commonly referred to as Protestant. I leave to others the task of exploring relations with the Orthodox and Jews.

One of my part time jobs is being a chaplain with the Arkansas National Guard. I remember when I was in basic training one of the instructors told us not to attempt to be ecumenical in our ministry but rather be pluralistic. Needless to say, we all scratched our heads at that one. However, when you think about it pluralism means that all the various sects co-exist side by side. Whereas, ecumenism seeks

---

[1] Information concerning the Diocese of Nashville is from Fr. Owen Campion, Diocesan Ecumenical Officer, 2400 Twenty-first Avenue South, Nashville, TN 37212.

to reconcile and unify the various faith traditions.

Although our country is pluralistic—I don't think the military is. Most career service people when asked their religion will say "we always attended the base/post chapel." For us Christians, though, the important issue is the unanswered prayer of Jesus: "that they all may be one as you Father are in me and I in you."[2]

The division among Christians openly contradicts the will of Christ, scandalizes the world and damages the most holy cause, the preaching of the gospel to every creature.[3]

Division, diversity and separation are not new to the Church.[4] Study of the New Testament and New Testament times shows there were Pauline churches, Johannine Churches, Jerusalem Churches and within them were Judaizers and followers of John the Baptizer (or in Nashville, let us say John the Baptist). But these were all in communion with each other. So the implication of Canon 1 of the 1983 Code re-inforced by cc. 111-112 that there are different rites and juridic systems within the church is not new.

From the earliest times there have also been heresies and schisms which the Church has sought to heal. However, the Great Schism of 1034 and the tragic events of the 16th century known as the Reformation have been different.

Because of the great suffering and cost that all sides paid, positions were hardened, extreme positions were taken. Can't we all remember the times we were not allowed to go to the YMCA? Permission from the bishop was needed to attend a non-Catholic college even if there was no Catholic college in the diocese. We could not read the King James version of the Bible. Some even wondered if they could contribute to the Salvation Army buckets at Christmas. And then, there were the jokes: Two nuns with their large flowing habits were standing in an elevator when a fellow behind them, obviously annoyed, said he wished he were somewhere where there are few nuns. One of the good sisters turned around and said "why don't you go to hell there aren't any nuns there." The Catholics were always the wise guys. The priest and the Protestant minister has a wreck. The irate minister said "If I weren't a man of God I would curse you." The priest said "If it weren't Friday I would chew your rear end." It's hard to respect people when you are always laughing at them.

No, those two tragedies, the Great Schism and the Protestant Reformation, have withstood efforts at reconciliation. Therefore, it is not an exaggeration to say the ecumenical movement of our time is unique. It involves the majority of non-Catholic Christian churches and centers for the most part around the World Council of Churches, the WCC.

---

[2]John 17,21. *New American Bible.* Translated by the Catholic Biblical Association. New York: P.J. Kennedy & Sons, 1968.
[3]*Unitatis Redintegratio* (UR) #7.
[4]The information on the "Ecumenical Movement," *The New Catholic Encyclopedia.* Vol. 5. New York: McGraw-Hill, 1967, pp. 96-100. and M. Marty, "Ecumenical Movement," *Encyclopedia Americana.* Vol. 9. Danbury, Conn., Grolier Press. 1972, p. 623.

Briefly, the WCC has undergone many developmental changes. They began working toward "non competitive" relationships, especially in missionary lands. They then began to work and serve together. Later, they saw the need for discussion concerning doctrine and church order.

The Roman Church, although not a member of the World Council, has always been an interested observer. The Catholic position has been that ecumenism is best served by clearly stating and maintaining one's theological beliefs regardless of how painful that might be.

For example: in 1896, Pope Leo XIII denied the validity of Angelican orders thus breaking with the Anglicans, the so-called bridge church between Roman Catholics and Protestants. In 1928 Pius XI in the encylical *Mortalium Animos* asserted unequivocally that unity must be based on acceptance of Christ's entire revelation, doctrinal compromise is inadmissible, and the Church cannot be a federation of independent bodies holding different doctrines.

In 1949 the Holy Office issued an "Instruction on the Ecumenical Movement" which was a charter of Catholic unionistic activity. It encouraged Catholics to pray for the success of the movement and to take part in it. It said the ecumenical movement should daily assume a more significant place within the Church's universal pastoral care.

Various organizations and groups arose throughout the world who worked, studied and talked together. New understandings and appreciations developed. In our own country problems stalled the ecumenical spirit. So many American Catholics, like myself, have deep, long, rich, Irish bloodlines. The memories of civil and social disabilities, struggles to maintain faith and build institutions died hard.

All the above notwithstanding, the pontificate of John XXIII gave the ecumenical movement in the Catholic Church its present impetus. His tone, his example, his encyclicals all encouraged a general spirit of confidence and friendship. In 1961 he established the Secretariat for Promoting Christian Unity under the leadership of Cardinal Bea. But it was his decision in that same year to convene a council and revise the Code of Canon Law that will have the most lasting effect.

We are familiar with the history of the Council. Ecumenists were deeply touched by the presence and limited participation of Protestant observers. The "Dogmatic Constitution on the Church," the "Decree on Ecumenism," the "Decree on the Church's Missionary Activity," the "Decree on the Eastern Churches," the "Declaration on Religious Freedom" and the "Declaration on the Relationship of the Church to Non-Christian Religions" were documents[5] which captured the ecumenical concerns of the Church and gave it direction in the post-conciliar era.

As we know, the revision of the Code could not begin until after the end of the Council. During those years of revision the Church lived in a time of experimentation and decretals. A quick glance at the indicies of the *Canon Law*

---

[5]See Walter W. Abbott, S.J., General Editor. *The Documents of Vatican II*. New York: Guild Press, 1966.

Digest after the Council shows a richness of activity—papers and interpretations from the Holy See as well as responses to initiatives in individual and local churches.[6] Covenants were being established between local Catholic churches and others. There were common youth programs, pre-marriage programs, Bible studies, and for a while we could even be Masons.

The most significant of the post-Conciliar documents is the "Ecumenical Directory" published in two parts by the Secretariat for Promoting Christian Unity in 1967 and 1970.[7] There may be some bewilderment as to whether it remains in effect since the promulgation of the Code. Cardinal Willebrands wrote that it was not a law in terms of canon 6 nor a general decree in terms of canon 29. There were even some difficulties in considering it a general executory decree as in cc. 31 and 33.[8]

The Directory still applies to the Oriental Church. Some canons in the 1983 code presuppose it,[9] so it still has some force with the Latin Church. According to the Secretariat the greater part of Part I remains in effect and the entirety of Part II remains in effect.[10]

Rumor has it that an updated version of the "Directory" is due out in the spring of 1988 which will take into account and incorporate any of the changes required by the 1983 Code.

It should be noted that in many ways the 1983 code is the last document of Vatican II. It does incorporate some post-conciliar legislation; i.e., *Matrimonia Mixta, Poenitemini* but in large part it uses the theology of the Council and when faced with theological problems or disagreements it simply restates the former position; i.e., vows.[11] Thus the Code should not be seen as the last word on a topic but rather realize the Code Commission wasn't taking sides on issues but giving time for a consensus to form.

The ecumenical value of the Code has been summarized by Cardinal Willebrands as:

> "From being centralising and biased toward uniformity, the code has become respectful of persons, of their fundamental rights and duties; it has given the laity active responsibility in the life of the Church; it emphasizes the importance of the Holy Spirit, of his gifts and Charismata; hence the care to respect particular autonomies according to the proper rights demanded by group identity and by ecclesial communities. At the service of a unity which respects legitimate and necessary

---

[6] See Bouscaren-O'Connor. *Canon Law Digest*, Vols. 6-9.

[7] "Ecumenical Directory" published by the Secretariat for Promoting Christian Unity. Part I *AAS* 59-584, Part II *AAS* 62-705 translated in *Canon Law Digest* Vol. 6. pp. 716-734, Vol. 7. pp. 801-819.

[8] Cardinal Willibrands, "An Introduction" "Ecumenical Aspects of the New Code of Canon Law." The Secretariat for Promoting Christian Unity Information Service. No. 60 (1986) 1-1. Vatican City. p. 54.

[9] C. 256, §2—Instruction of students about ecumenical affairs. C. 755, §1—The universal mandate for ecumenism. C. 383, 83—pastoral office of the diocesan bishop with regards to ecumenism.

[10] Cardinal Willebrands, op. cit.

[11] James Corriden, Thomas Green, Donald Heintschel, editors. *The Code of Canon Law A Text and Commentary*. Paulist Press. c. 1192; p. 842.

diversity, Church authority has to protect and promote them according to the pastoral needs of time and place."[12]

Some of the positive points about the Code and ecumenism have been mentioned by others. Briefly, some of these points are the following:

It's been said that we canonists don't design the Church—the theologians do—we are the plumbers and handymen who keep it running. The theological model upon which the Code is based is that of "communion."[13] Therefore, people are seen as being separated from or in varying degrees of communion with the Church. A person's rights and duties in the Church depend on the degree of communion he has.[14]

Canon 1 affirms that the Code is only for the Latin Church. In 1917 the Code in cc. 12 and 87 presupposed that the Church of Christ into which a person is baptized is contained exclusively within the Catholic Church, therefore ecclesiastical laws applied to all the baptized over the age of seven.

Canon 17 speaks of interpretation. In the 1917 Code reference was to be made to parallel passages in the Code.[15] By omitting this phrase we see that a true understanding of the law requires familiarity with the documents upon which it is based.

Canon 383 speaks of the bishop's obligation to those who are not in full communion and the non-baptized. It does not stretch the imagination too much to see the same obligation for the pastor who in many ways acts in the name of the bishop. It would be difficult for him to take his responsibilities listed in cc. 528 and 529 seriously and not come to that understanding.

Canon 751 gives some definitions which do not have the traditional applications. "Heresy" applies to those who are in full communion. The Decree on Ecumenism in article 3 states the sins of separation cannot be attributed to Christians baptized and raised in other Christian churches or ecclesial communities. Therefore, non-Catholics are not generally formal heretics. "Apostacy" could apply to any baptized Christian. "Schism" like heresy would normally only be attributed to Catholic Christians. The sanctions and penalties attached to these would no longer automatically apply to members of other churches.

Canon 755 is the universal mandate to work for the Christian unity which the "Church is bound by the will of Christ to promote."

There are several other examples of a positive tone in the Code but I would like to move on to some practical parochial issues created by the Code. There are of course some doctrinal items such as infant baptism, papal primacy, etc. which cause heartburn for the Orthodox and non-Catholic groups. However, I will by and large leave those matters to the theologians.

---

[12]"Ecumenical Aspects of the New Code of Canon Law," p. 57.

[13]*"Sacrae Disciplinae Leges."* translated by the Canon Law Society of America in *Code of Canon Law Latin-English Version.* p. xv. For an explanation of "communion" see *Jurist* Vol. 36 (1976) 1/2 and Avery Dulles, S.J. *Models of the Church.*

[14]C. 96.

[15]See C. 18 of the 1917 Code.

MEMBERSHIP

The first concern I would like to address is "membership." Who or what is a Catholic? I don't ask this as a Chancellor wondering about filling in the annual OCD statistics. Rather, I think this has bearing on several practical issues.

The code often uses the word *"christifideles."* But who are those people? By baptism a person is incorporated into the Church.[6] If a baptized person is joined with the visible structure of the Church by the bonds of profession of faith, of the sacraments and ecclesiastical governance she is in "full communion."[17] But there are other degrees of communion as well.[18] Then there is full Christian initiation *(plenam initiationem Christianam)*[19] which requires the reception of baptism, confirmation and first eucharist. I presume that one can be in full communion without being fully initiated but c. 205 does state that full communion is by means of the "bonds of the sacraments *(sacramentorum)*." Canon 512, §1, in describing the make up of the diocesan pastoral council limits membership to *"christifideles qui in plena communione sint."* Does this mean there are *christifideles qui non in plena communione sunt?* Canon 825, §2 uses the expression *"chrisitifideles catholici."* Does this mean there are also *"christifideles acatholici?"* The parish is defined as a definite community of the Christian faithful *(communitas Christifidelium).*[20] So to whom then do the merely ecclesiastical laws apply? Canon 11 tells us they apply to those baptized or received in the Catholic church who have reached the use of reason and are seven years of age. Does baptized or received in the Catholic church mean full communion? I believe it does.

Christifideles then is not a univocal word. To apply it we follow c. 17 and look at the text, context and parallel passages. Keeping in mind c. 512 describing the make up of the diocesan pastoral council, let's ask: Can a person not in full communion be a member of the parish pastoral council or even be the president of it? Canon 536 describes the make up of the parish council as *Christifideles* and those who help in the pastoral area. The hypothetical situation would be that a parish council is composed of elected members and the heads or chairpersons of various parish groups. The president of the PTA is a devoted parent who happens to be a Lutheran. According to the statutes of the parish council she is automatically on it. She might very well be elected its chair as well. What if she were non-baptized? What if it were a man and he were a Mason to boot? Using the diocesan pastoral council model, I think we would have to say she could not serve. However, in real life when a beleaguered pastor finds a competent willing person, she is going to serve.

Could a non-Catholic be a member of the parish? Membership on the parish

---

[16] C. 204.
[17] C. 205.
[18] See LG 13-15, UR 13-24, OE 24-29.
[19] C. 842.
[20] C. 515, 1.

council is probably restricted to members of the parish. Could a religiously mixed couple be listed as Mr. & Mrs. on the parish roster?

ASSOCIATIONS OF THE FAITHFUL

Fr. Leonard Pivonka and the Secretariat for Christian Unity[21] have already assured us that in considering whether a person not in full communion may join associations of the faithful we should keep in mind the dispensing power of the diocesan bishop and the particular statutes of that association itself. On the negative side of membership, the 1983 Code introduces the notion that someone can leave the Church by means of a "formal act" (e.g., c. 1124). This is a great leap forward ecumenically as it admits that someone can leave the "Catholic Church." Heretofore, once a Catholic, always a Catholic—juridically. However, as welcome as this admission might be, it also poses some problems.

The Code indicates that in leaving, something formal must be done. It however does not specify what that something might be. Someone checking out could hardly be expected to go through a liturgical or para-liturgical service of separation. Facetiously, we might ask whether it would be the turning in of her envelopes. Maybe it could be something along the lines of a written statement or as the Baptists would say "changing her letter."

As a canonist, I can see the need for the "formal act" of departure. We need something definite and something which can be used in the external forum. However, there are a lot of people who check out just by leaving. A person might find another church where she feels more at home. Or, for whatever reason, she does not want to belong to any church. In the former case perhaps a document of conversion or membership from the other denomination would suffice but what about the latter? Since baptism is incorporation into the community, once the indelible character is imprinted, a person belongs to some community regardless of how niggardly her membership may be. But, should she be required to observe canonical form when marrying?

I am afraid that if something on a consistent basis is not found and agreed upon, we will repeat the experience of c. 1099, §2 of the former code. Briefly, persons who were baptized Catholic but not raised Catholic (the wording was "persons who from infancy were raised in heresy, schism or infidelity or without any religion") were exempt from canonical form. It got to be such a hassle determining what a Catholic upbringing was that in 1948, Pius XII abrogated that phrase from the law and made all baptized Catholics subject to the requirements of form. We look to the *jurisprudentes* in the tribunals for help in sorting this one out.

---

[21]Leonard Pivonka, "The Revised Code of Canon Law: Ecumenical Implications," *Jurist* 45 (1985) 2, 533. and "Ecumenical Aspects of the New Code of Canon Law." p. 60.

RIGHTS

May we now talk about rights in the Church? As you know in the first part of Book II there are 23 canons (208-231) dealing with the duties and rights of all Christian faithful *(omnium Christifidelium)* and the obligations and rights of the lay Christian faithful *(christifidelium laicorum)*. Let us consider how these might apply. The extent of a person's duties and rights is determined by his condition and the extent of his ecclesiastical communion[22] but as we have seen above that is not so easy to determine.

It would seem that some of the rights enumerated would apply to any human being regardless of baptismal status: the right to privacy, a good name,[23] just remuneration.[24] Although because of baptism there exists a true equality of dignity and activity[25] some of the other rights would apply to all the baptized: the right to work for the spread of the gospel,[26] worship in her own rite and the right to her own form of spiritual life,[27] right to learn her religion.[28] Other rights apply only to Catholics: the right to fulfill the office of lector and acolyte,[29] to hold ecclesiastical offices and exercise ministries.[30]

Canons 528 and 529 list the obligations of the pastor towards the people *(christifideles)* living in his parish. Canon 1063 states that the pastor and the parish have an obligation to prepare *christifideles* for marriage even to the extent of giving them personal individualized instructions.[31] Do these obligations for the pastor constitute rights for the faithful and what degree of communion must these faithful profess to demand them?

Canon 221 reminds us that the faithful can legitimately vindicate and defend their rights . . . before a competent ecclesiastical court of law. As we Catholics know, rights go hand in hand with obligations. So if the non-Catholics have rights do they have obligations as well? Can they vindicate their rights with or without obligations?

It seems to me that all have the obligation to work for social justice,[32] and educate their children.[33] I suppose everyone is obliged to support the church[34] to the extent that if they come to bingo they do not play for free. But, non-Catholics would not have to maintain communion with the Pope.[35] For non-Catholics or even the

---

[22] C. 96.
[23] C. 220.
[24] C. 231, 2.
[25] C. 208.
[26] C. 211.
[27] C. 214.
[28] C. 229, 2.
[29] C. 230, 2-3.
[30] C. 228.
[31] C. 1063, 2.
[32] C. 222, 2.
[33] C. 236, 2.
[34] C. 222, 1.
[35] C. 209.

non-baptized to vindicate their rights in the Church is not without precedent, the matrimonial sections of our tribunals deal with them every day.

Let us now wonder about Catholics themselves. Can any baptized Catholic who has not left the Church by means of a formal act but who has not darkened the door of the church for years demand her right to a Christian education? How welcome will her opinions be when expressed to her pastor?

The vindication of rights is a matter we need to take seriously. During the Holy Father's recent trip to our country, time and time again the media spoke of how the American church and culture is different from others. One of the differences is the litigious society in which we live. People expect to be able to vindicate their rights. To be credible witnesses for social justice I believe we need to have a credible system of due process and conflict resolution. Precinding from the merits of the cases(s) the Church has been bloodied in the press in recent years because she seemed to ignore the rights of some of her children: e.g., Archbishop Hunthausen, Fr. Charles Curran, Sr. Agnes Mary Mansour. Many non-Catholics agree with the Church's position in these matters but disagree with the way they understand the Church enforces them. There are those who say the due process canons of the code (1732-39) are an American contribution to the law. We need to make it living law.

WOMEN

This leads into another thorny problem—the treatment of women in the Church. Meeting the requirements of c. 208, women possess that equality of dignity and activity. Yet one would not look too far for instances of real and perceived mistreatment. In many places and many times women are mistreated because some well-intentioned person tried to be holier than the Church and doesn't even allow what's permitted such as women readers, communion ministers, etc. A look at the papal Masses during his recent trip shows that all those things are okay with him, even while ordained men are sitting in the sanctuary behaving like the rest of the congregation. There are some who point out that the code discriminates in only three places: installing lectors and acolytes,[36] the age for a valid marriage[37] and the diriment impediment of abduction.[38] These would say that ordination of women is a theological problem and not a canonical one. Others would say everytime the code speaks of ministers it is discriminatory.

Regardless of your school of thought in this matter, it is a problem ecumenically. I don't know that our teaching on ordination needs to be changed. I am certainly not suggesting we change it because another church disagrees. I do think we need to remember that ordination does not only mean a person is empowered to preside

[36] C. 230.
[37] C. 1083.
[38] C. 1085.

at the liturgy but it also allows a person to be a part of the formal governance structure of the Church. In the present Code there are finally some offices which are open to women. For example she could be the defender of the bond[39] in a marriage case and could even be a judge but it has to be in a collegiate tribunal.[40] This is a country where a substantial number of tribunal practitioners are women. Canonists do not have the capability to examine the theology of ordination or non-ordination of women but we could study the connection between Orders and jurisdiction. Interestingly enough, as important as money is to any institution, the fiscal officer of the diocese could be a woman or even a non-Catholic.[41]

LITURGY

We now move for a while into the *munus sanctificandi*. Last year the bishops of the United States decided to implement c. 851, §1, requiring the catechumenate as the ordinary way for a convert to enter the Church. We know that since a person converts to God and not a particular church, the term convert applies only to the non-baptized. So what is to be done about those coming into full communion? Can we realistically expect parishes to conduct two different programs? Do not some baptized non-Catholic Christians need the formation as much as the non-baptized? Yet they are not to be enrolled or take part in the scrutinies.

More important is the need for catechizing those who work with the catechumenate. The seriousness with which the Church takes the catechumenate needs to be understood. This is not just another program—in fact it is not a program at all. The enrollment is serious. The catechumen does have a relationship with the Church that is real[42] and not just one of interest or curiosity as inquiry programs sometimes are. So, a catechumen has made some commitment to the Church and is not just one of interest or curiosity as inquiry programs sometimes are. As an aside, the catechumenate has been so popular in some places that some religious educators have been heard to remark "we have a catechumenate for confirmation" or "we're using the catechumenate for pre-cana." Obviously, they mean a step by step program of information and formation, which is good but it is not a catechumenate.

The Church has long taught that baptism is necessary for salvation. Probably for this reason I find more scrupulosity among priests concerning this sacrament than anything except mass intentions. The code is fairly straight forward in discouraging conditional baptism.[43] It is only to be done after a diligent inquiry

---

[39]C. 1435.
[40]C. 1421, 2.
[41]C. 494.
[42]C. 206.
[43]C. 869, 2.

fails to resolve the doubt about the validity or fact of a previous baptism.[44]

The *novus habitus mentis* is slow in this area. Most often there will be little doubt about the baptism, or the matter and form. But a pastor will be concerned because he cannot locate the minister of the doubtfully baptized and ascertain what he intended. Confusion enters because the Code does ask us to consider the intention of the baptized and the minister.[45] However, the Directory has been telling us that "sufficient intention in a baptizing minister is to be presumed unless there is serious ground for doubting that he intends to do what Christians do."[46] The insufficient faith of the minister never makes the baptism invalid.[47] The seeming difference between the code and the Directory will make most sin on the side of re-baptizing.

The plight of the priest is sometimes exacerbated by the wish of many non-Catholics to be re-baptized. It is not unheard of in some non-Catholic churches. The pressure mounts if the person is taking part in a catechumenate class and wants to be a part of the community she is experiencing there.

A related problem concerning baptism is c. 868, §2 which says that infants in danger of death are licitly baptized even against the wishes of the parents. Fr. John Robertson gives an excellent presentation of this canon in *The Jurist*.[48] Thirty years ago this law would not have raised an eyebrow. Baptism is necessary for salvation and we did not want the babies to go to Limbo so they were baptized. In the intervening years we decided we do not really teach Limbo, some of the pressure for baptism was removed.

The code now says the child should be baptized within the first weeks *(intra priores hebdomadas)*[49] as opposed to the former code which said as soon as possible *(quam primam)*.[50] No one is to accept the faith against his will[51] and the parents speak for the child so this would seem to be against the spirit of the Code. In considering this law I think we see a determination on the part of the Church not to weaken her teaching on infant baptism and thus all the above considerations are overridden by *salus animarum lex suprema est*.

Consistency is not our most common virtue. If the priest is scrupulous concerning the validity of baptism, he seems to be much less so concerning confirmation. When a person comes into full communion she is to be confirmed unless she has been confirmed in her previous religion.[52] Confirmation received in the

---

[44]ibid.
[45]C. 869, 2.
[46]Directory I, 12 b; CLD 6, p. 721.
[47]ibid.
[48]"Canons 867 and 868 and Baptizing Infants Against the Will of Parents" *The Jurist* 45 (1985) 2, pp. 631-638.
[49]C. 867.
[50]See C. 770 of the 1917 Code.
[51]C. 748, 2.
[52]*Rite of Reception of Baptized Christians into Full Communion with the Catholic Church*. Washington, D.C.: USCC Publications, 1976. p. 10, #17.

former church must be recognized as being valid by the Catholic Church.[53] Many think that because the other church thinks their sacraments are valid so should we.

One of the most familiar and most discussed canons of the code is c. 844 on *communicatio in sacris*. Nowadays we can say the "traditionalists" of Archbishop Lefebvre are to be considered in c. 844, §3; that is, just as the oriental churches who are not in full communion. They have valid orders but how could they be in communion with the pope when they don't think there's been one since Pius XII. This is quite a contrast to an episcopal priest I met who wanted to concelebrate Mass with me. I told him he couldn't until he recognized the Pope. He said "I recognize the Pope, he just doesn't recognize me."

Canon 844, §4 is also the subject of much discussion these days. As Fr. Provost points out the former norms prohibited non-Catholics from receiving the Eucharist unless, among other things, access to their own minister was impossible for a notable period of time or they were in prison or suffering persecution.[54] The 1983 code changed it to say merely they cannot approach a minister of their own community.[55]

The sacrament of Matrimony has in recent years been the occasion for demonstrations of ecumenical sensitivity. Examples of changes are numerous: *cautiones,* place of celebration, time of celebration, form, the impediment of mixed religion, etc. The *cautiones, qui semper requiruntur*[56] are a traditional sore spot in marriage preparation. There is a fine article in a recent *Jurist*[57] on this topic and argues for a change in practice. Although I don't think the fact that the Catholic population in Ireland is growing faster than the Protestant population is sufficient to do away with them the author does have a number of thought provoking points.

It seems that we have come full circle in dealing with the celebration of marriage. Years ago, a mixed marriage had to take place outside the sanctuary, many times in the rectory.[58] Now of course weddings can take place not only in the sanctuary but at Mass. The irony is some Catholics feel discriminated against because they have to be married in church.[59] Yes, permission can be given for them to be married elsewhere but they have to ask[60] and in different places the permission is given with varying degrees of reluctance. On the other hand, c. 1118, §3 allows a Catholic who marries a non-baptized to be married in a suitable place without asking permission. The diocesan bishop can and often does attach requirements affecting validity about the place of marriage which nullifies much

---

[53] *Rite of Reception of Baptized Christians into Full Communion* . . . p. 6, #8.
[54] "Directory" I Section 2 #55. CLD 6, 732.
[55] C. 844, 2.
[56] C. 1126.
[57] Eoin de Bhaldraithe, "Mixed Marriages in the New Code: Can We Now Implement the Anglican-Roman Catholic Recommendations?" *The Jurist* 46 (1986): 2 pp. 419 ff.
[58] See C. 1109 of the 1917 Code.
[59] C. 1118, 1.
[60] C. 1118, 2.

of that. However, it is ironic that the wonderful privilege of a nuptial Mass should be seen as a burden.

Sacramentals can be given to anyone unless there is a prohibition.[61] For years we've been blessing the throats of anyone of any age who approached the minister. Ashes have also been distributed rather indiscriminately. Ecumenical services have arisen in many places on the occasion of Ash Wednesday. According to the *Ordo*[62] the priest can get help in distributing ashes from deacons, eucharistic ministers, and other lay persons. Does this exclude protestant ministers who may be taking part in the service? After all, this is a sacramental of the Church, in imitation of the Sacraments it does give some spiritual effects.[63] So I think it does exclude Protestants although it's not that obvious to a priest who wants to please his non-Catholic brothers.

As mentioned before the prohibition of c. 1184, §1, 1° denying ecclesiastical burial rites to notorious apostates, heretics, and schismatics does not automatically apply to non-Catholics, in fact, it probably does not except rarely. In allowing a baptized member of a non-Catholic church ecclesiastical burial, the Church is careful to respect the wishes and conscience of the deceased. If she was an active member of some other church, she should be buried from that church. If on the other hand, she often attended the Catholic church and was active to some degree in the parish, then ecclesiastical burial would be in order. A reminder, persons in an invalid marriage are *not* to be denied ecclesiastical burial.[64]

EDUCATION

A last consideration is the *munus docendi*. Quite a bit of ink has already been spilled over c. 812 and the need for those who teach theological disciplines in institutes of higher learning to have an ecclesiastical mandate. It ignores the tradition of tenure and of academic freedom in this country, and creates some degree of entanglement between the church and the institution which may threaten the tax status of these institutions. The canon does not distinguish between Catholic and non-Catholic instructors. Many of our faculties today are very much ecumenically integrated.

We understand that the law applies to the whole church and in some countries the state may be choosing the teachers for the various faculties in the institutes of higher learning. If such a thing were even suggested here, there would be a

---

[61] C. 1170.
[62] *The Order of Prayer in the Liturgy of the Hours and Celebration of the Eucharist 1987.* Mahwah, N.J.: Paulist Press, 1987.
[63] C. 1166.
[64] *The Code of Canon Law Text and Commentary.* c. 1184.

louder outcry than is ever heard over the Church's *mandatum*. This is one of the areas where particular law would be appropriate.

Canon 804 could also be troublesome except that it is impossible to implement or observe. If you remember paragraph 1 says the bishop has vigilance and control over Catholic religious formation wherever and however it is imparted in his diocese. This includes the mass media. Most television programming in this country is produced in or around a few media centers which are outside the bulk of our dioceses. I understand the CTNA has had a hard time observing the local bishop's right of censorship.

But paragraph 2 of c. 804 could cause even more havoc. It gives the bishop the right to be concerned *(sollicitus)* about the pedagogical skills, the Christian witness and the correct doctrine of teachers of religion whether Catholic or not in any school whether Catholic or not. Fortunately, no American bishop would try to meddle in the schools of other ecclesiastical bodies. However, the mere fact that it has been written down and some levels and places in the Church might consider it their right can be troublesome to those who still view the Roman church as the beast of the apocalypse.

The scriptural renewal is very much alive and well among Catholics. In fact I would like to tout the Scripture Study program of my own diocese. It has introduced Catholics on the parish level to the exciting and rewarding world of reading and praying the inspired Word of God. This is one area where we definitely can talk and work with those of other faith traditions.

Canon 825, §2 encourages joint translations of scripture as long as they have the necessary permission of the episcopal conference and the appropriate annotations and explanations *(convenientibus explicationibus instructus)*. However, there may be some resentment on the part of the non-Catholic scholars to having their work approved by the Catholic bishops. In spite of the fact that the scriptural movement has been in the Church for a long time they may have reason to be suspicious. I recently looked at a copy of the Old Testament (Confraternity Version) and saw the *IMPRIMI POTEST,* the *NIHIL OBSTAT* and the *IMPRIMATUR.* Just below the *imprimatur* was the following disclaimer: "The *nihil obstat* and *imprimatur* are official declarations that a book or pamphlet is free of doctrinal or moral error. No implication is contained herein that those who have granted the *nihil obstat* and *imprimatur* agree with contents, opinions or statements expressed"[65]

CONCLUSION

Other people will find more interesting and more pressing issues in the Code. These are merely to prompt discussion and heighten awareness. As the cigarette

---

[65] *The Old Testament. Confraternity Version.* New York: Guild Press, Angelus Books. 1964.

ad says: "You've come a long way, baby." But there is still far to go.

Ecumenical understanding is not universally appreciated. Reciprocity is relevant in areas other than sacramental sharing. For us to proselytize people from other churches is considered bad manners. Others however, are not so squeamish. Some fundamentalist groups have introduced votive lights and Our Lady of Guadalupe in order to attract Hispanics. If your effectiveness as a pastor is measured by increasing the body count then you can feel the pressure to recruit wherever you can. The pastoral care teams of Catholic hospitals are employing ministers of other faiths but how many of their hospitals are seeking out Catholics to hire? And, who can forget the words of Bob Jones head of the university of the same name who on the occasion of the pope's visit said: "Any Baptist minister who shook the hand of the pope is a traitor to Jesus Christ"?

But there is good news too. The latest story is that while the Holy Father was in our country, he received a phone call from God. God said, "I hate to bother you but I have good news and I have bad news." The pope said "Great! Please tell me the good news." God said "After all these years, there will finally be one church. The Holy Spirit has been working so hard for so long and now finally he has been successful. You all really will be one." The pope answered "How wonderful! Praised be your name always! By the way what is the bad news?" God said "I'm calling from Salt Lake City."

Fr. Joe O'Donald of Glenmary who used to be in charge of their Baptist-Catholic dialogue tells the story of when he first went to pastor a small parish church in Kentucky. He attempted to join the local ministerial alliance. His membership was rejected 6-5. He was determined to join so he picked out a minister who had voted "no" and decided to befriend him. After several months of having each other for dinner, of discussing some common problems, of golfing and fishing together, Fr. Joe decided to try again. On the day of the vote, his new found friend told him: "You know, Joe, the last time you tried to join our association I voted against you. Since I've gotten to know you I have come to like you and discovered you are not the devil I thought. I know today they are voting on you again and I just wanted to let you know I am changing my vote—this time instead of voting no I am going to abstain." I'm afraid that if some of us are not against ecumenism we are however abstaining from active participation in its movement.

I would like to quote the words of Fr. Leonard Pivonka:

> "Pope John Paul II named ecumenism one of the special and distinctive qualities of the new Law . . . Pope John Paul has called the Church's commitment to ecumenism irreversible. The revised Code gives legal expression to the Church's commitment in this area and calls for the promotion of ecumenism among Catholics. This is in keeping with the spirit of renewal called for by the Second Vatican Council. Undoubtedly the revised code can be an effective instrument in promoting Catholic involvement in ecumenism. But ecumenism begins in the heart of a per-

son. Indeed in the same heart lies the heart of the ecumenical movement."[66]

All of us have asked the Lord to work to answer our prayers. Now, it is time for us to work to answer His.

---

[66]Leonard Pivonka, op. cit. p. 548.

NCCB IMPLEMENTATION OF THE
CODE OF CANON LAW

Donald E. Heintschel

It has been said so often that it has almost become a cliche that the reworking of the Code of Canon Law of 1917 so that it might reflect the theology of the II Vatican Council has been one of the turning points of the history of law and jurisprudence in the Catholic Church. Never since the golden age of canon law in the Middle Ages have so many spent so much time in shaping the text, in commenting on it once it was promulgated, and finally, in implementing and integrating it into the life and structure of the universal church and more particularly in the many and varied local churches of the world. Pope Paul VI perhaps said it best when he called upon the codifiers and lawyers to have a *novus habitus mentis* regarding the revised code.

The topic suggested for this seminar is the NCCB's implementation of the 1983 Code. Monsignor Hoye, our General Secretary, gave the keynote address in 1984 devoted to this topic. I have been asked to review for you what has taken place at the Conference since 1983 in adapting, where possible, the provisions of the revised Code of Canon Law to the pastoral needs of the U.S. Church.

The principal operating committee within the Conference that deals with canon law is the standing committee on Canonical Affairs. In the first year of the implementation, this committee was quite active in proposing adaptations. As time has passed, however, many questions have not been able to be resolved in so simple a fashion. Either the committee itself or the general assembly have asked that pastoral issues be resolved in an interdisciplinary fashion involving anywhere from one other committee or two or three committees within the Conference. All of this has had its effects upon the final outcome. As you will see later on, some issues have been in committee for several years and have yet to be resolved.

To begin with the Canonical Affairs Committee constructed a system to implement the Code. Eighty-four canons called for either mandatory or optional action by the Conference. These rubrics set by the committee were confirmed by a letter from Cardinal Casaroli (11/8/83) at the time of promulgation. Beginning as early as the spring meeting of the Administrative Committee, the Conference made several policy decisions concerning matters which the Conference had considered before, but which now needed formal action by way of reaffirmation in light of the new Code, e.g., it was decided to retain the norms on fast and abstinence as passed in 1966, with the caveat of Canon 97 wherein an adult is defined as someone who has completed their 18th year, rather than their 21st year. It was decided to retain the regulations concerning the cautiones for mixed marriages (Canon 1126) as well as the regulations concerning the dispensation from the form of marriage (Canon 1127, §2) with the change warranted by the

Code eliminating the possibility of the diocesan bishop of the place of marriage granting such a dispensation.

The final action taken in March 1983 was the adoption of a policy to permit the establishment of one or more courts of second instance in accord with the provisions of Canon 1439, §2.

November 1983 was the first general assembly when the bishops began to give consideration to the implementation of the revised Code. A cursory searching of the minutes shows that many issues were discussed and resolved while some were tabled for further study.

1. It was decided to permit auxiliaries and other titular bishops (454, §2) to have a deliberative vote in formulating the statutes of the Conference or in amending the same. This vote is just now coming into play, since the Conference has established an Ad Hoc Committee on Statutes and By-Laws to begin the rewording of the *Handbook* of the Conference. In this same area is the critical issue of the voting rights of Eastern Catholic Bishops. Working with the Inter-Rite Committee, language has been drafted which will be introduced into the statutes to cover this question. This becomes critical, for example, when issues of liturgy are debated in the Conference, and traditionally Eastern Rite Bishops have abstained, thus casting a negative vote. This can be critical when a 2/3 vote is necessary and the margin of difference is quite narrow. I do believe that the revision committee has resolved this question with new language in the statutes which will eventually need the *recognitio* of the Holy See.
2. It was determined that single judges could be used in marriage cases and that lay judges could be appointed to collegiate tribunals (Canons 1421, §2 and 1423, §4).
3. A third issue discussed was the question of the tenure of pastors (Canon 522). The issue was certainly of interest to the U.S. bishops. They voted 244 to 25 in favor of tenure, and then decided 240 to 12 to leave the question of renewability and the specific length of time to the diocesan bishop. This was submitted to the Holy See and I am sure that all of you are aware that this question was not finally resolved until September 1984 when the Holy See in its *recognitio* determined that tenure be specified as six years to give some sense of stability in office for pastors.
4. The age for confirmation (Canon 891) was also discussed, but was left unresolved. The Conference ruled to permit bishops to continue conferring confirmation at the age customary in their diocese until a study could be done. Well, the study was done by the Committee on Pastoral Research and Practices, along with the Committee on the Liturgy. It was brought to the floor once again in November 1984 and no consensus was able to be achieved. So the current stance of the Conference remains the individual discretion of the diocesan

bishop.

As I reviewed the minutes of the general meeting of the bishops for November 1984, I note that Bishop Bevilacqua, the chairman of the Committee on Canonical Affairs, reported that those canons having the rubric calling for immediate action by the Conference had been debated and passed during the previous year as noted above. He went on to say that the canons to be debated during the 1984 meeting were to be in the second category, i.e., those that are urgent but do not require immediate action. He suggested that these canons be sent to the appropriate committees of the Conference for research and recommendations so that unified norms might be promulgated for the Church in the United States. Here is a listing of the many issues and the current status of the research done and recommendations to be made:

1. Retirement and support of pastors (Canon 583). The Committee on Priestly Life and Ministry has developed a series of some 14 norms and these have been reviewed by the Committee on Canonical Affairs. The Committee on Priestly Life and Ministry accepted the critique of the Canonical Affairs Committee. Thus, the revised norms will be debated and voted upon during this year's general assembly.
2. Norms for the Catechumenate (Canon 788, §3). The Committee on the Liturgy has been developing these norms and are currently awaiting the approval of the Congregation for the Sacraments. The norms were inserted in the RCIA document submitted to the Holy See over a year ago.
3. The whole question of lay preaching (Canon 766). This issue was given to the Committees on Pastoral Research and Practices, Laity, Liturgy and Doctrine. Each of these committees has done a great deal of research into all of the issues. It has been most difficult to achieve some consensus, but with staff work and negotiations, it is hoped that these will be ready for debate and vote at a meeting during the coming year.
4. The whole question of pre-nuptial preparation (Canons 1062, 1067, 1083, 1112, 1120, 1121, 1126, 1127, etc.) is a complex issue involving the lives of most members of the Church. It is far more than a form for pre-nuptial investigation. It was assigned primarily to the Committee on Pastoral Research and Practices, and it was their decision to produce an all inclusive text dealing with all of the facets of pre-marital preparation, e.g., canonical, doctrine, phychological, sexual, liturgical, ecumenical, etc. It was also decided to select and hire a writer to prepare the manuscript. Father Joseph Champlin has been so designated. At this writing, it is still too early to say when the task will be finished.

Let me turn now to two issues which have preoccupied the Conference for some time. Each in its own way is a lesson in what the concept of implementation means in today's Church. I refer to the questions of alienation and leasing (Canons 1292,

1277, 1295), ordinary and extraordinary administration, and the controversial issue of general absolution (Canon 961).

First of all, then, to the generic concept of alienation. It was seen by Canonical Affairs as being a most important issue with Canon Law and Civil Law implications, and one that needed thorough treatment, clear norms for the guidance of diocesan bishops and their fiscal officers, and finally norms that took into consideration the population, economic conditions, geography, etc., of the many U.S. dioceses. A special ad hoc committee was developed by the appointment of the president to prepare the study and to make their recommendations to the Conference. Bishop James Griffin, a canon and civil lawyer, was asked to chair and he was assisted by bishop canonists as well as canon and civil law consultants.

It took two years for the committee to prepare its proposal. It was an excellent piece of work reflecting the study that had been undertaken. After a preliminary presentation to the March 1985 Administrative Committee meeting, it was set for the agenda of the November 1985 general assembly.

Since it is an intricate case in law and practice, the Administrative Committee moved that a workshop for bishops be prepared for presentation on the opening night of the general meeting. Some 170 bishops attended the workshop. In a comparative analysis of what other nations had done, it is easy to see how the U.S. took a unique approach. Recognizing that there is a great diversity in the size and economic conditions of the many local Churches a formula was developed; for example, in defining the maximum limit, the proposal states that one million dollars, or $5.00 per capita of the Catholic population, (whichever is the larger) up to a ceiling of five million dollars. The minimum was set at a half-million ($500,000) dollars. In light of this formula, acts of extraordinary and ordinary administration were defined and also the areas where the consent of the finance council and consultors were required and where the permission of the Holy See must be sought.

The workshop for bishops was successful, enabling them to understand and grasp for the first time the intricacies of the law on temporal administration.

When the debate and vote was held, the vote was 236 yes, 3 no, showing that the U.S. bishops were willing to accept the work of their committees.

The proposal was submitted to the Holy See for its *recognitio* on December 9, 1985, almost immediately after the meeting.

It was not until April 19, 1987 that Archbishop Laghi informed the Conference (Prot. No. 1782/86/8) that ". . . The maximum limit for the alienation of Church property shall be one million dollars. Both the ceiling amount of five million dollars and the alternate proposal of $5.00 per capita of the Catholic population have been determined to be *inappropriate.*"

This, of course, was not new law, nor an expression of the will of the Conference in implementing the Code for a particular country. I seriously wonder at times whether the canons which permit particular law for particular countries with their individual needs are not something that has been predetermined, and anything that a Conference might do is an exercise in futility and a waste of precious time. We certainly have two examples in the U.S., tenure of pastors and the whole alienation question.

Another serious question of a different kind has also been the source of pastoral research, particularly in Canon Law and Liturgy, and has not at this writing been resolved to the satisfaction of all. It is the question of general absolution and the norms and/or guidelines that should be used to (Canon 961) govern the use of Rite III. The Canonical Affairs Committee has been wrestling with this question for over three years. The question was finally brought into focus for the 1986 general assembly, when the Canonical Affairs Committee attempted to set forth criteria by which diocesan bishops might make judgments in their own dioceses regarding the use of general absolution. The debate was long and heated at times. A great number of bishops stood and spoke to the issue. In the end the President asked the house whether they wished to vote up or down the guidelines presented. The majority of the vote was in the negative, and so it was sent back to the committee with the direction from the floor that the proposal also be studied by the Committee on Doctrine, Liturgy and Pastoral Research and Practices. Again, at this writing the Committee on Canonical Affairs, after consulting with the named committees, was prepared to present a revised set of guidelines this November. A revised proposal was discussed at the September 1987 Administrative Committee meeting. After a lengthy debate, the chairman of Canonical Affairs was asked to send a copy of the canonical norms to all of the diocesan bishops for their guidance in setting norms in their local Churches, but the Administrative Committee also noted that the norms continue to be studied by the Committee on Pastoral Research and Practices so that the canonical norms might be interpreted into a larger study on the Rite of Reconciliation being prepared by the Committee so that pastoral sensitivity might be evident.

Finally, what other issues has the Committee on Canonical Affairs discussed during the past two years?:
  1. Guidelines for Preaching by the Non-Ordained (Canons 766-777)
  2. Age of Reason and the Reception of the Sacraments by the Mentally Handicapped (Canons 891, 914, 989, 104 passim)
  3. First Confession and First Communion (914)
  4. National Imprimaturs (C. 824-827)
  5. Forms for Pre-Nuptial Investigation (Canon 1067)
  6. Ecclesiastical Dress (Canon 284)
  7. Teaching Authority of Bishops and Theologians (a proposal presented to the NCCB by a joint committee of CLSA-CTSA)

As is evident from this cursory review, the NCCB has adopted a unique methodology in its attempt to implement the Code. Although the Committee on Canonical Affairs remains the "lead agent" in developing proposals to be presented to the body of bishops during their general meetings, it has frequently happened that either of these agencies of the Conference have asked that some proposals (canons) at least be reworked, researched, studied and prepared for formal presentation and debate. As I have watched this work, I have become deeply convinced of the U.S. bishops pastoral sensitivity in implementing the revised Code of Canon Law. I would interpret this as an example of the *novus habitus mentis* mentioned at the beginning of these remarks.

LAY PERSONS IN THE DIOCESAN CURIA: LEGAL STRUCTURES AND PRACTICAL ISSUES

ROSEMARY SMITH, SC

The impetus for this presentation is our contemporary experience as Church. In all likelihood there is not a single person in this room regardless of age, present employment or ecclesiology, who could not testify to a marked change in the personnel of the central office of your diocese. The lived experience, the present situation suggests serious reflection, in fact, demands it. This presentation is one attempt to do that.

This paper has three parts. The first focuses and lays the groundwork for what follows; it contains some definitions and general assumptions. The second part deals with legal structures and their parameters and possibilities; this is by far the longest part. The third part can best be described as considerations toward practice. This last part emerges from insights gathered from lay persons working in dioceses across the country as well as my own experience, reading and reflection.

Let us begin by clarifying terms. Since this is a presentation for canonists the canonical understanding of lay person as found in Canon 207 will be used. By lay persons are meant all members of the Christian faithful who are not clerics.[1] Many writers have pointed out that various understandings of "laity" appear in the documents of the Second Vatican Council.[2] The canonical definition is used for two reasons: 1) All of the legal issues and many of the practical issues affect all unordained persons, and, 2) it was the specific request of the Research and Development Committee that the topic be addressed in this manner.

A second clarifying point might be helpful at the outset. This paper is concerned with the diocesan curia. According to Canon 469, the diocesan curia consists of those institutions and persons which furnish assistance to the bishop in the governance of the entire diocese.[3] The focus of this paper on the diocesan curia consists consideration of any supra-diocesan activity, such as an interdiocesan tribunal,

---

[1] Canon 207, §1: "Ex divina institutione, inter christifideles sunt in Ecclesia ministri sacri, qui in iure et clerici vocantur; certeri autem et laici nuncupantur."

[2] For instance, Ferdinand Klostermann, "The Laity," in Herbert Vorgrimler, ed., *Commentary on the Documents of Vatican II* (New York: Herder and Herder, 1967), I, pp. 231-252; Joseph A. Komonchak, "Clergy, Laity, and the Church's Mission in the World," in James H. Provost, ed., *Official Ministry in a New Age* (Washington, DC: Canon Law Society of America, 1981), pp. 168-193; Edward Schillebeeckx, *The Mission of the Church* (New York: Seabury, 1973), esp. pp. 90-131; Rosemary Smith, *Lay Persons and the Munus Sanctificandi: Legal Development from the Second Vatican Council to the Revised Code of Canon Law*, Canon Law Studies, 512 (Washington, DC: Catholic University of America, 1984), pp. 59-96.

[3] Canon 469: "Curia dioecesana constat illis institutis et personis, quae Episcopo operam praestant in regimine universae dioecesis, praesertim in actione pastorali dirigenda, in administratione dioecesis curanda, necnon in potestate iudiciali exercenda."

a state Catholic conference or activities emanating from any national office. It likewise precludes consideration of the widespread involvement of lay persons in the parish, in lay organizations and in ministerial outreach. It might also be helpful to point out that any practical applications in this paper are based on recent experience in the United States.

Let us now proceed to some basic assumptions underlying these reflections. There are four. First, the Church is a living organism, an historical reality and a gradually unfolding mystery. The Church we experience and describe here has not always understood, organized and expressed itself in exactly the same way. It seems reasonable to expect that it will not always do so in exactly the same way in the future.

The second assumption is that the primary ecclesial experience is the lay experience. By primary is meant *first* chronologically for all members, numerically dominant, and sociologically normative. This realization has required a Copernican shift for many in our Church.

A third assumption is that where a person stands affects what a person sees. All persons—lay and cleric, women and men, third-world and first-world, insider and outsider—all persons filter external events through the sieve of their own experience. Every person operates, often unconsciously, out of his or her own presuppositions and frames of reference. For instance, the beauty of a consistent, coherent legal theory of interest to a canonist may well be lost on a divorced person waiting five years for a tribunal decision. Or, in an entirely different arena, one's perceptions and feelings about the antebellum South may be colored by the lineage one traces. The very least that this third assumption means is that each person, wherever he or she may stand, has much to learn.

The fourth assumption has to do with the teaching on charisms. In the last twenty-five years many insights and emphases of the Second Vatican Council have been well appropriated by the United States Catholic community. One deeply internalized teaching which has only begun to shape the Church's self understanding is the Council's re-emphasis on charisms, that is, the Spirit's distribution of gifts throughout the whole community. It is this whole community, both needy and gifted, which must be the entry point and the reference point for any discussion of service.

Having attempted to clarify terms, to circumscribe the topic, and to lay out ahead of time some of the underlying premises, let us now explore the legal structure itself. In doing so we will look, in summary fashion, at four different but interlocking areas of the Code. They are: (1) some canonical notions regarding lay persons; (2) legal requirements and strictures regarding the diocesan curia; (3) the nature of ecclesiastical office: and, (4) the exercise of the power of governance. Obviously the treatment of each topic will be quite limited. The intention is to review some basic "building block" canons and then attempt to make some connections with the topic of this presentation.

Let us move now to the first area—some canonical considerations on lay persons. According to canon 96, one becomes a person in the Church by baptism and together with that incorporation come certain duties and rights. The Latin words used here are *officium* and *ius*. These duties and rights, according to this same canon, are in keeping with the person's condition and are subject to a positive qualification, i.e., ecclesiastical communion, and to a negative barrier, i.e., ecclesiastical sanction.[4]

Book II of the revised Code is a remarkable development in the codified law of the Catholic Church for it contains a fuller treatment of the Christian faithful in general and the lay Christian faithful in particular. Three canons from this part of the Code have bearing on the present topic, canons 204, 208 and 228. Let us look at each of them briefly. Canon 204 states, among other concepts, that by reason of their baptism the Christian faithful ". . . have become sharers in Christ's priestly, prophetic and royal office in their own manner," and that ". . . they are called to exercise the mission which God has entrusted to the Church . . . in accord with the condition proper to each."[5] This is a description drawn from the Council document *Lumen Gentium,* 31, and it suggests that all the Christian faithful (both laity and clergy) participate in the threefold *munera* (functions) of the church but that the manner of this participation is qualified by one's "condition." It asserts an equality among the faithful based on their common baptism but, again, conditions the mode of actualizing this upon one's "condition and function."

Of most direct bearing on our topic is canon 228. Paragraph one states: "Qualified lay persons are capable of assuming from their sacred pastors those ecclesiastical offices and functions which they are able to exercise in accord with the prescriptions of law." The Latin words used are *officia* and *munera*. Paragraph two of the same canon states: "Lay persons who excel in the necessary knowledge, prudence and uprightness are capable of assisting the pastors of the church as experts or advisors; they can do so even in councils, in accord with the norm of law."[6]

Four brief comments on canon 228: (1) The first paragraph speaks of sacred pastors, a term reserved as a designation for bishops, while the second paragraph uses the term pastor which may include both presbyters and bishops so both paragraphs speak to the issue of lay persons in the diocesan curia. (2) In both paragraphs—as in many other canons in the Code—the word *laici* has qualifiers. The first paragraph speaks of qualified lay persons, the second speaks of lay per-

---

[4]Canon 96: "Baptismo homo Ecclesiae Christi incorporatur et in eadem constituitur persona, cum officiis et iuribus quae christianis, attenta quidem eorum condicione, sunt propria, quatenus in ecclesiastica sunt communione et nisi obstet lata legitime sanctio."

[5]Canon 208: "Inter christifideles omnes, ex eorum quidem in Christo regeneratione, vera viget quoad dignitatem et actionem aequalitas, qua cuncti, secundum propriam cuiusque condicionem et munus, ad aedificationem Corporis Christi cooperantur."

[6]Canon 228: §1 "Laici qui idonei reperiantur, sunt habiles ut a sacris Pastoribus ad illa officia ecclesiastica et munera assumantur, quibus ipsi secundum iuris praescripta fungi valent.

§2 "Laici debita scientia, prudentia et honestate praestantes, habiles sunt tamquam periti aut consiliarii, etiam in consiliis ad normam iuris, ad Ecclesiae Pastoribus adiutorium praebendum."

sons who excel in certain qualities.[7] It is the capabilities in which we have interest here, not qualifications. (3) Both paragraphs state that lay persons have the capacity *(habiles)* for doing these things; neither claims they have a right *(ius)* to do these things.[8] (4) Both paragraphs place this capacity squarely within the context of prescriptions or proscriptions found in other places in the law.

What can we learn from the four canons cited? First, canon 96, which is quite similar to its predecessor in the 1917 Code, deals mainly with the juridic effects of baptism on the individual. The other three canons cited have no counterpart in the previous Code. They situate the baptised person within the community and deal with the social effects of baptism. They speak of rights or capabilities possessed by all members, but exercised differently "according to one's condition."

Let us move now to the second interlocking area of the Code—legal requirements and strictures regarding the diocesan curia. For this we will look at the section of the Code entitled The Diocesan Curia, i.e., canons 469-494, and also include in a general way other canons to which these refer.

The first canon in this section, canon 469, states, as we have already noted, that the diocesan curia consists of both institutions and persons which furnish assistance to the bishop in the governance of the entire diocese especially in the directing of pastoral activity, in providing for the administration of the diocese and in exercising judicial power. This canon expands the understanding of who comprise the diocesan curia; it does not identify by name those who belong to the curia, as the 1917 Code had. Some persons and institutions are named in the canons which follow but the listing is not taxative. Although the diocesan bishop has ultimate responsibility for the governance of the diocese and the coordination of its many activities, he is largely free to organize this as he chooses.

A quick review of canons 469 to 494 and those to which they refer indicates that the only persons actually named and required by the Code are the vicar general; the chancellor; the judicial vicar, judges and a defender of the bond in the tribunal; and a finance officer. Of these, the Code requires that the vicar general and the judicial vicar be ordained to the order of presbyter. Also, in order to constitute a collegiate tribunal, a minimum of two judges must be ordained to at least the order of deacon. Lay persons may, by law, be appointed to the other required curial offices. The only institute of the diocesan curis named and required in the Code, the finance council, may have lay persons on it and may even be comprised entirely of lay persons.

In addition to the required elements of the diocesan curia, many other persons and institutions are either referred to or suggested by the canons of the Code. Among these other persons and institutions are: moderator of the curia, addi-

---

[7]The patronizing tone of this canon is noted by Michael A. Foley, S.J., "Diocesan Governance in Modern Catholic Theology and in the 1983 Code of Canon Law," in James K. Mallet, ed., *The Ministry of Governance* (Washington, DC: Canon Law Society of America, 1987), p. 132. Thomas J. Green cautions against the tendency to condition the formulations of rights so that their limitations seemed essential to the rights themselves rather than to their exercise. See Thomas J. Green, "Persons and Structures in the Church: Reflections on Selected Issues in Book II," *Jurist* 45 (1985) 67.

[8]In each paragraph of the canon the word used is *habiles* not *ius*.

tional vicars general, an episcopal council, episcopal vicars, notary, vice chancellor, and the other tribunal officers of auditor, assessor, procurator, advocate, and promoter of justice. Serious responsibilities of the diocesan bishop discussed in other parts of the Code also suggest the necessity of specialized persons and advisory bodies for such concerns as marriage preparation and family life, evangelization, catechesis, religious life, Catholic schools, and liturgy. In addition, imagination, experience and organizational consultants often suggest many other positions. If the diocesan bishop chooses to name a moderator of the curia, additional vicars general, episcopal vicars or an episcopal council persons ordained at least to the order of presbyter would have to be named.[9] For any other position in the diocesan curia either named in the Code or arising out of responsibilities expressed in the Code, a lay person may be named. In concluding this brief survey it is worth reiterating that the present legal understanding of diocesan curia is quite different from the understanding in the prior Code.

The third piece of legal structure which we will look at briefly is the concept of ecclesiastical office. This institute is addressed in fifty-two canons in the first book of the Code, General Norms. Only two of these, canons 145 and 150, are of interest here. Canon 145 incorporates into the juridic Code of the Church the new definition of ecclesiastical office which the Second Vatican Council changed almost twenty years previously.[10] Canon 145 states: "Ecclesiastical office *(officium)* is any function *(munus)* constituted in a stable manner by divine or ecclesiastical law to be exercised for a spiritual purpose."[11] Ecclesiastical office defined in this way clearly provides for the possibility of both lay persons and clerics holding such office, a point disputed under the 1917 Code. However, although lay persons may hold most ecclesiastical offices there are some for which they are not eligible. For instance, lay persons and deacons may not hold offices entailing the full care of souls for whose fulfillment the exercise of the priestly order is required.[12] Examples of this would be the ecclesiastical office of bishop for the diocese and pastor for the parish. It is difficult to imagine many such offices in the diocesan curia, that is, ones in which the full care of souls is entailed. However, elsewhere in the Code we find another restriction. Canon 274 articulates the general norm that "only clerics can obtain those offices for whose exercise there is required the power of orders or the power of ecclesiastical governance."[13] In conclusion we may say that lay persons are indeed capable of holding ecclesiastical office, but not *every* ecclesiastical office.

This brings us to the fourth interlocking area of the legal structure, the exercise of the power of governance. The discussion of this issue is wide-ranging

---

[9]Cf. ccs. 473 and 478.

[10]*Presbyterorum Ordinis*, 20: *AAS* 58 (1966): 1021.

[11]Canon 145, §1: "Officium ecclesiasticum est quodlibet munus ordinatione sive divina sive ecclesiastica stabiliter constitutum in finem spiritualem exercendum."

[12]Canon 150: "Officium secumferens plenam animarum curam, ad quam adimpledam ordinis sacerdotalis exercitium requiritur, ei qui sacerdotio nondum auctus est valide conferre nequit."

[13]Canon 274, §1: "Soli clerici obtinere possunt officia ad quorum exercitium requiritur potestas ordinis aut potestas regiminis ecclesiastici."

and long-standing; it has been strongly disputed both during the Second Vatican Council and since.[14] Framing the question in terms relevant to the topic at hand we ask, are members of the laity capable of exercising the power of governance and, if so, how?

Much of the current discussion by canonists revolves around Canon 129.[15] The first paragraph of the canon states, in part, "In accord with the prescriptions of law, those who have received sacred orders are capable of the power of governance . . ." The second paragraph states: "Lay members of the Christian faithful can cooperate in the exercise of this power in accord with the norm of law."[16] The first paragraph is similar to its predecessor, canon 118, in the 1917 Code. The second paragraph is an entirely new creation. Most canonists, regardless of which side of our question they come down on, admit that canon 129 is somewhat unclear. Some think it may have been left deliberately ambiguous in order to allow the Church itself to gradually live its way into an appropriate understanding of its meaning; others hold that the meaning of this paragraph must be deduced from and therefore circumscribed by other statements in the Code as well as prior understandings of the law.

Let us pause briefly to look more closely at the controverted statement, "Lay members of the Christian faithful can cooperate in the exercise of this power in accordance with the norm of law." The placement of this statement in the book of General Norms suggests its general nature, with implications for various subsequent canons in the Code. Its placement as paragraph 2 of the same canon which states in its first paragraph that those who have received sacred orders are capable of the power of governance, suggests that it has a relationship—perhaps of comparison, perhaps of contrast, perhaps of elaboration—to the capability of the clerics spoken of in the first paragraph. Let us also keep in mind that ascribing a capability to one group of the Christian faithful does not, by that fact alone, preclude it from another group of the Christian faithful.

Furthermore, the word cooperate *(cooperari)* is not a technically refined canonical term; it is a new and somewhat ambiguous word for a legal text and its framers

---

[14]Recent studies include Adriano Celeghin, "Sacra Potestas: Quaestio Post Conciliaris," *Periodica* 74 (1985) 165-225; James Cuneo, "The Power of Jurisdiction: Empowerment for Church Functioning and Mission Distinct from the Power of Orders," *Jurist* 39 (1979) 183-219; Gianfranco Ghirlanda, S.J., "De Natura, Origine et Exercitio Potestatis Regiminis Iuxta Novum Codicem," *Periodica* 74 (1985) 109-164; James H. Provost, "The Participation of the Laity in the Governance of the Church," *Studia Canonica* 19 (1985) 417-448; Alfonso M. Stickler, S.D.B., "La 'Potestas Regiminis' Visione Teologica," *Apollinaris* 56 (1983) 399-410; Francisco Javier Urrutia, S.J., "Delegation of the Executive Power of Governance," *Studia Canonica* 19 (1985) 339-355.

[15]For instance, see *Communicationes* 14 (1982) 146-151; Barbara Ane Cusack, "Cooperation in the Exercise of the Power of Governance by the Laity: Theoretical and Practical Issues of Canon 129, §2," paper delivered at the Midwest Canon Law Society meeting in Peoria, Illinois, April 29, 1987; John Huels, "Another Look at Lay Jurisdiction," *Jurist* 41 (1981) 59-80; David-Maria A. Jaeger, O.F.M., "The Relationship of Holy Orders and the Power of Governance According to the Revised Code of Canon Law or Are Laity Capable of the Power of Governance?" *Canon Law Society of Great Britain and Ireland Newsletter* 62 (1984) 20-38; Provost; and Stickler.

[16]Canon 129, §1: "Potestatis regiminis, quae quidem ex divina institutione est in Ecclesia et etiam potestas iurisdictionis vocatur, ad norman praescriptorum iuris, habiles sunt qui ordine sacro sunt insigniti."
§2: "In exercitis eiusdem potestatis, christifideles laici ad normam iuris cooperari possunt."

had to know that it would be a matter of keen interest in this rapidly developing area. Any attempt to construe the meaning of the word from parallel uses in the Code is less than helpful. For instance, in its various forms the word *cooperari* is used twenty-nine times in the 1983 Code in statements as diverse in context as the bishops acting with the Pope in Synod, priests cooperating among themselves in the work of the diocese and the sexual cooperation of spouses in marriage.[17]

It is not possible to repeat here in any detail arguments of proponents on both sides of our question. We can only summarize the general approach and the conclusions of the different positions. Those who argue that lay persons are capable of exercising the power of governance ground their answers in a carefully contextualized reading of the documents of the Second Vatican Council, developing theologies of ministry and laity, and a close reading of some seemingly contradictory statements in the present Code which, some suggest, gives rise to a *dubium iuris*. Those who argue that lay persons are not capable of exercising the power of governance emphasize the teaching of the Second Vatican Council on the unity of sacred power, operate out of the assumption that the 1983 Code does not contain inconsistencies nor does it depart from the prior understanding of the law on this matter, and some subscribe to the legal fiction that when lay persons act in consultative, administrative or judicial capacities the power operative is that of the ecclesiastical superior alone, not of the lay person acting in the office or function.

Whether or not lay persons can exercise the power of governance or what the phrase ''cooperate in the power of governance'' means has bearing on how we are to understand what it is that lay persons do in certain judicial or executive actions. There are two different questions embedded here. First, may lay persons be appointed to offices to which any exercise of governing power is attached? And, second, may lay persons be delegated—habitually or case by case—faculties which require some exercise of governing power? It is important to understand what lay persons do when they act as a judge in a collegiate tribunal or when they are delegated to assist at marriage in the name of the Church.[18] The first is an office and the second at least a function, both clearly provided for in the Code. Only after reflecting on these specific provisions should an attempt be made to define the phrase ''cooperate in the power of governance.''

We have looked briefly at four interlocking areas of the law critical to any understanding of the full incorporation of lay persons in the diocesan curia. We have reviewed some basic canonical notions regarding lay persons, looked at the requirements and strictures of the diocesan curia, commented on the new definition of ecclesiastical office and summarized varying approaches to the question of lay persons and the power of governance. With the Second Vatican Council and the subsequent revision of the Code, there have been developments in each

---

[17]Canons 334, 275 and 1096.
[18]Canons 1421, 1426 and 1113.

of these four areas of the law. Each area of development taken by itself offers some interesting possibilities and raises some questions. But the place where all four areas of legal development coalesce, which is the topic of this presentation, is inevitably a place of newness, excitement and growing pains.

Critical reflection on our recent experience—both what has been positive and life-giving as well as what has been negative—is one step toward creating the future we desire. This third and last section of the presentation will deal with some reflections on practical issues. Although this material is my own, I have augmented it with insights from lay persons in approximately 35 different dioceses across the country. The material in this last section will be grouped under three categories: (1) Personnel Policies, (2) Boundary Issues, and (3) Intangible Issues.

First, personnel policies. Lay persons are presently holding ecclesiastical offices of many kinds in diocesan curias across this country. A cursory look at the most recent *Official Catholic Directory* suggests that there are hundreds of lay persons in such positions.[19] It is my judgment that this situation is in keeping with the mind of the Second Vatican Council, is well within current legal parameters, and, even more, is a graced moment in our Church.

Coincidental with the growing phenomenon of lay persons in the diocesan curia is a growing awareness of the basic requirements of justice in the workplace. Many respected groups, among them the National Conference of Catholic Bishops, in their pastoral letter on the economy, the National Association of Church Personnel Administrators, and our own Society, have addressed the question of the Church as employer.[20] Every employer, by that very fact, enters into responsibilities over a whole range of personnel functions—recruitment, selection, training, formation, policy development, salary administration, benefits, due process, termination and retirement.[21] The Code itself as well as the Church's long-standing jurisprudential and social justice traditions offers guidance in this complex task.[22] Time after time the respondents to my survey confirmed the impression that many, if not most, dioceses are a long way from clear, comprehensive, fair and operative personnel policies. Placement based on competence, not status in the Church or privilege, was a concern which surfaced frequently. Inequities in fringe benefits, toleration of unacceptable or disruptive behavior, even toleration of incompetence, and the questionable resolution of conflict involving a lay person and a cleric are not lost on lay persons who work in the diocesan curia. They were usually named for what they are—injustice in the workplace. Also,

---

[19] *The Official Catholic Directory*, 1987 (New York: P.Y. Kenedy and Sons, 1987).
[20] NCCB, pastoral letter *Economic Justice for All: Catholic Social Teaching and the U.S. Economy*, November 13, 1986 (Washington, DC: USCC, 1986), nn. 347-358; National Association of Church Personnel Administrators, *Just Treatment for Those Who Work for the Church* (Cincinnati: NACPA, 1986); Canon Law Society of America "Canonical Standards in Labor-Management Relations: A Report," Canon Law Society of America Reports (1987) 62-93. This paper was approved by the Society at the Forty-Ninth Annual Convention in October 1987 and will be included in the *Proceedings* of that convention.
[21] *Just Treatment for Those Who Work for the Church*, p. 1.
[22] Cf. canon 1286.

the presence in many dioceses of priest personnel boards and the absence of any formal structure through which other personnel are handled suggests a diocese living in the past. Efforts have begun; they must continue. As a Church we must continue to write the vision down and make it work. Lay persons themselves, many with experience in the wider marketplace may be the most competent ones to do this.

The second category, Boundary Issues, is related to the first. I have entitled it Boundary Issues because it deals with identity and role, and in times of transition boundaries may shift. These shifts affect lay persons and clerics alike. Over many years, indeed centuries, the Christian community has tended to attribute almost all leadership qualities within the Church to the ordained. Such an attribution is not congruent with reality, and it creates unfair expectations on those so burdened while depriving the community of access to many of its best gifts. When lay persons and clerics work together in the diocesan curia there is a tendency to ascribe to the cleric competence in all areas whether theological, canonical, organizational, artistic, interpersonal, ministerial or administrative. The temptation to claim such competence or to allow that deference must be overcome. We must all learn to distinguish and heed different kinds of authority—*designated* authority, as in a department head; *expert* authority, which comes with learning or experience; and *personal* authority, which arises from integrity of life. These gifts are distributed throughout the community. Diocesan organization, job descriptions, even conversations and interactions in the office, in the lunchroom, in the conference room must incorporate more explicity the recognition of the giftedness of all persons.

Also under the rubric of Boundary Issues it is appropriate to place the delicate question of public life vs. private life. Public figures, whether lay or cleric, inevitably forego some measure of privacy, but as more lay persons offer their service to the Church through the acceptance of offices or functions in the diocesan curia, there arise questions about the scope, the degree and the content of the scrutiny to which those who work for the Church should be subjected. The questions are delicate and there are no easy answers. In al! likelihood any policies will remain unwritten, but the Church should be conscious of the message conveyed if the sole litmus test has to do with sexuality.

A third issue under the category of Boundary Issues is the anomalous situation of the laicized priest. After a grant of laicization and a dispensation from celibacy, the man remains a priest, but is freed from the rights and obligations of the clerical state. However, in some instances, because of conditions attached to the decree of laicization, this person may not function fully as a lay person participating in roles and activities open to other lay persons. This anomalous situation is noted here because it, too, can deprive the diocesan curia of some highly qualified persons with some sorely needed gifts.

In the last category of practical considerations, Intangible Issues, are grouped a few issues whose causes and remedies are harder to identify. These have more to do with attitudes than with facts or specific behaviors, but they have the effect of eroding the morale of presently-employed lay persons and discouraging others from long-term service.

The first issue is one of acceptance—by colleagues, by support staff and by the clergy of the diocese. In addition to institutional and social exclusions in language (e.g., the common connotation of the word "lay" meaning unprofessional), liturgy and law, there are also other "invisible barriers" or subtle non-inclusions. Examples would be information not shared, opportunities for personal formation and peer support not extended, the failure to include in travel plans or "carpooling" to professional meetings. Women have more difficulty than religious. There are dioceses in this country where the unwritten policy is to make positions available only to religious women because other women might get married, or pregnant, or even move because of the husband's employment. How can such attitudes and practices be reconciled with an official pro-family public stance?

A second and more insidious intangible concern is the lack of challenge many lay persons experience. This is particularly true of lay persons who are canonists. After a few years of learning and stretching many feel that their gifts are left to atrophy. Their expertise is not tapped for the wider range of church legal concerns as it is for many canonists who are ordained. Many intellectually active lay canonists see themselves sooner or later going elsewhere if their gifts are ignored or wasted.

This last part of the presentation has attempted to lay out some practical considerations which stand in the way of full incorporation of lay persons into the diocesan curia. The categories used—personnel policies, boundary issues and intangible barriers—are just one way of looking at the question.

In conclusion, the Church's organization and self-expression (i.e., both its legal structure and its lived reality) at any given moment in time are the result of the divine gift and human effort. In a presentation to church planners given last spring in this very city the noted ecclesiologist Joseph Komonchak captured the challenge of this human dimension. He said, "The Church is never realized once and for all; it comes to be in every generation and, indeed, every day."[23] Those of us who work in diocesan curias should realize that we are in fact servants of this daily unfolding mystery.

---

[23]Joseph Komonchak, "The Church: God's Gift and Our Task," *Origins* 16 (April 2, 1987) 735.

THE PERMANENT DIACONATE:
A COMMENTARY ON ITS DEVELOPMENT FROM THE END OF THE SECOND VATICAN COUNCIL TO THE 1983 *CODEX IURIS CANONICI*

RICHARD J. LYONS

INTRODUCTION

Among the significant developments which occurred as a result of the Second Vatican Council was the restoration of the office of the permanent diaconate to its rightful position in the hierarchy of the Roman Catholic Church.

The diaconate as an official ministry in the Church was revived to meet the demands of the contemporary Church for new forms of the ministry of service. Historically a recognized function of service, the diaconate emphasizes the servant nature of Jesus Christ and His Church.

The Second Vatican Council saw clearly that the nature of the Church was one of service to the world. In his article on the permanent diaconate, Joseph Buckley says:

> We stressed for so long the roles of Christ the king, prophet and priest, that we had become less aware that it was Christ the deacon (who came not to be served, but to serve) . . . Humble service is what Christ the deacon still gives to and through His Church. He expects His Church to be deacon.[1]

By the act of restoration the Church not only recommitted itself to the ministry of service but also to the diaconate as one of the many forms of that ministry. The Second Vatican Council stressed that all God's people are called to serve the Church in some way. Leon Croghan observes:

> The diaconal office, however, cannot be described simply on the basis of the Greek terms from which the words "deacon" and "diaconate" are derived. The Bible uses the terms *"diakonia"* and *"diakonos"* to designate "ministry" and "minister." The terms are used so widely that at times they refer to Christ, to the Apostles, to every Christian. Caution is required, therefore, in a theological study of the diaconate as a specific part of the Church hierarchy.[2]

The Church throughout the world is experiencing a need for more and more service, and the office of deacon can fulfill some of these needs as it did in the early centuries of the Church. Buckley writes, "the demand is not for the restora-

---

[1] Joseph C. Buckley, "The Permanent Diaconate," *The Furrow* 23 (1972): 477.

[2] Leo M. Croghan, "The Theology and the Spirit of the Diaconate's Restoration," *The American Ecclesiastical Review* 161 (1969): 295.

tion of an archaeological antique but for a rediscovery of a treasury of grace."[3]

The deacon in the early church was an assistant to the bishop and co-worker with the presbyter. Edward Echlin, in his article on the permanent diaconate in the *American Ecclesiastical Review,* observes:

> There is indeed an essence to the ministry, but the roles and functions of the hierarchy are adapted to the situations and needs of each succeeding age. We notice, for example, that in some times and places the deacon was exclusively the bishop's assistant, but that in other situations he served God's people by assisting the priest. Similarly, we notice that in the Rome of Justin the deacon administered communion under both species while in the later Rome of Hippolytus it was urged that the deacon's ministration normally be confined to distribution of the bread.[4]

In a later article on the diaconate which appeared in *Worship,* Echlin summarized the ministry of the deacon by saying, "the early deacon was the Church's official and ordained intermediary who mediated the love, concern and service of God's people to the world . . ."[5]

This mediation was accomplished by a threefold diaconal service. Echlin notes, "the primitive church carefully structured its diaconal function and deacons and deaconesses served in liturgy, word and charity in common with other church officers."[6] He goes on to say that though this is what service the deacon historically and traditionally performed, "the paramount challenge for God's servant people is to reorder themselves with a sense of history, to do so in continuity with past ministry, but to do so with daring originality."[7] This originality is further described by Echlin when he offers the following opinion on the future of the permanent diaconate:

> In Scripture, we experience the Church ordering itself and distributing functions. The forms these functions take today may differ from the forms of the Apostolic Church. The deacon of the secular age, while maintaining continuity with the deacon of history, will serve in forms appropriate to the secular age and some of these forms will be different than those of deacons in any preceding age.[8]

It was some of these forms of service, which led to the decline of the diaconate. James Barnett, in his book on the diaconate, links this decline to recurring problems between deacons and presbyters. He identifies some of the difficulties when he states:

> The matter of deacons presiding as Eucharistic celebrants was definitely settled in 325. Canon 18 of Nicaea, which states that according to neither

---

[3]Buckley, p. 477.
[4]Edward P. Echlin, "The Origins of the Permanent Deacon," *The American Ecclesiastical Review* 167 (1970): 96.
[5]Edward P. Echlin, "The Deacon's Golden Age," *Worship* vol. 45, no. 1 (1971): 46.
[6]Ibid., p. 38.
[7]Ibid., p. 37.
[8]Echlin, "Origins," pp. 96-97.

canon nor custom do the deacons have any right "to offer" the Eucharist and should not, therefore, administer to presbyters, who do offer, nor touch the Eucharist before the bishop. Further, the canon provides, the deacons are not to sit among the presbyters whose "inferiors" they are . . . The importance of the diaconate in this early period is to be seen as much as anything else in its lingering eminence, even as it slowly declined . . .[9]

Thus, it became apparent that the conflicts between the deacon and presbyter were the forerunner to the lessening of importance in regards to the office of deacon itself. Edward Echlin suggests three important events which contributed to the decline of the diaconate. He says:

As it originally developed the diaconate was a permanent ministry in communion with bishops and presbyters. But in the third century three significant developments occured. First, at Rome deacons, and especially archdeacons, became powerful out of all proportion to their numbers and history. Pope Fabian (d. 250) divided the Eternal City into seven administrative districts, each under the direction of a deacon. Henceforth seven would be the symbolic number for the diaconate; in many churches deacons were limited to seven. By the fourth century the office of archdeacon had developed in North Africa. Inevitably deacons and archdeacons, especially in communities with only seven deacons, aroused the resentment of presbyters and even of some bishops. Secondly, in the third century Cornelious of Rome (251-253) advanced through all clerical grades to the episcopacy. Therefore the diaconate very gradually became a preliminary step to the priesthood. Thirdly, as we have noticed in Tertullian and his admirer Cyprian, the sacralization of Christian ministry was underway, a development that would be sponsored by Ambrosiaster and Jerome in the fourth century at the expense of deacons and bishops.[10]

From the above, it becomes clear that the diaconate declined as bishops and presbyters began to take over the duties formerly reserved to deacons. The diaconate then became a stepping-stone in the hierarchial ranks, losing its unique and separate character.

An attempt was made at the Council of Trent to restore the office of deacon. On July 15, 1563, the Council Fathers decreed:

That the function of holy orders from the deacon to the porter, which have been laudably received in the Church from the times of the Apostles, and which have been for some time discontinued in many localities, may

---

[9] James M. Barnett, *The Diaconate—A Full and Equal Order* (New York: Seabury Press, 1981), p. 96.
[10] Echlin, "Golden Age," pp. 42-43.

again be restored . . .[11]

Unfortunately, this was never fully implemented, and it was not until the Second Vatican Council in its Dogmatic Constitution on the Church *Lumen Gentium,* that the restoration of the permanent diaconate was seriously considered.

The restoration of the permanent diaconate appears in several conciliar documents, the key one being Article 29 of *Lumen Gentium.* It is there that we read:

> At a lower level of the hierarchy are deacons, upon whom hands are imposed not unto the priesthood, but unto a ministry of service. For strengthened by sacramental grace, in communion with the bishop and his group of priests, they serve the People of God in the ministry of the liturgy, of the word and of charity. It is the duty of the deacon, to the extent that he has been authorized by competent authority, to administer baptism solemnly, to be custodian and dispenser of the Eucharist, to assist at and bless marriages in the name of the Church, to bring Viaticum to the dying, to read the Sacred Scriptures to the faithful, to instruct and exhort the people, to preside at the worship and prayer of the faithful, to administer sacramentals, and to officiate at funeral and burial services. Dedicated to duties of charity and of administration, let deacons be mindful of the admonition of Blessed Polycarp: "Be merciful, diligent, walking according to the truth of the Lord, who became the servant of all."
>
> These duties, so very necessary for the life of the Church, can in many areas be fulfilled only with difficulty according to the prevailing discipline of the Latin Church. For this reason, the diaconate can in the future, be restored as a proper and permanent rank of the hierarchy. It pertains to the competent territorial bodies of the bishops, of one kind or another, to decide, with the approval of the Supreme Pontiff, whether and where it is opportune for such deacons to be appointed for the care of souls. With the consent of the Roman Pontiff, this diaconate will be able to be conferred upon men of more mature age, even upon those living in the married state. It may also be conferred upon suitable young men. For them, however, the law of celibacy must remain intact.[12]

This conciliar statement concurs with the need for restoration expressed in Article 17 of the Decree on Catholic Eastern Churches, *Orientalium Ecclesiarum.* It says:

> In order that the ancient discipline of the sacrament of orders may flourish again in the Eastern Churches, this sacred Synod ardently desires

---

[11]*De Reformatione,* Sessio XXIII, caput XVII. "Ut Sanctorum ordinum a diaconatu ad ostiariatum functiones, ab Apostolorum temporibus in ecclesia laudabiliter receptae, et pluribus in locis aliquamdiu intermissae, in usum iuxta sacros canones revocentur . . ." - Johannes Dominicus Mansi, *Conciliorum Nova et Amplissima Collectio,* Tomus Trigesimus Tertio, Ab anno MDXLV ad annum MDXLV, (Parisiis: Expensis Huberti Welter, Bibliopolae, MDCCCCII), col. 246. (Translation in text from *The Diaconate—A Full and Equal Order,* cited above #9, p. 146.)

[12]Walter M. Abbott, ed., *The Documents of Vatican II* (New York: Build Press, 1966), pp. 55-56. For the Latin, *Acta Apostolicae Sedis* 57 (1965): 36. (Hereafter cited as *AAS*.)

that where it has fallen into disuse, the office of the permanent diaconate be restored. The legislative authority of each individual church should decide about the subdiaconate and the minor orders, including their rights and obligations.[13]

We also find reference to the permanent diaconate in the Decree on the Church's Missionary Activities, *Ad Gentes,* which states in Article 16:

Where Episcopal Conferences deem it opportune, the order of the diaconate should be restored as a permanent state of life, according to the norms of the Constitution on the Church. For there are men who are actually carrying out the functions of the deacon's office, either by preaching the word of God as catechists, or by presiding over scattered Christian communities in the name of the pastor and the bishop, or by practicing charity in social or relief work. It will be helpful to strengthen them by that imposition of hands which has come down from the apostles, and to bind them more closely to the altar. Thus they can carry out their ministry more effectively because of the sacramental grace of the diaconate.[14]

An emphasis on the *"communio"* idea in expressing the relationship between bishops, priests, and deacons, cited in Article 29 of *Lumen Gentium,* becomes an important point in the Decree on the Bishops' Pastoral Office in the Church, *Christus Dominus.* In Chapter Two, in the section of this document dealing with diocesan bishops, the focus is on the deacon and his relation to the bishop. It mentions, "Bishops enjoy the fullness of the sacrament of orders, and all priests as well as deacons are dependent on them in the exercise of authority . . . deacons are ordained for service and minister to the People of God in communion with the bishop and his presbytery."[15] Therefore, the hierarchical office of ministry serves the Church in a threefold variety of ways, episcopal, presbyteral and diaconal, a return to the early Church's ordering of ordained ministry, concentrating on the needs of the Church of today and tomorrow.

Having briefly looked at the restoration of the permanent diaconate in terms of its historical place in the hierarchy and life of the Church, and noting the conciliar statements which called for its restoration as a recognized ministry of service in the Church with its own specific duties, the remainder of this study will concern itself with two other areas. First, it is necessary to survey post-conciliar documentation on the permanent diaconate to see how the Council's call for its restoration continued to develop in the life of the Church and secondly, to study the diaconate in light of law; i.e., the office of deacon as it appeared in the 1917 *Codex Iuris Canonici,* the deacon in the 1980 *Schema,* and the present law on deacons found in the 1983 *Codex Iuris Canonici.*

---

[13]Ibid., pp. 380-81. *AAS* 57 (1965): 81-82.
[14]Ibid., p. 605. *AAS* 58 (1966): 967.
[15]Ibid., p. 406. *AAS* 58 (1966): 679.

POST CONCILIAR RESTORATION

In order to give some general direction as to how the diaconate should be restored, and what principles should be followed, Pope Paul VI issued in a *motu proprio* some general norms on June 18, 1967, beginning with the words *Sacrum Diaconatus Ordinem*.[16] Due to the importance of these norms for all subsequent legislation on the permanent diaconate, the document will be outlined topically and then analyzed in detail.

In outline form the document consists of an introduction and eight sections, these sections being subdivided into thirty-six articles. The topics discussed are outlined as follows:

1. *Sacrum Diaconatus Ordinem*
   A. Introduction
   B. Section I, Articles 1-3
      The Role of the Episcopal Conference and Ordinaries
   C. Section II, Articles 4-10
      Training and Education
   D. Section III, Articles 11-17
      Ordination, Age, Celibacy and Marriage
   E. Section IV, Articles 18-21
      Diaconal Support
   F. Section V, Articles 22-24
      Diaconal Functions
   G. Section VI, Articles 25-31
      Spiritual Exercises and Lifestyles
   H. Section VII, Articles 32-35
      Religious Deacons
   I. Section VIII, Article 36
      Conclusion

In his Introduction, Pope Paul explains the reason for the letter. He wrote:

> We therefore consider it not only proper but also necessary that specific and precise norms be given to adapt present discipline to the new precepts of the Ecumenical Council and to determine the proper conditions under which not only the ministry of the diaconate will be more advantageously regulated, but the training also of the candidates will be better suited to their different kinds of life, their common obligations and their sacred dignity.[17]

After mentioning that the diaconate has a rich and ancient tradition, and that

---

[16]Pope Paul VI, General Norms for Restoring the Permanent Diaconate in the Latin Church, *Sacrum Diaconatus Ordinem*, Apostolic Letter issued *Motu Proprio*, June 18, 1967. Translation (Washington, D.C.: United States Catholic Conference, 1967). For the Latin, *AAS* 59 (1967): 697-704.

[17]*SDO*, Introduction, USCC translation, p. 2. *AAS* 59: 698.

legislation regarding the deacon is already extant in the 1917 *Codex Iuris Canonici*, the Pope makes an important point when he points out that the restoration of the diaconate, "is not necessarily to be effected in the whole Latin Church since it pertains to the competent territorial Episcopal Conferences with the approval of the Supreme Pontiff, to decide whether and where it is timely that deacons of this kind be ordained for the care of souls ..."[18] This underscores the freedom of Conferences of Bishops throughout the world to assess their own needs and determine the proper ways of serving those needs.

Section I, Article 1, places the burden of restoring the permanent diaconate as a proper and permanent rank of the hierarchy on the "legitimate assemblies of bishops or episcopal conferences."[19] Article 2 insists that reasons for the restoration be given, "as well as the circumstances which give well-founded hope of success."[20] Article 3 leaves it up to the "powers of each Ordinary, within the sphere of his own jurisdiction, to approve and ordain the candidates ..."[21] and this can only come about "once the approval of the Holy See has been obtained ..."[22]

Section II, Articles 4 to 10, begin to list the requirements for age and training of the young deacon candidate. Article 4 states that "young men called to the diaconate are obliged to observe the law of celibacy."[23] Article 5 stipulates the minimum age, stating that the "permanent diaconate may not be conferred before the completion of the twenty-fifth year."[24] The remaining five articles of Section II determine the necessary education which must be provided for the deacon candidates.

Article 6 mandates that young men training for the diaconal office "be received in a special institute where they will be put to the test and will be educated to live a truly evangelical life ..."[25] Article 7 suggests that for the foundation of this institute, "let the bishops of the same country, or, if advantageous, of several countries according to the diversity of circumstances, join their efforts."[26]

Article 8 notes, "let only those young men be admitted to training for the diaconate who have shown a natural inclination of the spirit to service of the sacred hierarchy and of the Christian community."[27] Article 9 suggests a three-year period of training, with the curriculum of studies so arranged that "the candidates are orderly and gradually led to carrying out the various functions of the diaconate skillfully and beneficially."[28] Article 10 concludes Section II with an emphasis

---

[18] Ibid.
[19] *SDO*, Section I, Article 1, USCC translation, p. 3. *AAS* 59: 699.
[20] *SDO*, Section I, Article 2, USCC translation, p. 3. *AAS* 59: 699.
[21] *SDO*, Section I, Article 3, USCC translation, p. 3. *AAS* 59: 699.
[22] Ibid.
[23] *SDO*, Section II, Article 4, USCC translation, p. 3. *AAS* 59: 699.
[24] *SDO*, Section II, Article 5, USCC translation, p. 3. *AAS* 59: 699.
[25] *SDO*, Section II, Article 6, USCC translation, p. 4. *AAS* 59: 699.
[26] *SDO*, Section II, Article 7, USCC translation, p. 4. *AAS* 59:699.
[27] *SDO*, Section II, Article 8, USCC translation, p. 4. *AAS* 59: 700.
[28] *SDO*, Section II, Article 9, USCC translation, p. 4. *AAS* 59: 700.

on the pastoral education of the young diaconal candidate, suggesting that along with their academic subjects, other duties can be added, especially:

> Practice and training in teaching the elements of the Christian religion to children and other faithful, in familiarizing the people with sacred chant and in directing it, in reading the sacred books of Scripture at gatherings of the faithful, in addressing and exhorting the people, in administering the sacraments which pertain to them, in visiting the sick, and in general in fulfilling the ministries which can be entrusted to them.[29]

Section III concerns itself with the older candidate for the diaconate. Article II mentions that the older married candidate is "not to be admitted unless there is certainty not only about the wife's consent, but also about her blameless Christian life and those qualities which will neither impede nor bring dishonor on the husband's ministry."[30] Article 12 stipulates that "older age in this case is reached at the completion of the thirty-fifth year."[31] Article 13 presumes that the marriage of the older candidate is a stable and exemplary one, and Article 14 outlines the training of the older candidates, similar to that of the younger candidates, placing them "in a special school where they are to learn all that is necessary for worthily fulfilling the diaconal ministry."[32] If this is not feasible, then Article 15 states that the candidate "be entrusted for his education to an outstanding priest who will direct him, and instruct him and be able to testify to his prudence and maturity."[33] Article 16 mentions that "once they have received the order of deacons, even those who have been promoted at a more mature are, can not contract marriage by virtue of the traditional discipline of the Church."[34] Article 17 admonishes the local Ordinary to make sure that "deacons do not exercise an art or a profession which is unfitting or impedes the fruitful exercise of the sacred office."[35]

Section IV, Article 18, mentions that "any deacon who is not a professed member of a religious family must be duly enrolled in a diocese."[36] Presumably, this must mean that he has a formal attachment to some diocese either through domicile or an agreement with the diocese that he will offer them his services after ordination. Articles 19 and 20 refer to the proper sustenance and financial obligations that are owed to the deacon. Article 19 refers to "the norms in force with regard to caring for the fitting sustenance of priests and guaranteeing their social security . . ."[37] Here, the Pope is probably referring to Canon 979 of the *1917 Code*. It states:

---

[29]*SDO*, Section II, Article 10, USCC translation, p. 4. *AAS* 59: 700.
[30]*SDO*, Section III, Article 11, USCC translation, p. 5. *AAS* 59: 700.
[31]*SDO*, Section III, Article 12, USCC translation, p. 5. *AAS* 59: 700.
[32]*SDO*, Section III, Article 14, USCC translation, p. 5. *AAS* 59: 701.
[33]*SDO*, Section III, Article 15, USCC translation, p. 5. *AAS* 59: 701.
[34]*SDO*, Section III, Article 16, USCC translation, p. 5. *AAS* 59: 701.
[35]*SDO*, Section III, Article 17, USCC translation, p. 6. *AAS* 59: 701.
[36]*SDO*, Section IV, Article 18, USCC translation, p. 6. *AAS* 59: 701.
[37]*SDO*, Section IV, Article 19, USCC translation, p. 6. *AAS* 59: 701.

§1 The canonical title for the secular clergy is the title of a benefice or, in default of a benefice, of a patrimony or pension.

§2 This title should be really secure for the whole life of the cleric and truly sufficient for the proper maintenance of the cleric, according to the rules to be laid down by the Ordinaries in accordance with the needs and circumstances of the respective localities and times.[38]

Jose Medina in his doctoral dissertation on the diaconate, offers some suggestions for this question of supporting the permanent diaconate. He writes:

Three main points should be given consideration by the Conference of Bishops in issuing norms for the proper sustenance of the permanent deacons. First, the Conference should consider the principles laid down by the conciliar decree *Presbyterorum Ordinis* (nn. 20, 21). Second, the Conference of Bishops should give consideration to the special needs of married deacons. This applies not only to his needs but also to the needs of his family. Third, the Conference of Bishops should consider article twenty-one of the *motu proprio* which expects the married deacons to exercise a civil profession to provide, as far as possible, for the needs of his family.[39]

Section V, Article 22, lists the functions that the deacon may be allowed to perform in the exercise of his ministry. Article 29 of *Lumen Gentium* already listed as diaconal functions such things as administering baptism solemnly, being the custodian and dispenser of the Eucharist, assisting at and blessing marriages in the name of the Church, to bring Viaticum to the dying, to read the sacred books of Scripture to the faithful, to preside at the worship and prayer of the faithful, to administer sacramentals, and to officiate at funeral and burial services. To these, the *motu proprio* adds:

1. To assist the bishop and the priest during liturgical actions in all things which the rituals of the different orders assign to him.

2. To direct the liturgy of the word, particularly in the absence of a priest.

3. To carry out, in the name of the hierarchy, the duties of charity and of administration as well as works of social assistance.

4. To guide legitimately, in the name of the parish priest and of the bishop, remote Christian communities.

5. To promote and sustain the apostolic activities of laymen.[40]

Article 23 insists that all these duties be carried out "in perfect communion with the bishop and with his presbytery, that is to say, under the authority of

---

[38]*Canon 979:* §1 "Pro clericis saecularibus titulus canonicus est titulus beneficii, eoque deficiente, patrimonii aut pensionis.

§2 Hic titulus debet esse et vere securus protota ordinati vita et vere sufficens ad congruam eiusdem sustentationem, secundum normas ab Ordinariis pro diversis locorum et temporum necessitatibus et adiunctis dandas."

[39]Jose L. Casanas Medina, *The Law for the Restoration of the Permanent Diaconate: A Canonical Commentary.* Canon Law Studies 460. (Washington, D.C.: Catholic Univesity, 1968), p. 84.

[40]*SDO,* Section V, Article 22, USCC translation, pp. 6-7, *AAS* 59: 701-02.

the bishop and of the priests who are in charge of the care of souls in that place."[41] Article 24 suggests that deacons "should have their part in pastoral councils."[42]

Section VI, Article 25 to 31, give details concerning the obligations and lifestyle of the deacon. Exhorting them to "abstain from all vice and endeavor to be always pleasing to God . . . they must surpass all others in the practice of liturgical life, in the love for prayer, in the divine service, in obedience, in charity, in chastity."[43] Article 26 lists some of the spiritual obligations imposed on all deacons, and these are for the most part, the same exercises recommended in the *1917 Code* for clerics.[44] Deacons are urged in Article 27, to "recite every day at least part of the Divine Office, to be determined by the episcopal conference."[45] They also "must, at least every third year, attend spiritual exercises in a religious house or pious institution designated by the Ordinary."[46] Article 29 urges deacons, "not to neglect studies, particularly the sacred ones; let them read assiduously the sacred books of the Scripture; let them devote themselves to ecclesiastical studies in such a way that they can correctly explain Catholic teaching to the rest and become daily more capable of instructing and strengthening the minds of the faithful."[47] Article 30 admonishes deacons to "show reverence and obedience to the bishop . . ."[48] and Article 31 concludes this section with a statement on the wearing apparel of deacons. It notes, "in the matter of wearing apparel the local custom will have to be observed according to the norms set down by the episcopal conference."[49]

Section VII, Articles 23 to 35, pertain to those men in religious communities who wish to study for the permanent diaconate. Article 32 states that "the institution of the permanent diaconate among the Religious is a right reserved to the Holy See which is exclusively competent to examine and approve the recommendations of the general chapters in the matter."[50]

Article 33 obliges that "Religious deacons exercise the diaconal ministry under the authority of the bishop and of their own superiors according to the norms in force for religious priests."[51] Here, the Pope is most likely referring to the legislation on religious priests who become pastors in a diocese. (Cf. Canons

---

[41] *SDO*, Section V, Article 23, USCC translation, p. 7. *AAS* 59: 702.
[42] *SDO*, Section V, Article 24, USCC translation, p. 7. *AAS* 59: 702.
[43] *SDO*, Section VI, Article 25, USCC translation, p. 8. *AAS* 59: 702.
[44] *Canon 125:* §1 "Curent locorum Ordinarii: Ut clerici omnes poenitentiae sacramento frequenter conscientiae maculas eluant;
   §2 Ut iidem quotidie orationi mentali per aliquod tempus incumbent, sanctissimum Sacramentum visitent, Deiparam Virginem mariano rosario colant, conscientiam suam discutiant." *SDO,* Section VI, Article 26, USCC translation, p. 8.
[45] *SDO*, Section VI, Article 27, USCC translation, p. 8. *AAS* 59: 703.
[46] *SDO*, Section VI, Article 28, USCC translation, p. 8. *AAS* 59: 703.
[47] *SDO*, Section VI, Article 29, USCC translation, pp. 8-9. *AAS* 59: 703.
[48] *SDO*, Section VI, Article 30, USCC translation, p. 9. *AAS* 59: 703.
[49] *SDO*, Section VI, Article 31, USCC translation, p. 9. *AAS* 59: 703.
[50] *SDO*, Section VII, Article 32, USCC translation, p. 9. *AAS* 59: 703.
[51] *SDO*, Section VII, Article 33, USCC translation, p. 9. *AAS* 59: 704.

630-631 of *1917 Code*)

Article 34 mentions that "a Religious deacon who lives either permanently or for a specified time in a region which lacks a permanent diaconate may not exercise diaconal functions except with the consent of the local Ordinary."[52] Article 35 concludes this section with the reminder that "the provisions in nos. 32-34 regarding the Religious must be regarded as applying likewise to members of other institutes who profess the evangelical counsels."[53]

Section VIII, Article 36, concludes the *motu proprio* by stating "as regards the rite to be followed in conferring the sacred order of the diaconate and those orders which precede the diaconate, let the present discipline be observed until it is revised by the Holy See."[54]

As can be seen from the above analysis, *Sancrum Diaconatus Ordinem* was the document in which the order of deacon, restored in principle by the Second Vatican Council, began to take on form and substance, both healthy signs of growth and development in the post-conciliar Church.

The final article of the *motu proprio* studied above, Pope Paul noted that the rite conferring the diaconate would remain the same until revised by the Holy See. This revision took place when the Pope revised the whole Roman Pontifical in his Apostolic Constitution of 1968 entitled, *Pontificalis Romani*.[55]

In the final article of the *motu proprio* studied above, Pope Paul noted that the Roman Pontifical is prescribed in a general way by the Second Vatican Ecumenical Council . . . The greatest attention must be paid to the important teaching on the nature and effects of the sacrament of Order which was proclaimed by the Council in its Constitution on the Church."[56]

In reference to the ordination of candidates to the diaconate, the document takes note of the *motu proprio Sacrum Diaconatus Ordinem* and states, "in the ordination of deacons only a few changes were to be made, taking into account both the recent prescriptions concerning the diaconate as a proper and permanent grade of the hierarchy in the Latin Church . . ."[57]

Stressing that the ancient form of the imposition of hands in the conferral of orders must continue, the Pope decreed the following for the ordination rite of deacons:

> In the ordination of deacons, the matter is the imposition of the bishop's hands upon the individual candidates, which is done in silence before the consecratory prayer, the form consists of the words of the con-

---

[52]*SDO*, Section VII, Article 34, USCC translation, p. 10. *AAS* 59: 704.
[53]*SDO*, Section VII, Article 35, USCC translation, p. 10. *AAS* 59: 704.
[54]*SDO*, Section VIII, Article 36, USCC translation, p. 10. *AAS* 59: 704.
[55]Pope Paul VI, *Approval of a New Rite for the Ordination of Deacons, Priests and Bishops, Pontificalis Romani, Apostolic Constitution*, June 18, 1968. Translation (Washington, D.C.: United States Catholic Conference, 1968). For the Latin, *AAS* 60 (1968): 369-73.
[56]*PR*, Introduction, USCC translation, p. 3. *AAS* 60: 369-70.
[57]*PR*, p. 5. *AAS* 60: 372-73.

secratory prayer, of which the following pertain to the nature of the Order and therefore are required for the validity of the Act: "Send forth the Holy Spirit upon them, we ask you O Lord, that they may be strengthened by Him, through the gift of your sevenfold grace, for the faithful discharge of your service."[58]

On August 15, 1972, Pope Paul VI issued *motu proprio* two apostolic letters. *Ad Pascendum*[59] established further norms regarding the diaconate, and *Ministeria Quaedam*[60] reformed the discipline of First Tonsure, Minor Orders and Subdiaconate in the Latin Church.

Ad Pascendum is fundamentally different from *Sacrum Diaconatus Ordinem* in that this *motu proprio* considers norms for deacons in general, while *Sacrum Diaconatus Ordinem* concerned itself with general norms for restoring the permanent diaconate in the Latin Church. The norms *Ad Pascendum* offer are to be implemented so that "candidates for the diaconate should know what ministries they are to exercise before sacred ordination and when and how they are to take upon themselves the responsibilities of celibacy and liturgical prayer."[61]

After introducing his letter with a summary of the history of the diaconate, Pope Paul VI in the first norm mandates a new rite of admission for candidates to the diaconate and priesthood. The norm states:

> In order that this admission be properly made, the free petition of the aspirant, made out and signed in his own hand, is required, as well as the written acceptance of the competent ecclesiastical superior, by which the selection by the Church is brought about.[62]

The second norm requires that those who wish to be ordained either a deacon or priest must first receive the ministries of lector and acolyte. This is more clearly detailed in *Ministeria Quaedam*.[63]

Norms III and IV address the issues of how these ministries are conferred and the amount of time which should elapse between them. The document mentions, "the intervals established by the Holy See or by the episcopal conferences between the conferring—during the course of theological studies—of the ministry

---

[58] *PR*, p. 6. *AAS* 60: 372. (N.B. this is now the official rite for the ordination of deacons. Cf. *The Roman Pontifical*, revised by Decree of the Second Vatican Ecumenical Council and Published by Authority of Pope Paul VI (Washington, D.C., 1978), Chapter 8, *Ordination of Deacons*, no. 14).

[59] Pope Paul VI, *Apostolic Letter in Motu Proprio Form Laying Down Certain Norms Regarding the Sacred Order of the Diaconate, Ad Pascendum*, August 15, 1972. Translation (Washington, D.C.: United States Catholic Conference, 1972). For the Latin, *AAS* 64 (1972): 534-40.

[60] Pope Paul VI, *Apostolic Letter in Motu Proprio Form by which the Discipline of First Tonsure, Minor Orders and Subdiaconate in the Latin Church is Reformed, Ministeria Quaedam*, August 15, 1972. Translation (Washington, D.C.: United States Catholic Conference, 1972). For the Latin, *AAS* 64 (1972): 529-34.

[61] *AP*, Introduction, USCC translation, p. 5. *AAS* 64: 537.

[62] *AP*, Norm la, USCC translation, p. 6. *AAS* 64: 538.

[63] *Ministeria Quaedam*, XI: "Candidates for the diaconate and priesthood are to receive the ministries of lector and acolyte, unless they have already done so, and are to exercise them for a fitting time, in order to be better disposed for the future service of the Word and Altar. Dispensation from the reception of these ministries is reserved to the Holy See." USCC translation, p. 14. *AAS* 64: 533.

of lector and that of acolyte, and between the ministry of acolyte and the order of deacon must be observed."[64]

Norm V stresses the requisite mental state of a candidate prior to his diaconal ordination. The *motu proprio* states:

> Before ordination, candidates for the diaconate shall give to the Ordinary (the bishop, and in clerical institutes of perfection, the major superior) a declaration made out and signed in their own hand, by which they testify that they are about to receive the sacred order freely and of their own accord.[65]

Norm VI repeats the long-standing tradition of celibacy "observed for the sake of the kingdom of heaven and its obligations for candidates to the priesthood and for unmarried candidates to the diaconate . . ."[66] Norm VI further expands the law of celibacy mentioned in Article 16 of *Sacrum Diaconatus Ordinem* by stating, "a married deacon who has lost his wife cannot enter a new marriage."[67]

Norm VII suggests that those who will be ordained to the priesthood be not ordained until they have completed their required course of studies. It is also noted in Norm VII, "in regard to the course of theological studies to precede the ordination of permanent deacons, the episcopal conferences, with attention to the local situation, will issue the proper norms and submit them for the approval of the Sacred Congregation for Catholic Education."[68]

Norm VIII recommends the daily recitation of at least part of the Liturgy of the Hours for permanent deacons, as determined by the Conference of Bishops.[69]

Norm IX derogates from Canon 111, Paragraph 2, of the *1917 Code* where it is stated that a cleric is incardinated or attached to a diocese by the reception of first tonsure.[70] Now, "entrance into the clerical state and incardination into a diocese are brought about by ordination to the diaconate."[71]

As indicated in this section, the permanent diaconate, which had been restored by the Second Vatican Council, began to take on form and substance due to the publication of papal legislation and norms for the growth and development of the order of deacon. The next section will focus specifically on the issue of the diaconate in the *Code of Canon Law*.

---

[64] *AP*, Norm IV, USCC translation, p. 7. *AAS* 64: 539:
[65] *AP*, Norm V, USCC translation, p. 7. *AAS* 64: 539.
[66] *AP*, Norm VI, USCC translation, p. 7. *AAS* 64: 539.
[67] IBID.
[68] *AP*, Norm VII, USCC translation, pp. 7-8. *AAS* 64: 540.
[69] *AP*, Norm VIII, USCC translation, p. 8. *AAS* 64: 540.
[70] *Canon 111*, #2: "Per recetpionem primae tonsurae clericus adscribitur seu, ut aiunt, 'incardinatur,' dioecesi pro cuius servitio promotus fuit."
[71] *AP*, Norm IX, USCC translation, p. 8. *AAS* 64: 540.

THE CODE OF CANON LAW

In the introduction to this study, it was noted that the office of deacon, once an important ministry in the Early Church, had, over the course of time, declined to the point where it was considered merely a step in the hierarchial ranks, a stage a man passed through on his way into the higher ranks of the clergy. Also, the concept of specific diaconal ministry was mostly disregarded and their duties assumed by priests. It was not until the Second Vatican Council that both the dignity of the order and the ministry of service were reconsidered, and the restoration of the diaconate was seen as a positive step in the direction of serving God's people.

Thus, it should not be surprising to find that in the 1917 *Codex Iuris Canonici* (hereafter cited as the *17 Code*), the legislation which deals specifically with deacons is minimal. When the *motu proprio Sacrum Diaconatus Ordinem* was written, Pope Paul VI noted in the Introduction:

> Therefore, in the first place, all that is decreed in the *Code of Canon Law* about the rights and obligations of deacons, whether these rights and obligations be common to all clerics, or proper to deacons—all these, unless come other disposition has been made, we confirm and declare to be in force also for those who will remain permanently in the diaconate.[72]

The rights and obligations that the Pope referred to could be found in the *17 Code*, Book II: *De Personis*, Part I: *De Clericis*, Titles II and III.

For the purposes of this study, the canons of the *17 Code* concerning the qualifications, training and functions of deacons will be surveyed to show how these were expanded following the provisions of the Second Vatican Council and *Sacrum Diaconatus Ordinem*, and the canonical legislation which appeared in the 1980 *Schema Codicis Iuris Canonici* and the 1983 *Codex Iuris Canonici*.

PART ONE: 17 CODE

TRAINING AND QUALIFICATIONS

In Title VI of Book III: *De Rebus*, Part I: *De Sacramentis* on Holy Orders, we find the canons concerning diaconal qualifications and training.

Canon 949 states that the diaconate is one of the major orders of the clergy[73] and canons 968-978 give us the requirements and qualifications for ordination.

---

[72]*SDO*, Introduction, USCC translation, p. 2.
[73]*Canon 949:* "In canonibus qui sequuntur, nomine ordinum maiorum vel sacrorum intelliguntur presbyteratus, diaconatus, subdiaconatus; minorim vero acolythatus, exorcistatus, lectoratus, ostieriatus."

The person ordained must be of the male sex and be baptized.[74] He must be judged acceptable for service in the diocese by the proper bishop[75] and one must not be forced into accepting ordination.[576]

Canon 974 lists as requirements for ordination to the diaconate the following:

(1) previous reception of Confirmation
(2) moral character corresponding to the order a candidate is to receive
(3) canonical age
(4) due knowledge
(5) reception of inferior orders
(6) observance of the prescribed intervals between orders
(7) canonical title, if major orders are in question.[77]

Canon 975 gives the canonical age requirement for ordination to the diaconate: ". . . the diaconate should not be conferred before the completion of the twenty-second year . . ."[78] Canon 976 insists on the importance of the proper theological education prior to ordination by noting, ". . . diaconate should not be conferred until after the commencement of the fourth year of theology . . ."[79]

Canon 977 reflects the general understanding of the diaconate as an order which is part of the hierarchy of orders[80] and canon 978 prescribed the proper intervals of time between the orders themselves. The canon states:

. . . unless the necessity or utility of the diocese in the bishop's judgment demands otherwise, there must be at least one year's interval between the last minor order and the subdiaconate, and at least three months between the subdiaconate and diaconate . . .[81]

---

[74]*Canon 968, §1:* "Sacram ordinationem valide recipit solus vir baptizatus; licite autem, qui ad normam sacrorum canonum debitis qualitatibus iudicio proprii Ordinarii, praeditus sit, neque ulla detineatur irregularitate aliove impedimento."

[75]*Canon 969, §1:* "Nemo ex saecularibus ordinetur, qui iudicio proprii Episcopi non sit necessarius vel utilis ecclesiis dioecesis."

[76]*Canon 971:* "Nefas est quemquam, quovis modo, ob quamlibet rationem, ad satatum clericalem cogere, vel canonice idoneum ab eodem avertere."

[77]*Canon 974, §1:* "Ut quis licite ordinari possit, requiruntur:
1. Recepta sacra confirmatio;
2. Mores ordini recipiendo congruentes;
3. Aetas canonica;
4. Debita scientia;
5. Ordinum inferiorum susceptio;
6. Interstitiorum observatio;
7. Titulus canonicus, si agatur de ordinibus maioribus."

[78]*Canon 975:* "Subdiaconatus ne conferatur ante annum vicesimum primum completum; diaconatus ante vicesimum secundum completum; presbyteratus ante vicesimum quartum completum."

[79]*Canon 976, §2:* "Firmo praescripto can. 975, subdiaconatus ne conferatur, nisi exeunte tertio cursus theologici annop diaconatus, nisi incepto quarto anno; presbyteratus, nisi post medietatem eiusdem quarti anni."

[80]*Canon 977:* "Ordines gradatim conferendi sunt ita ut ordinationes per saltum omnino prohibeantur."

[81]*Canon 978, §2:* "Interstitia primam tonsuram inter et ostiariatum vel inter singulos ordines minores prudenti Episcopi iudicio committuntur; acolythus vero ad subdiaconatum, subdiaconus ad diaconatum, diaconus ad presbyteratum ne antea promoveantur, quam acolythus unum saltem annum, subdiaconus et diaconus tres saltem menses in suo quisque ordine fuerint versati, nisi necessitas aut utilitas Ecclesiae, iudicio Episcopi, aliud exposcat."

Canon 979 points out that:
>   1. The canonical title for the secular clergy is the title of a benefice or in lieu of a benefice, or a patrimony or a pension.
>
>   2. This title should be really secure for the whole life of the cleric and truly sufficient for the proper maintenance of the cleric, according to the rules to be laid down by the Ordinaries in accordance with the needs and circumstances of the respective localities and times.[82]

Cited as one of the requirements in canon 974 for those in major orders, the question of proper sustenance for the permanent deacon becomes a problem in the sense that supporting a man in the brief period of transitional diaconate is not the same things as supporting a married deacon, his wife and family. Yet, the deacon is a cleric in major orders and is deserving of support by the Church. As will be seen, this controversy continues to surface in later canonical discussions on the issue of the permanent diaconate.

FUNCTION OF THE DEACON

In regards to the functions a deacon could perform, the *17 Code* considered the deacon to be the:
> Extraordinary minister of baptism, but he cannot utilize his power without the permission of either the local ordinary or the pastor which may be given for a just reason; when necessity urges, that permission is legitimately assumed.[83]

Besides baptism, the deacon may also be the extraordinary minister of Holy Communion.[84] The deacon may expose the Blessed Sacrament to public veneration, yet not give the eucharistic blessing unless in accord with canon 845, Paragraph 2, he has brought Viaticum to the sick.[85] The *17 Code* empowers the deacon to give some blessings, but these are to be determined by the law itself.[86] The deacon has the faculties to preach,[87] he must recite the Divine Office[88] and

---

[82]*Canon 979, §1, 2:* "§1. Pro clericis saecularibus titulus canonicus est titulus beneficii, eoque deficiente, patrimonii aut pensionis.

§2. Hic titulus debet esse et vere securus pro tota ordinati vita et vere sufficiens ad congruam eiusdem sustentationem, secundum normas ab Ordinariis pro diveris locorum et temporum necessitatibus et adiunctis dandas."

[83]*Canon 741:* "Extraordinarius baptismi sollemnis minister est diaconus; qui tamen sua potestate ne utatur sine loci Ordinarii vel parochi licentia, iusta de causa concedenda, quae, ubi necessitas urgeat, legitime praesumitur."

[84]*Canon 845, §2:* "Extraordinarius est diaconus, de Ordinarii Loci vel parochi licentia, gravi de causa concedenda, quae in casu necessitatis legitime praesumitur."

[85]*Canon 1274, §2:* "Minister expositionis et repositionis sanctissimi Sacramenti est sacerdos vel diaconus; minister vero benedictionis Eucharisticae est solus sacerdos, nec eam impertire diaconus potest, nisi in casu qui, ad normam can. 845, §2, Viaticum ad infirmum detulerit."

[86]*Canon 1147, §4:* "Diaconi et lectores illas tantum valide et licite benedictiones dare possunt, quae ipsis expresse a iure permittuntur."

[87]*Canon 1342, §1:* Concionandi facultas solis sacredotibus vel diaconis fiat, non vero ceteris clericis, nisi rationabili de causa, iudicio Ordinarii et in casibus singularibus.

[88]*Canon 135:* "Clerici, in maioribus ordinibus constituti, exceptis iis de quibus in can. 312, 214, tenentur obligatione quotidie horas canonicas integre recitandi secundum proprios et probatos liturgicos libros."

is obliged to be celibate.[89]

As the survey has indicated, the canonical legislation on deacons in the *17 Code* was minimal and somewhat restrictive, especially as regards his ministerial functions, due to the fact that the diaconate was considered a transitional state in the clerical ranks. Article 29 of *Lumen Gentium* sought to restore the diaconate as a permanent office in the Church. *Sacrum Diaconatus Ordinem* offered norms as to how this restoration might be accomplished. It now remains to be seen how these norms were used to create new legislation which would regulate the reappearance of the diaconate as a full and equal order in the Church.

PART TWO: 1980 SCHEMA

RIGHTS AND OBLIGATIONS

This proposed legislation made its appearance in the *Schema Codicis Iuris Canonici* of 1980 (hereafter referred to as the *80 Schema*).

Canon 207, found in Liber II: *De Populo Dei,* Title I, Caput I: *De Clericorum Institutione,* echoes the suggestion of *Sacrum Diaconatus Ordinem,* Article II, Nos. 6 and 9, when it states:

> Aspirants to the permanent diaconate should be given a formation to lead an evangelical life and they should be duly instructed concerning the duties proper to this order. Such should be done in accord with the prescriptions of the Conference of Bishops. The following should also be observed:
> (1) for youth such training should extend for at least a period of three years while they are living in a special house, unless for serious reasons the local Ordinary should decide otherwise;
> (2) for men of a maturer age, whether celibate or married, such training should extend over a period of three years with a curriculum determined by the Conference of Bishops.[90]

Canon 237 indicates that presently one becomes a cleric by reception of the diaconate and is incardinated in the particular church for whose service he has been advanced.[91]

---

[89]*Canon 132, §1:* "Clerici in maioribus ordinibus constituti a nuptiis arcentur et servancae castitatis obligatione ita tenentur, ut contra eandem peccantes sacrilegii quoque rei sint, salvo praescripto can. 214, #1."

[90]*Canon 207:* "Aspirantes ad diaconatum permanentem secundum Episcoporum Conferentiae praescripta ad vitam evangelicam ducendam informentur atque ad officia eidem ordini propria rite sequenda instruantur:
1. iuvenes per tres saltem annos in aliqua domo peculiari degentes, nisi graves ob rationes loci Ordinarius aliter statuerit;
2. maturioris aetatis viri sive coelibes sive coniugati ratione ad tres annos protracta ab eadem Episcoporum Conferentiae definita."

[91]*Canon 327, §1:* "Firmo praescripto can. 691, per receptum diaconatum aliquis fit clericus et incardinatur in Ecclesia particulari pro cuius servitio promotus est."

The rights and obligations of deacons are once again those of clerics as was the case in the *17 Code*. They are urged to pursue holiness in their lives,[92] recite the Divine Office,[93] (cf. *SDO,* VI, 27), and observe celibacy, although canon 250, Paragraph 2, notes: "men who have been promoted to the permanent diaconate while they were living a married life are not bound by the prescriptions of paragraph one."[94] (N.B. This paragraph was later deleted in the 1983 *Codex Iuris Canonici,* Canon 277.)

Another area of rights the deacon enjoys is the right of remuneration already mentioned in canon 974 of the *17 Code* and *SDO* IV, 20. Canon 255, Paragraph 3, states:

> Married deacons who dedicate themselves completely to the ecclesiastical ministry deserve a remuneration by which they can provide for their own support and that of their families. Married deacons, however, who receive remuneration by reason of a civil profession which they exercise or have exercised, should first of all take care of their own and their family's necessities from the revenue acquired from that profession.[95]

The section of the rights of deacons closes with the statement in canon 263 that "permanent deacons are not bound to the prescriptions of the canons 258, 260, 261 and 262, paragraph two."[96]

We see that from the time of the *17 Code to the* 80 Schema, a development has occurred in the understanding of the diaconate, from considering it merely a stage of transition, to a permanent office and ministry in the Church. This permanent office has rights and obligations befitting any other clerical state. Their ministry of service, the threefold ministries of liturgy, Word and charity mentioned in *Lumen Gentium,* are covered in Books III and IV of the *80 Schema.*

---

[92]*Canon 249, §1:* "In vita sua ducenda ad sanctitatem persequendam peculiari ratione tenentur clerici quippe qui, Deo in Ordinis receptione novo titulo consecrati, dispensatores sint mysteriorum Dei in servitium Eius populi."

[93]*Canon 249, §3:* "Obligatione tenentur sacerdotes necnon diaconi ad presbyteratum adspirantes cotidie Divinum Officium persolvendi secundum proprios et probatos liturgicos libros; diaconi autem permanentes invitantur ut idem persolvant pro parte ab Episcoporum Conferentia definita."

[94]*Canon 250, §1, 2:* "§1. Clerici obligatione tenentur servandi perfectam perpetuamque propter Regnum coelorum continentiam ideaque ad coelibatum adstringuntur.

§2. Praescripto §1 non tenentur viri qui in matrimonio viventes ad diaconatum permanentem promoti sunt."

(N.B. As noted in the text, Paragraph 2 of this canon was deleted in the 1983 *CIC,* Canon 277. The question now arises whether or not married permanent deacons who became widowers, might be allowed to remarry. In the present law, the answer appears to be negative, barring the possibility of a dispensation.

Another interesting problem with this canon is in its relation to Canon 288 of the 1983 *CIC,* which lists those canons which do not bind permanent deacons. Canon 277 is not among those listed. Therefore, unless this was an oversight which might be corrected in the future, Canon 277 obliges permanent deacons who become widowers, to remain unmarried.)

[95]*Canon 255, §3:* "Diaconi uzorati qui plene ministerio ecclesiastico sese devovent remunerationem merentur qua sui suaeque familiae sustentatione providere valeant; qui vero ratione professionis civilis quam exercent aut exercuerunt remunerationem obtineant, ex perceptis prae aliis inde reditibus sibi suaeque familiae necessitatibus consulant."

[96]*Canon 263:* "Diaconi permanentes praescriptis canonum 258, 260, 261, 262 #2 non tenentur."

DIACONAL MINISTRY

In Book III: *De Ecclesiae Munere Docendi,* Title I: *De Divini Verbi Ministerio,* Chapter I speaks of the deacon's role in the ministry of the Word. Canon 712 insists on his right to share in the ministry of the Word with priests and bishops, and canon 719 grants him the faculty to preach, especially the homily, mentioned in canon 722.[97]

In Chapter II under Catechetical Formation, canon 731 mentions the assistance the clerics might give to the pastor of a parish in the catechesis of adults, youths and children,[98] while in Titulus II, *De Actione Ecclesiae Missionali,* canon 739 mentions clerics as those who might possibly be willing to serve the Church as missionaries.[99]

In Titulus IV, *De Instrumentis Communicationis Socialis Et In Specie De Libris,* canon 786 asserts that:

1. Without a just and reasonable cause the Christian faithful should not write anything for newspapers, magazines, or periodicals which are wont to attack the Catholic religion or good morals. Clerics and members of religious institutes should do so only with the license of the local Ordinary.

2. It is the responsibility of the Conference of Bishops to establish norms concerning the requirements enabling clerics and members of religious institutes of consecrated life to take part in radio or television programs which deal with questions concerning Catholic teaching or morals.[100]

Finally, in Title V, *De Fidei Professione,* canon 788 lists those who are obliged to make a profession of faith personally in accord with a formula approved by the Apostolic See. In Number 6 we find listed, "Those to be promoted to the order of diaconate."[101]

---

[97]*Canon 712:* ". . . diaconorum etiam est in ministerio verbi populo Dei, in communione cum Episcopo eiusque presbyterio, inservire."

Canon 719: "Salvo praescripto can. 720, facultate praedicandi ubique gaudent presbyteri et diaconi, nisi ab Ordinario competenti eadem facultas restricta fuerit aut sublata, aut lege particulari expressa requiratur licentia."

Canon 722, §1: "Inter praedicationis formas eminet homilia, quae est pars ipsius liturgiae et sacerdoti aut diacono reservatur . . ."

[98]*Canon 731:* "Parochus, vi sui muneris, catecheticam efformationem adultorum, iuvenum et puerorum curare tenetur, quem in finem sociam sibi operam adhibeat clericorum paroeciae addictorum . . ."

[99]*Canon 739:* "Missionarii, qui scilicet a competenti auctoritate ecclesiastica ad opus missionale explendum mittuntur, eligi possunt autochthoni vel non, sive clerici saeculares . . ."

[100]*Canon 786, §1:* "In diariis, foliis aut libellis periodicis qui religionem catholicam aut bonos mores manifesto impetere solent, ne quidpiam conscribant christifideles, nisi iusta et rationabili de causa; clerici autem et Institutorum vitae consecratae sodales, tantummodo de licentia loci Ordinarii."

§2. Episcoporum Conferentiae est normas statuere de requisitis ut clerici atque sodales Institutorum vitae consecratae partem habere valeant in tractandis via radiophonica aut televisifica quaestionibus, quae ad doctrinam catholicam aut mores attinent."

[101]*Canon 788, §6:* ". . . promovendi ad ordinem diaconatus; . . ."

Title VI of Book IV: *De Ecclesiae Munere Sanctificandi* on Orders in canon 962, lists the grades of orders as episcopacy, presbyterate and diaconate.[102] We notice the minor orders and subdiaconate have been suppressed as well as the addition of the episcopate to the list of orders, a change from canon 949 of the *17 Code*. The *80 Schema* repeats the injunction of the *17 Code* in canon 968 which stated that only baptized males may be the recipients of sacred orders.[103]

Canon 984, Paragraph 2, restates *SDO* II, 5, when it says, "a candidate for the permanent diaconate who is not married should not be admitted to the diaconate unless he is at least twenty-five years of age." When the canon states that "If the candidate is married, he should not be admitted to the permanent diaconate unless he is at least thirty-five years of age and has the consent of his wife," this echoes *SDO* III, 11 and 12. Paragraph 3 of canon 984 complies with *SDO* II, 5, when it states, "The Conference of Bishops is at liberty to establish a norm by which an older age is required for the priesthood and for the permanent diaconate."[104]

The legislation on deacons continues by requiring that the candidate for the diaconate go through the liturgical rite of admission,[105] receive the ministries of lector and acolyte (as mandated by the *motu proprio Ministeria Quaedam* in Article 11),[106] publicly accept celibacy if he is not married,[107] and provide the necessary documentation required by law, prior to his ordination.[108]

The ministry of liturgy and charity in the *80 Schema* mentions that the deacon is the ordinary minister of the sacrament of baptism,[109] and the ordinary minister of Holy Communion.[110] Canon 892 refers to the exposition of the Blessed Sacra-

---

[102]*Canon 962:* "Ordines sunt episcopatus, presbyteratus et diaconatus."

[103]*Canon 977:* "Sacram ordinationem valide recipit solus vir baptizatus."

[104]*Canon 984, §2, 3:* "§2. Candidatus ad diaconatum permanentem qui non sit uxoratus as eundem diaconatum ne admittuntur, nisi post expletum vigesimum quintum saltem aetatis annum; qui matrimonio coniunctus est, nonnisi post expletum trigesimum quintum saltem aetatis annum, atque de uxoris consensu.
§3. Integrum est Episcoporum Conferentiis normam statuere, qua provectior ad presbyteratum et ad diaconatum permanentem requiratur aetas."

[105]*Canon 987, §1:* "Ad diaconatum vel presbyteratum adspirans ne ordinetur nisi qui prius ritu liturgico admissionis ab auctoritate de qua in cann. 969 et 972 adscriptionem inter candidatos obtinuerit post praeviam suam petitionem propria manu exaratam et subscriptam atque ab eadem auctoritate in scriptis acceptatam."

[106]*Canon 988, §1:* "Antequam quid ad diaconatum, sive permanentem sive transeuntem, promoveatur, requiritur ut ministeria lectoris et acolythi receperit et per congruum tempus exercuerit."

[107]*Canon 990:* "Candidatus ad diaconatum permanentem qui non sit uxoratus, itemque candidatus ad presbyteratum, ad ordinem diaconatus ne admittatur, nisi ritu praescripto publice coram Deo et Ecclesia obligationem caelibatus assumpserit."

[108]*Canon 1003:* "Documenta quae requiruntur sunt sequentia:
1. testimonium de studiis rite peractis ad normam can. 985, §1 et §2.
2. si agatur de ordinandis ad presbyteratum testimonium recepit diaconatus;
3. si agatur de promovendis ad diaconatum, testimonium recepti baptismi et confirmationis, atque receptorum ministeriorum de quibus in can. 988; item testimonium factae declarationis de qua in can. 989, necnon, si ordinandus sit uxoratus qui promovendus est ad diaconatum permanentem, testimonia celebrati matrimonii et consensus uxoris."

[109]*Canon 815:* "Minister ordinarius baptismi est Episcopus, presbyter et diaconus, firmo praescripto can. 469."

[110]*Canon 863:* "Minister ordinarius sacrae communionis est episcopus, presbyter et diaconus."

ment, and in Paragraph 3 we read, "the minister of the exposition of the Blessed Sacrament of the Eucharistic blessing is a priest or a deacon . . ."[111] Canon 1123 allows the deacon to impart blessings noting "only those blessings which are expressly permitted to deacons by law."[112] Deacons are permitted to officiate at weddings with delegation from the local Ordinary or pastor,[113] and they have the faculty to dispense from the form of marriage and each and every impediment of ecclesiastical law, according to the norms of canon 1032, Paragraph 2.[114] The *80 Schema* does not give any specific details on the ministry of charity deacons might perform in the service of the Church. Presumably, it would be the task of the various Conferences of Bishops to give these specifics in the particular law regarding deacons which they may create for their own regions and/or nations.[115]

PART THREE: 1983 CODEX IURIS CANONICI
TRAINING AND QUALIFICATIONS

Much of the legislation found in the *80 Schema* was transferred into the 1983 *Codex Iuris Canonici* (hereafter referred to as *CIC*). Canons which deal with the office of deacon are found in three of the seven books of the *CIC*; i.e., Book II: *De Populo Dei*, Book III: *De Ecclesiae Munere Docendi*, and Book IV: *De Ecclesiae Munere Santificandi*.

In Title III of Book II: *De Populo Dei* on *De Ministris Sacris Seu De Clericis*, we find the canons which pertain to the formation and training of candidates for the diaconate.

Canon 236 substantially repeats the legislation already found in the *80 Schema* in reference to the mandatory training period for ordination.[116] Canon 266 states that one becomes a cleric "through the reception of diaconate and is incardinated into the particular church or personal prelature."[117] Canon 276, Paragraphs 2

---

[111]*Canon 892, §3:* "Minister expositionis Sanctissimi sacramenti et benedictionis eucharisticae est sacerdos vel diaconus . . ."

[112]*Canon 1123, §3:* "Diaconus illas tantum benedictiones impertire potest, quae ipsis expresse iure permittunter."

[113]*Canon 1065:* "Loci Ordinarius et parochus, quandiu valide officio funguntur, possunt facultatem intra fines sui territorii matrimoniis assistendi, etiam generalem, de legare sacerdotibus et diaconis."

[114]*Canon 1032, §2:* In eisdem rerum adiunctis de quibus in §1 et solum pro casibus in quibus ne loci quidem Ordinarius adiri possit, eadem dispensandi facultate pollet tum parochus, tum minister sacer rite delegatus, tum sacerdos vel diaconus qui matrimonio, ad normam can. 1071, §2, assistit."

[115]This is evident from the *Guidelines* which the NCCB published in 1971 and which were analyzed in Chapter Two of this study.

[116]*Canon 236.* This corresponds to Canon 207 of the *80 Schema* with two changes in wording. The phrase "ad vitam evangelicam" in the *80 schema* becomes "ad vitam spiritualem alendam" in the 1983 *CIC*, and "loci Ordinarius" of the *80 Schema* becomes "ob rationes Episcopus diocesanus" in the 1983 *CIC*. (Cf. footnote #19.)

[117]*Canon 266.* This corresponds to Canon 237 of the *80 Schema*. One word change is made in the 1983 *CIC*. Inserted in Canon 266 is the phrase, "Praelaturae personali." (Cf. footnote #20.)

and 3, restate the suggestions for spiritual growth made in the *80 Schema*[118] and Canon 281, Paragraph 3, once again addresses the issue of remuneration for married deacons.[119] Canon 288 of the *CIC* follows canon 263 of the *80 Schema* in listing what canons do not affect permanent deacons.[120]

DIACONAL MINISTRY

In Title I of Book III: *De Divini Verbi Ministerio,* canons 757, 764 and 767 stress the deacon's role in the ministry of the Word;[121] and canons 776, 784, 831 and 833 repeat the legislation mentioned in the *80 Schema.*[122]

In Title VI of Book IV: *De Ordine,* canons 1009 and 1024 once again list the orders as ". . . episcopacy, the presbyterate, and the diaconate."[123] Canon 1024 restates the fact that "only a baptized male validly receives sacred ordination."[124] Canon 1031 also repeats the norms of the *80 Schema* regarding the questions of age and marital status.[125]

Canon 1034 speaks of the liturgical rite of admission.[126] Canon 1035 repeats the injunction of *Ministeria Quaedam* #11 about receiving the ministries of lector and acolyte before the diaconate.[127] Canon 1036 tells of the necessity that ordination be a free act on the part of the candidate, and Canons 1037-1039 pertain to the issues of celibacy, impediments to ordination and retreats.[128]

---

[118]*Canon 276.* This canon is taken verbatim from the *80 Schema,* Canon 249. (Cf. footnotes nos. 21 and 22.)
[119]*Canon 281.* This canon is taken verbatim from the *80 Schema,* Canon 255. (Cf. footnote #24.)
[120]*Canon 288.* This corresponds to Canon 263 of the *80 Schema.* Inserted in the 1983 *CIC* is the phrase, "nisi ius particulare aliud statuat." (Cf. footnote #25.)
[121]*Canon 757.* This canon is taken verbatim from the *80 Schema.* (Cf. footnote #26, Canon 712.)
    Canon 764. This canon corresponds to Canon 719 of the *80 Schema.* The 1983 *CIC* adds the phrase, "de consensu saltem praesumpto rectoris ecclesiae exercenda." (Cf. footnote #26.)
    Canon 767. This canon is taken verbatim from the *80 Schema.* (Cf. footnote #26, Canon 722.)
[122]*Canon 776.* This canon corresponds to Canon 731 of the *80 Schema.* The 1983 *CIC* adds the phrase, "necnon societatum vitae apostolicae" and "Munus parentum, in catechesi familiari, de quo in can. 774, #2, promoveat et foveat." (Cf. footnote #27.)
    Canon 784. This canon is taken verbatim from the *80 Schema.* (Cf. footnote #28, Canon 739.)
    Canon 831. This canon is taken verbatim from Canon 786 of the *80 Schema.* (Cf. footnote #29.)
    Canon 833. This canon is taken verbatim from Canon 788, #6, of the *80 Schema.* (Cf. footnote #30.)
[123]*Canon 1009.* This canon is taken verbatim from the *80 Schema,* Canon 962. (Cf. footnote #31.)
[124]*Canon 1024.* This canon is taken verbatim from the *80 Schema,* Canon 977. (Cf. footnote #32.)
[125]*Canon 1031.* This canon is taken verbatim from the *80 Schema,* Canon 984. (Cf. footnote #33.)
[126]*Canon 1034.* This canon is taken verbatim from the *80 Schema,* Canon 987. (Cf. footnote #34.)
[127]*Canon 1035.* This canon is taken verbatim from the *80 Schema,* Canon 988. (Cf. footnote #35.)
[128]*Canon 1036.* This canon is taken verbatim from the *80 Schema,* Canon 989, which states: "Candidatus, ut ad ordinem diaconatus aut presbyteratus promoveri possit, Episcopo proprio aut Superiori maiori competenti declarationem tradat propria manu exaratam et subscriptam, qua testificetur se sponte ac libere sacrum ordinem suscepturum atque se ministerio ecclesiastico perpetuo mancipaturum esse, insimul petens ut ad ordinem recipiendum admittatur."
    Canon 1037. This canon corresponds to Canon 990 of the *80 Schema.* The 1983 *CIC* adds the phrase, "aut vota perpetua in instituto religioso emiserint." (Cf. footnote #36.)
    Canon 1038. This canon is taken verbatim from the *80 Schema,* Canon 991, which states: "Diaconus qui ad

Diaconal functions include having a "part in the celebration of divine worship in accord with the prescriptions of the law."[129] The deacon can baptize,[130] distribute Holy Communion,[131] officiate at the exposition of the Blessed Sacrament,[132] assist at marriages,[133] and dispense from certain impediments regarding marriage when there is the danger of death,[134] as well as impart certain blessings.[135]

Another form of the ministry of service which the deacon might be able to perform is found in canon 517, Paragraph 2, which was not explicitly stated in canon 456 of the *80 Schema*. Canon 517, Paragraph 2, states:

> If the diocesan bishop should decide that due to a dearth of priests a participation in the exercise of the pastoral care of a parish is to be entrusted to a deacon or to some other person who is not a priest or to a community of persons, he is to appoint some priest endowed with the powers and faculties of a pastor to supervise the pastoral care.[65]

The inclusion of the word "deacon" in the *CIC* text, which would not be found in the *80 Schema*, may perhaps indicate that the office of deacon has gained more and more importance in the post-Vatican II Church.

CONCLUSION

This ministry of service has flourished in the Church and the legislation which appears in the Code of Canon Law assures the permanent diaconate of a serious commitment to it on the part of the whole Christian community.

(Footnote 128 *Continued*)
presbyteratum promoveri renuat ab ordinis recepti exercitio prohiberi non potest, nisi impedimento detineatur canonico aliave gravis, de iudicio Episcopi dioecesani aut superioris maioris competentis, obsit causa."

Canon 1039. This canon is taken verbatim from the *80 Schema*, Canon 992, which states: "Omnes qui ad aliquem ordinem promovendi sunt, exercitis spiritualibus, per quinque saltem dies, vacent, loco et modo ab Ordinario determinatis; Episcopus, antequam ad ordinationem procedat, certior factus esse debet candidatos rite issdem exercitiis vacasse."

[129]*Canon 835, §3:* "Diaconi in divino cultu celebrando partem habent, ad normam iuris praescriptorum." (This canon is found in the *80 Schema*.)

[130]*Canon 861.* This canon is taken verbatim from the *80 Schema*, Canon 815. (Cf. footnote #38.)

[131]*Canon 910.* This canon is taken verbatim from the *80 Schema*, Canon 863. (Cf. footnote #39.)

[132]*Canon 943.* This canon is taken verbatim from the *80 Schema*, Canon 1065. (Cf. footnote #40.)

[133]*Canon 1111.* This canon is taken verbatim from the *80 Schema*, Canon 1065. (Cf. footnote #42.)

[134]*Canon 1079. This canon is taken verbatim from the 80 Schema,* Canon 1032, #2. (Cf. footnote #43.)

[135]*Canon 1169, §3.* This canon is taken verbatim from the *80 Schema*, Canon 1123, #3. (Cf. footnote #41.)

[136]*Canon 517, §2:* "Si ob sacerdotum penuriam Episcopus dioecesanus aestimaverit participationem in exercitio curae pastoralis paroeciae concredendam esse diacono aliive personae sacerdotali charactere non insignitae aut personarum cummunitati, sacerdotem constituat aliquem qui, potestatibus et facultatibus parochi instructus, curam pastoralem moderetur." (This canon corresponds to Canon 456 of the *80 Schema*, the word "diacono" being inserted in the 1983 *CIC*.)

BIBLIOGRAPHY

Acta Apostolicae Sedis, Commentarium Officiale. Romae: 1909-1929. Civitate Vaticana, 1929.

Codex Iuris Canonici. Romae: Typos Polyglottis Vaticanis, 1917.

Codex Iuris Canonici Auctoritate Ioannis Pauli II Promulgatus. Romae: Libreria Editrice Vaticana, 1983.

Mansi, Johannes Dominicus. *Conciliorum Nova et Amplissima Collectio.* Tomus Trigesimus Tertio, Ab Anno MDXLV Ad Annum MDLXV (Parisiis: Expensis Huberti Welter, Bibliopolae, MDCCCCII).

Pope Paul VI. *Apostolic Constitution, Pontificalis Romani, Approval of a New Rite for the Ordination of Deacons, Priests and Bishops.* June 19, 1968. Washington D.C.: United States Catholic Conference translation.

_____. *Apostolic Letter in Motu Proprio Form Laying Down Certain Norms Regarding the Sacred Order of the Diaconate, Ad Pascendum.* September 15, 1972. Washington, D.C.: United States Catholic Conference translation.

_____. *Apostolic Letter in Motu Proprio Form By Which the Discipline of First Tonsure, Minor Orders and Subdiaconate in the Latin Church is Reformed, Ministeria Quaedam.* September 15, 1972. Washington, D.C.: United States Catholic Conference translation.

_____. *General Norms for Restoring the Permanent Diaconate in the Latin Church, Sacrum Diaconatus Ordinem, Apostolic Letter Issued Motu Proprio.* June 18, 1967. Washington, D.C.: United States Catholic Conference translation.

Reference Works

Abbott, Walter M., ed. *The Documents of Vatican II.* New York: Guild Press, 1966.

Barnett, James M. *The Diaconate: A Full and Equal Order.* New York: Seabury Press, 1981.

Medina, Jose Casanas. *The Law for the Restoration of the Permanent Diaconate: A Canonical Commentary.* Canon Law Studies 460. Washington, D.C.: The Catholic University of America, 1968.

Buckley, Joseph C. "The Permanent Diaconate." *The Furrow* 23 (1972): 476-482.

Croghan, Leo M. "The Theology and the Spirit of the Diaconate's Restoration." *American Ecclesiastical Review* 161 (1969): 293-301.

Erchlin, Edward P. "The Deacon's Golden Age." *Worship* 45 (1971): 37-46.

_____. "The Origins of the Permanent Diaconate." *American Ecclesiastical Review* 163 (1970): 92-105.

HEARING ON THE C.L.S.A. SCHOLARSHIP FUND

William A. Schumacher

Leonard G. Scott, the Vice-President, had served as liaison for the Board of Governors for the successive committees which had worked on this project in the past year. He began the session by explaining that the presenter of each topic would make a rather short presentation, and since there was a small group in attendance this hearing would serve not only to inform the membership about the plans of the Board of Governors regarding the scholarship fund, but would also serve as a working session in which the Board could refine its own motions which would be presented to the body at the annual business meeting.

1. The history of the scholarship fund.

William A. Schumacher made the first presentation. He noted that the notion of a scholarship fund began in 1984 when a resolution was presented to the body and the Canon Law Society of America established a task force to study the feasibility of a scholarship program. This motion was adopted by the body at the 46th Annual General Meeting [*CLSA Proceedings 1984*, pp. 291-293]. In January, 1985 the Board of Governors met and adopted a series of questions which had been raised by James Mallett of the Diocese of Nashville. These indicated the areas which should be explored by the ad hoc committee to study the feasibility of the scholarship program. That spring William Varvaro, President of the Canon Law Society of America, established a task force to look into the matter. This task force reported to the Board of Governors prior to the 47th Annual Meeting that such a project would be feasible given certain conditions [*CLSA Proceedings 1985*, pp. 183-189].

As a result of the adoption of this report by the body (*CLSA Proceedings 1985*, pp. 214-216], a goal was set and established of raising $50,000 from the membership of the Canon Law Society of America as a beginning of attaining a goal of $500,000 by the completion of the project.

During 1985 and 1986 there was a mailing from the Executive Coordinator's office which resulted in some contributions being received. Following the 48th Annual Meeting in 1986, Richard Cunningham, President of the Canon Law Society of America, established a committee which would organize a campaign to solicit all the members with the goal of raising the $50,000. A telephone and mail campaign succeeded in raising this money [cf. *below*, pp. 206-208].

Once this was accomplished, President Cunningham then established an ad hoc committee to look into the issue of how a Board of Trustees should be structured and empowered to administer these funds. This report was returned to the Board of Governors in April, 1987. Consultation was held with Peter M. Shannon, Esq., who serves as a general counsel for the Canon Law Society of America, with Mr. Lawrence G. Hickey, Chief Executive Officer of Stein, Roe & Farnham, Inc., investment counselors, and Mr. Walter Hansen, professional fundraiser for the Archdiocese of Chicago. Father Michael Connolly was also very helpful with practical suggestions which were contained in the report to the Board of Governors. This report gave rise to two Board resolutions presented in the pre-convention packet which was discussed later in this meeting.

Since this presentation was merely an historical review, there was little discussion following. Some merely wished to be reassured that we had indeed raised $50,000 from the membership by this campaign. Total contributions to date stood at $52,000.

2. The task of the project directors.

Following the meeting of the Board of Governors in April, 1987, President Richard Cunningham acted on one of the suggestions in that report and asked that James Coriden and William Varvaro serve as Project Co-Directors. Their task was to gather the remaining part of the half million dollars which was the goal of this fund. Edward Pfnausch, Executive Coordinator of the Canon Law Society of America, would serve as liaison with the Project Directors. As a beginning the Project Directors stated that they identified 16 Area Coordinators throughout the country with whom they would work in raising these additional funds.

Just prior to the 49th General Meeting in Nashville seven of these Area Coordinators met with the Project Directors and Mr. Paul Rohling of Nashville, a professional fundraiser for a Catholic high school there, whoe presented to them another pssible method of raising the remaining funds, namely, to use the Area Coordinators to identify 3 members of the Canon Law Society of America who are influential and well-respected in the local region. These members would be asked to identify potential large, local contributors who would contribute $25,000 or more to the Scholarship Fund over a period of 3 to 5 years.

Another direction would be for the Project Directors, using Area Coordinators, to make a consistent, well founded, well thought out approach to various foundations throughout the country who are interested in Catholic causes.

The presentation of Coriden and Varvaro was followed by a very lengthy discussion which focused on how to approach both individual donors and foundations for contributions to this Scholarship Fund. Some expressed concern that using members to identify donors would simply be putting more burden on the membership, whereas we seem to have made an implicit promise to the membership not to come back to them for more contributions in the future. Concerning potential membership donors in the future, a suggestion was raised that when a new member joins the Society, in the initial packet that person receives along with a copy of the constitution of the Society, should be contained a pledge card and envelope with a covering letter simply indicating that, as a new member you should be informed that this is one of the things we do as members, to support this one-time contribution. The sense of the meeting was that the Project Directors should confine themselves at this stage of the Society's development, to raising the remaining $450,000 needed to implement the Scholarship Fund. The further development of funds from the general membership of the Society might follow in the future once this goal has been achieved.

3. Board Resolutions implementing the Committee reports:

Lynn Jarrell, Secretary of the Society, also served as a liaison to the various committees working on the Scholarship Fund. She explained the two resolutions brought forward by the Board and distributed in the mailing prior to the convention.

The first of these, Resolution #2 at that stage, was concerned with the separate incorporations of the Scholarship Fund. This was seen as an implementation of the resolution passed in 1985 [*CLSA Proceedings 1985,* pp. 214-216]. The other resolution brought forward by the Board, #3 at that stage, was concerned with the structure, makeup and selection of the Board of Trustees for the Scholarship Fund.

A great deal of discussion followed Lynn Jarrell's presentation. Questions were raised such as: Why a separate incorporation from that of the Canon Law Society of America? What relationship has the Board of Trustees to the Board of Governors? What would be the cost of separate incorporation and a separate Internal Revenue Service ruling for tax purposes? How would the Board be composed? How would the Board hold its annual meetings? What would be the liability to be undertaken by the Board?

After a great deal of discussion of some of these technical points, the sense of the house was that there must be an easier way to do this than to have this elaborate structure, a separate Board of Trustees and a separate incorporation. From this discussion the Board of Governors later reformulated its two resolutions into a subsequent resolution #2 which was presented and amended at the annual business meeting [cf. *below,* p. 364].

4. CLSA Scholarship Criteria:

Paul Golden had been appointed by President Cunningham to chair a small committee to determine the criteria for the granting of the scholarships. The report of this committee was published with the other committee reports in the convention packet [cf. *below,* 280-282]. The committee also presented an enabling resolution #4 which was adopted at the annual business meeting [cf. *below,* p. 368]. Following Paul Golden's report there was a lengthy discussion. It seems that various schools of canon law use different terminology regarding the first year of their program. This would have to be clarified because the general intent of the membership seems to be that the scholarship program would not fund any necessary theological studies to qualify someone for entrance into a school of canon law. A great deal of discussion followed regarding the statement, "Applicants must be members of Roman Catholic Church and be in good standing." It was pointed out that the phrase "canonical status" in the criteria referred not to a person being in full communion with the Church, but rather the fact that the person need not be a cleric or religious to qualify for such a scholarship. It was noted too that affirmative action resolution #3 [cf. *below*, pp. 367-368] should be taken into account.

The final discussion centered on the question of marketing the scholarship funds, namely, advising those who would be concerned and interested: 1) that the monies would be available; 2) that criteria for selection had been established; and 3) that a set method for application should be followed.

At the conclusion Vice-President Scott thanked all the presenters and those who came and gave input, which helped the Board of Governors to clarify further their own thinking in regard to the resolution which they would present at the business meeting.

DEFERENCE OR NEUTRAL PRINCIPLES: THE DUAL APPROACH BY CIVIL COURTS TO ECCLESIASTICAL DISPUTES

Peter M. Shannon, Jr.

In our presentation this morning, I intend first to describe the two alternative approaches employed by the Supreme Court of the United States in resolving intra-Church disputes and secondly to discuss how these alternative approaches might apply to current disputes within the Catholic Church in the United States.

Churches are like other institutions in that the American legal system permits them to function according to their own rules as long as those rules are not in conflict with civil laws. Churches are unlike other institutions in that the American legal system sometimes sanctions ecclesiastical resolution of ecclesiastical disputes even though civil courts, presented with almost identical disputes involving secular institutions, had rendered or would render decisions diametrically opposed to the ecclesiastical decisions. This is so, of course, because of the First Amendment religion clauses which bring an added dimension in the resolution by civil courts of ecclesiastical disputes.

For over 100 years, civil courts utilized only one approach in resolving ecclesiastical disputes. This one approach was enunciated in 1871 by the Supreme Court in the famous case of *Watson v. Jones*.[1] There the Supreme Court announced that the proper rule to employ in resolving intra-church disputes was the "deference" approach, i.e. a court should ascertain and defer to the decision of the church's highest governing body that already resolved the ecclesiastical controversy pending before the civil court. At issue in *Watson* was which faction of a local Presbyterian church had proper title to church property. The Watson court held that a civil court must defer in such circumstances to the decision of the Presbyterian General Assembly.

According to the *Watson* court, the deference approach preserves the separation of church and state by allowing religious associations to decide questions of religious belief, church discipline, and ecclesiastical government without state interference.[2] The court summarized the deference approach as follows:

> The rule of action which should govern the civil courts is that whenever the questions of discipline, or faith, or ecclesiastical rule, custom, or law have been decided by the highest . . . church judicator[y] . . ., the legal tribunals must accept such decision as final, and as binding on them.[3]

Some 50 years after *Watson v. Jones,* Justice Brandeis in *dictum,* announced a modified version of the deference rule in *Gonzalez v. Roman Catholic Archbishop*

---

[1] *Watson v. Jones,* 80 U.S. (13 Wall.) 679 (1871).
[2] *Id.* at 728-729, 733.
[3] *Id.* at 727.

of Manilla.[4] Under the modified deference rule, courts are allowed to disregard church court determinations of ecclesiastical matters if there is evidence that the church's decision is the result of fraud, collusion, or arbitrariness.[5]

The deference approach, however, continued to prevail as the sole approach for civil court resolution of ecclesiastical disputes until 1979 when the Supreme Court posed an alternative approach—the so-called "neutral principles of law" approach. This neutral principles concept was first introduced in *dictim* in 1969 in the case of *Presbyterian Church v. Mary Elizabeth Blue Hall Memorial Presbyterian Church.*[6] In *Hall*, the Supreme Court indicated that the First Amendment establishment clause would not prohibit courts from resolving church disputes by applying the same law which governs other institutions, *i.e.*, traditional contract, property, and trust law.

Yet the "neutral principles" approach was not clearly articulated and developed until ten years later when the Supreme Court in the 1979 case of *Jones v. Wolf,*[7] delineated the nature and significance of the neutral principles approach and applied the approach in resolving a church property dispute, again involving the Presbyterian Church. At issue in *Jones* was whether a civil court could apply "neutral principles of law" to decide a church property dispute among competing groups of a local Presbyterian congregation in the State of Georgia without running afoul of the religion clauses of the First Amendment. The court identified as the primary issue in the case the following: whether civil courts could resolve church property disputes by using the neutral principles of law approach or whether civil courts had to defer to the resolution of the dispute by an authoritative tribunal of the respective Church.

Writing for the majority of the court, Justice Blackmum noted that the First Amendment places strict restraints on the role of civil courts in resolving church property disputes. He conceded that in matters of religious doctrine or polity, the First Amendment religion clauses require civil courts to defer resolution of these issues to the highest ecclesiastical authority. Where, however, doctrine or policy is not the basis of the dispute, civil courts may adopt a "neutral principles of law" approach by interpreting and applying secular provisions of the church's governing documents such as deeds, church constitutions, and other documentary evidence.[8]

Parenthetically, "polity"—which is frequently the focus of Church-property disputes—refers to the particular system of church government agreed upon by the church members, including the structural allocation of authority within the church and the established grievance procedures for resolving internal disputes.[9]

Under the neutral principles of law approach, a court must conduct a two step inquiry into church property disputes. First, the court must examine deeds to the

---

[4]*Gonzalez v. Roman Catholic Archbishop of Manilla*, 280 U.S. 1 (1929).
[5]*Id.* at 16.
[6]*Presbyterian Church v. Mary Elizabeth Blue Hall Memorial Presbyterian Church*, 393 U.S. 440 (1969).
[7]*Jones v. Wolf*, 443 U.S. 595 (1979).
[8]*Id.* at 602-606.
[9]*See* Adams and Hanlon, *Jones v. Wolf: Church Antonomy and the Religion Clauses of the First Amendment*, 128 U. of Pennsylvania Law Review 1291, 1292, note 5 (1980).

property as well as any other relevant documents such as the church constitution or bylaws to determine if title to the property is vested or held in trust by the general church. Second, if the court finds that the local congregation and not the general church owns the property, it must then apply neutral principles to decide who constitutes the local congregation. Under the deference approach, the court would have honored the church's decision as to the identity of the local congregation. After *Jones,* the court, unless obligated by particular state law to follow the deference approach, need not accept the church's resolution of the matter but can proceed to adjudicate it according to neutral principles.

Where civil courts have employed the neutral principles approach, they have almost always done so in deciding disputes involving church property. But my reading of these court decisions and my analysis of the neutral principles approach lead me to conclude that the neutral principle approach is also applicable to non-property, intra-church disputes.

Thus, in the 2nd part of our presentation this morning, I would like to discuss how the Supreme Court might apply these two alternative approaches in resolving current disputes within the American Catholic Community.

A number of examples (of current issues) come readily to mind. Termination of an unmarried pregnant teacher in a parochial school; termination of a doctor's sterilization surgeries within the hospital or, the more difficult case, apart from the Catholic hospital; or, in a very recent situation where I was privileged to represent the Sisters, a pastor's termination of two Sisters as pastoral assistants without due process of law.

However, the controversy surrounding Father Charles Curran and The Catholic University is probably the best example for us to focus upon in applying the deference and neutral principle approaches to current disputes within the American Catholic Community, not simply because of the notoriety of the dispute but also because at last year's CLSA meeting the report of the Ad Hoc Committee on Canon law/Civil law indicated that the issue of tenure of university professors at Catholic universitites is one of the critical legal issues within the United States' Catholic community.

In the summer of 1986, for the first time in the Continental United States, the Vatican's Congregation for the Doctrine of Faith found a Roman Catholic theologian unsuitable and ineligible to continue teaching Catholic theology at The Catholic University because he allegedly refused to conform his teachings to official Catholic doctrine. Pope John Paul II approved the Congregation's finding. Thereupon, The Catholic University's Chancellor, Archbishop James Hickey, suspended Father Curran and began proceedings to revoke his ecclesiastical license to teach; and the University President, Father William Byron, cancelled Father Curran's scheduled classes. In March 1987, Father Curran filed suit in the Superior Court of the District of Columbia against The Catholic University challenging his suspension and the cancellation of his classes.

The question I would like to discuss today is how and why the civil court or courts considering Father Curran's suit might or might not employ the deference or neutral principles approach and, depending on the approach utilized, the probable consequences for the involved parties. In applying these two approaches to the Father Curran situation, I wish to emphasize that in no way am I prejudging preparing the case; that I have not read the pleadings by any of the parties to this controversy; and that I have not discussed the case itself with any of the parties. Indeed, my sources for the "facts" in the matter are all secondary sources, i.e. law reviews, periodicals and newspaper articles.

In 1965, Father Curran joined the theology faculty at The Catholic University, one of the few pontifical faculties in the United States. As you know, according to the Code of Canon Law, theology professors are required to have a mandate to teach ("mandatum"—formerly termed "missio canonica") from "the competent ecclesiastical authority."[10] At The Catholic University, Archbishop Hickey grants the mandate to faculty members who will teach theology at the University. As we have already noted, in addition to suspending Father Curran from teaching, Archbishop Hickey began revocation of Father Curran's canonical license according to the procedures set fourth in the university statutes and faculty handbook. Under these statutes, the chancellor is permitted to withdraw the mandate "only for the most serious reasons and after providing information regarding specific charges and for cause."[11] Pursuant to these statutes, Father Curran has asked The Catholic University to comply with due process procedures for dismissal for cause outlined in the faculty handbook. Last December, a faculty committee was formed to evaluate the charges and hold hearings. The Faculty Committee reports to the University's Board of Trustees for a final decision on the controversy.

FATHER CURRAN'S CONTRACTUAL RIGHTS AND REMEDIES

Since The Catholic University has suspended Father Curran because of the Vatican's actions, Father Curran is seeking relief through the civil court, primarily on the basis of contract law. At a January 15, 1987 press conference, Father Curran summarized his lawsuit as follows: "As a tenured professor, I have a legal binding contract. The question is, can an external authority break that contract?"[12]

To prove that the University has breached his employment contract, Father Curran must establish that the University dismissed him without adequate cause or violated his contractual due process rights by failing to follow dismissal procedures outlined in the faculty handbook. In resolving these issues, the court would likely consider whether or not revocation of his license to teach Catholic theology constitutes cause.

---

[10] Canon 812, Code of Canon Law.
[11] Note *Recent Development: Church Licensed Professors: the Curran Controversy*, 13 Journal of College and University Law 375, 376 (1987).
[12] *Id.* at 395.

The starting point in determining the rights of The Catholic University vis-a-vis Father Curran is to examine the nature of Father Curran's contract with the University. The contract itself is in the form of a letter of appointment. Even though the letter of appointment does not make any specific reference to religious criteria, it arguably does incorporate the ecclesiastical statutes.[13]

Universities adopt tenure systems to give professors freedom to pursue studies and teaching without the threat of arbitrary dismissal. At the same time, the tenure system restricts the university's power to dismiss a tenured professor when the professor does not act in accordance with university practices.

According to The Catholic University's tenure plan, it can terminate Father Curran's contract only for a financial emergency of the University, his inability to teach due to a medical condition, cessation of his ecclesiastical obligations, and cause. Cause for dismissal includes "demonstrable incompetence or dishonesty in teaching or research, manifest neglect of duty, or other adequate cause."[14] The cause for dismissal must directly relate to Father Curran's inability to perform his duties. The court would consider whether withdrawal of Father Curran's canonical mandate constitutes cause under the contract's definition. No reported cases address whether the failure of a tenured professor to fulfill specific *religious* criteria constitutes just cause for dismissal.

If The Catholic University is unable to classify withdrawal of Father Curran's mandate as "demonstrable incompetence," it will be forced to defend its termination of Father Curran on the basis of "adequate cause." If Father Curran were offered and he accepted a teaching position at The Catholic University in a non-theological department, it would have been extremely difficult to dismiss Father Curran from this teaching position because of one significant fact: Father Curran does not need a canonical mission to teach in a non-theological department.[15] Father Curran contended that neither the Vatican nor Archbishop Hickey has the authority to stop him from teaching in the Theology Department since 75% of his theology students are civil degree candidates. The University awards civil degrees, such as a master of divinity, under powers it receives from the District of Columbia. Civil degrees, unlike ecclesiastical or Vatican accredited degrees, are not regulated by the Vatican. Nevertheless, the fact that 75% of Father Curran's students are civil degree candidates is irrelevant, according to Archbishop Hickey, because the entire theology faculty receives its authorization from the Vatican. Father Curran's proposal of removing Vatican degree candidates from his classes was rejected by The Catholic University because of the additional costs and confusion such changes might create.

---

[13] For an overview of the statutes, faculty by law etc. of Catholic University, *see generally* Note, *The Curran Controversy, supra* note 11.
[14] *Id.* at 379.
[15] See Coriden, Green and Heintschel, *The Code of Canon Law: A Text and Commentary,* at 576 (1985).

FREE EXERCISE RIGHTS

If a court decides that Father Curran's dismissal was not for adequate cause, and thus was a breach of contract, the court must then decide a more troubling issue. Will court enforcement of Father Curran's contract infringe The Catholic University's First Amendment free exercise rights? Traditionally, courts have refused to adjudicate claims between members of religious organizations, because to do so would simultaneously establish one view as correct, and inhibit the free exercise rights of the other side. If the court determines that the doctrinal provisions cannot be severed from the secular ones, the court will refuse to accept jurisdiction to hear the case. In opposition to the court's jurisdiction over the dispute, The Catholic University would argue that any attempt by a court to enforce the licensing dimension of Father Curran's contract may burden it's free exercise rights with respect to the hiring of its religious faculty. Based on the tradition of judicial deference to church regulation of its internal affairs, such an argument might well prevail.

Given the judicial history against secular interference in church matters, even when church decisions may be arbitrary or contrary to the church's own rules,[16] a court might still refuse to overturn the Church decision. In order for a court to determine what is arbitrary, arguably at least the court would have to examine the Catholic Church's canonical and ecclesiastical laws. Consequently, even if Father Curran is found suitable to teach theology by the *ad hoc* committee formed pursuant to mandatory administrative procedures, should the Board of Trustees approve the decision to terminate Father Curran's contract, a court might refuse to review that decision. Moreover, because the Vatican may select and authorize theology teachers, arguably it is empowered to determine the eligibility and fitness of those faculty members.

Even though traditionally courts have adopted a handsoff approach to resolving most church disputes, the Supreme Court in recent decades has used a two part balancing test in free exercise cases: first, the plaintiff must establish that the law burdens the free exercise of his or her religious beliefs; and second, such a burden will be sustained only if the least restrictive means is used by the state to fulfill a secular purpose.[17]

In cases involving the church as an employer, the court has invalidated state enforcement of statutes or hiring practices which infringe on the free exercise of the *church's* religious belief if there are no overriding government or state interests. For example, a Wisconsin court refused to review Marquette University's decision not to hire Marjorie Maguire as a theology professor because her views on abortion did not conform to official church teaching, citing a lack of jurisdiction over the matter as its reason for declining to review the case.[18] In

---

[16]See *Serbian Orthodox Diocese v. Milivojevich*, 426 U.S. 696, (1976).
[17]*Sherbert v. Verner*, 374 U.S. 389 (1963).
[18]*Maguire v. Marquette University*, 627 F. Supp. 1499 (E.D. Wis. 1986).

the court's opinion, to order Marquette University to hire the plaintiff would be to impose its interpretation of Catholicism on the university and its students. "Such a ruling would not only interfere with the theology department's right to freely exercise its religion, through the explication and analysis of Catholicism and other religions, but would also result in a governmental imprimatur of approval on a particular set of beliefs as Catholic."[19]

Based on the Supreme Court's consistent refusal to inquire into claims involving religious criteria in employment contracts, it is *improbable* that a court applying the *deference approach* would accept jurisdiction over Father Curran's claims because it could hardly avoid examining and interpreting the Vatican's licensing practices and the appropriateness of religious criteria for teaching theology at The Catholic University.

On the other hand, if the court used the neutral principles approach, the court could decide to accept jurisdiction and rule on the purely substantive matters. As we have seen earlier, courts use the neutral principles of law approach where a standard, noncontroversial body of law can resolve internal church disputes. The neutral principles approach has generally been used to adjudicate disputes involving church property although at least one state court[20] has extended it to employment contracts.

An example of how the courts use the neutral principles of law approach to resolve church property disputes is illustrated by the New York case of *Morris v. Scribner*.[21] Church members of New York City's St. Bartholomew's Church challenged the expenditure of Church funds by church officials in contesting the city's designation of St. Bartholomew's as a landmark edifice. The church officials sought to construct a high rise office tower on a portion of the Park Avenue church property. In order to do so, the church must obtain a certificate of appropriateness from the city's Landmark Preservation Commission permitting alteration of the landmark.[22]

As a preliminary matter, the court invoked the neutral principles of law approach in accepting jurisdiction over the resolution of the dispute. Because the court concluded that it could decide the case on the basis of statutory interpretation and common law precedent without reference to matters of religious belief or dogma, the court found no violation of the First Amendment's prescription that religious bodies be left free to decide Church matters for themselves.[23]

Church members argued that Section 5 of the New York Religious Corporations Law was violated when monies donated to an incorporated church were used by church oficials to pursue development plans. They also argued that the plan constituted an "improper diversion from the trust purposes" because the

---

[19]*Id.* at 1503.
[20]*See Reardon v. LeMoyne*, 454 A. 2d 428 (N.H., 1982).
[21]*Morris v. Scribner*, 69 N.Y. 2d 418, 508 N.E. 2d 136 (1987).
[22]*Id.* ar 137.
[23]*Id.* at 138.

disputed funds were "not invested for the support and maintenance of the church, but rather were wasted in a highly speculative profit-seeking scheme and are now beyond recoupment."[24]

In rejecting the church members' arguments, the court stated that churches are not limited to the performance of strictly religious activities. More importantly to the court's decision, the church never ceased to perform its primary religious activities. In fact, church officials instituted the development plan to improve the church's financial condition. Because the plaintiffs did not allege that the trustees acted dishonestly or unfairly, or that they abandoned church purposes in favor of engaging in a commercial enterprise, the court refused to second guess the trustees' prudence in pursuing the development plan.[25]

The New Hampshire case of *Reardon v. LeMoyne*,[26] illustrates how a court might use the neutral principles of law approach to adjudicate the employment dispute involving Father Curran. The New Hampshire Supreme Court applied contract law in settling a dispute over the termination of four Sisters' teaching at a parochial school. In reversing the trial court's dismissal of the suit, the New Hampshire Supreme Court held that adjudication of the sisters' contract rights would not violate the First Amendment, as long as a "neutral principles of law" approach is used. Based on the neutral principles approach, the New Hampshire Supreme Court believed it could apply "well-defined, objective and secular rules of law, thereby avoiding any impermissible inquiry into religious doctrine."[27]

Jurisdiction was proper in this case, according to the court, because an inquiry into whether the sisters were entitled to dismissal procedures listed in their contracts "would not have touched upon doctrinal matters and would not have placed plaintiffs in a posture different from other lay persons who entered into employment contracts with defendants."[28] As a guideline to the local court as to when jurisdiction is proper, the New Hampshire Supreme Court stated that jurisdiction lies only in non-doctrinal matters, not matters involving doctrine, faith, or internal organization. Significantly, the court also indicated that religious organizations may restrict the likelihood of judicial review of its internal non-doctrinal decisions, if they properly so provide.[29]

If the court employs the neutral principles of law approach to Father Curran's case, the court may be able to limit its review to the employment contract itself, or the letter of appointment, and determine Father Curran's rights under the applicable civil law. Yet, a court may decline to decide Father Curran's case if it determines that resolution of the dispute would involve applying or interpreting catholic doctrinal matters. Although Father Curran's contract does not expressly

---

[24]*Id.* at 139.
[25]*Id.* at 140.
[26]*Reardon v. LeMoyne, supra,* note 20.
[27]*Id.* at 432.
[28]*Id.*
[29]Most probably, the more the American Catholic Church establishes fair and adequate internal procedures for resolution of Ecclesiastical disputes, the more likely it is that civil courts will defer to the Ecclesiastical decisions.

mention any religious criteria, it may prove too difficult to separate the contractual provisions because The Catholic University requires a professor to possess a canonical mission from the Vatican to teach in its theological department. Since the Vatican has already determined that Father Curran is unsuitable to teach theology, a court may refuse to enforce Father Curran's contract rights, because such rights may appear to be conditioned on a license awarded only after resolution of the parties' disputes over internal religious doctrines and beliefs.

An examination of the Father Curran controversy shows a weakness of the alternative theories adopted by the Supreme Court to resolve intra-church conflicts. Under the deference test, courts have to locate the locus of authority in a church and defer to its determination. In applying this test, the Supreme Court has classified churches as either hierarchical or congregational. Hierarchical churches are characterized by local churches that are subordinate to "some general church organization in which there are superior and ecclesiastical tribunals with the general and ultimate power of control more or less complete, in some supreme judicatory over the whole membership of that general organization."[30] Under the deference test, courts are required to take the general church's highest authority determination as the final word. The court is not allowed to examine the procedures or methods used by the church in reaching its decision.[31] Under the deference test, the Catholic church is clearly hierarchical.

There are several fallacious assumptions inherent in the deference test. The test assumes that church members submit totally to the church's internal authority. For instance, the Supreme Court held: "It is the essence of the religious faith that ecclesiastical decisions are reached and are to be accepted as matters of faith, whether or not rational or measurable by objective criteria."[32] Although under the deference test courts are not competent to examine the reasoning behind the church's decision, the deference test does allow a court to pinpoint the center of the church's authority, to determine that the church has rendered a decision, and to state what the decision is. Thus, even though the Supreme Court purports to adopt a hands-off approach to resolving church disputes, in fact it actually requires courts to investigate internal church procedures, documents, and church doctrine. The totality of these assumptions inherent in the deference approach leads to greater immunity from judicial review of church decisions than to decisions reached by other American institutions.

The neutral principles test, by contrast, assumes that secular provisions in church documents, standing alone, correctly reflect the expectations of the church and its members. Another faulty assumption is that the formal documents and not extrinsic writings, words, or conduct regulate relationships among the church and its members. The neutral principles further assumes that courts are compe-

---

[30] *Watson v. Jones, supra* at 722-723.
[31] *See Serbian Eastern Orthodox Church v. Milivojevich, supra,* note 16.
[32] *Id.* at 714-715.

tent to identify which provisions are secular and which are religious.[33] Moreover, as noted by Justice Powell in his dissenting opinion in *Jones v. Wolf,* under the neutral principles approach courts are unable to consider all the evidence relevant to ownership or control of local church property. In Justice Powell's view, the neutral principles of law approach violates the First Amendment in some cases by imposing both the form of church government and a doctrinal resolution contrary to that reached by the general church.[34]

In its decision in *Jones v. Wolf,* the U.S. Supreme Court indicated that the doctrine of judicial deference to a church's governing body remains a constitutionally acceptable alternative approach in resolving intra-church disputes. In other words state courts, depending on the law of their particular state, may constitutionally adopt either the deference approach or the neutral principles of law approach. Thus, the *Jones v. Wolf* decision, even though it purported to clarify state courts' resolution of ecclesiastical issues, may have created additional confusion because now not only is it unclear whether a court will accept jurisdiction over an ecclesiastical matter, but it is also unclear which approach a court will adopt to resolve the dispute, what provisions of the church documents a court will examine, how a court will interpret church documents if expert testimony is allowed to be admitted, etc. etc. etc.

Therefore, we are where we began—pondering over the dual approach by civil courts to ecclesiastical disputes, but unable to predict with any semblance of certitude the likely outcome of a given ecclesiastical dispute. Thus, in this matter, as in many others, we continue to walk through the valley in the shadow of darkness . . .

---

[33]For a comprehensive description of the questionable assumptions inherent in the neutral principles approach as well as the deference approach, *See generally* L. Sirico, Jr., *Church Property Disputes: Churches As Secular And Alien Institutions,* 55 Fordham L. Rev. 335 (1986).

[34]*See Jones v. Wolf, Supra* at 613, note 2 (Powell, J., disent).

CANON 1098 OF THE REVISED CODE OF CANON LAW

KEVIN W. VANN

INTRODUCTION

The promulgation of the 1983 *Codex Iuris Canonici* has afforded canonists and theologians many new opportunities in the past four years to deepen their insights and knowledge of the Church's law, and to study the law's ultimate sources in theology and the Church's self-understanding. One area which will be the source of much research and study for years to come is the area of matrimonial jurisprudence. The urging of continued study comes from many places, including that of the Holy Father himself.[1] One of the areas within the broad framework of matrimonial jurisprudence which is in need of much further study and reflection is Canon 1098, which specifically establishes *dolus* (deceit, fraud) as a *caput nullitatis* for the first time. At this time, there is not a great deal of jurisprudence as a background for interpretation. Study of this topic is also made more challenging by the fact that the definition, sources, and explanations of *dolus* and its effect (in both contractual and penal law) are found scattered throughout the centuries: from Roman Law up to the present day. In these various sources, the explanations of dolus and its effects are confusing and ambiguous. I believe that before any consideration can be given to Canon 1098, some minimal grasp of the history of *dolus* must be had. Therefore, in this presentation, I will:

1) Set forth the more significant moments in this history pf *dolus* and its relationship to contractual law and matrimonial consent. In twò parts I will work to summarize the important points in the history of *dolus* and matrimonial consent. Part I will treat the older history, and Part II will concern itself with the more recent currents of thought. This history can give the tools which I believe the norms of interpretation (found in Book I of the Code) require.[2]

2) Offer what I hope are some practical observations dealing with issues in interpretation. I will consider the wording of the canon in a "phrase-by-phrase" fashion, and comment on available jurisprudence.

3) Since various synonyms are possible for a translation of the Latin word *dolus* (of which I will note later), I will simply use the word dolus as an English word. Hopefully, this will result in a clearer and more precise presentation, and avoid confusion in alternating synonyms.

---

[1] John Paul II, "Ad Praelatos Auditores S. Romane Rotac coram Admissos, "26th January 1984, *Acta Apostolica Sedis,* LXXVI (1984): 648.

[2] Canon 17 of the 1983 Code of Canon Law.

PART I: SOME OF THE EARLY HISTORY OF DOLUS

Roman Law is the initial source for a definition of dolus. A typical textbook of Roman Law would describe dolus thusly:

"Any craft or deceit employed for the circumvention or entrapping of another person."[3]

More specifically, the following definition of dolus, given by Labeo, is found in the *Digest* of Justinian:

"Dolus malus is every craft, trick, deceit, or machination having been employed for cheating, tricking, deceiving another person."[4]

This concept of dolus was to have a long history in law. Its effect was studied and considered in two different areas of law: contracts (civil law) and penal law. In penal law, dolus is understood as bad will for the deliberate intent to do something wrong.[5] In the area of contracts, or civil law, the meaning is more restricted, that of tricking or deceiving. What effect does dolus have on the placing of a given juridical act . . . a contract, for example? This two-fold application of dolus is seen down to our present day, with the Revised Code of Canon Law.[6] Since the focus of this article is the consideration of the effects of dolus in something which may be considered under a contractual aspect (matrimony), the emphasis here will only be the effect of dolus in juridical acts—that is, contracts.

The *Digest* of Justinian contains some forty examples of contractual agreements carried out under the influence of dolus: for example, the sale of a slave, or dealings in inheritance.[7] What, then, was the effect of dolus in the carrying out of a contract? It seems that in Roman Law, a contract carried out under the influence of dolus was considered binding, despite the dolus. Buckland reports:

"In *stricti iuris* transactions the fraud had, till the time of Cicero, no effect on the liability. Thereafter, the *exceptio doli* could have always been pleaded in reply to a claim on a contract induced by fraud, and there was an *actio doli* when the matter had been completed. In *bonae fidei* contracts, the words *ex fide bona* in the formula enabled the injured party to prove the fraud, if he was sued, and conversely, to claim on account of it if he sued."[8]

It seems, then, that originally there was no more redress for mere deceit any

---

[3]W.W. Buckland, *A Textbook of Roman Law from Augustus to Justinian* (London: Cambridge University Press, 1921), 594.

[4]*Corpus Iurus Civilis*, 3 vols. 14th Stereotype Edition (Berlin: Weidmann, 1922), vol. I, *Institutiones*, revised by Paul Krueger: *Digest,* revised by Theodore Mommsen, reviewed by Paul Krueger. *Digest,* Book IV, Title III, N. 1.

[5]Professor A Gauthier O.P., Lecture notes on Roman Law, University of St. Thomas Aquinas, Rome, Italy, 1983.

[6]1983 Code of Canon Law, the two-fold application of dolus is seen in this manner: dolus in contracts in Canon 125, and dolus in penal law in Canon 1321.

[7]*Corpus Iuris Civilis, Digest,* Book IV, Title III, N. 7 and 9.

[8]Buckland, *Roman Law,* 415.

more than for threats. For example, if a man had been cheated into making a conveyance of his property, nevertheless he had made it. There is evidence that in very early times the deceit was not regarded as morally reprehensible.[9]

Why, then, would a transaction or contract—brought about because of the influence of dolus still be valid? A study of ancient juridic acts (in this time of Roman Law) indicates that dolus was not taken into consideration. In the primitive notion of contract, the words and symbolic actions made the contract effective. It was only later in history that the *praetor* (a Roman judge) began to take motives like dolus into consideration, but still realizing what a difficult thing it is to prove while so easy to assert. The *praetor* would at least discuss the charge and perhaps discern enough evidence to declare that the contract was valid. The point of focus in the consideration was the victim of dolus. The remedy, then, in these cases was the *actio de dolo* or the *exceptio doli*. It gave only simple damages for the loss which had been inflicted by the dolus, and was available only if the plaintiff had no other remedy open to him.[10]

Given this basis in Roman Law, the later centuries also need to be examined. Then, some insights may be seen as to why dolus was never seriously considered as having a nullifying effect on a matrimonial contract.

Looking toward the Middle Ages, the focus will not be on dolus and contract in general, but will shift to the specific mention of dolus and its effect on marriage. The relevant works to be considered would be the *Decretum of Gratian,* the *Decretals* of Pope Gregory IX, and the *Summa* of Saint Raymond of Penyafort.[11] In these works the authors (canonists and glossators) set forth a theory which evidently was to be held for many centuries: that of *dolus in spiritualibus* (deceit in spiritual things). This opinion held that if an individual was brought a spiritual good or into a spiritual state (such as marriage or profession of religious vows), then such vows or marriages were considered to be valid: because one had been brought into a better state of life, or Sacrament, because of dolus. To be specific:

> "Thus, it is evident, because although dolus occur in spiritual things of this nature, nevertheless for the one having suffered dolus, no aid is given . . . the same thing in matrimony . . . likewise observe that in spiritual things, complete restitution does not have place: because they do not seem deceived, who have chosen a better life."[12]

---

[9]H.F. Jolowicz and Barry Nicholas, *Historical Introduction to the Study of Roman Law,* 3rd ed. (Cambridge University Press, 1972), 278.

[10]Ibid., 279.

[11]Gratian, *Decretum* (Lyons: Hugo a Porta, 1548), *glossa Cognatur,* C. XX, Q. III, c.5, C. XXIX, Q. II, c.5, *Cum dicitur;* Gregory IX, *Decretales* (Lyons: Hugo a Porta, 1550), *Ad fauitem* to c. VI, *Cum dilectus* X, I, XL, *Captiose* to c. VI *Veniens* X, III, XXXII, *Falsa sit causa* to c. XIC, *Ex parte tua* X, III, XXXII, and *Spes* to c. XXX, *Dudum* X, III, XXXII; and Raymond of Penyafort, *Summa de paenitentia,* vol. I of *Universa Bibliothica Iuris,* edited by Xavier Ochoa and Aloysius Diez (Rome: Commentarius pro Religiosis, 1976).

[12]"Sic patet, quod licet dolus interveniat in huiusmodi spiritualibus, non tamen subvenitur dolus passo, licet dolus det causam contractui . . . idem in matrimonio . . . item nota quod in spiritualibus non habet locum in integrum restitutio: quia non videntur decepti, qui meliorem vitam elegerunt."Gregory IX, *Decretales* (Lyons: Hugo a Porta, 1550), *Ad fatuitem* to c. VI, *Cum dilectus* X, I, XL. English translation by Kevin W. Vann.

Ironically enough, this opinion was evidently abandoned as far as religious vows are concerned, because the *Codex Iuris Canonici* of 1917 specifically treats of the matter of dolus and its effects on religious vows. Such vows, taken under the influence of dolus, were considered invalid.[13]

Another reason for the non-inclusion of dolus as a *caput nullitatis* in 1917 can be found in the sixteen century. In this era (after the promulgation of the *Corpus Iuris Canonici*), canonists such as Anacletus Reiffenstuel, Francis Schmalzgruber, and Francis Xavier Wernz commented considerably on dolus and its effect on contracts.[14] Their discussions are couched in scholastic terminology. Their conclusions were that if dolus brought about an error in the substance of a contract, then such a contract was null and void. If, however, dolus was directed at or concerned the so-called "accidental" qualities in a contract, then the contract was valid . . . because the essence or substance of a contract/bargain/agreement remained the same and was untouched. In any of these particular discussions, it should be noted that the reason for the nullity of a contract brought about by dolus was not dolus in itself, but the error which it generated. It follows, then, that as far as matrimony is considered, such an error would have to involve the actual physical person: the physical person being the substance of the contract. Any other errors would touch the accidental properties of the marriage contract: these would be the various qualities of a person, etc. The contract, then, would be considered binding, since the substance (the same physical person) was intact.

In conclusion: even though dolus was considered in relationship to the matrimonial contract, at various times in history, and although its effects were considered in a number of canons in the 1917 *Codex Iuris Canonici*,[15] it was not in itself considered as nullifying the matrimonial contract because:

1) dolus was seen to be able to procure a "spiritual good" (such as religious profession or marriage), so one was better off because of dolus. In essence this says that "One who received the Sacrament could not attack the validity of the marriage for dolus, because he/she had obviously gained by the reception of the Sacrament."[16]

2) of the relationship between dolus and error. Any dolus which was so significant as to cause an error in the substance of a contract resulted in the nullity of the contract. As far as the marriage contract was concerned, this would have to be the actual physical person, which would be the substance of the contract. Since the majority of errors which could

---

[13]Canon 572, §1, 4⁰ of the 1917 Code of Canon Law.

[14]Anacletus Teiffenstuel O.F.M., *Ius Canonicum Universum*, 6 vols. (Antwerp: From the expenses of the Society, 1755), Lib. II, Titl XIV, N. 3; Francis Schmalzgruber S.J. *Jus Ecclesiasticum Universum*, 5 vols. (Rome: The Apostolic Camera, 1844), Tome II, Pars II, Tit XIV, No. 2; Francie Xavier Wernz S.J., *Ius Decretalium*, 6 vols. (Prato: Giachetti, 1914), Tome V. Tit XXVI, N. 517.

[15]The following canons of the 1917 Code concern dolus: 48§2; 52; 103§2; 169§1, 1⁰; 572§1, 4⁰; 637; 647§2, 2⁰; 1321; 1625§1; 1684; 1685; 1686; 1857§2; 2049; 2199; 2200; 2387.

[16]Professor Jose M. Serrano, Class lecture notes on *Rotalis Iurisprudentia Circa Causas Matrimoniales*, University of St. Thomas Aquinas, Rome, Italy, January 9th, 1984.

be induced by dolus involved accidental qualities (equivalent to personal qualities of the parties involved in the marriage), the substance of the contract would remain untouched. Therefore, the consent directed toward a given person is not destroyed.

PART II: CONTEMPORARY TRENDS IN THE HISTORY OF DOLUS AND MATRIMONIAL CONSENT

As the twentieth century progressed from the time of the promulgation of the 1917 *Codex* to the decade of the 1950's, there seemed to be a new interest in the question of the effect of dolus on matrimonial consent. This was prompted, in part, by the various ways in which Canon 1083 was applied to certain marriage cases: those cases in which a petitioner was trapped into a disastrous marriage due to the deception of the intended spouse. It will be remembered that for an error to be invalidating, it would have to be a substantial error . . . which is equivalent to an error in person. Attempts were made to prove that this dolus could result in an error in the quality of a person which redounded into error of person. Yet, this type of argumentation was exceedingly complex.

This weakness of Canon 1083 in dealing with these types of marriage cases, and the problems in formulating argumentation for cases introduced under this canon, led to new interest and speculation on the relationship of dolus to matrimonial consent. Some of this speculation came from a professor of Canon Law at the University of Tubingen, Heinrich Flatten. He wrote two articles[17] which gave a number of concrete examples of marriages contracted under the influence of dolus. He stated that canon law does not even minimally protect (from dolus) a person who married. According to him, some examples of marriage that concretely involved dolus were:

1) A hidden homicide, in which the perpetrator of this crime did not become known until after he had married the daughter of the person whom he had killed.

2) Feigned affection for the Catholic Church, as well as feigned promises in order to marry a Catholic.

Flatten wrote in a time of much theological and canonical ferment and many of the works of the period resulted in concrete suggestions to the Preparatory Commission for the Second Vatican Council. This was certainly true in the case of Flatten, because a number of the canonical suggestions to the Preparatory Commission involved proposals from the German Bishops to modify Canon 1083 to take dolus into consideration. One even mentioned Flatten's article by name.[18]

---

[17]*Irrtum und Tauschung bei der Eheschliessung nach Kanonischem Recht*, reviewed by G. Oesterle, O.S.B. in *Monitor Ecclesiasticus*, LXXXII (1957); and *Quomodo matrimonium contrahentes iure canonico contra dolum tutandi sint* (Cologne: editio auctoris, 1961).

[18]*Acta et Documenta Concilio Oecumenico Vaticano Appardando*, Series I, vol. II, part I, 367, 565, 600, 607, 620, 628, 654, 674.

Besides the episcopal proposals, similar sentiments were found echoed in the proposals submitted by the Canon Law Faculties of Gregorian University and the Catholic University of Tolouse. The Congregation for the Discipline of the Sacraments also had some input relative to dolus.[19]

Following the close of the Council, a new wave of speculation on dolus and matrimonial consent appeared. This speculation, this reconsideration of dolus, seemed to have been prompted by the conciliar teaching on marriage, found in *Gaudium et Spes'* teaching on marriage.[20] More importantly, another influence in the new interest in dolus was the revision of the 1917 *Codex Iuris Canonici,* which was underway by this time. The time period in which these writings and opinions are to be found would be about from 1966 to 1981. These writings were comprised of the works of various canonists and theologians, and Tribunal sentences. Examples of decisions which respond to the allegations of dolus in contracting marriage came from Ireland, England, and the Roman Rota.[21]

Contemporary with the theological and canonical speculation on dolus, the late 1970's produced the first drafts of a new canon on dolus, which had no equivalent in the 1917 Code. This new canon specifically names dolus as a *caput nullitatis* for marriage. This drafted canon was to eventually become Canon 1052 of the 1980 Schema, and finally Canon 1098 of the 1983 promulgated version of the Code. It is almost as if a straight line could be drawn through thirty years which would highlight the history of this canon. The starting point would be Heinrich Flatten in the 1950's, and the end point would be Canon 1098 in 1983.

It is worthwhile, in studying the genesis of this Canon, to look closely at the work of the Code Commission. Their work, in the 1970's, records discussion about the introduction of a defect of consent coming from dolus into the new Code.[22] The first formulation of this possible new canon is found, numbered SDS 300:

> The one who enters matrimony having been entrapped by deceit, having been committed for obtaining consent, regarding a certain quality of the other party which is made for gravely disturbing the consortium of the conjugal life, contracts invalidly.[23]

---

[19] Ibid, vol. IV, part I-I, 43; part II, 595; I, vol. III, 95.

[20] The following articles would demonstrate the connection with *Gaudium et Spes:*

Angela Maria Punzi Nicolo, "Il Dolo nel Matrimonio Canonico in una Prospettiva di Riforma del Codex," *Il Diritto Ecclesiastico,* LXXXII (1971), 588-604.

Aldo M. Arena, "The Jurisprudence of the Sacred Roma Rota: Its Development and Direction after the Second Vatican Council." *Studia Canonica,* XII (1978), 292.

Philip T. Sumner, *"Dolus* as a Ground for Nullity of Marriage," *Studia Canonica,* XIV (1980), 183.

Peter Huizing S.J., "Nota sul Dolo Causa di Nullita del 'Foedus Matrimoniale,'" in *Ius Populi Dei* (Rome: Gregorian University Press, 1972), 597-601.

[21] *coram* Sheehy (August 28th, 1979), *Canon Law Society of Great Britain and Ireland Newsletter,* XLV (1979-1980), 51-52; *coram* Dunderdale (March 29th, 1973), *Studia Canonica,* VII (1973), 129; *coram* DiFelice (March 26th, 1977), *Ephermerides Iuris Canonici,* XXIV (1978), 162.

[22] *Communicationes,* III (1971), 76.

[23] "Qui matrimonium init deceptus dolo, ad obtinendum consensum patrato, circa aliquam alterius partis qualitatem, quae nata est ad consortium vitae conjugalis gravieter perturbandum, invalide contrahit." Ibid., 373. (Vatican City: Vatican Polyglot Press, 1983). English translation by Kevin W. Vann.

SDS eventually became Canon 1052 of the 1980 draft, and 1098 in the final promulgated version:
> The one who enters matrimony having been entrapped by deceit, having been committed for obtaining consent, regarding a certain quality of the other party which by its very nature is able to gravely disturb the consortium of conjugal life, contracts invalidly.[24]

In all of this, there was only a slight change in wording from Canon 1052 to Canon 1098. *Quae nata est ad consortium vitae* (which is made for gravely disturbing the consortium of conjugal life) was changed to *quae suapte natura consortium vitae conjugalis* (which by its very nature is able to gravely disturb the consortium of conjugal life). The meaning of this change could be interpreted as a precision, an indication that the quality in which the deception is situated must by its very nature be able to disrupt the *consortium vitae*. An indication of such a quality can be found in reference to the canon on sterility.[25]

In review, then, this brief sketch of thirty years of history has attempted to show how contemporary interests in an ancient concept resulted in Canon 1098 of the revised Code of Canon Law . . . a canon which has no correspondence in the 1917 Code. The key elements in this story would be:

> 1) Canon 1083 of the 1917 Code (on error) was perceived to be inadequate to deal with marriage cases in which dolus played a significant part in the contracting of the marriage. Heinrich Flatten, among others, attempted to address the question of solutions for these types of cases.
>
> 2) A new interest in Canon 1083 (partly endangered by Flatten) resulted in various suggestions and observations being forwarded to the Preparatory Commission for the Council. These suggestions particularly mentioned dolus and Canon 1083.
>
> 3) The Post-conciliar interest in the question of dolus and matrimonial consent was wide-spread. This interest seemed to come from many quarters: Reflection on *Gaudium et Spes'* teaching on marriage, the work of various canonists and theologians, tribunal sentences, and the work of the Code Commission itself.

With this background in mind, it would be important to turn to some additional considerations: Dolus and related concepts, an analysis of Canon 1098, and some practical thoughts for Tribunal practice.

---

[24]"Oui matrimonium init deceptus dolo, ad obtinendum consensum patrato, circa aliquam alterius partis qualitatem, quae nata est ad consortium vitae conjugalis graviter perturbandum, invalide contrahit." *Codex Iuris Canonici* Vatican City: Vatican Polygot Press, 1983). English translation by Kevin W. Vann.

[25]Canon 1083 §3: "Sterility neither prohibits nor invalidates marriage, with due regard to the prescription of Canon 1098.

PART III
A STUDY OF DOLUS AND RELATED CONCEPTS: AN ANALYSIS OF CANON 1098: PRACTICAL TRIBUNAL CONCERNS

The history of dolus in Roman Law, and its discussion in terms of its effect on marriage consent reveals a synonymous use of several terms, and a convergence and overlap of topics related to dolus. This can tend to give any discussion on dolus a rather ambiguous slant, and certainly would make any attempt at interpretation "foggy." In an effort to make the discussion of Canon 1098 more precise, there are certain related concepts which must be understood as different, yet related to dolus in Canon 1098. I would offer a brief consideration of some of these concepts.

A. Dolus Bonus and Dolus Malus

It will be remembered that the definition of dolus found in the *Digest* of Justinian was referred to as *dolus malus*. This qualification of *malus* was given, because *dolus bonus* was also known to exist. This was not seen as bad. Ulpian would classify dolus bonus as the shrewdness which would be used against an enemy[26] while Black's law dictionary would state that dolus bonus is justified or allowable deceit, employed for self defense or another permissable purpose. In contrast to this, Black would say that dolus malus exists where one intentionally misleads another or takes advantage of another's error wrongfully, by any form of deception, fraud, or cheating.[27] Given this distinction, it is safe to say that in Canon 1098 we are concerned with only *dolus malus*. Dolus in this canon is perpetrated for the purpose of tricking someone into marital consent . . . the circumvention of entrapping of the person into marriage. This is not the protection from an enemy, or the shrewdness which is considered as *dolus bonus*.

B. Dolus and Fraud

This can be a source of great confusion, as these two terms are often used as synonyms. But, at the same time, the synonymous use is not consistent, because the terms are often differentiated. Encyclopedias of law define *dolus* and *fraus* (fraud) separately, yet these definitions sound very similar. A brief examination of this phenomenon would be helpful as a background for interpretation of this canon.

---

[26]*Corpus Iuris Civilis, Digest,* Book IV, Title III, n. 1.
[27]Henry Campbell Black, *Black's Law Dictionary,* 4th revised edition (St. Paul, Minnesota: West Publishing Company, 1968), 570.

A setting for the use of *dolus* and *fraus* is given by the *New Catholic Encyclopedia* when it says that "classical Roman jurists distinguished *fraus* from *dolus,* considering dolus to be any action purporting to deceive a person, while fraud was envisioned as being directed against the law."[28] St. Thomas would also speak of a difference between dolus and fraud, noting that

> . . . they seem to be different, because dolus pertains universally to the execution of craft whether it be done through words or deeds; fraud, however, more properly pertains to the execution of craft, and in accordance with that which is done only through deeds.[29]

This same nuanced distinction between dolus and fraud is carried into this century, in such works as Black's Law Dictionary, and a commentary by Gommary Michiels, O.F.M. on Canon 52. Black would say that dolus would be "guile, deceitfulness, and malicious fraud," while fraud would be "an intentional perversion of truth for the purpose of inducing another in reliance upon it to part with some valuable thing belonging to him or to surrender some legal right."[30] Michiels believes that the two terms are different, yet are the same.[31] In the Code of Canon Law of 1917, dolus and fraud are linked together in Canons 52, 2049, and 2361. In other canons, they are differentiated: dolus being either simple deceit, or fraud directed against the law.[32] The same interchangeability is also seen in the Code of 1983. The English translation of the code by the Canon Law Society of America uses fraud as the word of choice when translating Canon 1098.

Given the foregoing complex history of dolus and fraud, my personal choice for a translation of dolus in Canon 1098 would be deceit, rather than fraud . . . deceit being the English rendering of *dolus*. I would suggest this for two reasons: 1) Since there is a separate Latin root for fraud *(fraus)* it would appear to me to be more precise to use the original Latin *dolus* without any reference to fraud, and simply translate it as "deceit." The use of one word only is less confusing. 2) Dolus translated as deceit carries with it the idea of tricking another person. This would certainly be in line with the intent of Canon 1098, and carries with it a highly personal dimension. Canon 1098 (as all of the marriage law) understands marriage as a communion of life as two persons. Fraud, on the other hand, can be understood as simply being directed against a given law . . . as an intent to get around the law.[33] There would be no persons involved here, and the understanding of trapping or leading another person into something he/she would not want (if the truth were known) is missing from this understanding of fraud. For these

---

[28]An Editorial Staff at the Catholic University of America, eds., *New Catholic Encyclopedia* (New York: McGraw-Hill, 1967), s.v. "Fraud (Canon Law)," by W.J. LaDue.

[29]*Summa Theologiae,* II-II, 55, 5.

[30]Black, *Black's Law Dictionary,* 788.

[31]Gommar Michiels, O.F.M. Cap., *Normae Generales Juris Canonici,* 2 vols. (Tournai: Desclee, 1949), II, 439.

[32]Jose F. Castano O.P. "Il Dolus—Vizi del Consenso Matrimoniale: Commentario al Canone 300 dello Schema." *Apollinaris,* LV (1982), 664-665.

[33]LaDue, "Fraud (Canon Law)," p. 82.

reasons, my personal preference would be to avoid fraud altogether as a synonym for dolus. Again, this is a personal preference only and not a major criticism.

C. Dolus: Contractual Law vs. Penal Law

In considering dolus as it is found in Canon 1098, it is important to be precise as to exactly what is intended by dolus in this canon . . . remembering that there are two senses for dolus in canon law. In the opening remarks of this presentation, it will be remembered that mention was made of the different applications of dolus in penal and civil law: deliberate intent to violate a law vs. the effect of dolus in a contract. This double application was taken into the 1917 Code of Canon Law, where Canon 103 concerns itself with the effects of dolus in juridic acts and Canon 2200 offers a definition of dolus in penal law. (The 1983 Code offers the same in Canons 125 and 1321.) Canon 2200 says:

§1. Dolus here is understood as the deliberate will of violating the law, and a defect of cognition is opposed to it from the part of the intellect, and a defect of liberty from the part of the will.
§2. Once an external violation of the law has been posited, dolus in the external form is presumed, unless the contrary is proven.

For a synonym for dolus in this context, Woywod offers "evil will."[34] A similar explanation for dolus in penal law in Italian civil law is "the expectation and the will of the event, the consequence of criminal conduct."[35] A survey of these various understandings of dolus in penal law certainly indicates a broader concept than Labeo's original words of "every craft, trick, deceit, or machination having employed for cheating, tricking, deceiving another person." In a like manner, Victor De Reina contends that dolus regarding matrimonial consent differs from dolus in penal law, where the concern is the injury produced.[36]

Since the concern of Canon 1098 is the effect of dolus in consent for a definite juridic act (marriage), the wider application of dolus in penal law is not of direct concern here.

D. Dolus and Violence (Metus)

Another facet of the question of dolus which was posed during various discussions and articles was the relationship of dolus to various forms of moral

---

[34] Stanislaus Woywod O.F.M., *A Practical Commentary on the Code of Canon Law*, revised and enlarged edition of combined volumes I and II, revised and enlarged by Callisstus Smith O.F.M. (New York: Joseph F. Wagner, 1957), 450.

[35] Marcello Gallo, "Dolo (Diritto Penale)," *Enciclopedia del Diritto*, XIII, 751.

[36] Victor De Reina, *Error v Dolo en el Matrimonio Canonico* (Pamplona: Navarre University Press, 1967), 291-292.

violence—specifically force and fear *(vis et metus)*. A consideration of these two phenomena—their differences and similarities—is nothing new, because such a consideration is found as far back as the *Decretum* of Gratian. This reference to dolus and metus is found in the *Decretum:*

> . . . and it is astonishing that in spiritual matters a contract having been entered by dolus holds: but a contract having been entered by fear does not hold: since according to the laws, it is entirely contrary. For according to the laws the contract having been entered upon by fear holds, although it is rescinded by legal action because fear was the reason.[37]

The glossator seems to be wondering why there is a difference in the effect of *dolus* and *metus* on marriage—why the idea of procuring a spiritual good through fear is not the same as for dolus.

Centuries later, these two concepts continued to be considered differently in relationship to marriage. For example, the Code of Canon Law of 1917, without admitting dolus as a *caput nullitatis,* does admit force and fear. The Code says:

> Canon 1087. §1. The matrimony having been entered because of force or grave fear having been occurred unjustly from the outside is also invalid, so that someone might liberate himself from which (fear), he is compelled to choose matrimony.
>
> §2. No other fear, even if it gives the cause of the contract, brings with itself the nullity of the matrimony.

This discrepancy of treatment between dolus and metus in regards to the marriage contract can be considered a specific choice of "political legislation" according to Giacchi. He believed that this choice (of violence over against dolus) was made since it was held that a defect of consent due to violence could be proven with precision.[38] More recent reflection on the relationship of dolus and metus is offered by Monsignor Jose Serrano of the Roman Rota, and Father Jose Castano of the Pontifical University of St. Thomas Aquinas. Serrano's conviction is that dolus could be seen as a means of coercion, and further believes that too much strength is attributed to the difference between intellect and will in the classical treatment of dolus and error. In dolus there is an unjust invasion of privacy, and could it not be interpreted therefore as an authentic form of violence? He contends:

> "Dolus is related to *metus* (violence) because even though dolus produces an error in the intellect (and thus indirectly the will), while metus directly involves the will, the will and the intellect touch and therefore the will influences by the choice of the intellect.[39]

---

[37]". . . et est mirum, quod in spiritualibus contractus dolo initus tenet: sed contractus metu initus non tenet: Cum secundum leges penitus contrarium sit. Nam secundum leges contractus dolo initus nullus est sed contractus metu initus tenet, licet rescindatur per actionem quod metus causam." Gratian, *Decretum,* glossa *Cogantur,* C. XX, O. III, c. 5. English translation by Kevin W. Vann.

[38]Orio Giacchi, *Il Consenso nel Matrimonio Canonico,* 3rd edition (Milan: Giuffre, 1968), 157.

[39]Monsignor Jose M. Serrano, Interview by Rev. Kevin W. Vann, November 16, 1984.

In a similar vein, he held that dolus has an autonomous treatment that is situated outside of error, inasmuch as there is an outside malicious intervention.[40]

Professor Castano of the Angelicum, writing on Canon 103 of the 1917 Code, says that although dolus and violence are different (since dolus acts directly on the intellect and violence directly on the will) they have in common the fact that they are extrinsic principles. Thus, what the legislator did in applying violence to matrimonial consent, he does now also in regard to dolus.[41]

E. Dolus and Error

The understanding of the relationship of dolus and error has a long and complex, and ambiguous history. One need only to briefly study the works of Reiffenstuel, Schmalzgruber, Wernz and Sanchez to see how these two concepts were connected. The philosophical discussions about dolus before the Council, and the proposals which were forwarded to the Preparatory Commission, all treat dolus in reference to Canon 1083 on error. This is likewise found in the discussions of the Code Commission.[42] The work of several canonists in recent years, such as Mostaza and Ahern, speak in the same way. For example, Ahern would say that "when deception occurs, error in the person deceived accompanies it of necessity."[43] Sumner echoes a similar sentiment,[44] as does Castano, who speaks of a specific "deceitful error."[45] Since, as most authors seem to agree, dolus is simply another cause of error (as is ignorance, inadvertence, etc. would be), why is there need of a separate *caput nullitatis* for dolus? Sumner attempts to deal with the question by stating that since marriage involves the consent of both parties, dolus affects both parties to this consent. According to him, the one who deceives does not consent with an act of self-bestowal, and the one who is deceived is manipulated into giving consent. This could not be called an act of acceptance by the other partner. Thus, there would be no mutual convenant.[46] Sumner's conclusion for the uniqueness of a *caput nullitatis* for dolus alone finds its basis in *Gaudium et Spes*. Because the element of entrapment is involved, it is impossible for the self-bestowal of the *consortium vitae* to occur. This would be the opinion of Rev. Peter Huizing, S.J., also.[47]

---

[40]Monsignor Jose M. Serrano, "El Dolo en el Consentimento Matrimonial," *Revista Espanola de Derecho Canonico*, XXIX (1973), 184.
[41]Castano, "Il Dolus," 666.
[42]*Communicationes*, IX (1977), 371-373.
[43]Maurice B. Ahern, "Error and Deception as Grounds for Nullity," *Studia Canonica*, IX (1977), 246.
[44]Sumner, "Dolus as a Ground for Nullity," 179.
[45]Castano, "Il Dolus," 661.
[46]Sumner, "Dolus as a Ground for Nullity," 1979.
[47]Peter Huizing S.J., "Nota dul Dolo Causa di Nullita del 'Foedus Matrimoniale,'" in *Ius Populi Dei* (Rome: Gregorian University Press, 1972), 800.

AN ANALYSIS OF CANON 1098

Having considered the similarities/differences of dolus with various related concepts, this presentation will now shift to an analysis of Canon 1098, considering each phrase separately.

A. *Qui matrimonium init deceptus dolo*

The work of many canonists of this century leads precisely to this point, where the effect of dolus on matrimony is brought into the Church's juridic framework. What is being applied to matrimony is dolus as understood by Labeo, or "every craft, trick, deceit, or machination having been employed for cheating, tricking, deceiving another person."

The sense of this definition, then, excludes here such things as ignorance or negligence. In addition, dolus here is understood as *dolus malus*. The works of Labeo imply a concerted, conscious, premeditated effort. This is more than a "white lie," or even, it seems, a one-time lie.

The focus of dolus here is related to the specific juridic act of marriage. This would mean that the wider understanding of dolus as general evil will would not be applicable here.

B. *ad obtinendum consensum patrato*

The intention of this phrase is that the dolus must be committed, or perpetrated, for the purpose of marrying. In other words, the focus of this phrase is the finality or purpose of dolus. The central issue here is that the dolus has the finality of obtaining the consent for marriage. For example, current opinions here in the United States would say that: 1) dolus must have been perpetrated prior to the consent, for the purpose of obtaining the consent to marriage, and that the dolus, that is the cunning trick, did work that error in fact was effected at the time of the consent,[48] and 2) that "it is central, none the less, that the deceived contractant must be ignorant or in error as a result of the cunning execution of the deceiver."[49]

C. *alterius partis*

Here the concern is the quality of dolus and its source. The classical understand-

---

[48]J. James Cuneo, "Deceit/Error of Person as a *Caput Nullitatis*," in Canon Law Society of America, *Proceedings* (Washington, D.C.: Canon Law Society of America, 1984), 165.
[49]Ellsworth Kneal *et al.*, "A Proposed *In Iure* Section for the New Statute of Fraud," *The Jurist*, XXXII (1982), 220-221.

ing of dolus involves a transaction between two persons. This is the case here, as matrimony involves two persons: the future husband and wife. The dolus and the associated quality must only involve the two parties. However, there is some speculation that the dolus could also be involved with someone very close to one of the parties. For example, Castano would speculate that "we do not see why a quality that does not belong to the partner but to a third person very close to him or her—for example, the mother-in-law—is not also able to be gravely a disturber of the consortium of conjugal life, and therefore render that matrimony invalid." He would go on to say, however, that the words *alterius partis* do not admit such a possibility.[50] From another angle, there is discussion if the dolus can come from a third party, and not just one of the contractants. It does seem that such a hypothesis can be admitted, because of the silence of the canon on this point. Kneal would hold this very clearly, by saying that "parents of a respondent who deliberately and by a concerted plan, of silence or of a web of lies, conceal the presence of a serious defect in their child, are perpetrating 'fraud' in the intended sense of the canon."[51] James Cuneo would be of the same opinion, illustrating this by means of concealment of a prison record by the parents of an intended spouse.[52] It does appear that when there is a possibility of a third party being involved in such deceit, this third party would have to be in close connection with one of the marrying parties. This the case of a sentence from England, *coram* Dunderdale.

D. *circa aliquam qualitatem*

The interpretation of these words about a quality must be made in conjunction with the words which immediately follow this phrase, *quae suapte natura*. In other word, discussion of a certain type of quality cannot take place without considering what the effect of this quality is to be. This entire consideration of the quality is a facet of the question of dolus and matrimony that is in need of further study and delineation. It is an area which, according to Serrano, has to be defined more and will involve a certain amount of relativity.[53] This particular aspect is an area of great concern. This canon would be doing a great disservice to marriage and to tribunal work if it resulted in many declarations of nullity based on trivial qualities. Certainly, the origins of this canon are not to be found in trivial qualities. Flatten's examples of concealing homicide and deliberately faked good will toward the Catholic Church and the pre-nuptial promises do not indicate such

---

[50]Castano, "Il Dolus," 674; See also Castano, "L'Influsso del Dolo nel Consenso Matrimoniale," *Apollinaris*, LVIII (1984), 581.

[51]Kneal, *et al.*, "A Proposed *In Iure* Section," 218.

[52] Cuneo, "Deceit/Error," 165.

[53]Serrano, Personal Interview, November 16, 1984.

trivialities.[54] And Flatten himself says it would be foolish to establish such things as deception regarding hair color as invalidating.[55]

The proposed *in iure* section by Kneal *et al.* holds that mere personal qualities of the respondent which may be unpleasant or unwanted cannot of themselves be held to render a marriage invalid if their presence has been deceitfully concealed, and then continues:

> It goes without saying that the latter allegation, or subjectively grave and objectively trivial circumstances, requires the strongest structures of proof. To hold seriously that the unsuspected presence of addiction to pro-football TV watching made conjugal life literally impossible, and the marriage invalid, would require the most rigorous proof imaginable.[56]

Francis Morrisey, O.M.I., discussing possible qualities, such as concealing sterility, previous invalid marriage and a concealed prison record, adds that:

> In some instances, there could be a temptation to go all the way to the case where a person could say, "He never told me he ate peanuts in bed!" This, it goes without saying is not the meaning of the canon.[57]

The Code itself gives a hint of a type of concealed quality that would be relevant in the canon concerning sterility (1084, §3). Several other references may be useful in this area. Roger Label, S.J. writes about the deliberate concealment of a serious genetic disease which is inherited, and Benito Gangoiti, O.P. provides an extensive list of qualities which are adverse to matrimony. He includes such qualities as permanent sterility, homosexuality, certain contagious diseases, children by another person, intention to desert the spouse after a determined time, criminal record which would have consequences for marriage, and pathological addiction to drugs.[58]

E. quae suapte natura consortium vitae conjugalis graviter perturbare potest

This phrase must be seen in the same context with the quality. In other words, what is the effect of the deliberate concealment of a quality? It must be capable of seriously disturbing or destroying the marriage. Castano would say that the quality in question has to be objectively capable of this.[59] If there is a certain relativity to the type of the quality, there could also be a certain relativity as to the effect. What might affect one marriage would not necessarily affect another one. The type of quality must have the potential of causing a serious disturbance

---

[54] Oesterle, Review of "Irrtum and Tauschung," 520; Flatten, "Quomodo Matrimonium," 3.
[55] Flatten, "Quomodo Matrimonium," 11.
[56] Kneal *et al.*, "A Proposed *In Iure* Section," 220-221.
[57] Francis Morrisey O.M.I., "Revising Church Legislation on Marriage," *Origins*, IX (1979), 217.
[58] Benito Gangoiti O.P., "Error, Nullatenus Dolus, est Causa Directa Nullitatis Matrimonii," in *Quaestiones de Matrimonio Hisce Diebus Controversae* (Rome: Herder, 1974), 33-34.
[59] Castano, L'Influsso del Dolo," 582.

of the marriage. Sumner says the result is the non-establishment of the *consortium vitae*.[60] Monsignor Mario Pompedda of the Rota states that qualities are not able to be treated which are not strictly connected with the conjugal life.[61]

Some additional insights in this regard (as to the type of quality and its effect) can also be gained by an examination of civil law—in this case the law of the State of Illinois concerning marriage and dissolution. And perhaps somewhat ironically, it is found that fraud (the word of choice) is seen as invalidating a marriage civilly. But the critical questions are what constitutes fraud, and its extent. Among other things noted, the law of Illinois states that

"Fraud, in order to vitiate a marriage must go to the very essence of the contract, and fraudulent misrepresentations of one party as to birth, social position, fortune, good health, and temperament cannot, therefore, vitiate the contract . . . Marriage will not be annulled for false representations as to fortune, character, social standing, and personal qualities . . . Fraudulent representations must be of something essential to marriage relation, rendering performance of its duties and obligations impossible or its assumption and continuance dangerous to health or life, to warrant, annulment . . . misrepresentation warranting marriage annulment must be of existing fact, not promise as to future conduct . . ."[62]

The law goes on to state that another requirment for civil annulment is that if the fraudulent statement would not have been made the marriage never would have been entered into.[63] How similar these sound to the considerations of the church's law in these matters.

Practical Considerations and Tribunal Issues

These remarks are made in the light of practical Tribunal experience, both in the level of First Instance and Appeal level. They should be considered complementary to any historical analysis of Canon 1098, and any analysis of its components.

The Code of Canon Law: A Text and Commentary notes that the following essential elements are to be proven if dolus is to be considered an invalidating marriage consent:
  A. It (the deceit) is deliberately perpetrated in order to obtain consent.
  B. The quality is real, grave, and present at the time of the consent.

---

[60]Sumner, "Dolus as a Ground for Nullity," 183.

[61]Mario F. Pompedda, "Il Consenso Matrimoniale," in Zenon Grocholewski *et al.*, *Il Matrimonio nel Nuovo Codice di Diritto Canonico* (Padua: Libreria Gregoriana, 1984), 67.

[62]Illinois Revised Statutes, Chapter 40, Section 301 (1), 1985.

[63]Ibid.

C. The quality must be unknown to the other party.
D. The discovery of the absence or presence of the quality must precipitate the end of the marriage.[64]

Taking these elements into account, a Tribunal accepting a case involving dolus should have the following in mind:

1) If deceit is alleged in the *libellus,* the presiding judge must consider the motivations for this deceit. There should be some indication of this in the petitioner's statement. For example, marrying an individual in order to escape from one country into another could be a very concrete example of deceit to entrap someone into marriage. Finding in the petitioner's statement evidence of a lie about pregnancy to marry, or finding the actual words "lying" or "he lied" in regard to certain qualities (such as the ability to have children) can give indication that there is a good possibility of a marriage based on deceit.

Keep in mind that this deception must be carried out with the intention of bring about marriage. Simply discovering some unwanted quality years after a marriage is not necessarily indicative of "deception perpetrated to obtain consent."

It would probably be good to include deceit in the initial setting of the grounds, if it is a possibility. For example, the *contestatio litis* might be:

Deceit on the part of the petitioner and/or total simulation on the part of the respondent

OR

Deceit on the part of the petitioner and/or lack of due competence on the part of the respondent.

It is important to keep in mind the various roles played by each party in contracting this marriage because there will be difference in emphasis during the instruction process. For example, if the Court is dealing with a case of possible condition (Canon 1102) or error (Canon 1097 . . . without any reference to dolus) then the instruction should center on the petitioner. In other words, the petitioner in these cases is the active subject, and the proofs should take this into consideration. If, on the other hand, there is a very strong possibility of dolus, then the petitioner would be the passive subject, and the respondent the active subject. The instruction would no longer center primarily on the petitioner, but on the respondent who is alleged to have perpetrated this deception in order to marry the petitioner. (This is with the assumption that most cases of this type would come to the Tribunal with the petitioner alleging to have been deceived. There is no reason, however, that a petitioner could not admit to have deceived to marry. But, there still would be an active and passive subject involved).

2) A part of the task of jurisprudence at this time is the focus on the

---

[64]Thomas P. Doyle O.P., "Title VII: Marriage ((cc. 1055-1165)," in *The Code of Canon Law: A Text and Commentary,* James A. Coriden et. al., eds, (New York Mahweh: The Paulist Press, 1985), 781.

quality connected with the deception. The quality must be present at the time of marriage, and not merely imagined. The concern of the canon are qualities which are capable of disrupting the marriage. The CLSA commentary notes:

> The quality must be an actual feature of the individual and not an isolated action from the past which is no longer relevant to the person. It must be grave. This means that it is so serious that its concealment would be commonly accepted as an injustice to the other party (objective) or so serious in the estimation of the other party that, although it might not adversely affect others, it causes profound reaction on the part of the person deceived (subjective).[65]

Again, this quality should be evident in the *libellus*. Connected with 1) above, questions concerning pregnancy and concealed sterility come to mind. So do deliberately concealed illnesses, such as drug dependencies which have the potential for serious disruption of lives. Concealed homosexuality might be another possibility. Statements like "If I had known, I would never have married" *could* be indicative of a case involving covering up of a serious problem in order to bring marriage about.

3) It might be well for a Tribunal to compose a series of questions for witnesses, such as:

    A. Was the petitioner/respondent inclined to dishonesty in life? Did he/she frequently lie?

    B. As far as you know, what was the motive for this marriage?

    C. Did you know of the deception which is being alleged by the petitioner/respondent?

    D. Describe, as best as you are able, what N.N. claims not to have known about the petitioner/respondent before their marriage.

    E. Do you think that this marriage would have taken place if the other party had been aware of this problem before the marriage?

4) With so little material at hand at the present time, there is very little available as a model, especially in terms of sentence-writing. However, there are two sequences (one hypothetical, the other an actual case) that could give some guidance for method of argumentation, weight of proofs, etc.[66]

Another very "practical" issue for Tribunals is whether this canon can be applied retroactively or not. It is well known that the concept of retroactivity of

---

[65]Ibid.
[66]Kneal *et al.*, "A Proposed *In Iure* Section," and *coram* Sheehy (August 28th, 1979).

law is very central to its application, because as Canon 9 states, "Laws deal with the future and not the past, unless specific provisions be made in the laws concerning the past."

The fundamental issue here is whether this canon is founded in natural law or positive law: because if it is purely a matter of "political legislation," in other words, positive ecclesiastical law, then it cannot have retroactive application. If on the other hand, it is based in natural law, it could have retroactive application. Opinion is certainly divided in this matter. Some authors argue that this new canon is positive law[67] while others hold for a natural law base.[68] The Church does have the ability, as Gasparri noted,[69] to establish dolus as nullifying matrimonial consent, but more study and clarification is needed to establish with certainty this basis. It has been said that Canon 1099 could be considered a written expression of natural law, and would apply to any act of consent.[70] It also has been observed that the discussion of the Code Commission during the formulation of this canon "were based more on the philosophical arguments than on the political argument of the Church's authority to establish the impediment.[71] It must be noted too, that by way of official response to this question, the Code Commission stated that this canon was seen to be of positive law, and therefore could not be applied to marriages which occurred before November 27, 1983 (the date of the promulgation of the Code). This response was a private letter, upon an inquiry to the Pontifical Commission for authentic interpretation of the Code.[72]

It would seem that the best solution (given the disparity of opinions and the response from the Code Commission) would be to seek out alternate grounds when a case is received in the Tribunal which alleges deception as the reason for a contested marriage, and the date of the marriage is before November 27, 1983. For example, instead of deceit on the part of the petitioner, a *contestatio litis* might be a grave lack of discretion of judgment on the part of the petitioner, and some sort of simulation on the part of the respondent. Another possibility would be to consider an inability to assume the rights and duties of Christian marriage on the part of the respondent, if a case involved the concealment of some permanent illness or psychological incapacity.

In any case, as time passes, this could prove to be less and less of a concern. From a personal point of view, of the three cases involving dolus which have

---

[67] Joseph Bank, *Cannubia Canonica*, (Rome: Herder, 1959), 360; Carlo Gullo, "Error Qualitatis Redundans in Errorem Personae," *Il Diritto Ecclesiastico*, XCII (1981), Fasc. III, Pt. I, 357-358, believes the statute is founded in positive law, but should have been founded in natural law; Flatten, "Quomodo Matrimonium," 5; Ahern, "Error and Deception as Grounds of Nullity," 253.

[68] Urbano Navarrete S.J., "Schema Iuris Recogniti 'De Matrimonio.' Textus et Observationes," *Peridica*, LXIII (1974), 638; Castano, "L'Influsso del Doto," 578; Cuneo, "Deceit/Error of Person," 166; *coram* Sheehy (August 28th 1979).

[69] Pietro Cardinal Gasparri *Tractatus Canonicus de Matrimonio*, 2 vols. (Vatican City: Vatican Press, 1932), II, 21.

[70] Cuneo, "Deceit/Error," 166.

[71] Ibid.

[72] A private response from Cardinal Castillo-Lara, President of the Pontifical Commission for Authentic Interpretation of the Code of Canon Law, dated February 8, 1986 (Prot. N. 843/86).

been accepted by the Tribunal of the Diocese of Springfield in Illinois, only one of these marriages was celebrated before the promulgation of the New Code. Therefore, the issue may not be as pressing as first perceived.

Another consideration (related to the retroactivity issue) is whether this new canon would be considered binding for non-Catholics, since as Canon 11 states "merely ecclesiastical laws bind those baptized in the Catholic Church or received into it and who enjoy sufficient use of reason . . ." This is very relative in light of the number of baptized Catholics who approach Catholic Tribunals, so that they may be free to marry a Catholic. Also, Canon 1055 speaks of "this covenant between baptized persons," making no distinction between baptized Catholics and those of other ecclesiastical communions. If this canon has its origin in natural law, then its provisions would apply to baptized non-Catholics. However, if it is positive law only (and therefore "merely ecclesiastical") then it would not be binding for non-Catholics.

CONCLUSIONS

In this presentation I have tried to briefly sketch some of the history of dolus and matrimonial consent, and to surface issues which would be relevant to future Tribunal use. Since our law does not originate in a vacuum, but in the real history of people who form a part of civil society and the Church, a "backward glance" may help give us the keys to the interpretation of this new canon. Likewise, since Canon 17 states that "ecclesiastical laws are to be understood in accord with the proper meaning of the words considered in their text and context," a study of the construction and words of Canon 1098 can offer that text and context for proper interpretation.

Much further study needs to be done. Any of the sources to which I have reffered can be a valuable resource for this further study. Lastly, since by its very nature the content of this canon is concerned with the "dark side" of human nature, I would suggest that the opposite content should be a part of the lives of all involved in this work: an uncompromising honesty and integrity as we seek to serve Christ in our respective vocations in His Church.

SECULAR INSTITUTES:
CAN THEY BE BOTH CLERICAL AND LAY?

Sharon L. Holland IHM

Can secular institutes be both clerical and lay? The obvious answer is "yes." It is a fact that both clerical and lay secular institutes exist with full ecclesiastical recognition. The 1947 document *Provida Mater Ecclesia*[1] officially recognizing secular institutes as a true and complete form of consecrated life, acknowledged that they could be both lay and clerical (art. I). The 1983 code repeats this (cc. 588, 711, 713, 715).

For decades, however, the questions were even more basic: Could there be a consecration of life outside of religious institutes? Could one profess the evangelical counsels and remain fully a lay person?

Canonists, theologians, and popes wrestled with the questions posed by those who believed in such a vocation. At last they said "yes." "Yes," the Spirit has called men and women to consecration as lay persons living in the world. "Yes" the Church has received a new gift of the Spirit which is well described as "consecrated secularity." "Yes" priests too may make this commitment to the evangelical counsels in institutes called secular, without changing their status as members of a diocesan presbyterate.

The Church, most recently in the 1983 code and the 1983 SCRIS Plenaria, has indeed said "yes" to all of these things. Still, the more frequent and fundamental question today remains: What is a secular institute?

Canon 710 sets forth a working definition:

> A secular institute is an institute of consecrated life in which the Christian faithful living in the world strive for the perfection of charity and work for the sanctification of the world especially from within.

To further consider the question, we will begin briefly from the point of view to history, of papal expressions and, of course, the canons. Then we will turn to some of the on-going contemporary questions—with no promise of definitive answers. These questions include: 1) Should secular institutes of priests really be called secular? and 2) Should secular institutes of laity really be grouped among institutes of consecrated life?

Today secular institutes report some 80,000 members. They are the descendants of inspired men and women from as early as the sixteenth century. They belong to some 148 recognized institutes, fifty-two of which are pontifical.[2] For our purposes here, a few examples from history may be helpful.

---

[1] *AAS* 39 (1947) 114-24.
[2] Mario Albertini, *Dialogue* (Jan./Mar. 1987).

The women who form the Company of St. Ursula today take inspiration from St. Angela Merici who began her company in Italy in 1535 to give service and education in homes. In her day, all women religious were cloistered, and Angela wished to respond to needs they could not meet. After her death many of her followers became cloistered, but the founding spirit is alive today.

When the Jesuits were suppressed in eighteenth century France, Pere Cloriviere organized a group of priests, no longer officially religious, who would live the evangelical counsels in the world while exercising civil professions. His institute continued from 1791 to 1835. It disappeared, but was reorganized in 1918 and recognized as a secular institute—the Society of the Heart of Jesus—in 1952.[3]

The persecution of the Church in nineteenth century Poland produced many institutes modeled on the hidden life of Jesus at Nazareth. They were founded by Cappucian Father Honorat Kozminski[4] who saw this as a way to keep those desiring a consecrated life from leaving Poland.

Another Franciscan, Agostino Gemelli, together with his co-worker Armida Barelli, founded the Missionaries of the Kingship of Christ in Italy in 1919. Theirs was a concern for the decaying intellectual and moral fiber of their society in which official representatives of the Church were often spurned. Their original inspiration was "Associations of Laity Consecrated to God in the World"[5] but the Kingship now includes institutes of lay women, lay men and priests.

Institutes have grown much more rapidly in Europe than in the United States. A 1984 editorial in the World Conference's publication estimated that 63% of all secular institute members are in Italy, France and Spain.[6] The 1985 Official Catholic Directory lists seventeen secular institutes in the United States, of which one is explicitly listed as a U.S. foundation.

Perhaps more important than numerical growth is the fact that understanding of secular institutes has grown. After the long struggle of seeking official recognition from the Church, Pius XII issued *Provida Mater*. Response was mixed however, as some felt that the document did not really capture the newness of their vocation. The description of their life as "substantially religious" seemed simply to make secular institutes an extension of the category "religious." A year later, with the Motu proprio *Primo feliciter*[7] Pius XII affirmed that this form of Christian perfection was truly secular. His eloquent description of institute members as light, salt and leaven in a dark and savorless world, set a new tone of understanding.

---

[3] Jean Beyer, *Les Instituts Seculiers* (Burges, 1954) pp. 35-50.

[4] Pauline Brzozowska, "La secularite, element de la vie religieuse selon la pensee de P. Honorat Kozminski (1829-1916)" *Vie Consacree* 56 (1984) 296.

[5] Agostino Gemelli, "Le Associazioni di laici consacrati a Dio nel mondo," in *Secolarita e Vita Consacrata*, ed. A. Oberti (Milano, 1966) pp. 361-442,

[6] *Dialogue* (March, 1984) 2.

[7] *AAS* 40 (1948) 283-86.

This year secular institute members celebrate the fortieth anniversary of *Provida Mater*. In the intervening years, papal allocutions have added many expressions descriptive of institute members. The addresses of Paul VI, and later of John Paul II, are reflective of an increasingly integrated and positive understanding of the secular institute's identity.

Paul VI repeatedly used synthetic terms such as "consecrated secularity."[8] Addressing the 1970 International Congress, he reminded members that they were in the world, not of the world, but for the world.[9] He insisted that this not be heard as a simple play of words. Theirs was truly a mission of salvation for humanity today. In Paul VI's sight, secular institutes clearly had become a sign of how the Church was to relate to the world. He spoke of them as a "model" of the untiring impulse toward the new attitude the Church wished to incarnate before the world.[10] They were, further, "providential instruments" through which the charism of consecrated secularity could be transmitted to the world.[11] Finally, they were the "laboratories of experience" in which the Church verifies the concrete modalities of its relationship with the world.[12] During the 1983 Plenaria on the life and mission of secular institutes, Pope John Paul II added a new phrase, praising institutes as "eruptions of grace" in the life of the Church.[13]

This, of course, is not the type of language one would expect to find in canon law. Nevertheless, the same theological reality should be recognizable. First of all, by their inclusion in the section entitled institutes of consecrated life, secular institutes are recognized for the first time in the Church's universal law. The common norms for all institutes of consecrated life apply to them (cc. 573-606). In response to a vocational call they are consecrated through life-long commitment to the evangelical counsels of chastity, poverty and obedience. Institutes are then specifically treated in cc. 710-730.

Canon 710, as noted above, identifies secular institutes as a form of consecrated life in which members seek the sanctificaiton of the world *ab intus*. From within the world, their lives will leaven it with Christ. This notion of leaven recalls that important expression from *Primo feliciter* which now appears in canon 713, §1:

> The members of these institutes express and exercise their own consecration in their apostolic activity and like a leaven they strive to imbue all things with the spirit of the gospel for the strengthening and growth of the Body of Christ.

This is, of course, the language of *Lumen gentium* 31, as well as of Pius XII. The first article of canon 713 is addressed to all secular institute members. Canon 711 has already stated that the consecration of these persons does not alter their canonical condition. They remain therefore, laity or diocesan clergy—members

---

[8] "In questo giorno," *AAS* 64 (1972) 208, 212.
[9] *Acta Congressus* (Milano, 1971) p. 693.
[10] "In questo giorno," pp. 209-212.
[11] Ibid, p. 208.
[12] "C'est bien volontiers," *Commentarium pro Religiosis* 57 (1976) 369.
[13] *Informationes* 9 (1983) 122.

of an institute of consecrated life. In the words of *Perfectae caritatis* 11, they are not religious.

The subsequent articles of canon 713 specify distinct roles of laity and clergy in the building up of the Body of Christ. The language of canon 713, §2 on the lay member's role in the ecclesial mission of evangelization reinforces the notion of consecrated seculars. The phrase, similar to the canon's *in saeculo et ex saeculo,* first appeared in Father Gemelli's apologia for ecclesial recognition of his proposed associations of laity consecrated to God in the world. Gemelli's phrase *in saeculo ac veluti ex saeculo* was repeated in *PC* 11. The omission of the rather tentative *veluti* is seen by some today as an opportune change, seeming to remove the previous hesitation to recognize lay members' full secularity.[14] Lay members of secular institutes are seen as living and working in the world, playing a role in salvation in and through the world.

The canon's description of the consecrated lay person's role of evangelization begins with witness. A contribution is made toward the sanctification of the world simply through Christian witness in fidelity to one's consecration of life. Further, their efforts must be expended toward ordering the temporal according to God's plan and informing the world with values of the Gospel. Here again, we recognize the language which *LG* 31 addressed to all of the laity.

Here they are addressed specifically to lay men and women whose entire lives are consecrated toward this end. Canon 714 reinforces this by stating that members live in the ordinary circumstances of the world. Seeking to radicalize the vocation received in baptism, they have undertaken a life of the evangelical counsels for this transformation of the world from within—within the halls of government and the ranks of the military; within science laboratories and banks, classrooms and medical centers; within every sphere of life. Canon 722, §2 echoes *Primo feliciter* in insisting that members be formed in such a way that the whole of their lives is transformed into apostolate.

There is also provision for cooperation in service to the Church community, in keeping with their secular way of life. Lay secular institute members, like any other lay persons, may serve as catechists, lectors, commission members, extraordinary ministers etc. This is, however, in addition to the primary apostolic role of consecrated presence in the world.

As lay secular institutes penetrate more deeply the notion of secularity, the nagging question of clerical institutes recurs. According to canon 713, §3, the immediate "world" in which a priest member bears witness through his consecrated life is that of the diocesan presbyterate. In the wider sphere of the People of God, he labors to bring about the sanctification of the world through his sacred ministry. If we recall that diocesan priests have long been referred to as secular—meaning not religious—there is nothing so new or strange in this. In most cases, the cleric is incardinated in a diocese and relates to the bishop as do the other priests of

---

[14]O. Montevecchi, unpublished manuscript.

the diocese, except in matters which pertain to consecrated life in their particular institute (c. 715). It is only by concession of the Apostolic See that members may be incardinated in the institute (c. 715, §2; c. 266, §3).

Because there is already great similarity between the life of a priest and the life of the evangelical counsels, entrance into an institute implies a particular call to somehow further radicalize priestly consecration.

Despite ecclesial recognition and new understandings, the old questions recur in new forms and perhaps with new implications. For example, today some ask:
1. Should secular institutes of priests really be called secular?
2. Should secular institutes of laity really be grouped among institutes of consecrated life?

In considering these questions, some authors have found it helpful to distinguish vocation and mission. The beginning point must be the universal call to holiness, to growth in charity, which is the vocation of all through baptism. In a 1974 article, Francois Morlot then distinguishes the vocation to the evangelical counsels and the vocation to ministry. The former is a vocation within the Christian vocation, not substantially different from the universal call, but sufficiently characteristic to be called a particular vocation.[15]

While vocation and mission are always intimately related, Morlot distinguishes the call to holiness from the call to service—the invitation to participate in Christ's life of union with the Father and to participate in Christ's action of drawing all to Him.

The call to live the evangelical counsels according to a particular rule of life is not necessarily identifiable with a particular ministry. Ministry demands the life of charity to which all are called, but does not presuppose profession of the evangelical counsels.

While all secular institute members make a permanent commitment in a life of the evangelical counsels, there is diversity in ministry. Morlot contends that distinguishing profession of the counsels and ministry helps explain secular institutes of priests. He finds the two calls—to the counsels and to priesthood—distinct but mutually reinforcing.[16]

The working paper published in preparation for the Synod on the Laity, entitled "Vocation and Mission of the Laity,"[17] also distinguishes vocation and mission. In this explanation, vocation is used as the broader of the two concepts. It embraces a call to both *communio* and mission. The call to *communio* is fundamental, involving the two-fold union of love of God and others. It is an everlasting reality. Mission is a consequence of *communio* and lasts throughout earthly existence (n. 14).

Because of the two dimensions of Christian life, every vocation involves a cor-

---

[15] Francois Morlot, "Vocation a un ministere, Vocation a la vie consacree," *Studia Canonica* 8 (1984) 75.
[16] Ibid, 89.
[17] *Origins* 17 (1987) 1-19.

responding mission. The diversity of participation in the Chursh's mission is illustrated in broad strokes by speaking of laity and clergy. "The mission of the laity," the document states, "receives its specific character by their immediate involvement in worldly affairs" (n. 18). In a separate paragraph, the Synod working paper recognizes the special vocation of secular institute members and the role they can and do play in exemplifying the universal call to holiness and the lay role within the world (n. 61). Ordained ministries are "in service to this vocation which the laity fulfill in the world" (n. 16).

We can conclude then, that a vocation to profess the evangelical counsels does not, of itself, specify the way in which one is to participate in the Church's mission. In turn, this conclusion reaffirms that both clerics and lay persons may be called to consecrated life (c. 207, §2) in secular institutes.

Returning to the question of clerical institutes called secular, we have seen in canon 713, §3 that a priest member's role in the sanctification of the world is through sacred ministry. Armando Oberti, a well known author on secular institutes, sees in canon 713, §3 the Church's understanding that secular institutes of priests have a particular mission. Writing as President of the World Conference of Secular Institutes (CMIS) Oberti notes that the Church and all its members have a secular character. Each however, is called to live this "being in the world" in a different way.[18]

A study of the "secular characteristic" of priest members was begun in 1980 by the Directors General of clerical institutes. A summary of their preliminary research recognizes Jesus, through the Incarnation, as the first to be consecrated and as the "secular" par excellence. This Jesus communicates his secularity to the Church, and thus one summary conclusion reads:

> Since secularity is one of the essential aspects of the Church, the priest
> is also minister of the Church's secularity.[19]

Composed of human beings and existing in history, the Church has a secularity which represents her human earthly side. This is lived out in diverse forms so that secularity cannot be reduced to "being lay." While laity and clergy are essentially diverse with regard to ordained priesthood, with regard to secularity, the difference between them is not substantial. By analogy, the secularity of priests and laity—their spiritual immersion in earthly realities and commitment to the ordering of worldly activities—is a difference of density and modulation. Secularity is typical of the lay state, but not exclusive to it. The priest, representing Christ, is truly present in the "here and now" of the local Christian community.

The "sacred ministry" of the priest, then, is as broad in scope as the lives of the persons to whom he ministers in concrete world situations. He is said to be "secular" because he lives among and for the people.

The words of Pope John Paul II are cited, urging all secular institute members

---

[18] Armando Oberti, "Les Instituts Seculiers dans le nouveau Code de Droit Canon," *Vie Consacree* 55 (1983) 211.
[19] "The Secular Character of Priests: Why and How," unpublished draft.

to widen and deepen their understanding of temporal realities and values as these relate to evangelization. This will make priest members increasingly concerned with the situation of people in the world. Further, it will enable them to contribute to the diocesan clergy both through their life of the counsels and their sense of the true relation between the Church and the world.[20]

In its conclusion, the draft document addresses the relationship of secular consecration to sacerdotal consecration. First, the secular consecration of the priest is described as "a function of his ministry, as radicalization, development and fulness of the mission and grace bestowed upon him by sacred orders." Secondly, his priestly consecration is better specified and is enriched by "a new aspect of grace deriving from the particular charism of the Holy Spirit."

The priest member of a secular institute is not set apart from his brothers in the diocesan presbyterate, nor is he given a different mission. His secularity involves becoming aware of his place in the world and his responsibility toward it. Through a particular call of grace he has undertaken a further focusing of his orientation and dedication as priest. The research document speaks of this special gift of the Spirit as having the newness of a "greater light," and "more urgent call," a "more lucid and radical commitment." One is led, then, to the conclusion that these institutes can be called secular, with this understood in a sense proper to clerics.

We turn next to the second question, that of categorizing lay institutes among institutes of consecrated life. The distinction made above between vocation to the evangelical counsels and one's particular share in ecclesial mission illustrates that it it entirely possible to have consecrated lay persons "living in the world." Further, what has just been said about deepening and radicalizing a priest's life and mission may likewise be said of the laity. Given the fundamental Christian consecration of baptism and the resultant sharing in the three-fold mission of Christ and the Church, lay members of secular institutes, responding to a vocational call, radicalize their responsibility for the Christian penetration and transformation of the world.

All that the Church says to the laity—characteristically as found in *Luman gentium, Apostolicam actuositatem* and *Evangelii nuntiandi*—is taken to heart by those who have consecrated their secularity through life-long commitment to the evangelical counsels.

The lay members' consecrated celibacy places them in sharper contrast with the rest of the laity than is true of priest members among the secular priests in the Latin Church. However, the practice of reserve in many lay institutes helps guard against elitism and preserves the potential for leaven-like penetration of temporal realities. It is clear that the call to embrace the evangelical counsels in an institute approved by the Church is a particular vocation within the univer-

---

[20]"To Change the World from Within," (Aug. 28, 1980) *Secular Institutes: The Official Documents* (Rome: CMIS, 1981) n. 16.

sal call to holiness. The lay member's mission remains that to which the Church continually calls all of the baptized.

In his recent address to the United States laity, Pope John Paul II used terms especially familiar to secular institute members.[21] He urged them to consecrate the temporal through lives which are leaven, salt, and light. Such lives, he notes, will sometimes be signs of contradiction—not by imposing their religious beliefs on others, but by witnessing to justice, faith, hope and charity.

The critical importance of this broad service of the Gospel is also highlighted in a statement by Morlot. A Church without interest in the world, he writes, will give rise to a world which does not interest itself with God.[22]

Vatican II's new expression of Church-world rapport, and its renewed emphasis on the role of laity, have played an important part in today's better understanding of secular institutes. What the institutes sought to be and do, well before their official recognition in 1947, was in fact, as Paul VI recognized, an experimental lab for testing out the possibilities of a new Church-world rapport.

In this decade, Oberti sees the institutes at the center of a dynamic intersection of Church and world, and this point of intersection is at the heart of the mystery of salvation. Institutes enable the Church to offer the world the content of revelation, and enable the Church to listen to the Spirit speaking in daily historical reality. They are, in a sense, the Church in the world and the world in the Church.[23] They are, Oberti suggests, in some way living in anticipation of the Church's yet developing consciousness of its own secular nature and of the role of laity within the Church in the world.[24]

Like priest author Morlot, lay author Oberti notes that every secular institute member's canonical status remains unchanged (c. 711). Their consecration reinforces and radicalizes their ecclesial identity. Secularity becomes consecrated secularity, more strictly lived through permanent and total commitment, with and for the world.[25] Though silent and discreet, there is in the lay member's life, a radical witness to the Paschal Mystery, entered into through baptism.

There is, then, neither theological nor juridic reason why lay secular institutes cannot be included under the title institutes of consecrated life. The newness of the secular institute vocation which many felt was not really understood or clearly expressed in *Provida Mater* surely is better understood today. *Primo feliciter* quickly added emphasis on the characteristic of secularity and both Paul VI and Vatican II contributed to an enhanced understanding of this vocation. Inclusion in the 1983 Code has concretized the institutes' universal juridic identity.

In view of this, it might seem ironic that Germana Sommaruga, who remembers

---

[21] St. Mary's Cathedral, San Francisco, Sept. 18, 1987.
[22] Morlot, pp. 80-81.
[23] Armando Oberti, "La vocation des instituts seculiers dans l'Eglise," Vie Consacree 42 (1982) 239.
[24] Oberti, "Les instituts," p. 204.

the Church's "no" to consecration outside religious institutes, and who has experienced the growth of understanding over these decades, now asks if secular institutes will survive to the year 2000? Her question flows from a concern over whether the new understanding of consecrated secularity came too late. It also flows from a concern over whether bishops understand the vocational distinctness of institutes sufficiently to avoid encouraging quasi-religious secular institutes.[26]

In this context, the author recalls a distinction which Father Larraona of SCRIS made at a 1957 conference. He had spoken of two types of secular institutes: institutes of penetration and institutes of collaboration. Institutes of penetration were those which entered the more difficult frontiers such as bureaucracy, public assistance, politics and international affairs. In contrast, institutes of collaboration served selflessly and silently on parochial, diocesan and national levels, involved in Catholic action and the lay apostolate.[27]

Commenting today, Sommaruga notes that institutes of collaboration are more numerous, despite Vatican II's emphasis on the meaning of the world, of laity, and of Christians totally committed in the world to the service of humanity (cf. *SC* 9, *AA* 2, *GS* 3). Clearly she hopes that it is not too late for these institutes to reconsider and deepen their proper characteristic of secularity.[28]

Will secular institutes exist in the year 2000? In response to her own question, Sommaruga says "yes . . . if." Secular institutes will exist in the year 2000 if institutes of penetration exist even in a plurality of forms. They will exist if others come into being, and

> If secular institutes of collaboration reflect on the words of popes, in particular on the specific call of the Holy Spirit to a form of secular consecration which is truly secular, to a consecrated secularity which is truly consecrated.[29]

Finally, Simmaruga poses another important condition. Secular institutes will exist in the year 2000 if those presenting themselves to CRIS's section on secular institutes, all, or at least in the majority, present a true psysiognomy of a secular institute with its full identity. And, conversely the institutes will continue to exist if that section of CRIS dedicated to them will take a stand, even in the face of bishops, for truly secular institutes. This will involve renouncing, above all, common houses, para-religious works, and a variety of quasi-parochial activities which could be handled by others.[30]

---

[26]Germana Sommaruga, "Les Instituts Seculiers en route vers l'an 2000," *Vie Consacree* 59 (1987) 248-50.
[27]Ibid., 247.
[28]Ibid., 248.
[29]"Si les Instituts séculiers de collaboration réflechissent aux paroles des papes, en particulier à l'appel specifique du Saint-Esprit à une forme de consecration séculière vraiment séculière, à une sécularité consacrée vraiment consacree." Ibid, 251.
[30]Ibid, 251-52.

The author acknowledges that this requires courage and attentiveness to the Holy Spirit, to the needs of the Church today and to the needs of humanity. She who witnessed the Church's "no" to a secular consecration turn to "yes," is hopeful for the continued vitality of this gift of the Spirit to the Church. The hope and vision of those who live this life can serve to encourage others in the Church to ever deeper understanding of this, and their own vocation and ecclesial mission.

ISSUES IN SACRED ORDERS

DAVID M. HYNOUS, OP

INTRODUCTION

In a certain Catholic school in Philadelphia, the third-grade class was given a written project as an assignment: Please put down in writing what you want to be when you grow up and tell me why.

The following was submitted by a nine-year-old and is dated February 5, 1987:

"Since I was three years old, I've wanted to be a priest . . .

As a priest, I would celebrate liturgies, help people with their problems and tell people about God.

"Priests have to spend many hours doing their work. Sometimes they get up early in the morning and don't go to bed until late at night. They don't make a lot of money, their salary is below the poverty level. But they do their work because they love God. They only get one day off each week and sometimes they don't see their families for a long time. Even though this is hard work, I still want to be a priest. I will keep on praying that I can be a priest someday.

[I have left one sentence for the last.] I am going to send a letter to Pope John Paul II asking him to allow women to be priests."

Signed: Katie Link

[Accompanying this class report is a color snapshot of Catherine Link dressed in black trousers, a black clergy shirt and Roman collar. And she is nine-years old.]

I therefore propose to you that we have some of the issues in the ordained priesthood, those elements that comprise the call to Sacred Orders:

A priest is someone who loves God.

He wants to tell people about God and help them with their problems.

He celebrates liturgy.

He is asked to give of himself from early in the morning until late in the evening.

He sacrifices not only contact with his own family but the option to raise a family.

He is underpaid and overworked.

His vocation is not necessarily of his own choosing; even a three-year old can be inspired to seek out Sacred Orders.

It is well for me to say at the beginning what I will not treat in this seminar presentation. The first issue I cannot address is the question of the ordination of women, and the second, which I will allude to but not treat, is the issue of clericalism and its impact on preparation of candidates for the ordained ministry.

First of all, I cannot speak of women's ordination. It is a topic for another type of presentation. I must speak directly to the canons on formation.

Secondly, the issue of clericalism looms in any discussion on the type of person who presents himself for ordination and in any discussion on the process of formation. Although I am presuming that I can set clericalism aside, it permeates the atmosphere. Eventually, as I conclude my remarks, you may find that subtly and unconsciously clericalism is still the main issue.

Let me share the essence of a letter I had to respond to at the end of August. A letter was addressed to the Chancery. The author of the letter was a brother of a religious congregation and he insisted in strong language that we were to stop addressing letters to the *Fathers* of this particular unnamed religious congregation. He insisted on the brotherhood taking precedence over the priesthood. The community was composed not just of priests but of brothers as well—the unordained. Here's what he said:

". . . There are two terrible diseases that destroy people on this planet in our day. One is AIDS; the other is clericalism. I believe a cure will be found for AIDS . . . [but for] clericalism? I just wonder??? Since it originates in the heart and isn't a virus, it will take some doing . . .

"Last year I wrote a similar letter . . . it ended up on my Provincial's desk. Proof positive that clericalism is alive and working overtime. My Provincial didn't put me on bread and water or have me kneel for meals . . . (apparently someone in your office did!) I did tell him I would not recant, as Martin Luther 'could not recant.' I told him that I'd stop into the chancery to speak about the 'Servant Jesus,' but he didn't encourage the idea . . .''

Allow me one comment. This charge of clericalism should not be viewed as male vs. female; men vs. women. The issue is very much one of the ordained vs. the non-ordained. The non-ordained religious brother can equally be a victim.

FORMATION QUESTIONS

In addressing canonical issues of priestly formation, there are present simultaneously the theological, psychological, and practical aspects involved. As one who taught seminarians, served as their religious superior, and ended up as the Personnel Director for the entire province, I can attest to the presence of the theological and the psychological as well as the canonical.

One of our seminarians put it bluntly to me. When I challenged him about his negative reaction to formation, he said in a tone of frustration:

"I know what you want out of me. There are two issues involved in my being ordained. Can I do anything and can you live with me."

Pragmatically, I could only agree with him. A formation program testing a vocation is much more than an employment agency screening applicants. It is a process harking back to the words of Jesus: "You have not chosen me; I have chosen you."

Yes, Lord, we say. But canon law is a fallible instrument for the work of identifying the "chosen."

The Goals of Priestly Formation:

In any investigation of a topic, I think it worthwhile to begin with the end-product, the goal of priestly formation is obviously the ordination of a man to the ministerial priesthood. As the philosopher says: the final cause is the cause of all the other causes. Therefore, my first question is: what is the ministerial ordained priesthood or who is an ordained priest?

In a talk given recently at a meeting of bishops and major superiors of religious men, the Rev. Howard Gray, S.J., gave four aspects of Christian spirituality used by the Church to characterize the priesthood:[1]
 1. The priest is a disciple;
 2. The priest is an apostle;
 3. The priest is a presbyter;
 4. The priest is one who presides at the Eucharist.

He later proposes three theological trends in today's theology of priesthood:
 1. The priest is a leader of the community;
 2. The priest is servant-shepherd of the Mystery of Christ;
 3. The priest is prophet.

The goal of priestly formation will have to take into account:

1. An individual who possesses the intellectual capacity to teach and preach to his people, the pastoral insight to lead them in the scaramental life of the Church, and who has developed his own faith-life, including a dedication to celibacy, with the graces of the Spirit.

2. A program that can develop these personal aspects and assist the individual to integrate them into a life-long ministry.

THE SELECTION OF CANDIDATES

A. *The type of candidate:*

1. The pattern has been to seek suitable candidates from the ranks of the younger generation. We know now that the age of decision-making is being postponed in the middle to later 20's.

2. The restrictions *against* beginning seminary training are much more relaxed:
  a. No longer is there a prohibition against the illegitimate son; the son of divorced parents; the son of non-Catholics; a man afflicted with certain specific illnesses such as epilepsy.
  b. The permanent impediments [irregularities] are fewer:
  c. The simple impediments are equally few.

3. However, we are being faced with a variety of cases which we have not had before:

---

[1] Howard Gray, S.J., "Assumptions and Issues on the Theology of Priesthood," unpublished talk to the Second Assembly of Bishops and Rectors, June 29-July 2, 1987.

a. The physically handicapped:

1) In the past we concerned ourselves with blindness in the left eye [you've heard of the canonical eye: you had to be able to see with your left eye because of where the missal sat.] We were concerned with deformity of the fingers or hands ["Can he break a host?" was the question Rome asked].

2) Today, the questions are broader, the tolerance greater, but the problems remain. Now, we are asked: Will you accept someone totally blind—not partially—not just legally—but sightless? I have been asked: would the Church accept a young man who has artificial arms? [I watched this young man slowly raise his artificial arm, close the fingers on a ciborium, and carry it out to the altar.] But, should these men be priests?

The answer sometimes given is, yes, but maybe he should be a religious. That is not a satisfying answer because the religious clerical institutes are strongly resisting the concept of priesthood for everyone. Indeed, the spectre of the past still haunts us, that of the "Mass priest," ordained not to a full ministry but ordained as one to say Mass and hear confessions.

b. addictive behavior:

1) Whereas alcoholism was not an issue in a previous generation, today it is quite possible, especially if you are entertaining acceptance of a "late vocation." Do you accept recovering alcoholics? With what conditions? The demands of an AA program are significant. The factors that accompany the disease of alcoholism are equally operative in a man's life.

The question has arisen about the permission to use *mustum*, normally given to one already ordained. Could permission be given to a man, a recovering alcoholic, before he was ordained, as it is after ordination.

The following case appears in *Roman Replies* of 1987:[2] A particular bishop petitions the Congregation for the Doctrine of the Faith to allow a seminariam to make use of the indult for *mustum* even before his ordination to the diaconate. The Congregation replied that it could not grant the permission requested. Why? Two ponts:

  1. "Such an indult is envisioned only in the cases of priests who have developed problems of health so serious that not even intinction is possible."

  2. "Furthermore, this Congregation is obliged to ask Your Excellency to consider whether the seminarian's inability to receive the Eucharist under the ordinary conditions may not affect his suitability as a candidate for ordination. If the medical judgment in his case is correct, it would hardly seem justifiable to encourage his aspiring to the priesthood, given that his condition would hinder his offering the Mass in the normal manner the Church prescribed . . ."

2) I would hope that the topic of AIDS would not be one that we have to consider. In my inquiries, I find that the admissions groups are not asking for AIDS testing because of the uncertainty of the testing and the inconclusiveness of the results.

---

[2] Wm. A. Schumacher and J. James Cuneo (eds.), *Roman Replies & CLSA Advisory Opinions, 1987*, CLSA, Washington, D.C., 1987.

c. the formerly married:

1) This class of men come from varying situations:
   a. The widower is the easiest to consider.

   b. The married who have had their marriages annulled supposedly have no impediment, but to me there is still a serious issue present. Let me explain in a moment.

   c. The married who have not sought or cannot seek an annulment do have an impediment; but should they be considered? Briefly, the answer is yes; the Holy See under unusual circumstances will grant a dispensation.

2) The underlying issue for the married man who has received an annulment goes beyond the canons. The basic question to answer remains: does this man have a vocation to the married state? Or to the clerical state? To me, it is insufficient to say, he has no impediment; therefore his previous marriage is of no consequence. It indeed is, and especially if there are minor children. The parental and family vocation is God-given, and the relationship between father and children is of primary importance.

There is also the distinct possibility that the gentleman who has an annulment was granted one by reason of his lack of due competence, and a prohibition has been placed against a remarriage. What effect does this have on pursuing ordination? Much!

d. attempted suicide:

I wish to single out one of the irregularities, and that is the caution against accepting one who had made a suicidal gesture, as pointed out in c. 1041, 5. I have been in the midst of a process of termination of seminarian who had made a dramatic suicidial gesture. Some will say: time has passed; every situation is unique. I respond: the canon has merit. Such a man is not to be accepted, and yet the man I am speaking of is today a candidate for priesthood in another religious Institute.

e. one last observation:

There is no longer any impediment of being illegitimate by reason of a conception by a parent who was in either sacred orders or in the vowed life. Sons of an adulterine or sacrilegious union in the old Code were barred from entry into the priesthood.

But there is a new category of candidates for the priesthood. They are the sons of resigned and laicized priests and their wives. As two wives of former priests have said to me: "Our sons are extremely proud of their fathers; they want to emulate their dads." And one confided: "Our younger son is extremely attracted to everything his father represents, and one of those elements is the priesthod."

What will you do with the son of a resigned priest?

B. *The process of admission:*

1. We must seriously inquire about the process of admission. Most processes incorporate the same elements: baptismal, confirmation records, etc.

We are also encouraged to make use of psychological experts for the determination of any psychotic disorder, as stated in c. 1041, §1.

However, the psychologists say back to us: what is it that you want us to investigate. For example, they say to us: what do you want us to ask in the area of sexuality? As priests, we vacillate between being confessors and administrators. If the candidate says that there have been transgressions in the past, we absolve. But we are administrators, i.e., those accepting and preparing men for a life of celibacy. It cannot be compromised by a man saying to us "you will forgive me, won't you, if I can't maintain celibacy perfectly."

The psychologists caution us that we are being very simplistic, accepting the testimony and credentials of a man without sufficient investigation into his past. Allow me one example:

> Some years ago, as a member of the admissions board, I came across a 41-year old gentleman, applying to be a priest. What had he done since he left college? He had worked 7 years here, three years there, etc. As a 41-year old, I asked him how he would relate to men who were 22, 23, or 24—much younger. He said: I refuse to play games. I quickly learned that it was he who was playing games.
>
> I was at that time the dean of the seminary, so when the interview was concluded, I asked the vocation director for the transcripts from this man's college years. There, at the top, was his name. Let's call him "Joe Smith." But the name was not Joseph on the transcripts but Brother Matthew. On the next line was not the name of his parents, but the name of Brother Mark. Except for one thing: some Registrar had put the transcript back into the typewriter, X-ed out the religious name and typed in "Joseph."
>
> I investigated and learned that he had been a teaching brother for 13 years, tried priesthood in a clerical Institute, had not presevered, and then finally left the brothers. On his application, he denied he had ever been a religious. In giving us his resume, he had conveniently omitted 13 years of his life.
>
> When challenged by the vocation director who asked: "why did you do it, Joe?", his reply was: "I didn't want to compromise my application." I would like to suggest that c. 643, §1, 5⁰, might have some benefit. For someone applying to a religious clerical institute, concealing previous religious membership automatically makes the admission process invalid.

In accepting a candidate for priesthood who clearly admits to membership in another clerical institute or diocese, it is absolutely necessary, in my opinion, to seek letters of recommendation from the previous seminary and/or formation program. And yet, invitations come from former members to attend their ordination to the priesthood and yet never once did anyone write and ask about an individual's performance, character, or suitability.

PRIESTLY FORMATION

As canon 1027 states: "candidates are to receive an accurate formation in accord with the norm of law." These norms have been set up by the NCCB and are known to us all as "The Program of Priestly Formation," published in its 3rd edition in 1981. Many of us have had our seminary visited or have part of a visitation team. It is not necessary, therefore, to do more than pick out some significant issues.

The formation requirements have three definite aspects: spiritual, academic, pastoral:
1. Spiritual formation = a life according to the Gospel;
2. Academic formation = philosophy and theology harmoniously organized;
3. Pastoral formation = serious attention given to pedagogics, psychology, and periodic practical field experience.

1. *Spiritual Formation:*

> I purposely chose to place the spiritual formation as the first concern. In my experience as a member of a visitation team for programs of priestly formation, the two most important issues were that of the caliber of the formation directors and the quality of the spiritual direction. We were interested in celibacy as a key element of the ministerial priesthood. But the key to promotion to Orders lies in the realm of spiritual formation. The decision whether to promote a man to priesthood is not made so much academically, at least for me. Perhaps the decision is made more so on the basis of ministerial performance. Certainly, the decision is made in regard to one's faith and ability to make a commitment to ministry as well as to celibacy.

At this juncture, it is an obvious fact that the best of one's clergy are to be selected as directors of formation. And to this end, I will add that those selected are to be trained. If I was impressed by anything in visitations it was the quality and preparedness of formation directors. They are versed not only in theology, but in psychology and counseling as well. I must also add that the faculty of the seminary must share in the design and vision of the formation program.

Secondly, the choice of spiritual directors is an essential element. As an almost universal conclusion, the visitation team will recommend:

1) the spiritual directors be known to the seminary directors;

2) the spiritual directors meet as a group with the directors to discuss common concerns, and

3) if the spiritual director is not the confessor, that it be clear that the Sacrament of Reconciliation is the necessary counterpart of direction.

---

[3]Bishop James Keleher, in an unpublished address, "Three Critical Factors in Creating a Positive Seminary Environment," to the Second Assembly of Bishops & Rectors, June 29-July 2, 1987.

2. *Pastoral Preparation:*

Bishop James Keleher of Belleville, in a recent talk to bishops and seminary rectors, has put it this way:[3]

". . . Only pastoral personalities should be admitted to the seminary community . . . It is a waste of the seminary's time; it is detriment to the rest of the community; and it is a danger to the institution to accept persons without pastoral bent."

He accepts the fact that good academic training will assist a student to understand the pastoral aspects of theology. But the watchword is from Scripture, the disciples on the way to Emmaus exclaimed "Were our hearts not burning within us?" If their hearts are not burning, then someone needs to light a fire.

Bishop Daniel Buchlein of Memphis is quoted as saying:[4]

"The rate of change in Church and in society has been so rapid that the momentum of the times may easily propel a candidate toward equally unacceptable extremes in regard to priestly identity . . . [A man may well come with] a generalized identity as a minister of the Gospel who views priesthood as an anachronism. Or, he may have a rigid understanding of the priesthood which only grudgingly acknowledges other ministries in the Church and the legitimate role of an active and engaged laity. One extreme is as much to be avoided as the other."

3. *Academic Training:*

Bishop Keleher quotes this conversation between two bishops:[5]

"One bishops says to the other: "I'd be satisfied if they knew the Creed. The other Bishop responded, 'Yes, and perhaps the teachings of Vatican II as well.'" And as Bishop Keleher concludes: nothing can be assumed and nothing can be presumed.

It is one thing for canon 1042, §3, to caution us about accepting recent converts to Catholicism. But a more perilous situation develops when we accept men from Catholic backgrounds, but of widely varying quality.

Eugene Hemrick quotes the following statistics:[6]

Today only 44% of seminarians have attended Catholic schools for all eight years as compared with 70% 20 years ago. Only 44% have attended all four years of Catholic high school compared to 80% twenty years ago. A more striking statistic is that 36% of today's seminarians never attended a Catholic high school compared with only 1% twenty years ago.

---

[4]Ibid.
[5]Ibid.
[6]Eugene F. Hemrick, in an unpublished address, "The State of Today's Seminarians," to the above-mentioned Assembly.

Above all, in the training of a candidate for ministerial priesthood matters of concern for the Church, as Bishop Keleher outlines them, are in the following areas: psychosexual identity, collaborative style, pastoral charity, and interior obedience. Anything less than full integration of these elements will be the detriment of all.

THE CALL TO ORDERS

Canon 1029 says that when all is accomplished—a suitable candidate, of the proper age, with adequate training, etc.—the candidate is admitted to Orders. To this we add canon 1030 which states that the diocesan bishop or competent religious superior cannot deny access to the priesthood to a qualified deacon *unless* he has canonical reasons. The Commentary tells us that one such reason for denial of priesthood is *non-fulfillment of one of the criteria of canon 1029*. The deacon may have recourse. Let me raise 2 concrns.

The first is obvious. If a man is not qualified academically, pastorally, or spiritually, then I take the position that the man is not to be promoted. No one has a right to ordination to the priesthood, especially if the Church will be disserved. However, I do have to admit that the situation would call for some extraordinary circumstances. How could an individual get that far without someone, somewhere, pointing out his deficiencies? It happened to a community of religious whom I know. It had to do with the promotion of a man over 50 years of age. In order for him to finish his educational requirements, he was literally tutored each and every step of the way. The tutoring masked his inability to be a counselor, a preacher, and a teacher. The diaconate internship proved to be an embarrassment. He was refused priesthood.

One fact to note from *Roman Replies* of 1986. The Holy See will not entertain a request for a transitional deacon to become a permanent deacon. The two approaches are to remain separate.[7]

The second and last concern is the transfer of a candidate for priesthood from a diocese to a clerical religious institute. Priests are concerned about what the bishop will do to them when they tell him that they have applied to a religious institute. I now have a deacon in my canon law class who has waited eleven years to be allowed to enter a religious novitiate. College seminarians have met strong resistance from seminary rectors when they indicate that they are making application to a religious clerical institute. My hope is that we do not see each other, religious and diocesan, as being in competition for priestly vocations.

---

[7] Wm. A. Schumacher and J. James Cuneo (eds.), *Roman Replies & CLSA Advisory Opinions, 1986*, pp. 16-20, CLSA, Washington, D.C., 1986.

CONCLUSION

Everyone wants to know when and how something ends. We ask "how did the late movie end?" Or, we ask, "How did the ballgame end? What was the final score?" We read the last chapter of the novel or the mystery thriller because we don't have the patience to plow through the details.

The same thing is true of preparation for ordination to the ministerial priesthood. A man, as he concludes formation, says: "now, it's all over. I'm on my way with no further hurdles to overcome." But the truth of the matter is that there is no conclusion to formation, there is only a beginning. On-going formation is the next and even more crucial problem. The final chapter on priesthood has not yet been written; it has just begun. However, good beginnings make for good endings.[8]

---

[8] Many of the points raised in this paper are also contained in the Letter of Cardinal William W. Baum, on the "State of the U.S. Free-Standing Seminaries," October 5, 1986. This letter may be found in *Origins*, October 16, 1986, vol. 16, #18, pp. 313-325.

ISSUES OF AGGREGATION, MERGER AND DISSOLUTION

Ellen M. O'Hara, C.S.J.

In beginning this presentation, I wish to limit my treatment specifically to religious institutes of women. My intent is not to be discriminatory, but rather to avoid the necessity of treating a host of allied issues, e.g. issues involving clergy and issues involving institutes with both lay members and clerical members. The basic sources for the presentation are the 1983 Code of Canon Law, *Perfectae Caritatis*, articles 21 and 22, and *Ecclesiae Sanctae*, II, 39-41. The definitions, while not used consistently in the same fashion by Vatican practice or U.S. practitioners, are those presented by the Code or by the Congregation for Religious and Secular Institutes.[1] The four foci of the paper are Aggregation, Federation, Amalgamation and Merger. In conclusion, I will present some questions and some processes and issues.

Aggregation: This term is referred to in Canon 580, "The aggregation of one institute of consecrated life to another is reserved to the competent authority of the aggregating institute, always safeguarding the canonical autonomy of the aggregated institute." The term applies to two institutes of consecrated life; therefore, the term is not applicable to the associations of the faithful mentioned in Canon 677, §2 or Canon 725.[2] One implication of this non-applicability is that the variety of groups known variously as co-members, extended members, lay members, lay associates, etc., would not be eligible for aggregation to their allied religious institute.[3] The wording of the canon does allow for the possible aggregation between a secular institute and a religious institute, although I am not aware of any such aggregation at the present.

Aggregation itself is a faculty or privilege granted by the Apostolic See to first orders. An assumption in aggregation is that the institutes share some commonalities, such as spirituality and nature. Unlike other forms of "joining" of

---

[1] Leone Murabito, "Unione fra Instituti e Monasteri in Decadenze," *Informationes*, 2, 1985, pp. 294-301.

[2] Canon 667, 2 reads, "A stricter discipline of cloister is to be observed in monasteries ordered to the contemplative life." Canon 725 reads, "The institute can associate to itself, by some bond determined in the constitutions, other members of the Christian faithful who strive toward evangelical perfection according to the spirit of the institute and share its mission."

[3] The suggestion has already been made that such groups as public or private associations could attain juridic autonomy (for reasons of ministry or identity) but then be aggregated to the religious institute which initiated the group. This idea tends to occur when the extended members or associates identify through local groups or communities of their own, and not simply as individuals associated for purposes of prayer or a temporary ministry commitment. The whole issue of the purposes, identity and spirituality of these groups, as well as their relationship to the parent religious institute needs more time for observation and analysis. The nature and purpose of such groups varies too greatly to deal with here: subsequent serious studies of the phenomenon will need to distinguish among the various types.

institutes, the juridic process and accomplishment of aggregation is not reserved to the Apostolic See, but to the competent authority of the institute which processes the faculty of aggregating.[4]

Basically, there are two legal outcomes of aggregation:

1) the *aggregated* institute obtains the spiritual benefits and favors (such as liturgical privileges) of the *aggregating* institute.

2) the *aggregated* institute and the *aggregating* institute both retain their juridical autonomy. There *may* be some juridical effects of the aggregation: if so, they must be elaborated in the fundamental code or *constitutiones* of the *aggregated* institute.

Two legal issues associated with this topic are found in Canons 614 and 615.[5] Canon 614 speaks of monasteries of nuns "associated" *(consociata)* with institutes of men. This concept, as outlined in the canon, seems to include aggregations of second orders to first orders, but does not limit itself to that. Canon 615 speaks of autonomous monasteries not "associated" *(consociatum est)* with any other institute so that the latter enjoys "true power" over the monastery. This concept would not seem to include aggregation since canonical autonomy is maintained in aggregation. "Association" is also the term used in *Perfectae Caritatis* 22: "Let them enter into associations *(associationes)* if they are engaged in external activities of an identical or similar nature" (as opposed to a federation or union).

A specific problem which has occurred here in the U.S. is the aggregation of small independent institutes to one of the Orders. This aggregation involved various phenomena, but I would like to point out only two. In some cases, a small local community was founded to meet local needs (e.g. care of an immigrant or ethnic population, nursing, teaching) rather than with a distinct founding charism. The spirituality of the aggregating Order was, at least in some cases, imposed on the group (either by the founding/supporting priest or bishop or by canonical necessity) not arising from within the group or necessarily consonant with its apostolic aims. Thus, the study of charism in post-Vatican II times is somewhat difficult (if not impossible) for some smaller institutes. Secondly, there were cases (one exam-

---

[4]The previous Code spoke of aggregation in Canon 492, §1 and referred to "tertiaries living in common" (or third orders). Aggregation is a privilege granted to some first orders: Franciscans, Dominicans, Carmelites, Servites and Augustinians. The Benedictines are somewhat different, since individual tertiaries (usually called "oblates") are affiliated to a particular abbey/priory, not to the Order *per se*, and not by the Abbot Primate. The Apostolic See has aggregated at times (as in 1911 with the Ursulines), but most aggregation is internal to the first order. Vermeersch-Creusen (*Epitome*, I, n. 551) comments that consultation with the Holy See would be necessary only if matters already approved by Rome (e.g. constitutions) require changes. This means that a diocesan institute could be aggregated without Rome's involvement. A summary of the issue in the previous Code appears in Clement Raymond Orth, *The Approbation of Religious Institutes* (J.C.L. dissertation, Catholic University of America, 1931), pp. 121-125.

[5]Canon 614 reads, "Monasteries of nuns which are associated with an institute of men maintain their own order of life and governance according to the constitutions. Mutual rights and obligations are to be so defined that the association is spiritually enriching." Canon 615 reads, "An autonomous monastery which has no other major superior beyond its own moderator and is not associated with any other institute of religious in such a way that the superior of the latter enjoys true power over such a monastery determined by the constitutions in committed to the special vigilance of the diocesan bishop according to the norm of law."

ple being the Eucharistic Missionaries of St. Dominic) of institutes already established within an apostolic orientation who were compelled to aggregate. The effect was to change the spiritual orientation of the institute.

Federation: This term has two distinct meanings, one Benedictine and one non-Benedictine. In the Benedictine tradition, one goes back to the Council of Trent (1545-1563) for the mandate that Benedictine monasteries should form congregations. In the Benedictine sense, monastic congregations were and are sometimes referred to also as federations.[6] The concept required a joining (sometimes referred to as a "union") of autonomous monasteries under a superior. Members were religious.[7]

Within the Benedictine model, several issues arise:

1) Benedictines themselves interchange at times the terms "congregation" and "federation." Currently, the three American (Canadian and U.S.) congregations of women Benedictines all use the term "federation": The Federation of St. Gertrude, St. Benedict, and St. Scholastica.[8]

2) Among Benedictines, some make vows in context of priory/abbey, while some pronounce vows within the federation. Women Benedictines in the federations pronounce vows to the priory in which they enter.

3) In 1893, Pope Leo XIII established the office of Abbot Primate. The office, as developed by Benedictines, appears to be one of honor, but not jurisdiction.

4) In 1964, a Benedictine "confederation" *(confederatio)* was established as a "union of several federations." The confederation model itself holds no particular authority.

5) The 1983 Code uses the term "supreme moderator" for the highest internal superior of an institute. The term "institute" itself can be applied at best in an analogous fashion to a Benedictine federation. The term "supreme moderator" is totally inapplicable.[9] Each of the three federations has separate legal status as a public juridic person and its President is considered a major superior, with little or no authority over the federation members and priories.

Within the Benedictine model also, priories are either dependent or independent. The establishment of a dependent priory (also known sometimes as a filial house) is by chapter vote of an independent priory; the long-range goal is for

---

[6] For a good summary of distinctions in this area between European and American usage of the terms, cf., Daniel Ward, O.S.B., "Monastic Life and the New Code" in *Handbook on Canons 573-746,* (Collegeville, Liturgical Press, 1985) pp. 307-330.

[7] Women Benedictines in the U.S. especially have as part of their story, the history of being made to forego solemn vows [as nuns] for the sake of the apostolate, when they came to the U.S. from European monasteries. U.S. Benedictine women then took simple vows and regained their status as religious in 1900-01.

[8] Besides these three Federations, there are also Benedictine Nuns, a diocesan Benedictine congregation in Little Rock, and other Benedictine Sisters in the U.S. whose motherhouse is in Europe.

[9] There are places in the section of the Code for religious institutes where the Supreme Moderator is identified as the competent superior. (Examples include c. 647—regarding novitiate; c. 668, §4—renunciation of patrimony; c. 684, §1—permission to transfer; c. 686, §3—granting exclaustration or requesting imposed exclaustration; 6. 690, §—re-admission; c. 691—departure; c. 694-700—dismissal).

the dependent house to become an independent priory itself.[10] How this occurs depends on the statutes of the federation to which the priory belongs. In reverse, the closing or suppression of a filial house also is dependent upon the chapter vote of its independent sponsoring priory. Depending on length of time, human investment of resources, and the decision-making process itself, such a closure may or may not be traumatic.

The question of suppression of an independent Benedictine priory is more complicated. The custom of visitation [regularly scheduled evaluations by an outside team] provides one mechanism for bringing the topic to conscious discussion. An extraordinary visitation specifically for this purpose is another possible method. The suppression itself could be done according to the statutes of the Federation, after a chpater vote of the priory itself. Should the suppression be agreed upon, several options arise. Some members of the priory to be suppressed may choose to seek an indult to leave religious life. Others may choose to seek transfer to another priory, either of the same federation or to a priory of another federation [The option to transfer to another institute of consecrated life also exists. Within the context of religious who entered when there was not much difference between monastic communities and apostolic communities, it is entirely possible that some members would choose to reject the return to monastic practices in favor of an apostolic institute.].

Yet another option is to seek to maintain a filial house, dependent upon another priory. The attraction of this concept is that it allows members to remain in a particular geographic area where there may be longstanding ministerial commitments or family ties. The concern would be the need for members who are in ill-health or among the frail elderly (not necessarily all retired or all above a certain age) the criterion being inability to care for one's own well-being, to understand and agree to return to the independent priory for care (in other words, to prevent duplication of health-care facilities and expenses).[11]

It is clear to me that an independent priory who chooses *not* to seek suppression despite strong evidences in support of suppression remains independent. Legally, the statutes could provide for federation suppression anyway, with possible appeal to the CRIS if necessary. The CRIS could also act to suppress the priory, usually after a request by the diocesan bishop, an apostolic visitation, and lack of alternatives. Questions then arise about at what point the priory may be forbidden to accept novices or new members, who has authority to make such a decision, and what support (financial, personnel-wise, and human services) can be given by its Federation.

The second and non-Benedictine use of the term "federation" occurs in two ways: federations of nuns and other federations of independent apostolic institutes

---

[10] One unusual exception to this process in the Priory of St. Scholastica, Chicago, Illinois. This priory has had a dependent house in Colorado Springs, Colorado, for almost 100 years.

[11] In some cases, members already in outside nursing homes could probably remain, especially if there are several at the same facility or if they are no longer legally or morally capable of making such decisions.

with a common heritage.

On November 21, 1950, Pope Pius XII issued an Apostolic Constitution, *Sponsa Christi* (implemented by the *Inter cetera,* 23 November 1950, Sacred Congregation for Religious and Secular Institutes).[12] In the papal document, autonomous monasteries are encouraged to form federations in order to avoid "harmful effects which more seriously and likely befall individual monasteries" and in order to foster spiritual and temporal interests. These federations were to have four purposes:

1) "legally recognized and canonically sanctioned" mutual assistance;
2) a common novitiate (to overcome lack of trained personnel);
3) interchange of specifically trained members, especially for governance and formation;
4) transfer possibilities for health, moral or other reasons.

In 1974, a fifth purpose was added: to exchange books and media.[13]

The federations formed are of pontifical right, made up of separate juridic persons, based on a geographical or "regional" factor, and non-interfering in the internal autonomy of the member monasteries. In the U.S., such federations were formed. In North America, Visitation Nuns chose to form two federations: the first federation for strictly contemplative monasteries and the second federation for monasteries with schools attached. The federations, while respecting the internal autonomy of monasteries, worked on "core documents" for all.

"Core documents" have also been written as a unifying factor in federations of apostolic institutes. These federations are an outgrowth of *Perfectae Caritatis* which expanded federations beyond *Sponsa Christi* for nuns. Usually, these federations do *not* have separate juridic status; they are voluntary in membership, with no authority other than joint agreement and moral suasion. Again, these federations of apostolic institutes are usually based on common heritage and some historical connection in founding. In some cases, as in the Mercy tradition, the federation serves as a common ground for the Union and the smaller, independent Mercy institutes.

Amalgamation: This concept can involve simultaneous suppression of some juridic person(s) and erection of a new juridic person, or simply the erection of a new juridic person involving several other (previously established) juridic persons. Let me demonstrate some amalgamations:

1) The Sisters of the Presentation (P.B.V.M.) in San Francisco were, at one time, several autonomous houses. They were "amalgamated" into one institute.

2) In Great Britain, there were two amalgalmations of independent Mercy Houses into one institue: Westminster (1922) and Birmingham (1932). Westminster was originally of diocesan right, but became pontifical in 1925. Bir-

---

[12]See *AAS,* v. XVIII, pp. 5-24 for *Sponso Christi* and *AAS,* v. XVIII, pp. 37-44 for the Instruction.

[13]In a private reply, published in 1974, the Sacred Congregation for Religious and Secular Institutes drew up a model for drawing up statutes for federations of nuns. Cf. *Canon Law Digest,* vol. 8, pp. 391-406.

mingham was pontifical from its beginning. [In 1976, these groups formed a union (with movement toward a new institute). In 1983, the Federation (union and independent groups) moved toward a new Institute.][14]

3) On December 15, 1981, the Mercy Sisters of the Union and the other independent Mercy congregations, all of whom formed the Mercy Federation, became a new institute, The Institute of Sisters of Mercy of Australia (I.S.M.A.). ISMA is of pontifical right and all 17 member congregations remain pontifical also. ISMA has a national president who is a major superior [with no particular powers], an executive council [for administrative pusposes] and a plenary council.[15] In contrast, the Presentation Sisters of Australia have recently "merged" (six congregations into one but retaining juridical autonomy) but the President was not allowed to be a major superior.

4) The Mercy Federation (also composed of a union and independent congregations) in the U.S. is moving toward an amalgamation also - ISMA (Institute of Sisters of Mercy of the Americas). The Federation, through its projects, Mercy Futures and Core Constitutions, already has CRIS approval of its constitutions and of the process for decision-making within each institute. ISMA is projected for 1988 or 1989.

"Amalgamation" is the term used in the English translation of *Perfectae Caritatis,* 21, to speak of an institute or monastery with little hope of further development and its being "amalgamated" to another institute with similar aims and spirit. The sense of amalgamation here is that used with another term, "fusion" (cf. below). In the Latin official text, it simply says that such institutes or monasteries should be *"uniatur."*

Merger: The term itself is not one used in canonical documents or Roman curial praxis. Actually, "merger" describes one of several phenomena: fusion or union, with both terms at times also used for the result of an amalgamation process.

At times, the term "fusion" is used. When used, it refers to the suppression of an institute or monastery as a separate juridic person and its absorption into another institute or monastery. "Union" is used to refer to the joining of two or more institutes (and their suppression as separate juridic persons) in order to form a new institute. A caution is that terminology is not always used consistently.[16]

---

[14]A succinct history can be found in *Sisters of Mercy of Great Britain,* ed. Sr. Imelda King, 1977, published by the Sisters of Mercy of Great Britain.

[15]Much of the Australian documentation is available directly from ISMA, Buffalo Road, Ryde, NSW 2112, or from the Mercy Federation Futures Project in the U.S.

[16]Sr. Cathleen Toomey prepared a paper for LCWR entitled, "A Choice for Life." The paper describes the "fusion/merger" of the Sisters of Mercy of Worcester, Massachusetts with the Sisters of Mercy of the U.S. Union. In her paper, Sr. Toomey remarks, "Fusion and merger are words used interchangeably. Technically, however, the union of the two congregations whose founder is the same is a fusion." "Fusion" is the term used in the decree (prot. no. V. 131-1/85) allowing the merger (the term "merge" is also used in the decree) of these two congregations. The term does not always mean that and "founder" may refer to basic spirituality rather than the actual historical founder (e.g. Mercys acknowledge Catherine McAuley as their "foundress" even though she did not actually found each house).

With regard to the phenomenon of merger, there are several resources currently or soon to be available:

1) Sr. Melanie Bair, O.S.F., is doing her doctoral dissertation in canon law on this topic at St. Paul's, Ottawa.

2) The April 1987 bulletin on Issues of Religious Law (vol. 3, #1) is devoted to this topic. The article, written by Sr. Melanie Bair and Rev. Jordan Hite, T.O.R. is an excellent summary.

In addition, the 1987 national assembly of LCWR addressed discussion to a test case on this issue.[17] Interestingly enough, Elizabeth Kolmer's work, *Religious Women in the U.S.: A Survey of Influential Literature 1950-1983* does not even list the issue as a topic!

The documents, or at least some of them, for several mergers are available as resources for canonists working on the topic.[18] For purposes of this paper, I received information on the following:

1) Merger of Sisters of St. Francis of Rice Lake, Wisconsin with Sisters of St. Joseph, Third Order of St. Francis. Merger occurred in 1967 and involved diocesan and pontifical congregations (diocesan merged into pontifical).[19]

2) Merger of Sisters of St. Joseph of Fall River, Massachusetts with Sisters of St. Joseph of Springfield, Massachusetts. Merger occurred in 1974 and involved two diocesan congregations. (One community merged into the other.)[20]

---

[17]The test case, graciously supplied to me by Sr. Janet Roesner, Executive Director of LCWR, was as follows:

CASE STUDY 2

The Sisters of St. Dymphna are a congregation of 100 women whose median age is 60. In the past ten years, they have had one new member. The congregation was founded 50 years ago to care for the orphans in an eastern U.S. diocese. Their works are very diverse. The motherhouse is a large building in the central city, and most of the members live there. The community did not choose to join Social Security and it has only savings of $900,000 at the present time. During the summer the congregation held its annual assembly of the membership. The agenda focused on some difficult questions:
—whether to allow for more diverse living situations
—how to provide for the increasing numbers of ill, elderly members
—how to deal with the deficit in the budget which has been encountered for the first time this year.
During the assembly a member (in her 40's) rose to suggest that the community actively pursue the question of a merger with another community.

****

1. Put yourself in the place of leadership of this congregation faced with the question on the floor of the assembly and afterwards.
—what is your initial reaction?
—what are some of the questions that you will have to deal with from yourself and others?
—what aspects of the situation of this congregation point to the advisability of a merger?
2. If you were called by the leaders of this community for advice on this question, what would you say to them?
3. If you were contacted about receiving this congregation into your own community, what would be your response?

[18]A Complete listing of mergers (world-wide) in the 1960's appears in *Vida Religiosa* 25 (1968), pp. 277-278. There were 14 in 1965, 13 in 1966 and 15 in 1967.

[19]Decree published in *Canonical Documentation on Consecrated Life*, St. Paul's University, 1977, pp. 121-122.

[20]Documents available through Sisters of St. Joseph, Springfield, Massachusetts.

3) Various Mercy mergers mentioned above.

4) Merger of Sisters of St. Francis, Maryville, Missouri and Sisters of St. Mary, St. Louis. Merger occurred in 1983 and involved two pontifical congregations. (One community merged into the other. The decree mentions their being "united again.")[21]

5) Merger of Sisters of St. Joseph, Superior, Wisconsin with Sisters of St. Joseph of Carondelet. Merger occurred in 1986 and involved a diocesan congregation merging into a pontifical.[22]

Several other instances are currently in process. Among these are the pontential merger of the Franciscan Sisters of the Immaculate Conception of the Order of St. Francis (diocesan) with the Sisters of the Third Order of St. Francis (pontifical) and the potential merger of Holy Family Convent (Benedictine) with Mt. St. Benedict Monastery, Erie, Pennsylvania.

Questions I Asked:

A. *How the idea got started and when.* I found that the idea usually started within the community itself, and usually with someone in administration.[23] The person(s) who first raised the idea were not always appreciated for the action. In one case, the idea was first proposed seriously twenty-five years before it was acted upon. Also, those in administration are likely to see the merits of the idea and be less threatened than the membership at large. Leaders are more used to contacts with their counterparts in other institutes, have more contact with the other institute, and are quicker to see an end of duplication of meetings, personnel, and projects, as well as unnecessary expenses. Bringing community awareness and agreement took more time and process.

B. *Status of those involved.* I asked about sizes of the congregations, ages of members and whether each congregation was diocesan or pontifical. In general, I found that none of these was considered essential, although, in hindsight perhaps some should have been. Relative size was often among the data collected, but perhaps without attention to the implications [e.g. loss of voting power for superiors or chapters, identity.]

C. *Were there meetings and what process was used.* In all cases, it was clear thar there had been many meetings over a long period. The meetings included input, discussion and prayerful reflection for all members. Outside experts and

---

[21] Material available directly from Sisters of St. Mary. Also, material can be found in *CLSA Roman Replies*, 1986, pp. 49-52 and "An Experience of Reunion: One Divided-Becomes One," by Mary Teresa Noth, SSM, *Review for Religious* 46 (1987), pp. 383-406.

[22] Documents available through Sisters of St. Joseph of Carondelet, Generalate. A Summary appears in *CLSA Roman Replies*, 1986, pp. 46-48.

[23] In contrast to this, I have found that processes leading to suppression alone, tend to be initiated externally, i.e. from a priest, a canonical visitator, a Vicar for Religious; ecclesiastical authority.

facilitators were used in most cases. Joint meetings, retreats and social get-togethers were also part of the plan.

D. *What decision-making process was involved.* These processes varied, but included the meetings described above, referendum of all members and chapter votes: 75-80% majorities were considered as minimum necessary; in these cases, the agreement was much higher. A summary of Roman requirements appears in CLSA *Roman Replies* (1986), pp. 46-47. Basically, the procedural requirements for the merging are adequate preparation and, toward the time of decision: a secret formal vote of all members, written opinion and approval of the diocesan bishop, at least a preliminary agreement on disposition of temporalities, a declaration of acceptance for the receiving institute, a list of Sisters (dates of birth and profession), a brief history of the process and the reasons for the request.

E. *Was Rome involved prior to the final approval.* In all cases, the answer was affirmative, although how Rome was involved varied. In some cases, there was informational exchange, in other cases processes were suggested or approved. Decisions or processes (what percentage vote for change is required, how/who to consult, how to insure members are aware of their options and are voting freely) and constitutional documents are most prominent.

F. *Involvement of local bishops.* In all cases, the diocesan bishop was involved, obviously much more so when at least one of the congregations was diocesan. In all cases, the opinion and support of the local bishop was/is seen as important. In almost all cases, the local community made first contact with the bishop and involved him/them in the processes.

G. *Distribution of assets and liabilities.* This was usually not a major issue but was handled competently, with assistance of both canon and civil lawyers.

H. *What alternatives were present as options.* This answer was uniform. Sisters were told that they had these options (merger having been approved): to join the new/other institute, to transfer to another institute of consecrated life or society of apostolic life, or to seek an indult of secularization.

I. *What human processes were used* — prior to the decision, subsequent to the decision and subsequent to merger. Again the answers varied greatly. This leads to the final section of my paper.

Processes and Issues to Consider:

Bair and Hite summarize issues to be considered in their article. Specifically, they mention charism, lifestyle, ministries, culture, geography, spirituality, governance, size, psychological effects, civil law structures and finances.[24] I would like to comment on some of these and some other issues of which I am aware.

---

[24]*Op. cit.*, p. 3.

A. *Consultants:*

One important and basic concern is for the experts or facilitators with whom and on whom the community in transition (or considering transition) relies. These outside consultants must be competent professionally, humanly sensitive and scrupulously concerned with avoiding manipulation of decisions by taking advantage of their trusted status. Outside consultants bring assistance, not solutions.

B. *The human process:*

Human processes in transition are primary. *Ecclesiae Sanctae,* II, 39, states, "A union of any sort between different Institutes presupposes adequate spiritual, psychological and juridic preparation." To this I would add adequate physical preparation, in a process which involves member-intensive collaboration and sharing in an adequate way. Massive doses of information in short time spans are not a guarantee of a highly informative process. Presentations, chances for interchange and input, time for assimilation and repetition, if necessary, are all important to ensure that information is shared in a qualitative manner and not just quantitatively.

The human process also needs to take into account the need for time, stages of grieving and dying, and respect for the fears and history (both individual and corporate) of the merging community. Another factor of the human process, and a very important factor, is the mingling of different cultural backgrounds and expectations.

The human process can begin with an intervention, if needs be, from outside the community. The intervention can be due to financial status (NATRI is an excellent resource for evaluation teams in this area) or to concerns about the quality of life.

C. *Some fears and concerns:*

One of the greatest fears which emerges is the fear of the unknown—how ministry and lifestyle will change and where retirement will take place. A second fear is a loss of identity, a fear of being "taken over" or "swallowed up." The Sisters of St. Joseph (Superior) rejected the notion of expecting representation, at least on the council of the new institute; the decree reunifying the Sisters of St. Francis of Maryville and the Sisters of Mary specified that the superior general of the former institute was to function as a General Counsellor until the next General Chapter to be celebrated within two years. Loss of identity ties in directly with the question of relative sizes of the two groups and also with any corporate ministries of either group.

Allied with this loss of identity is the real fact known to sociologists as "cognitive dissonance," an inability to reach certain conclusions because of pre-selected "filters" for what one wants to hear. My experience is that denial and cognitive dissonance should never be underestimated as one works with a community in transition. One example may suffice. A particular community decided to enter a process to evaluate itself and its preferred future. Numerous consultants, studies, and meetings followed over a several year period. Ecclesiastical authorities and friends of the small community fervently hoped the sisters could see "the handwriting on the wall." Instead, despite all the facts and studies, the sisters chose, as a preferred future "revitalization" to use the terms developed by Raymond Hostie and later the study of Fitz *et al.*[25] No amount of intellectual input or discussion was sufficient in itself to help them deal with their future realistically.

In some cases, denial/cognitive dissonance can be handled appropriately as one reviews areas of finances [operating budgets, restricted funds, actuarial projections for retirement, income], ministry responsibilities, available personnel, and an assessment of community-owned facilities. An estimate and evaluation of the facilities may show the need for major overhaul within the next few years (a result of deferred repairs, lack of funds, or simply wearing out) or that the operation of the facility is neither cost-efficient nor safe for the persons living there.

Another concern is the guilt or sense of failure experienced by members of a community contemplating transition. There is a real sense of having let down the people they serve, the church (especially the local church), and the sisters who have gone before them. In a real sense, there is a sense of failure because, despite hard work and much prayer, they cannot continue and succeed in adversity as the oral and written traditions of their community say of earlier generations of sisters. Guilt also becomes a factor as the group begins to discern whether or not they will stay together. Hope that the group will stay together on the part of the majority becomes a burden of guilt for those who choose to transfer or seek dispensation.

Two other concerns which surface are geographical and health-related. The community may have strong geographic ties to an area, either for family ties or ministry. Alleviating the concern (if possible) by allowing those who can to stay in the area is one possibility. On the other hand, lack of strong geographical ties may make transition easier. Knowing the relationship between the sisters and the area in terms of family ties or ministry is a factor of the human process, as is knowing the health of the sisters. Health problems related to stress and overwork can be an issue in both the decision and timing of the transition.

Finally, the human process requires both grieving and bonding. Searching for another community with which to unite means looking for real and potential areas of bonding. Family ties, geography, shared ministries, shared educational training and personalities, as well as similar charism and lifestyle, all need to be ex-

---

[25]Raymond Hostie, S.J. *Vie and Mort des Ordres Religieux.* Paris: Desclee de Brouwer, 1972. and Lawrence Cada, Raymond Fitz, Gertrude Foley, Thomas Gardino and Carol Lichtenberg, *Shaping the Coming Age of Religious Life.* New York: Seaburg Press, 1979.

plored for what they can contribute to easing transition and bonding members. Past hurts or stereotypes may need to be dealt with and reconciled. The involvement of the local bishop as an informed, trusted and compassionate part of the whole process brings the dimension of larger ecclesial concern and caring.

There are a number of things which the receiving community could do to ease the transition. Simply replying in a gracious thank-you for the privilege of being considered a possibility for merger could assist a great deal. Considerations for ministry and living accomodations and a respect for, and incorporation of, the heritage of the merging community are other factors. Finally, the telling of the stories, both past and present, and the opportunity to share these can be an excellent beginning.

D. *Criteria to use in the discussion:*

According to *Ecclesiae Sanctae,* II, 40, a number of factors must be considered, the first being the good of the church. Secondly, the character of the institute is a consideration. If a community is an apostolic institute and, in all honesty can no longer function as such, the orientation and purpose of the institute is no longer being served. The group may be living a conventual or even contemplative lifestyle, but they are not the institute as intended. This is not a criticism of the members, but an acknowledgement of what has occurred and something to be considered in a decision. *Ecclesiae Sanctae* is also concerned about the members' informed freedom of choice about options and by a secret formal vote at the time of decision.

In its next article, 41, *Ecclesiae Sanctae* gives three further considerations: the number of members remains small, no candidates come to enter and the age of members continues to rise. The papal document was promulgated in 1966. Sixteen years later, Sister Marie Augusta Neal published her survey of sisters and her survey indicated that the three most pressing concerns of sisters were the rising age of members, fewer members and finances.[26] According to LCWR, several years ago 25% of women religious in the U.S. had 32 members or less. While I believe some caution is in order (e.g. some communities have historically always been small and have remained constant) with regard to looking at numbers alone, I believe that only "cognitive dissonance" could not see the need to address the issues of this paper in today's context.

One final concern for this section is my concern for "pregnant" communities, communities which, while aging and losing membership in the U.S. are, at the same time, giving birth to institutes of the future, not yet ready for independence but definitely alive and growing. Any move toward merger of any kind must, in my opinion, be mindful of its effect on these fledgling groups.

---

[26]Marie Augusta Neal, SND de Namur, *Catholic Sisters in Transition: From the 1960's to the 1980's.* Wilmington: Michael Glazier, 1984.

E. *Civil law structures and temporal goods:*

In the course of a transition, the congregation which is losing or significantly changing its juridic status (e.g. being suppressed or moving from independence to provincial/regional status) may need to retain its civil corporate structures for awhile in order to complete civil transactions. If these civil corporations are retained beyond the merger completion, the merger itself should contain, in my opinion, an agreement on the time by which these corporations are to be dissolved.

With regard to the assets of the juridic person, I would like to make four comments:

1) Canon law (c. 1283, §2) requires an accurate and up-to-date inventory of these assets, along with appropriate legal documents.

2) At the time of the suppression of the juridic person, canons 123 and 584 are applicable. The Apostolic See, according to c. 584, is to determine what is done with the temporal goods of the institute. Canon 123 indicates due regard for the will of the founders or donors and for acquired rights. U.S. law regarding the dissolution of a 501c3 coporation (the category under which many institutes come) is fairly specific about what happens to the temporal goods of the coporation at the time of dissolution. Fulfilling the requirements of both laws could come into conflict. In the decrees of suppression of two Visitation Monasteries in the Archdiocese of Baltimore, the decrees of suppression came "with the understanding that their net assets would become the property of a successor corporation for the sake of preserving these assets for the Order as such, ensuring that they remain ecclesiastical and also provide for any nuns not accepted by another monastery. After the debts were paid and the nuns re-located, the new corporation . . . absorbed the two prior corporations that represented in civil law" the two monasteries.[27]

3) It appears clear that the distribution of the goods of the institute is provided for canonically. I do not see any way canonically that members could believe that the assets would be distributed among the remaining members. Yet I have frequently been asked if this were true. In one case, some members were happy to think a few members would be transferring to another institute (apart from where the bulk of the group was considering). These members thought the assets of the institute would be divided among the fewer people, thus enriching themselves!

The question does remain, though, about what would happen if the civil law corporation (which would not automatically end when the juridic person is suppressed) dissolved and distributed its assets to the corporation members. This would be difficult for a 501c3 corporation, but other civilly legal corporations of the institute might be eligible. Thomas Doyle discusses this in an article and he concludes that it is probably "that the civil law courts would enforce the claim of church authorities" in the matter.[28] The matter has not been tested yet in the courts, to my knowledge.

---

[27] Information graciously supplied by Monsignor Porter J. White, J.C.D., Pro-Chancellor, in a letter to me.
[28] Thomas Doyle, O.P. "The Status of Religious Institutes," *Monitor Ecclesiastias* vol. CX (1985), p. 236.

4) The institute may also have some restricted funds, funds which have been restricted both canonically and civilly by endowment, wills, intentions of donors, or even the institute itself (as in an irrevocable trust or pension/retirement plan). Canon 1310 §2 provides that the "Ordinary can diminish them equitably." The involvement of the Ordinary prior to suppression or when suppression is not occurring may resolve the distribution of some of these assets, although the procedures and requirements of civil law remain.

Conclusion:

Some concluding thoughts, my areas of hope for the future, are in order here. According to *Pro Mundi Vita,* there are as many new groups being born as there are groups dying and new forms (not just new institutes) of religious life are emerging.[29] That new groups/forms are emerging is, in my opinion, evidence of one more paradigm shift, in T.S. Kuhn's words, in religious life. Jean Leclerq describes it this way and I believe his comments about monasticism are applicable to our religious life:

> If spontaneity disappears, if everything is minutely spelled out in writing, is catered for and controlled in a more or less bureaucratic way, monastic institutions may survive . . . but no longer the spirit of monasticism. Monasticism will then inevitably reappear outside the institutions: ascetics, God-seekers living as individuals or small groups, who have rescued their freedom vis-a-vis the corpus of legislation. When personal vocation is sacrificed to this institution, to the order, to the uniformity imposed by a detailed system of laws, then such a system is nothing more than a surrogate of a genuine inspiration.[30]

J.M. Tillard, O.P. also addresses the phenomenon of endings and beginnings in the context of the cross and Easter: new life through death. He speaks of this "dynamic of growth" and says that "it may well come to the point where it severs the umbilical cords through which links are still maintained with the original congregations" in order to birth new and smaller groups. In short, the current reduction of some communities and mergers in this country (and in some other parts of the world) stands in contrast to the growth surge in communities in other parts of the world, but in consistency with the mystery of God's spirit. In our particular society, an additional hope is that those religious who are in transition as a community will offer their counter-cultural witness to a society that does not value aging, limitation, loss of independence or death.

---

[29]Pro Mundi Vita, "New Beginnings: Religious Life Evolves," Bulletin 92 (Speing, 1983). This article discusses the evolution of religious life, shifts in thinking about some of the essential values of religious life, and 32 "experiments" in new forms in Europe.

[30]Leclerq is quoted in an article by van Bovel, *The Future of Religious Life* Concilium, p. 64.

CANONICAL AND CIVIL LIABILITY FOR LAY MINISTERS

MELANIE DIPIETRO, S.C.

I. INTRODUCTION

There is no doubt that the topic of "Canonical and Civil Liability for Lay Ministry" is one of current and pragmatic interest. There are currently more than 2,000 cases pending nationwide involving houses of worship, clergy and religious groups and ministers.[1] A survey conducted in 1981 indicated that 18% of all members of the clergy were threatened or actually sued in connection with ministry.[2]

The most serious of these cases involves allegations of child abuse, paternity and embezzlement, but an increasing number of them are charging clergy with inadequate teaching or improper counseling. In an 18 month period more than $1,000,000 had been awarded to those groups that were suing clergy and religious groups.[3] This fact not only has pastoral significance for the Church, but obviously, economic interest. The institutional question has been stated as "not whether it is desirable or worthwhile for the faithful to use civil courts to resolve Church disputes, but rather—how can Churches protect their resources, their autonomy and their mission in the face of increasing judicial scrutiny."[4] I will suggest in this paper that if we focus on ministry from our own theological and canonical values, we will protect, as much as possible, our autonomy and our resources.

To begin a legal discussion, we must necessarily define terms. The practical orientation of this seminar necessitates a selection of some pragmatic parameters for the terms "canonical and civil liability" and lay "ministry." In an effort to be practical, I shall narrow our discussion to the area of tort liability. Within that general area, I will address three causes of action that represent the types of lawsuits the Church is most likely to experience: Intentional Torts, Ordinary Negligence and, possibly, Ministerial Malpractice.

Within these areas, I shall consider the liability of the individual person and the potential vicarious liability for the Church.

In this context, the Church means the Bishop, the Diocese or the parish. Corporations, not themselves constituted as a public juridic person, governed by a board of directors, lay and religious or all lay, will be considered separately. From these general considerations, I will present the following statements for

---

[1] "Suing the Clergy," N.Y. Times, Sept. 7, 1986, §3 at 1, col. 1.
[2] Burek, "Clergy Malpractice: Making Clergy Accountable to a Lower Power," 14 Pepperdine Law Rev. 1:154 (1986).
[3] N.Y. Times, §3 at 1, col. 1.
[4] William W. Bassett, "Christian Rights in Civil Litigation: Translating Religion Into Justiciable Categories," THE JURIST 46 (1986): 230.

your consideration:
1. The question posed as civil and canonical liability for lay ministers is, I believe, stated inappropriately. Rather, the question should be stated in terms of responsibility for ministry, not liability.
2. If viewed as responsibility for ministry rather than liability, our action will be ministry because the originating values are theological and governed by Church standards. If the question is framed this way, some canonical norms may be relevant. I shall suggest that attentiveness to these canons promotes our integrity as Church, and to the degree that is reasonably possible, will reduce the civil law liability exposure in the tort areas that I shall discuss.

I will conclude this presentation with some practical suggestions for daily operations.

LIABILITY IN GENERAL

Civil Law

The area of private law that imposes liability on one person for injuries that he or she may allow to happen to another person, either directly or vicariously, is called tort law. Tort law is defined as a private or civil wrong or injury that is independent of a contract.

There are three divisions of Tort law. Intentional torts involve the actor's desire to bring about the act and its consequences which invade a person's interest which the law will not sanction.[5] Tort liability sounding in ordinary negligence involves several elements. First, the existence of a legal duty to conform to a certain standard of conduct which the defendant, in this case, the Church, owes to the plaintiff. The second element is a breach of that duty measured according to legally recognized standards. The third element is legal causation; the breach of duty must proximately cause the injury. Finally, the injury is legally recognized and compensable in money damages.[6] Malpractice is similar to ordinary negligence except that the duty and standard of care are measured by a specific professional standard.[7]

Canon Law

Obviously, when one attempts to define canonical liability, one does not get such an explicit paradigm on the face of the code. However, the principle that

---

[5]W. Prosser, *Law of Torts*, §8 (4th ed. 1971).
[6]Ibid, §30.
[7]Speiser, Krause, and Gans, *The American Law of Torts* §15:1 (Lawyers Co-op, 1987), p. 321.

parties should be compensated for injury is really based in natural justice. The Code does contain a concept of liability for negligent actions. Canonical negligence is analogous to the concept of negligence found in tort law but not to its application.

The Code in C.128[8] recognizes that a perpetrator of an injustice or a harm, through the exercise of authority, or otherwise, should be liable for remedying injury. The concept of *culpa* in private wrongs approximates the common law concept of negligence, which embodies the notion of liability for the foreseeable harm resulting from one's inappropriate actions. In the Roman quasi-delicta sphere, distinct from contract, negligent fault lies between dolus, evil intent or fraud, and accident. However, canon law and practice do not support a developed substantive or procedural law for remedying injury from breach of duty, distinct from a breach of contract or the negligent exercise of authority.

Canonical tradition, following Roman civil law, recognized compensation of damage, but this was not codified until C.128 in the 1983 Code. In C.128, one who posits a "juridic act" or "any other act" may be liable for negligently inflicted injury. This canon, however, does not seem to be authority for remedying injury or unintended damages arising from the "breach of duty" that our common law has developed[9] in its system of tort law. While C.128 suggests liability for negligent harm and C.221[10] suggests a remedy for the violation of a right, the substantive law centers on injury resulting from a commission of a crime or the negligent exercise of authority. Even if one could argue that these canons invite the potential development of a substantive law similar to tort law, some practical procedural issues would remain in pursuing a remedy.

Procedurally, most Code remedies are administrative[11] and judicial remedies are limited to prosecuting or vindicating rights or imposing penalties.[12] Civil trials in ecclesial courts concern more the clearing of title, possessory rights or restitution for or rescission of acts[13] than they do in distributing the risk for social interaction between private parties. Finally, the fact is that in contentious actions, the Church does not possess a direct judicial means of enforcing judgments.[14] Even if it had a substantive law, a credible fact finding process and the power

---

[8]Translation of this canon and subsequent citations are taken from the 1983 *Code of Canon Law, Latin-English Edition*, (Washington: CLSA, 1983). 1983 Code of Canon Law, C.128: "Anyone who unlawfully inflicts damage upon someone by a juridic act, or in deed by any other act placed with malice or culpability, is obliged to compensate for the damage inflicted."

[9]Richard A. Hill, S.J. in *The Code of Canon Law: A Text and Commentary*, ed. James A. Coriden, et al. (New York/Mahwah: Paulist, 1985), p. 92.

[10]1983 Code of Canon Law C.221: "The Christian faithful can legitimately vindicate and defend the rights which they enjoy in the Church before a competent ecclesiastical court in accord with the norm of law."

[11]Rev. Matthew Ramstein, O.F.M., *A Manual of Canon Law*, (Hoboken, New Jersey: Terminal Printing and Publishing Co., 1947) p. 575.

[12]Ibid., p. 579.

[13]Ibid. p. 576; Rev. Stanislaus Woywod, O.F.M., L.L.B., *A Practical Commentary on the Code of Canon Law*, (Rev. Callistus Smith, O.F.M., J.C.L., (New York: Joseph F. Wagner, Inc., 1948) II: 239, 268.

[14]Fernando Della Rocca, *Manual of Canon Law*, (Milwaukee: Bruce Publishing Co., 1959) p. 333.

to enforce judgments, one amusing practical problem remains. At what premium rate and what insurance company would indemnify the defendant for its self imposed judgments!

At first glance, it would appear that canonical liability is not relevant in the area of tort liability. I hope to show in this presentation that it may be relevent if the question is restated.

II. PRINCIPLES OF TORT LIABILITY

Intentional Torts

Intentional torts are those acts in which, at the time of commission, the actor desires to effect the consequence of the act. If one pulls the trigger of a gun, he/she intends to fire it and if he/she is aiming at an object, he intends to hit it.[15] Some examples of intentional torts affecting persons are assault and battery, defamation of character, false imprisonment, invasion of privacy, fraud, infliction of emotional distress, alienation of affection of spouse or child, interference with advantageous economic relations, or contracts, and kidnapping. All of these have been a cause of action against persons acting in a religious context.[16] However, most of the cases involving religious persons acting in a religious context in the area of intentional tort have involved the alienation of affection between spouses; the false imprisonment of persons, for example, in order to brainwash or to deprogram them; and the intentional infliction of emotional distress. The First Amendment defense of free exercise of religion is inevitably set forth by the Church defendants in these cases. The judicial response distinguishes between the absolute protection given to religious belief and the qualified protection given to religious action.[17] Whether or not the plaintiff was successful in these actions turned on the facts and the relevant state requisites for stating a claim, but the First Amendment has not been a successful defense. There is no question that a minister or a person acting in a religious context is liable for intentional torts occurring as an incident of the minister—communicant encounter in a religious context.

Ordinary Negligence

There is also no question that legal remedies exist for injuries resulting from ordinary negligence that occurs in the context of a minister-communicant relation-

---

[15]Restatement Second of Torts, *88A (1965).
[16]See discussion in Klee, "Clergy Malpractice: Bad News for the Good Samaritan or a Blessing in Disguise?", 17 Toledo Law Rev. pp. 209, 212, n. 23, (1985); Funston, "Made Out of Whole Cloth? A Constitutional Analysis of the Clergy Malpractice Concept," 19 Cal. W.L. Rev. 507, 512, n. 31 (1983); See also *Hester v. Barnett,* 723 *S.W.* 2d 544 *(Mo. App. 1987) n. 3 p.* 552.
[17]*Cantwell v. State of Connecticut,* 310 U.S. 296 (1940),

ship or religious activities. The motive or the good intent of the actor does not relieve the actor of the liability for the foreseeable consequences of one's actions.[18]

In a case sounding in ordinary negligence, the focus is on the duty of the actor. Breaching one's duty may result from omitting to act; failing to act, as well as from performing specific acts below a reasonable standard of care. The standard of care by which one's conduct is judged comes from several sources; statutes, past judicial decisions or instant judicial decisions, and the common law standards of the "reasonable person."

Note that the standard of care in ordinary negligence is determined by what the "reasonable person" in similar circumstances would know or do. Minimally, this means that one has the ordinary intelligence and training for carrying out the activities he or she undertakes; that one has ordinary knowledge of relevant statutes and circumstances relevant to the activity; and that one has the capacity to make reasonable judgments[19] concerning the foreseeable risks of harm inherent in the activity.

The legal duties that individuals owe to others are linked to public policy decisions concerning who and what interests get protected in the balancing of the risks inherent in commercial or social transactions. While it is the norm to speak of the "reasonable person" standard, it is interesting to note the Court's discussion in a recent case involving the duty of a church toward children taken on a summer camp trip. The court indicated that the church's duty must be measured according to "the ordinary care for protection of a child." That care is measured in accord with the child's ability to care for himself or herself.[20] It is interesting to note the court's perception of the duty of care owed by churches, especially toward a protected class, children. In a footnote in this case,[21] the court indicated that there is some authority for the proposition that a higher duty of care might exist where organizations receive a benefit from the relationship or is in a position of moral authority over the child. I think is is important for us in our discussion to note this criteria for duty. Earlier in this presentation, I indicated that ordinary negligence is measured by the "reasonable person" standard. If one studies this comment, the reasonableness standard has been used. However, I believe the court is suggesting that a determination of reasonableness may be influenced by the actor's identity and moral power as well as the status of the injured person. What I am suggesting is, that in the areas of intentional tort and in the areas of ordinary negligence, religious actors, whether we call them clerics or lay ministers, may have a differently perceived duty than non-religious persons. This perception is, I suggest, internal and subjective to the fact finder and not a quantifiable or explicitly stated legal standard.

---

[18]*Malloy v. Fong*, 37 Cal. 2d 356, 232 P. 2d. 241 (1951).
[19]Restatement Second of Torts, §§284-285, 289-290 (1965).
[20]*Cutler v. St. John's United Methodist Church of Edwardsville, Ill.*, 489 So. 2d. 123, 125 (Fla. App. 1 Dist. 1986).
[21]Ibid., n. 3, p. 125.

Malpractice

In addition to the general area of liability called ordinary negligence there is a separate cause of action also based on negligence concepts but distinguished as malpractice. Sometimes the word 'professional' negligence and the word 'malpractice' are used interchangeably. The differentiating characteristic between ordinary negligence and malpractice is that the undertaking usually involves a profession or a calling, a trade or business.

The defendant has a special form of competence that creates a different standard of care from that of the "reasonable person." In malpractice, the standard of care is defined by the profession of the defendant which identifies the degree of skill and learning ordinarily used under the same or similar circumstances by members of a specific profession.[22] It means by very definition a breach of a professional duty which is unique to that profession. Thus, malpractice is distinguishable from ordinary negligence or from that of an intentional tort. In cases of ordinary negligence or intentional tort, any person may be liable regardless of his/her "professional or religious color." A minister is amenable to suit for any injury to a person independent of the fact of his/her clerical or ministerial status. In order to get at a functional theory of clergy or ministerial malpractice, the Court must address the specific and differentiating incidents of the clergy/minister-communicant relationship that is not already actionable under intentional tort or ordinary negligence. This is the major difficulty in Court's accepting a clergy malpractice cause of action.[23] The source of conduct that has been the object of most ministerial malpractice cases to date has included sexual misconduct, molestation of children, and improper counseling. The leading case, a California case, has involved the activity known as pastoral counseling. The gravamen of the malpractice action concerns failure to meet the professional standards of counseling, specifically in failure to refer the suicidal communicant to a psychiatrist. Because of this failure, it was alleged that the depressed counselee eventually committed suicide. The action for a wrongful death was filed by the counselee's parents who are Roman Catholics and not members of the defendant Church.[24]

In ministerial malpractice, it is the essential incident of the ministerial activity that is at issue. Ministerial malpractice imposes liability, not for tangential consequences, but for the failure to execute properly the specifically ministerial duty.[25]

Many law review articles presented argumentation for and against recognizing a ministerial malpractice action in the fact situation involving pastoral counsel-

---

[22]Speiser, Krause, Gans, *The American Law of Torts*, p. 321; Restatement Second of Torts, §299A (1965).
[23]*Hester*, p. 551.
[24]*Nally v. Grace*, 240 Cal. Rptr. 215, 194 Cal. App. 3d. 1147, 195 Cal. App. 3d. 956A (1987).
[25]See discussion: Bergman, "Is the Cloth Unraveling? A First Look at Clergy Malpractice," 9 U. San. Fern. V.L. Rev. 47 (1981); Ericsson, "Clergyman Malpractice: Ramifications of a New Theory," 16 Val. L. Rev. 163 (1981).

ing in the California case. The articles raise some interesting constitutional issues. However, the California Court has finally decided the case and refused to recognize a new cause of action for ministerial malpractice in the facts of that case. As of this presentation, no state has yet recognized a separate ministerial malpractice cause of action, though several cases are still pending.[26] Other courts have avoided recognizing a specific malpractice action but have implied that in a given set of circumstances, such an action may be recognized.[27] This development deserves our attention, not only because of an additional exposure to liability, but also for the determination of the specific standards and identification of the ministerial duty. Since this involves definitions of ministry, it is an area that invites some scholarly attention. However, for the limited practical concern of this seminar, it may be well to focus on existing liability potential. These three areas of tort liability: intentional tort, negligence and clergy or ministerial malpractice can be reduced to some practical principles.

1. Regardless of the identity of the actor and the incidents of religion that appear in the situational context, a person is liable for intentional or reckless actions that cause injury.

2. Religious identity is not a shield. A state's compelling interest in protecting family, children, and the availability of a judicial forum to remedy injury is a compelling state interest overriding a religious defense.

3. In ordinary negligence, the religious identity and the religious context are no shield. One has a duty to prevent injury and to complete actions in accord with a reasonable person standard of care.

4. However, the Church's duty may be different because of its unique fiduciary character and its unique influence over the plaintiff, particularly if the plaintiff is a child or a member of a protected class.

5. Activities that require special training, such as counseling, should be done in accord with the standards common to counseling or the relevant profession and only by trained persons.

The discussion so far has simply addressed the direct liability of the actor. The seminar question concerns liability transferable to one other than the actor, namely, the Church.

Vicarious Liability

As a general principle, one person is not liable for the intentional torts of another. If, however, the conduct and injurious consequences, may be foreseeable within the nature and scope of the activity done in the Church's name, vicarious liability may attach. In a recent 1986 case, the court indicated that a Church may be

---
[26]Funston, 19 Cal. W.L. Rev. 508, n. 7, 8, 9.
[27]Lund v. Caple, 675 P. 2d. 226, 230 (1984).

held liable for intentional torts of its officers and members if conduct is carried out as part of the Church's religious practices.[28] Usually, however, the circumstances must be egregious for vicarious liability to attach in most of the circumstances in matters of the intentional torts identified earlier in this presentation.

However, in torts sounding in ordinary negligence, the Church or the employer may be liable for the ordinary negligence of an employee, labeled minister or not, on two bases. One, it may be liable for the breach of its own duty to provide adequate training or supervision. Secondly, it may be liable for the negligent action of the employee, agent or representative on the doctrine of *respondeant superior.*

For example, in the *Nally v. Grace* ministerial malpractice case mentioned earlier, the plaintiff stated a cause of action against the church and pastor for negligent failure to require proper psychological training for spiritual counselors. This is negligence in performing its own duty owned to the communicant. Similarly, if the church should have supervised one acting in its name, but did not, it failed in its duty of supervision owed to the communicant.

If the Church places the counselor and invites others to come to the counselor as part of the Church's activities, the Church has a duty to require training and to monitor and supervise counselors.

The Church may also be liable for the negligence of his/her employees under the doctrine of *respondeat superior.* The doctrine extends liability to the employer (the Church) for those acts within the scope of employment that the employer has the right or duty to control.[29]

The relationship of employer/employee is distinct from that of an employer and independent contractor or of a principal and agent. The characterization of the relationship of the actor to the Church is significant for the application of a particular legal theory of vicarious liability, both in ordinary negligence and in the area of potential liability of ministerial pastoral or clergy malpractice. While these relationships are technically different for evidentiary purposes, for the purposes of this seminar, the pragmatic concern is the identification of the actor as one empowered or allowed to act by the Church in its name. This is the significant fact question for this seminar. While the exact characterization of employer/employee etc. will control evidentiary questions relevant to the burden of proof in a cause of action, the empowerment by the Church is the threshold fact to potential liability. These are the most common theories for imposing vicarious liability upon the Church.

There is a newer theory being recognized by the Court's in the area of hospital liability for cases of medical malpractice. It is interesting to note it briefly. This

---

[28]*Mermon v. Holy Spirit Association for the Unification of World Christianity,* 506 N.Y.S. 2d 174, 119 A.D. 2d 200 (1986).

[29]Black's Law Dictionary 1475 (Rev. 4th Ed. 1968); Restatement Second Agency Section 219 (1958).

more recent developing doctrine is known as "ostensible agency."[30] It seeks to impose liability on the hospital for the acts and omissions of someone whom it empowers to work on its premises, regardless of the technical classification as an employee or independent contractor or the hospital's ability to control his/her actions. The doctrine of ostensible agency, flips the attention of the court to the injured party's perceptions. By analogy of Church to hospital, it may be that in the future the Church may be held responsible vicariously for the acts, errors and omissions of independent contractors and employees or other, if considering all of the facts, the communicant reasonably believed that the minister was an employee of the Church or parish or empowered or allowed by the Church to act in its name.

By analogy, if a separate ministerial malpractice action is recognized and matures, one can assume the theories of vicarious liability in ministerial malpractice will also expand as they are in medical malpractice arena. This necessarily focuses our attention on the definition of "lay minister" and "ministry."

Lay Minister

The definition of lay minister presents a rather interesting problem for the purposes of this analysis. As I began to reread some ministry articles from the perspective of the topic, I became very frustrated from a legal perspective. What is a lay minister? In the Code there is no definition of lay ministry other than C. 207[31] which indicates that the laity are those that are not ordained. The difficulty with the word minister or "ministry" is that the Code almost exclusively limits minister to sacred ministers. Theologically, one could say that deputation to the apostolate is sacramental rather than merely ecclesiastical or juridical. For lay persons ministry, too, is a sacramental state[32] if one uses the term in its fullest conciliar meaning. In reviewing the literature on ministry, one begins to see that words like "ministry" or "institutional ministers, ordained or not ordained," "apostolate" or "ecclesiastical office" are sometimes used interchangeably and sometimes are differentiated. Not being able to find comfort for purposes of factual and legal analyses in one definition, I began calling different dioceses to see what persons and activities were being labeled as "lay ministry." The answers varied from those who are solely involved in liturgy, to those lay persons working in tribunals, to those who are catechists, to teachers, community organizers, and parish hosts and hostesses and social service persons. References are also made to ministry for activities in separate corporations, such as hospitals.

---

[30] See Jeddeloh, "The Ostensible Agency Doctrine: More to the Point Than Darling," 20 Hospital Law 4 (April, 1987): 49-54.

[31] 1983 Code of Canon Law, c.207: §1. "Among the Christian faithful by divine institution there exists in the Church sacred ministers, who are also called clerics in law, and other Christian faithful, who are also called laity."

[32] John Allesandro, "Law & Renewal: A Canon Lawyer's Analysis of the Revised Code," CLSA Proceedings (Washington: CLSA, 1982) pp. 20, 38.

When I listed the different activities that I found labeled lay ministry, I came up with just a random listing of over twenty (20) activity descriptions with very little commonality of functions. When I began to list in a column what kind of liability those kinds of activities could invite, I came up with a list of twenty two (22) different causes of actions. Obviously, that approach doesn't work to get a common definition to narrow my focus for a liability analysis in a one hour seminar. Therefore, for the purposes of this analysis, I will use Cardinal Bernadin's definition. A lay minister is someone who is not ordained as a priest or deacon. Secondly, a person's specific activities are called ministry by the Church because it is supported and designated as such by the Church.[33] The Bishop is the endorsing agent for ministers, both ordained and not ordained. This endorsement may be civilly characterized as employee, or agent, or even independent contractor. The triggering event is the Church's endorsement and classification as "ministry." First, the deputation and identification of an actor as a minister and the placement of that activity in a Church related environment will be the fact event that triggers the application of the principles of vicarious liability to reach the Church. Secondly, if an activity is labeled ministry with professional training, it may be a source of liability on a malpractice level, if such develops, in addition to the existing ordinary negligence actions.

Finally, before reaching the theses of this seminar, I would like to acknowledge a more remote potential for Church liability in relation to separate corporations.

Church Liability for Separate Incorporations[34]

The act of incorporation creates an artificial legal person. The presumption of law is that each legal person is liable for its own acts. Liability cannot be transferred fom one artificial legal person to another without a compelling fact situation. The transference of liability from one corporation to another corporation is referred to as "ascending liability" or "piercing the corporate veil." I began this presentation with identifying the Church as the Diocese or Parish. Sometimes the Diocese is linked to a separate corporation. This link may be in several forms. The Diocese may be the title owner of the property leased to a separate corporation to carry on its activities; or in matters of hospitals or schools, there may be some statement in the corporate documents that indicates that this activity is a ministry of the Church; or, there may be some corporate language that indicates that this corporation has some type of affiliation with the Diocese.

---

[33]John J. Myers, "Ecclesial Ministries for Lay Persons Within the Diocese: Development and Integration," Proceedings of the Forty-Seventh Annual Convention (Washington, D.C.: CLSA, 1986) p. 72.

[34]For a more complete and helpful discussion, see Edward McGlynn Gaffney, Jr., Philip C. Sorensen, *Ascending Liability in Religious and Other Nonprofit Organizations,* Mercer Studies in Law and Religion 2, ed. Howard R. Griffin, (Macon, GA: Mercer University Press, 1984).

Most of these corporations are placed in the Official Catholic Directory. Often times, because of the theories of certain canonists, the bishop, or certain authorities in the Diocese, are ex-officio, in a governing capacity in these corporations either as members or directors.[35]

In and of itself, an affiliation or even an ex-officio limited governing position for certain ecclesial offices does not itself create a liability. However, any name, public identification, or overlapping governance structure does create the potential to be joined in a lawsuit for the tortious or contractual activities of a separate corporation based on legal theories of agency. These structures must be carefully created, understood and respected in implementation.[36]

Ultimately, whether the courts will actually "pierce the corporate veil" depends on a fact analysis. A successful fact analysis to "pierce the corporate veil" and transfer liability from the corporation to the Church requires a showing of economic gain by the Church; of undue influence and control in the governance of the corporation; and perhaps a non-economic but valuable benefit to the Church. Basically, if corporate formalities are not followed in the daily operations of a corporation, and authorities from the Church unduly participate in or influence the activities of a separate corporation in a capacity other than as a member or a director in accord with the bylaws of the corporation, the potential for liability is increased.

Most of the litigation in the area of the Church's liability for the activities of a separate corporation have been contract actions involving the failure of a residential or retirement facility to meet their contractual obligations. The link to the Church in those separate corporations has either been through the way in which the retirement home was identified as a "ministry" or by references in the promotional materials and contracts of the corporation to the Church. The plaintiffs in *Barr v. United Methodist Church*, used references to the Church in the promotional materials and in the contract to make the argument that they were relying on the stability of the Church behind the particular corporation with which they contracted. This case involved contracts between the plaintiffs and the corporation which created guarantees for retirement. The retirement facility became insolvent. The plaintiffs in this case attempted to name as a defendant all the Methodist congregations in addition to the specific corporation. The type of relationship existing in the *Barr* case is not uncommon and this case should be studied carefully for it does raise serious questions concerning affiliation and "sponsorship" structures.

Though the state court rulings suggest that an entire denomination can be a

---

[35] Adam J. Maida, *Ownership, Control and Sponsorship of Catholic Institutions*, Harrisburg, Pennsylvania: Pennsylvania Catholic Conference, 1975), Adam J. Maida, Nicholas P. Cafardi, *Church Property, Church Finance, and Church—Related Corporations*, (St. Louis: Catholic Health Association, 1983).

[36] McGlynn, Sorensen, *Ascending Liability in Religious and Other Nonprofit Organizations*, pp. 77-93.

legal entity and exposed to suit for activities of its affiliates, the Supreme Court has declined review. This specific case was settled out of court for twenty one million dollars.[37]

The fact questions in these cases involve the agency principles that I addressed under Intentional Tort and Ordinary Negligence. Basically, the question turns on the degree of autonomy, legally and functionally of these corporations. These questions are fact questions, and the Court will look to such things as whether or not the corporate form and formalities have been observed. The court will consider, not only at what corporate documents say on their face, but also to what is the actual, factual practice. How is governing power really exercised in the corporation? What is the degree of influence and control by non members and directors, namely Church authorities? The critical question is whether Church authorities use ecclesiastical position and authority or corporate position and authority to act in the corporation. What is the economic or benefit relationship between the two corporations? At this point, whether the Church is ultimately held accountable on ascending liability theories for activities of a separate corporation is going to depend upon a given fact situation. Potential liability may be raised on a "piercing the corporate veil" legal theory if the following exists:

1. The activity is labeled a ministry of the Church.

2. The corporation carries on business either through use of promotional literature or stationery that suggests to the public, that is, to any reasonable person, that it is not a separate and autonomous corporation but the instrumentality or agent of the Church.

3. The corporation does not respect the formalities of the corporation, its own bylaws.

4. There is a blurring of governance authority between the corporation and the Church. Ecclesiastical authorities, mix the use of ecclesiastical authority with the use of corporate authority.

A properly structured corporation and a properly functioning corporation reduces the potential for "piercing the corporate veil." My experience leads me to suggest that structures to address canonical concerns are not the problem. People, lacking a conceptual understanding of the structures or appropriate management skills, are, I believe a greater source of risk.

We must educate ourselves, attorneys, accountants, bishops and managers to both principles and practice. We must understand both the functions and limitations of corporations with pluralistic boards and pluralistic funding. Finally, we must address catechetical and theological problems in Church forums and address service delivery problems in corporations. Frankly, the directors should understand that being Catholic does impose a different value paradigm for decision making. If all participants clearly and competently differentiate their roles

---

[37]Ibid., pp. 12-13. *Barr v. United Methodist Church*, 90 Cal. app. 3d. 259, 153 Cal. Rptr. 322 (1979), cert. denied, 444 U.S. 973 (1979).

and functions, fewer situations would develop that give rise to the factual situations supporting an actual "piercing of the corporate veil."

III. FROM CIVIL LAW TO CANON LAW

Tort law is the battleground of social theory.[38] The simple goal underlying the distribution or risk in society through the development of tort law is simply responsible social interaction so that order is maintained in a society, so the commonweal is protected.

Analogously to the function of tort law in social policy, canon law suggests rules and procedures of social life "that attempt to bring alive the Gospel's values in the Church's orderly conduct" of itself[39] and presumably ministerial or sacramental interaction among communicants.

It seems to me that this goal of canon law should control our analysis. Liability is not, it seems to me, a driving force in canon law nor should it be. The very nature of the Church and the nature of its legal system should encourage more affirmative goals than those which fear of a civil suit or of financial liability may produce.

If the question is framed in terms of responsibility for ministry instead of liability, it becomes manageable and canon law becomes relevant. If we look at canonical responsibility, the thrust will be affirmative action for ministry. This is the distinctive quality of Church activities. I believe this approach is not only more truly ecclesial but, I suggest, it will meet the standards of care and public policy issues contained in the general tort principles discussed above.

Perhaps this will be clearer if we look at this question: what is the responsibility of the Church for the ministerial experience of its people from its own theological and canonical definitions as distinct from society's tort law developments? Rather than a code analysis by numbers, it seems more appropriate for one to attempt a value analysis of the code.

I think a comparison of the norms of some selected canons and the actual torts principles in some selected cases will illustrate my point.

Canons 96 and 205[40] establish that the relationship of minister and communicant is rooted in a sacramental bond. It is not merely that of members in an unincorporated association such as a labor union. The relationship is not created by

---

[38] W. Prosser, *Law of Torts*, §14 (1964).

[39] Peter Chirico, S.S., "The Expression and Actualization of Values Toward a Theology of Canon Law," *THE JURIST* 42 (1982): 503.

[40] 1983 Code of Canon Law, C.96: "By Baptism one is incorporated into the Church of Christ and is constituted a person in it with duties and rights which are proper to Christians, in keeping with their condition, to the extent that they are in ecclesiastical communion and unless a legitimately issued sanction stands in the way."

C. 205: "Those baptized are fully in communion with the Catholic Church on this earth who are joined with Christ in its visible structure by the bonds of profession of faith, of the sacraments and of ecclesiastical governance."

the parties because of common commerce or social interaction. Civil tort theory measures liability by the identity of the actor and injured party and the nature of the transaction, i.e. employer-employee, trespasser, invitee, principal-agent, a member of a protected class etc. While there are incidents of these civil relationships in church relationships, there should be a sacramental quality in the encounter that defies containment in these civil categories. I suggest that this canon may be relevant to the civil analyses in the following ways: First, is every employee a minister; is every activity in a Church environment a ministry? Is the communicant only a purchaser or vendee of services? I'm suggesting that if one consciously reflects on the sacramental potential in actions we choose to label 'ministry,' one must give serious attention to the standards of care and competency that are involved in the particular service rendered that is to be means of a sacramental, not merely a social, interaction. This leads to some thoughts concerning the element of duty that is the essential issue in causes of action sounding in ordinary negligence.

Duty

Canon 209[41] may be relevant to the standard of conduct and the duty questions. Canon 209 creates an expectation among members of the Church in their "own pattern of activities." That expectation is diligence. In intentional torts, the defendant action, to create legal liability, must be reckless, intentional and outrageous. In ordinary negligence, the standard of care is reasonableness. In malpractice, it is a standard of care determined by the standards of the professional training involved.

I think that Canons 228, 229 and 780[42] speak of professional qualification and knowledge for office and for one's role in the apostolate. These qualifications

---

[41] 1983 Code of Canon Law, C. 209 "§1. The Christian faithful are bound by an obligation, even in their own pattern of activity, always to maintain communion with the Church. §2. They are to fulfill with great diligence the duties which they owe to the universal Church and to the particular church to which they belong according to the prescriptions of law."

[42] 1983 Code of Canon Law, C. 228 "§1. Qualified lay persons are capable of assuming from their sacred pastors those ecclesiastical offices and functions which they are able to exercise in accord with the prescriptions of law." §2. Lay persons who excel in the necessary knowledge, prudence, and uprightness are capable of assisting the pastors of the Church as experts or advisors; they can do so even in councils, in accord with the norm of law.

C. 229 "§1. Lay persons are bound by the obligation and possess the right to acquire a knowledge of Christian doctrine adapted to their capacity and condition so that they can live in accord with that doctrine, announce it, defend it when necessary, and be enable to assume their role in exercising the apostolate. §2. Lay persons also possess the right to acquire that deeper knowledge of the sacred sciences which are taught in ecclesiastical universitites of faculties or in institutes of religious sciences by attending classes and obtaining academic degrees. §3. Likewise, the prescriptions as to the required suitability having been observed, lay persons are capable of receiving from legitimate ecclesiastical authority a mandate to teach the sacred sciences.

C. 780—Local ordinaries are to see to it that catechists are duly prepared to fulfill their task correctly, namely, that continuing formation is made available to them, that they acquire a proper knowledge of the Church's teaching, and that they learn in theory and in practice that norms proper to the pedagogical disciplines.

extend to formation for the apostolate both in theory and in practice and the range of human services and interpersonal relations.

The canons suggest values governing the way in which one prepares for and carries out one's community obligations. The standard of diligence means prudence, attentive, active, steadily application in doing something. Certainly, if the purpose and care of activities labeled ministry is rooted in canon 96 and 209; and ministers are diligent in integrating their beliefs in their "own pattern of activities," such actions will meet the standards of the civil law. Certainly, one's diligence would preclude outrageous, reckless conduct in intentional torts; would meet the standards of the reasonably prudent person for purposes of ordinary negligence and would meet the professional standard of care relevant in malpractice actions.

If one looks at the values in canons such as (but not only) 218, 220, 221, 308, and 793,[43] as a whole,—spirit, principle and language,—there exists protection of reputation, the care for personal privacy, prudent expression, protection of family and protection of the prerogative of parents. There is also protection for associational and dismissal rights and relationships between and among the laity.

These are the natural rights that tort law seeks to protect. They are at issue in the kidnapping and deprogramming cases, the tortions interference with business relations cases and the excessive zeal in proselytizing cases which are the fact situations of the intentional torts enumerated earlier in this presentation. Proper training and attention to the diligence standard should provide the type of honest supervision of ministers that will allow the identification of incompetency or questionable situations and preventive, curative, supervisory actions that are likely to reduce the potential for negligence and malpractice claims.

Canons 216, 300, 305, 323, and 394[44] speak of authorization of, vigilance of

---

[43] 1983 Code of Canon Law—C. 218—Those who are engaged in the sacred disciplines enjoy a lawful freedom of inquiry and of prudently expressing their opinions on matters in which they have expertise, while observing a due respect for the magisterium of the Church. C. 220—No one is permitted to damage unlawfully the good reputation which another person enjoys nor to violate the right of another person to protect his or her own privacy. C. 221—§1. The Christian faithful can legitimately vindicate and defend the rights which they enjoy in the Church before a competent ecclesiastical court in accord with the norm of law. C. 308—No one who has been legitimately enrolled may be dismissed from an association except for a just cause in accord with the norm of law and the statutes. C. 793—§1. Parents as well as those who take their place are obliged and enjoy the right to educate their offspring; Catholic parents also have the duty and the right to select those means and institutions through which they can provide more suitable for the Catholic education of the children according to local circumstances. §2. Parents also have the right to make use of those aids to be furnished by civil society which they need in order to obtain Catholic education for their children."

[44] 1983 Code of Canon Law "C. 216—All the Christian faithful, since they participate in the mission of the Church, have the right to promote or to sustain apostolic action by their own undertakings in accord with each one's state and condition; however, no undertaking shall assume the name Catholic unless the consent of competent ecclesiastical authority is given. C. 300—No association shall assume the name "Catholic" without the consent of competent ecclesiastical authority, in accord with the norm of can. 312. C. 305—§1. All associations of the Christian faithful are subject to the vigilance of competent ecclesiastical authority, whose duty it is to take care that integrity of faith and morals is preserved in them and to watch lest abuse creep into ecclesiastical discipline; therefore that authority has the right and duty to visit them in accord with the norm of law and the statutes; such associations are also

and pastoral supervision of ministry. These canons parallel the theories of vicarious liability and the fact situations that may lead to imposing vicarious liability upon the Church. As I mentioned earlier, the definition that I accepted for this presentation focused upon deputation and endorsement. The civil theories set forth also turn on authorization and public representations that may lead a reasonable person to think that the actor is authorized by another principal. The basic principle of any of the theories of vicarious liability is fair distribution of risk for activities and social responsibility. Minimally, society is going to distribute the risk among the one who wants a benefit, society's interest in facilitating the exchange of benefits, and the one who directly or indirectly empowers or facilitates the exchange relationship. All three should be reasonable. If the one authorizing the ministry combines to a diligent degree the training and formation of the actor and vigilance and supervision of the actor, it is reasonable to believe the civil standards of reasonable care or professionalism will be met.

There is also a parallel between the autonomy recognized in the Code for the governing and operational integrity of private and public juridic persons [45] and the principles of civil law governing the form and formalities of separate corporations. If Church persons respect the autonomy and separateness of a corporation which is similar to the respect for the governance integrity for juridic persons, explicit and implicit in the canons governing them, fact situations creating the risk for "piercing the corporate veil" will be minimal.

It is my suggestion that a reflection on the values implied in these canons would encourage, from a legal perspective, actions that reduce liability exposure, but more importantly lend themselves to being defined and experienced as ministry. Responsibility born of this reflection, not only promote Church integrity but, pragmatically, is the best action that can be advised to reduce exposure to civil liability for tortious actions.

These canons are, I hope, illustrative of value interpretations instead of a numbers analysis of the Code. If we consciously held our selves responsible for the values stated in these types of canons and the rich norms and values of the theological and conciliar literature which ground these norms, the way in which we do ministry would meet the minimal standards of civil law.

(Footnote 44 *continued*)
subject to the governance of the same authority according to the prescriptions of the following canons. §2. Associations of any kind whatever are subject to the vigilance of the Holy See; diocesan associations and also other associations to the extent that they work in the diocese are subject to the vigilance of the local ordinary. C. 323—§1. Although private associations of the Christian faithful enjoy autonomy in accord with the norm of can. 321, they are subject to the vigilance of ecclesiastical authority in accord with the norm of can. 305, and are subject to the governance of the same authority. C. 394—§1. The bishop is to foster the various aspects of the apostolate within his diocese and see to it that within the entire diocese or within its individual districts all the works of the apostolate are coordinated under his direction, with due regard for their distinctive character. §2. He is to urge the faithful to exercise the apostolate in proportion to each one's condition and ability, since it is a duty to which they are bound; he is also to recommend to them that they participate and assist in the various works of the apostolate in accord with the needs of place and time."

[45]See 1983 Code of Canon Law, Canons 113-123 and 1257; 1279 and Canons 298-329.

IV. PRACTICAL ACTIONS

Integrating the Code and the cases, I suggest the following practical actions that can be taken to promote responsibility for ministry:

1. Each minister should evidence both study and formation in church values. Some vigilance should be exercised in access to ministerial positions. There should be affirmative vigilance for supervision of performance.

2. The Pastor or Bishop should explicitly approve the designation of a work as done in the name of the Church or as ministry and it should be a policy that the term is used for public identification only with permission and with assurance that the criteria in number one above is consistenly operative.

3. The legal "ministry" ought to have some selectivity and definition about it particularly if it involves professional or quasi-professional services. Standards of admission, and performance should be defined and implemented consistently. Religious motivation is not enough.

4. Some reasonable administrative decisions need to be made concerning standards for the adequacy and training of sufficient supervisory professionals to support ministries. These standards should be articulated in terms of the recipient of the ministry, not the institution. This standard may be an interesting one.

   a). It challenges the potential institutionally protective disposition of staff and the possible institutionally protective expectations of leadership.

   b). It challenges leadership. Leadership gives both formal and informal messages to staff. One needs to know whether the formal message is ministry, but the informal message is inappropriate protectionism.

5. There should be a clear professional expectation of the "duty" and "standard of care" of minister and ministerial action by the person who deputizes or empowers. The person who is the supervisor ought to have enough multi-discipline training and experience to recognize competency and incompetency. That person must understand the foreseeable consequences of theoretical and practical incompetence, especially where he/she is placing a minister in a position relating to minors or the disabled.

6. Affirmative attention to the norms of these canons should result in substantive educational and formation programs for ministers.

7. In regard to separate incorporations, there ought to be adequate corporate documents, separate management, accounting and governance processes. Political issues should not be stated as moral or doctrinal issues. There simply must be vigilance in formation and appointment of trustees. They must have a sophisticated understanding of the relationship of separate corporations to the Church. The bishop and his staff

must be equally honest and sophisticated in understanding operational integrity of a separate corporation. Ecclesial authority should be used in the Church; corporate authority in the corporations.

8. There must be a reasoned criteria for identification of "Catholic" in a public work and for placement in the official Catholic directory. The interpretation of the criteria should not violate in theory or practice the autonomy and separateness of the authority and operations of a separate corporation.

Affirmative responsibility primarily by a theological standard and by canonical standards, I submit, is the only integral way to handle potential liability for ministry. From a liability perspective, the civil law may appear to be frighteningly paralyzing and canon law may appear to be irrelevant. From a responsibility perspective, civil law creates no greater or unmanageable standard than that which the essence of ministry creates.

THE ECONOMIC PASTORAL:
FOUNDATION IN THE CHURCH'S MISSION;
CHALLENGES FOR THE CHURCH'S LIFE

JOHN J. MYERS

The 1986 Pastoral Statement of the Catholic Bishops in the United States entitled "Economic Justice For All: Catholic Social Teaching and the U.S. Economy" has called forth interest both keen and broad among the American people. This is especially true of Catholics in the United States. A major segment of U.S. Catholics is increasingly well educated, increasingly affluent and increasingly influential in the life of the United States society. Another significant portion of American Catholics is composed of recent immigrants and others who have yet to benefit from the blessings of our economic and political system. Each of these groups has reason to attend to the Economic Pastoral. The moral and ethical principles are intended to ground specific suggestions and proposals for economic policy which would affect all such persons.

Each individual must face the questions in terms of his or her own life:
    What does this Pastoral mean to my family?
    What does it mean to my employment or my business or my profession?
    What does it mean to me as a consumer, a voter and a participant in forming public policy?
    What does the Pastoral mean to me as a member of the Roman Catholic Church?

Such questions are obviously not canonical for the most part, but they must be in the background of any consideration of the Economic Pastoral. On the other hand, this seminar will not attempt to analyze or critique the moral and ethical principles presented in the Pastoral or their specific applications. That is the role neither of canon law nor of the canon lawyer. There are, however, pertinent canonical issues and there are areas where moral/ethical teaching is connected with canon law.

As the title suggests, I think that there are canonical issues in the very notion of a pastoral letter and message. These represent teaching from a national group of bishops organized into an episcopal conference. How does this teaching relate to the mission of the Church, to the role of bishops, to the responsibilities of lay persons both with regard to Church teaching and with regard to the sanctification of the world? I am not certain that canon law answers or clarifies these questions in every instance, but there are some clear canonical reference points.

First of all, let us acknowledge that the Catholic bishops in the United States have spoken out as individuals and then as a group on issues of public order and policy since the time of Bishop John Carroll. Even if one does not agree with all of his conclusions, the fine book of George Cweigel demonstrates that the involvement of United States bishops in issues of war and peace, for example, has been present practically from the beginning of the American hierarchy. This teacher incorporated serious reflection solidly founded in Roman Catholic tradition. The *praxis* of the Church has indicated, therefore, the propriety of such public discourse and teaching. The Code of Canon Law supports the role of Catholic bishops in this teaching responsibility.

> Canon 747 §2. To the Church belongs the right always and everywhere to announce moral principles, including those pertaining to the social order, and to make judgments on any human affairs to the extent that they are required by the fundamental rights of the human person or the salvation of souls.

The Constitution on the Church of the Second Vatican Council speaks of this special teaching role of the bishops together with the corresponding responsibilities of Catholics to submit their bishops' decisions and teachings and to adhere to them with a ready and respectful allegiance of mind. (LG 25) Nor can there be any doubt that social teaching is part of the proclamation of the gospel. The 1971 World Synod of Bishops spoke of it as a "constitutive element" of proclaiming the gospel. The Code of Canon Law would certainly echo that thought.

> Canon 768 §2. They [those who proclaim the Word of God to the Christian faithful] are also to impart to the faithful the teaching which the magisterium of the Church proposes concerning the dignity and freedom of the human person, the unity and stability of the family and its duties, the obligations which men and women have from being joined together in society, and the ordering of temporal affairs according to God's plan.

This final phrase clearly mandates the proclamation of the principles of social justice in the ministry of the word.

Moreover, pastors of parishes are to "foster works by which the spirit of the gospel, including issues involving social justice, is promoted." (Canon 528, §1) Not only pastors have this responsibility, but all the Christian faithful have the duty of promoting social justice. (Canon 22, §2).

These canons echo the Constitution on the Church in the Modern World of the Second Vatican Council, several other Council documents and the 1971 World Synod of Bishops which emphasized that proclaiming social justice is a "constitutive element" in the proclamation of the gospel.

The matter becomes more complicated when one inquires about the responsibility other persons in the Church have to submit to the social teaching of episcopal conferences. A fine recent doctoral dissertation addresses this issue. Father James P. Green, a priest of the Archdiocese of Philadelphia, wrote at the Gregorian University. (*Conferences of Bishops and the Exercise of the Munus Docendi,* Romae, 1987: Gregorian University Press.) In general, there is a correspondence between the acceptance expected of the faithful and the authority of the Ecclesiastical Magisterium. The Christian faithful have the obligation to stay in communion with the Church, even in their own patterns of activity (canon 209). To the ordinary magisterium of the Church is due that *"obsequium religiosum"* which is not the assent of faith but is a true, internal assent motivated by religious convictions.

Canon 753, which addresses the issue at hand, is not entirely clear.

> Canon 753. Although they do not enjoy infallible teaching authority, the bishops in communion with the head and members of the college, whether as individuals or gathered in conference of bishops or in particular councils, are authentic teachers and instructors of the faith for the faithful entrusted to their care; the faithful must adhere to the authoritative teaching of their own bishops with an "obsequium religiosum."

Father Green indicates that, while conferences of bishops are not representative of collegial action in the strict sense, they are an example of effective collegial action. The teachings exercised by the bishops gathered in the episcopal conferences is rooted in their ordination as bishops and their membership in the College of Bishops. According to him, conferences of bishops as organized canonical bodies do not enjoy a mandate to teach with authority. When they teach, it is not the episcopal body which teaches, but the bishops, in conference, "conjointly" exercise their magisterium (p. 293).

When the bishops of a particular conference present the ordinary magisterium in union with the Pope and the rest of the Episcopal College, they are to be accepted with the *obsequium religiosum.* When they make practical judgments, however, they cannot demand acceptance from this religious motivation.

Always, the individual bishops who do not agree with the presentation of Church teaching or with specific recommendations made by the episcopal body could simply refrain from giving a document authoritative force in their own diocese. One must note, on the other hand, that *The Directory On the Pastoral Ministry of Bishops* encourages bishops to recognize unity of the College and only withhold consent for very serious reasons.

This distinction between various levels of authoritative teaching was very clearly recognized by the bishops of the United States in the Pastoral on Peace (n. 331). It is recognized in this pastoral too (n. 19 and n. 20) but I am not certain that it is as consistently followed out in the document itself.

One must recognize that a great deal of the material in this Economic Pastoral, especially when practical judgments are involved, is presented in a dialogical mode: "Let's think about this together." Material presented from this point of view can hardly be understood as being presented to the faithful to be accepted because of the religious authority involved.

There is yet another matter involved: The legitimate freedom of lay persons in secular matters.

> Canon 227. Lay Christian faithful have the right to have recognized that freedom in the affairs of the earthly city which belongs to all citizens; when they exercise such freedom, however, they are to take care that their actions are imbued with the spirit of the gospel and take into account the doctrine set forth by the magisterium of the Church; but they are to avoid proposing their own opinion as the teaching of the Church

in questions which are open to various opinions.

The Constitution on the Church in the Modern World serves as a background for this canon. ". . . [I]t is up to the layman to shoulder the responsibilities under the guidance of Christian wisdom and with eager attention to the teaching authority of the Church." (GS/43)

Lay persons, then, when the questions are not authoritatively addressed and in a way that reflects the College of Bishops in the strict sense or the clear teaching of their own diocesan bishop, are not bound to submit from their religious motives. Respect, of course, is always due. Sincere seeking of gospel values is always called for. But genuine disagreement is possible about the best methods for incarnating the gospel values in any particular situation.

This legitimate freedom of lay persons has real consequences, in my opinion, for the manner in which such matters are treated in homilies, education classes and other *fora* which are created or sponsored in the name of the Church. In Central Illinois where the Diocese of Peoria is situated, for example, our people tend to be politically more conservative. It can be very confusing and legitimately upsetting for them if homilies begin to sound like the recent platform of the Democratic Party. While the gospel must be proclaimed and social justice and the ethical principles upon which it is founded must be genuinely and honestly proclaimed, the people have a right not to have church pulpits or other ecclesial situations used to propound matters with which they legitimately and honestly disagree.

The Economic Pastoral moves on, near the conclusion, to speak of challenges to the Church. In reflecting on the Christian vocation in the world, the bishops remind us that action for social justice must be rooted in the Grace of God as it touches the human heart (n. 328). Worship and common prayer are seen as "wellsprings that give life to any reflection on economic problems and they continually call the participants to greater fidelity to discipleship" (n. 329). It seems to me that we could understand many canons and many sections of the Code of Canon Law as recognizing this same fundamental reality. Especially Book IV which concerns the Sanctifying Mission of the Church would be related to this teaching of the pastoral.

Education is also seen as one of the important ways in which the Church can work towards economic justice. First of all, we must maintain quality schools for the poor whenever it is feasible. More than that, the bishops quote their own 1972 statement on Catholic Education in which they taught that ". . . the educational efforts of the Church must encompass the twin purposes of personal sanctification and social reform in the light of Christian values."

The Code of Canon Law certainly recognizes and encourages Catholic schools of all kinds. To that degree it supports this assertion of the bishops. At the same time, it must be recognized that the Code does not make specific mention of these points. There is no contradiction, but complementarity.

One of the ways in which the Church can help work for social justice in society is by being very supportive of families (nn. 344-346). The code several times recognizes the rights of families and the importance of families. The pastor is to visit families and help them, sharing their cares and worries and helping to strengthen them (Canon 529). The parish and diocese are to provide assistance for those already married so that they might lead holier and fuller lives in their families and the local ordinary is to make provision that such assistance is duly organized'' (Canon 1063, 4° and Canon 1064).

One of the greatest challenges to the Church is to the Church as an actor in the economic life of the nation. The bishops provide a very significant affirmation: "All the moral principles apply to the Church and its agencies and institutions; indeed the Church should be exemplary" (c. 347).

Five areas of church life were selected for special reflection: wages and salaries, rights of employees, investments and property, works of charity, and working for economic justice.

The Code of Canon Law surely supports very strongly the affirmations of the bishops that the Church must pay just wages.

> Canon 231, §2. With due regard for can. 230, §1, they have a right to a decent remuneration suited to their condition; by such remuneration they should be able to provide decently for their own needs and for those of their family with due regard for the prescriptions of civil law; they likewise have a right that their pension, social security and health benefits be duly provided.
>
> Canon 1286: Administrators of goods:
>
> 1° are to observe meticulously the civil laws pertaining to labor and social policy according to Church principles in the employment of workers;
>
> 2° are to pay employees a just and decent wage so that they may provide appropriately for their needs and those of their family.

It is the duty of the diocesan bishop to see that administrators in the Church fulfill their responsibilities (Canon 392, §2). Surely a just wage and just working conditions would be among the things a diocesan bishop must attend to. The bishops point out that in order for them to be able to meet this responsibility, the members of the Church will have to provide the financial means for doing so.

The Economic Pastoral surely recognizes the right of employees to organize. "The Church fully supports the rights of workers to form unions or other associations to secure their rights to fair wages and working conditions." (n. 104) This clear affirmation of the Economic Pastoral is rooted in the long social teaching of the Church. It must be stated that the Code of Canon Law does not speak of unionization. In addition, it is important to note that the pastoral itself suggests that perhaps more collaborative models than unionization would be desirable in the worker-management relationship.

The code does recognize the right of association both for purely religious purposes and for "promoting the Christian vocation in the world" as well as for animating "the temporal order with a Christian spirit." (Canon 298, §1 and Canon

215) It does not seem accurate to interpret these canons as addressing the right to unionize, but surely the right of association is recognized.

The Conference of Bishops teaches that any property and investments held by the Church must be examined in the light of social criteria. Holdings in companies which are engaged in unjust or immoral activity are not appropriate for the Church. This does not always mean immediate divestiture, however, since other actions to promote social change are possible. Also, the holding of property by the Church when it can affect a local tax base or might have other adverse social consequences is to be examined.

Canon law does not formally require social justice criteria for property and investments of the Church, even though it presumes the Church will have both. At the same time, it would not be correct to say that canon law is insensitive to these issues. The sole purpose for which the church may hold temporal goods is specified in canon 1254, §2: ". . . to order divine worship; to provide decent sustenance for clergy and other workers; to perform works of the apostolate and of charity, especially towards the needy." It is my opinion that it would be very much in accord with the very purpose of the temporal goods of the Church that the social consequences of such holdings always be taken into account. I would say that this position is more implicit than explicit in the law but is certainly not contradictory to it.

It is very clear that the poor always have a special hold on the goods of the Church. I need only mention Canon 1254 as quoted above and also point out Canon 1285 which reads "Within the limits of ordinary administration only, it is permissible for administrators to make donations for purposes of piety or Christian charity from movable goods which should not pertain to the stable patrimony." This gives Church administrators rather broad discretion in coming to the aid of needy persons.

We are also to work for economic justice, not simply talk about it. Canon 528 states the responsibility of the pastor to see that *action* towards economic justice takes place. Furthermore, all the Christian faithful are to promote social justice (Canon 222, §2). These may not be the most ringing of exhortations, but at the same time they show that the matter of promoting and working for economic justice was considered by the drafters of the code and has been included in its provisions.

The Catholic bishops of the United States after broad and deep consultation and after long and serious discussion among themselves have offered to the Catholics of the United States and to all people of good will their thought and guidance in very complicated economic matters. Their efforts have produced a significant contribution to national dialogue on ethical values in our economic system. They have forced us to ask pointedly how this system serves human well-being.

They teach with authority insofar as the ethical principles reflect the ordinary magisterium of the Universal Church, although they do not teach with authority as a conference, according to the opinion which this seminar has followed. And yet they do choose to exercise their teaching office conjointly. The process of formulating the Pastoral as well as the resulting document offer an important aid to individual bishops as they fulfill their teaching responsibilities. While many different levels of teaching authority are incorporated into their work in a manner which might confuse some people, their general dialogical model will serve to invite discussion and serious thought.

At no time is the document in contradition to the law of the Church. Most of the time the law of the Church supports and is in line with their teachings. At times there is no specific mention but the teaching of the Economic Pastoral serves to complete or compliment provisions of canon law.

PRESBYTERAL COUNCILS AND COLLEGES OF CONSULTORS: CURRENT LAW AND SOME DIOCESAN STATUTES

JAMES H. PROVOST

When those responsible for planning this convention asked for a seminar on presbyteral councils and colleges of consultors, I gathered they were particularly interested in the relationship between these two bodies in terms of how this is working out in practice. This seminar, therefore, will be divided into four parts: some background to illustrate why the issue is worthy of discussion; the key element in the relationship between these two bodies as the 1983 code presents it, namely, membership; questions concerning the competencies of the two bodies; and finally a few other issues.

I. SIGNIFICANCE OF THE ISSUE

Diocesan consultors were originally an American invention, adopted (or, as some might say, imposed) in the United States Church instead of cathedral chapters as a senate of the bishop.[1] This legal structure was adopted in the 1917 code, although first preference was still given to the cathedral chapter.[2] The consultors were to be the major advisors to the bishop especially in finance questions. Often they were the only check on a bishop's financial adventures. In addition, the consultors had special functions *sede vacante*.[3]

During Vatican II there was a concerted effort to provide effective means for consultation in the Church. A decision was made to broaden the role of the existing *senatus* of the bishop, the cathedral chapter or, in our case, the diocesan consultors.[4] As is evident from a note inserted in the decree by the council itself,

---

[1] See Robert F. Trisco, "An American Anomaly: Bishops without Canons," *Chicago Studies* 9 (1970) 143-157; Gerald P. Fogarty, *The Vatican and the American Hierarchy from 1870 to 1965* (Wilmington, DE: Michael Glazier, 1985), pp. 33-35; and comments in Stephanus Sipos, *Enchiridion Iuris Canonici*, 7th ed. rev. by Ladislaus Galos (Rome: Herder, 1960), p. 243.

[2] See 1917 code, cc. 423-428. In c. 427 the diocesan consultors were said to function in the place of the cathedral chapter, "qua Episcopi senatus." Membership was to be entirely of secular clergy, religious and even secularized religious being excluded—see response of the Code Commission, January 29, 1931: *AAS* 23 (1931) 110; *CLD* 1: 242-242. The vicar general, however, could be a member provided the number of consultors were not too small; see declaration of the S. Consistorial Congregation, February 27, 1914: *AAS* 6 (1914) 111; *CLD* 1: 242.

[3] See 1917 code, cc. 429-444.

[4] See the decree on the ministry and life of priests, *Presbyterorum ordinis*, 7. In addition to the standard commentaries on Vatican II, see: Jacques Denis, "Voix consultative, voix deliberative: avenir du conseil presbyteral," *Revue Theologique de Louvain* 5 (1974) 198-210; Heribert Heinemann, "Was wird aus dem Priesterrat?" *Theologisch-praktische Quartalschrift* 122 (1974) 361-370; Anthony T. Padovano, "Ecclesiastical Authority and the Senate of Priests," *Chicago Studies* 9 (1970) 203-222; Jean Passicos, "Reflexions sur le conseil du Presbyterium," *Revue de Droit Canonique* 20 (1970) 146-183; W. Dean Walz, "The Juridical Status of the Senate of Priests," JCL dissertation, Catholic University of America, Washington, 1968.

the intent seems to have been to expand both the breadth of representation and the seriousness of involvement of the existing body, rather than to create something new or even parallel to the existing *senatus*.

In 1966 Paul VI issued practical norms to implement the conciliar decree.[5] In addition to providing several norms for presbyteral councils, the decree also retained existing bodies such as the cathedral chapter or diocesan consultors. One purpose for keeping the existing bodies seems to have been to avoid complicating arrangements in civil law, whether through concordats or, in several States in this country, the existing provisions of statutes about corporations sole. Although there was some discussion in drafting the revised code about retaining only one *senatus,* the presbyteral council,[6] the new code requires each diocese to have both bodies, a presbyteral council and a college of consultors (cc. 495-502).

Soon after the council a number of dioceses established presbyteral councils—or "Priests' Senates" as they were first popularly called in keeping with the determination of the council that these bodies would be the *senatus* of the bishop. Early in this experience a number of problems were encountered as dioceses attempted to insert this new entity into existing diocesan structures. Problems arose both in relating presbyteral councils with the existing diocesan consultors, and in a wider context.

A. *Relating Councils with Diocesan Consultors*

Presbyteral councils and diocesan consultors were both bodies of priests whom the bishop was supposed to consult. Three types of problems developed after Vatican II: competence, "divide and conquer," and too many meetings.

The competencies of the two bodies were not clearly distinguished at first, and it was difficult to coordinate them. In some dioceses presbyteral councils became so enmeshed in concerns of priests that they seemed to lose sight of their wider function of aiding the bishop in the pastoral governance of the diocese.[7]

There was also a fear that the bishop would consult the two bodies independently, and by a "divide and conquer" approach go ahead and do whatever he wished, without the restraints envisioned in the law. Indeed, in some cases this fear was not without foundation. In other dioceses, the two groups often were so opposed on various issues that the bishop was left without effective advice. Most frequently, however, they were just not informed about what each other was doing, and their advice was therefore less useful because not adequately informed.

Finally, the complaint arose that there were "too many meetings." Bishops found themselves attending all sorts of meetings, sometimes discussing the same

---

[5]Paul VI, motu proprio *Ecclesiae Sanctae,* August 6, 1966, nn. 15-17: *AAS* 58 (1966) 765-767; *CLD* 6: 274-275.
[6]See "Relatio" to the animadversions of the commission members to the 1980 schema, *Communicationes* 14 (1982) 217-218.
[7]See *Ecclesiae Sanctae,* n. 15, §1.

items with many of the same people, but one time at a consultors' meeting and the next at the presbyteral council or diocesan pastoral council sessions. Little time was left for effective pastoral activity.

B. *Wider Context*

Presbyteral councils also ran into problems in relating with two other diocesan structures: deans, and the diocesan pastoral council.

As dioceses attempted to implement the council, many turned to the system of deans to provide regional level leadership, and asked deans to assume a more creative role in the life of the diocese. At the same time priests were being asked to serve on presbyteral councils, diocesan pastoral councils, etc. In each diocese only a limited number of qualified clergy were able and willing to assume these various middle-management tasks which require more meetings and time away from the parish; in many dioceses, there were not enough priests to release some for such non-parochial work full time. It was difficult to coordinate these various positions, and conflicts in competencies or mixed expectations about the roles led to frustration.

The problem of competencies has also been an acute question in relating presbyteral councils and diocesan pastoral councils.[8] Pastoral councils are supposed to look toward planning, while presbyteral councils are to be involved in advising on governance of the diocese. Yet in practice, as presbyteral councils became so focused on priests' concerns, diocesan pastoral councils sometimes took over the task of providing effective advice on financial and other governance issues. Moreover, the same concerns about "divide and conquer" and "too many meetings" also exist in relating pastoral and presbyteral councils.

C. *Code's Solution*

These problems did not go unnoticed. Several approaches were considered in drafting the revised code, but eventually the following solution was adopted: two distinct bodies were retained which are distinguished on the basis of the selection of their members, and on the basis of their competencies; yet they are interrelated bodies because a priest must be a member of one body (presbyteral council) in order to be selected for the other (consultors).

They are distinguished first by the selection of their members. The presbyteral council is composed of three types of members: elected, ex-officio, and perhaps

---

[8] See James H. Provost, "The Working Together of Consultative Bodies—Great Expectations?" *The Jurist* 40 (1980) 257-281.

some appointed by the bishop (c. 497). There is only one type of consultor, and all members of the college of consultors are "freely selected by the diocesan bishop" (c. 502, §1).

Their competencies, which will be discussed in more detail below, also distinguish these two groups. The presbyteral council "is to aid the bishop in the governance of the diocese according to the norm of law" (c. 495, §1). It is named the "senate" of the bishop (c. 495, §1), indicating it is the "preeminent" consultative body.[9] Its concerns are quite broad, extending to all that may apply to the governance of the diocese.

The college of consultors, however, has a limited scope. *Sede plena* the law specifies the issues on which it must be consulted; it appears to have no competence beyond these.[10] *Sede vacante* the consultors have an expanded, special role.

Yet these two bodies are still interrelated; the presbyteral council's broader scope can include the issues which the consultors must address as diocesan governance issues. So the code has decided to draw upon the membership of the presbyteral council in order to form the college of consultors. Thus in order to be appointed to the college of consultors a priest must be currently serving on the presbyteral council (c. 502, §1).

Two reasons were given in the development of the code for retaining two distinct but related bodies.[11] The first is that some issues are so urgent that it is not possible to take the time to convene the whole presbyteral council to deal with them. In practice these appear to be only finance issues, the chief areas in which the consultors have a responsibility *sede plena*. The other reason is that some issues are so delicate they should be addressed only by a restricted group. Such issues could also relate to finances. They might also be personnel issues—but the only personnel issue that the consultors address *sede plena* is the hiring and firing of the fiscal officer, in which their advice is to be sought (c. 494, §§1-2). It is said that some have also argued the bishop should be free to choose his own advisors, but such a reason was not advanced by the code commission and does not seem entirely in keeping with the idea that consultors are to be a check on the bishop's autonomy.

II. MEMBERSHIP LINK

We now take a more in depth look at the linking of these two bodies as envisioned by the code, namely the relationship through membership. First, some

---

[9] See S. Congregation for the Clergy, circular letter, April 11, 1970, n. 9: *AAS* 62 (1970) 462; *CLD* 7: 388.

[10] This, at least, is the opinion of those who drafted the new code; cf. "Relatio," *Communicationes* 14 (1982) 218. This response is given to an objection by one commission member to the 1980 draft, who feared there would be confusion between the two: "There will be no confusion (between the presbyteral council and college of consultors) because the functions of the college of consultors are determined in each place, by reason of the matter *(ratione materiae)*; it does not have other functions *(alias functiones non habet)*."

[11] See comments by Wilhelm Onclin, Secretary to the Code Commission, *Communicationes* 5 (1973) 230.

key legal elements need to be recalled; then we will examine some of the practical arrangements which have been developed in United States dioceses.

A. *The Law*

To be appointed to the college of consultors, a priest must be currently serving on the presbyteral council (c. 502, §1). Members of the presbyteral council can be elected, ex-officio, or appointed; there is no provision in the code restricting selection of consultors to one or another of these classes of presbyteral council members. Unless particular law has determined otherwise, the diocesan bishop is free to select whomever he wishes from among the presbyteral council members, including just the ex-officio or appointed members.

Note that it is only required that a priest be on the presbyteral council at the time of his appointment to the college of consultors. If his term on the presbyteral council expires prior to the expiration of his term on the college of consultors, he remains a consultor even though he is no longer a presbyteral council member. The Commission for the Authoritative Interpretation of the Code has confirmed this in one of its early responses.[12]

In regard to terms of office, presbyteral council members can have rotating terms (c. 501, §1). Thus members could have staggered terms, or the whole council could be rotated as a body (i.e., all members start at the same time and their terms expire at the same time). The code does not set the length of term for presbyteral council members; this pertains to the council's own statutes (c. 501, §1).

Can members of the college of consultors also have rotating terms? The code establishes a five year term for the college (c. 502, §1). But it is the *college* itself which has the five year term, not just the individuals who serve on it.[13] It is the *college* which, at the end of the five year term, "continues to exercise its proper functions until a *new college* is established" (c. 502, §1; emphasis added). So it seems to me from a strict reading of the text that consultors do not have rotating terms, but rather are named as a group and remain in office as a group for the five year period, or even longer if a new group has not been named.[14]

Unlike the presbyteral council, the code does not leave it up to the college's statutes to determine the term of office (which is fixed at a five year period), nor does it mention the possibility of rotating some members. Under the former

---

[12]Commission for the Authoritative Interpretation of the Code, response of June 26, 1984: *AAS* 76 (1984) 746.

[13]The Latin text reads: "Inter membra consilii presbyteralis ab Episcopo dioecesano libere nominantur aliqui sacerdotes . . . qui collegium consultorum ad quinquennium constituant . . .; expleto tamen quinquennio munera sua propria exercere pergit usquedum novum collegium constituatur."

[14]For a different view, see John A. Alesandro in *The Code of Canon Law: A Text and Commentary,* ed. James A. Coriden et al. (New York/Mahwah: Paulist, 1985), p. 407.

code, the consultors were named as a group and served "ad triennium" with a replacement being named to fill out the remaining three-year period if someone went off the consultors for any reason whatever.[15] The same concept seems to underlie the provisions of the new code, with adjustments as to length of time for each college.

The code does not set any maximum number for the membership on the presbyteral council; for the consultors, however, it limits the group to twelve, with a minimum of six. Under the former code, the same minimum existed but no maximum was fixed.[16]

So, while at the beginning of any given five-year period the members of the consultors will all be drawn from priests currently serving on the presbyteral council, there could be more members of the presbyteral council than there are consultors, and those who are consultors might not remain on the presbyteral council for the duration of their time as consultors. Given the earlier concerns about coordinating these two bodies, the "divide and conquer" fear, and "too many meetings," how has the code's solution of basing appointment to the consultors on membership in the presbyteral council worked out in practice?

B. *The Practice*[17]

In June 1987 I wrote to the chancellors of the 172 Latin rite dioceses in the United States. I requested a copy of the statutes, or constitution and by-laws, of the diocesan presbyteral council and of the diocesan college of consultors. By October 1, 1987 I had received 130 responses, or a very good rate of return at 76%. Seven responses were in the form of a letter or unrelated material; 123 sent usable documentation. Two of these sets of documents were not statutes, but they did provide sufficient information for these dioceses to be included in the results of the survey. 121 sets of presbyteral council statutes were submitted; 4 sets of statutes for colleges of consultors, distinct from the statutes for the presbyteral council, were also submitted. In another fifty-one dioceses specific provisions about the college of consultors are contained in the statutes of the presbyteral council.

---

[15]1917 code, c. 426. §1 states the office is "ad triennium," §2 begins with "exacto triennio," and §3 specifies that a replacement is to be named who remains in office "usque ad expletum idem triennium."

[16]See 1917 code, c. 425, §1—dioceses with few clergy could have a minimum of four consultors, but the general rule was six. The canon makes no mention of a maximum number. However, it does call for them to live in the episcopal see or in neighboring areas.

[17]Here I am limiting the study to the experience of dioceses in the United States. For a review of similar concerns in Spain, see the excellent study by Luis Martinez Sistach, "Consejos presbiterales y colegios de consultores," in *Derecho Particular de la Iglesia an Espana* (Salamanca, 1986), pp. 27-66. For other studies on the experience of presbyteral councils, for several Canadian dioceses see Roch Page, "Le Conseil presbytéral, dix ans apres le decret Presbyterorum ordinis," *Studia Canonica* 8 (1974) 237-254; for presbyteral councils and diocesan pastoral councils in Spain, see Louis Martinez Sistach, "Consejos Presbiterales y Pastorales Diocesonas en Espana. Bilance de su situacion," *Estudio Eclesiasticos* 51 (1976) 147-182.

1. *Members of the Consultors and Presbyteral Council*

In eleven dioceses, the presbyteral council serves as the college of consultors; the two bodies are co-terminus. The members of the presbyteral council are elected for a five year term. In two other dioceses, each of which has a three year term for the presbyteral council, if a member of the consultors goes off the presbyteral council that priest also ceases to be a member of the college of consultors. In one diocese this is stated without further explanation; in the other, the priest is invited to resign from the consultors. If he were to decline to do so, however, he would remain on the presbyteral council as an ex-officio member for the duration of his term on the consultors.

Indeed, this is the most common solution, namely that if a consultor ceases to be a member of the presbyteral council, he becomes an ex-officio member for the duration of his term on the consultors. Thirty-seven dioceses have this provision explicitly. In another diocese, consultors whose term on the presbyteral council expires remain as non-voting members of the council for the duration of their term on the college of consultors.

Thus in many dioceses the code's approach of relating these two bodies has been extended to provide for concomitant membership on both bodies by consultors. In this way the consultors are informed of what is happening in the presbyteral council, since they are part of it; in a few instances the members of the presbyteral council are also fully informed of what is taking place within the college of consultors, since they are also all members of it. Even if some problems may remain as to which body is competent in a given issue, communications are open and there is some assurance of continuity.

In one diocese the statutes explicitly state if a consultor ceases to be a member of the presbyteral council, he remains on the college of consultors for the duration of the five year period but is no longer on the presbyteral council. In nineteen other dioceses which have a specific section on the consultors in the presbyteral council statutes, the question of remaining on the presbyteral council for the duration of a consultor's term is not raised; presumably in these dioceses it is also true that when one's term on the council expires, the consultor remains on the college but not on the council. In these, and presumably in the remaining dioceses which make no mention of consultors in their presbyteral council statutes, some approach to coordinating the work of the two bodies has to be developed other than full membership of the consultors on the presbyteral council.

Finally, in regard to membership, there are some dioceses in which the consultors are, in effect, elected by the priests. This is true of the elected members of those presbyteral councils which also serve as the college of consultors. In two dioceses the deans are elected by the priests, serve on the presbyteral council, and form the college of consultors. In another, the consultors are the diocesan priests who serve on the presbyteral council plus the vicar general. One diocese has a college of consultors formed by the executive board of the presbyteral council, while another has the members of the presbyteral council elect the consultors.

All of these could be ways in which the diocesan bishop has decided to structure the exercise of his discretion to select members of the college of consultors; he has done this, for example, in approving the statutes of the presbyteral council.

2. *Numbers on the College and Council*

It is difficult to determine the statutory size of many presbyteral councils because of ambiguous or open-ended language in the statutes themselves. Some do not specify how many and which positions will serve as ex-officio members; some do not specify the number of additional members the bishop may appoint. Indeed, in a very few, it is not specified how many elected members there will be. For some councils a formula is set in the statutes, such that the ex-officio and appointed members combined cannot surpass a certain percentage of the elected members.

Even in light of these cautions, it is clear that presbyteral councils range in size from 95 members (in Chicago) to 7 (for Saginaw). Over 50% of the councils are in the range of 12 to 18 members.

Membership on the college of consultors is limited to a maximum of twelve. Thirty-five dioceses have presbyteral councils of twelve members or less, and could solve the question of relating the presbyteral council and college of consultors in the fairly simple manner of have the same membership serve on both bodies for the same term. However, as reported earlier, only eleven of these thirty-five dioceses have adopted that approach. On the other hand, at least eighty-six dioceses have presbyteral councils with more than twelve members, so need some other solution.

In regard to statutory size for the college of consultors, two of the statutes for consultors and twenty of the presbyteral council statutes state that the number of consultors will be "from six to twelve," merely citing the canon and not specifying an exact number.

Six dioceses specify that the consultors will be six in number, which is the minimum number. The Commission for the Authoritative Interpretation of the Code has determined that while a bishop is not ordinarily bound to fill a vacancy on the consultors if one occurs within the five year term of a given *collegium*, he is to do so if the number would fall below the minimum.[18] Thus in these six dioceses any vacancies on the consultors would have to be filled; it should be noted that in filling them, the bishop is limited to selecting from among those priests who are serving on the presbyteral council at the time he makes this appointment. The appointee is to complete the unexpired term, rather than begin a new five-year term.[19]

---

[18]Commission for the Authoritative Interpretation of the Code, reply of June 26, 1984, *ad mentem: AAS* 76 (1984) 747.

[19]While the code is silent on this detail, it was the provision of the 1917 code, and follows from the fact that the *collegium* is appointed for a five-year term, not its individual members. The new appointment is to this *collegium*, at whatever stage in its five-year life it may be.

3. Term of Office

In regard to elected members of the presbyteral council, the largest number of dioceses (67, or over half of those responding) have a term of three years. For thirty-two dioceses the term is five years. Smaller numbers have various other terms.[20] So, for only thirty-two dioceses are concomitant terms possible for presbyteral council members and consultors, although as reported above many dioceses have solved this by providing for continued ex-officio membership on the presbyteral council for its members whose terms have otherwise expired but who are also serving as consultors.

For consultors, most dioceses specify a term of five years, as in the code. However, there are some exceptions. In two dioceses consultors have a three-year term; in another, the diocesan priests on the presbyteral council form the consultors, but terms on the presbyteral council are only three years. As noted earlier, one diocese limits the term on the college of consultors by requiring that if a consultor ceases to be a member of the presbyteral council, he ceases to be a consultor. In another diocese, consultors in that situation are asked to resign from the college of consultors.

While many dioceses provide for consultors to be named as a group and to serve as a group, in a number of others they have staggered or flexible terms.

There are some serious questions of legality here, questions which have a wider impact than might appear at first glance. We are dealing with statutes. While a diocesan bishop can dispense from the general law of the Church in individual cases (c. 87, §1), this does not apply to establishing statutes, where an exception would be more in the form of a privilege than a dispensation. If the statutes are not in conformity with the general law of the Church, the legitimacy of the college itself could be called into question. Consultors exercise a significant role in the validity of certain transactions *sede plena,* and as will be discussed below, have certain governance and even civil law functions *sede vacante.* The legality of certain transactions could be challenged if the consultors who perform them are themselves illegitimately constituted.

4. Summary on Membership

The code proposes to structure the relationship between the college of consultors and the presbyteral council primarily through the requirement that to be appointed a consultor, a priest must be currently serving on the presbyteral council. Many United States dioceses have found this to be insufficient, and have extend-

---

[20]Nine dioceses have terms of 2 years; eight dioceses have 4 year terms; 1 diocese has six year terms. In four dioceses, the elected members have differing terms; that is, some are elected for two, and other for three year terms, etc. The range for these variable terms is between two and five years.

ed the structured relationship on the basis of membership so that at least all consultors are on the presbyteral council for the duration of their term on the college of consultors.

Some of the approaches to achieve this arrangement are clearly in keeping with the law. In some cases the presbyteral council is composed of at most twelve members elected for a five year term, and the entire council also serves as the college of consultors. In many other cases, consultors are guaranteed continued membership on the presbyteral council for the duration of the college's five-year period, through the use of ex-officio membership on the council. Some other solutions have also developed, but need further study since a first evaluation indicates serious canonical and civil law questions.

III. COMPETENCY

In an effort to avoid conflicts in competency between these two bodies, the revised code specified a limited set of issues on which the consultors are to be consulted. It was clearly the intent of those drafting the law that the consultors were to be limited to these issues.[21] Yet this does not entirely resolve the problem. There are three possible approaches here.

From one perspective, the presbyteral council can seem to have a very broad scope: "to aid the bisop in the governance of the diocese . . . in order that the pastoral welfare . . . may be promoted as effectively as possible" (c. 495, §1). So from the diocesan bishop's point of view, he could consult the presbyteral council about those matters in which he must consult the college of consultors, provided he also consults the college of consultors. However, from the perspective of the two bodies, each can insist on being consulted only in matters specified for it in law.

A second opinion focuses on the limitation stated in canon 495: "to aid the bishop in the governance of the diocese *according to the norm of law*" (emphasis added). It would restrict the bishop to consulting the presbyteral council only in those matters specified in law, and clearly distinguish those which the law gives to the college of consultors. This has the advantage of clearly distinguishing the two bodies *ratione materiae,* i.e., in virtue of their specific competencies. But it reflects a very weakened notion of "aid . . . in governance," to say nothing of the meaning of *senatus* in canon 495 or the injunction of canon, 500 §2 that the bishop is to listen to the presbyteral council "in matters of greater moment."

A third opinion focuses on the initiative of the bishop. He is free to consult whomever he wishes. He could therefore broaden the competence of the college of consultors to include whatever he might also bring to the presbyteral council.

---

[21]See note 10, above.

If he were to do this by particular law, then the college of consultors would indeed be "responsible for the functions determined in the law" even though this would be much more extensive than the provisions of the code. It should be noted, however, that this raises questions about the meaning of *senatus* as applied to the presbyteral council in canon 495, to say nothing of the intention of Vatican II as expressed in *Presbyterorum ordinis,* n. 7.

Leaving this theoretical discussion aside for the moment, what are the competencies specified for these two bodies in the new code? They can be discussed in terms of three conditions of the diocese: *sede plena* with a diocesan bishop in charge; *sede impedita* when there is a diocesan bishop, but he is unable to communicate with the people of the diocese; and *sede vacante,* when there is no diocesan bishop.

A. *Sede Plena*

The presbyteral council is to "aid the bishop in the governance of the diocese" (c. 495, §1). It is to be heard "in matters of greater moment" (c. 500, §2). Here are some specific instances in which it must be consulted:

1. To hold a diocesan synod (461, §1)
2. To modify parishes (cc. 515, §2; 813)
3. Concerning the use of offerings by the faithful on the occasion of parish services (c. 531)
4. In order to issue norms for parish councils (c. 536)
5. Before the construction of a church or conversion of a church to secular use (cc. 1215, §2; 1222, §2)
6. Before imposing diocesan taxes (c. 1263)
7. To approve the list of pastors which the bishop is to propose for consultation in certain personnel issues (c. 1742, §1).

The college of consultors "is responsible for the functions determined in the law" (c. 502, §1). These are:

1. Receive the apostolic letters of appointment of coadjutor bishop (c. 404, §1)
2. Advise in hiring and firing the finance officer (c. 494, §1)
3. Advise in more important acts of administration (c. 1277)[22]
4. Consent for acts of extraordinary administration (c. 1277)
5. Consent for alienation of certain ecclesiastical property (c. 1292, §1).

---

[22]The statutes for colleges of consultors submitted as part of the survey all miss this item; it is also missing from Alesandro's list in the CLSA commentary, p. 407.

B. *Sede Impedita*

This situation may not be so rare as once thought. For example, in the Summer of 1987 Archbishop Donnellan of Atlanta suffered a stroke which rendered him incapable of communicating. The college of consultors were required to elect an administrator even prior to the eventual death of the Archbishop (who died October 15, the day the CLSA convention closed).

There are no specific provisions in law concerning the presbyteral council *sede impedita*. One opinion is that it continues to function, and the administrator would function in the place of the diocesan bishop in its regard. I am inclined toward this strict interpretation since a right to exist is in question. Unless the presbyteral council is clearly terminated, as it is in the case of *sede vacante* (c. 501, §2), then its right to exist should not be questioned. Another opinion is that there is a *lacuna legis* here, and recourse is to be taken to parallel places in law. The obvious parallel is the *sede vacante* situation, and if this were to apply then the presbyteral council would cease to exist *sede impedita*.

The college of consultors has a special role *sede impedita* if there is no coadjutor, and if the bishop failed to compile a list of persons to whom the governance of the diocese is to pass in case of *sede impedita* (c. 413, §1). This role is to "select a priest who is to govern the diocese" during the time the see is impeded (c. 413, §2). In addition, a coadjutor or auxiliary bishop takes possession of his office *sede impedita* by presenting the apostolic letters to the college of consultors (c. 404, §3). There are no other specific provisions relating to the consultors *sede impedita*, although by analogy it may have to give its consent for certain acts by the priest who governs the diocese *sede impedita*.[23]

C. *Sede Vacante*

The presbyteral council ceases, and its functions are fulfilled by the college of consultors (c. 501, §2).

The consultors have various responsibilities at different stages of the vacancy. If there are no auxiliary bishops, the governance of the diocese "devolves upon the college of consultors unless the Holy See has provided otherwise" (c. 419). While the college must elect a diocesan administrator within eight days (c. 421, §1), in the meantime the college exercises governing power in the diocese as a collegial body. The consultors cannot innovate and are restrained from certain

---

[23] The code does not term this priest a "diocesan administrator," but attributes to him the obligations and power "which belong by law to a diocesan administrator" but "only for the time during which the see is impeded" (c. 414). Hence the consultors may need to consent if the priest wishes to remove the chancellor or notaries (c. 485), and perhaps if the see has been impeded for over a year and the priest in charge wishes to grant excardination or incardination (c. 272—although this canon specifies *sede vacante*).

activities (c. 428); nevertheless they are responsible collegially for the proper administration of the diocese during this time. They also are to notify the Apostolic See of the vacancy in the diocese (c. 422).

Once they have elected an administrator (c. 421, §1) the consultors cease to exercise the functions of the presbyteral council during the remainder of the interregnum (c. 501, §2). Moreover, if the diocese is vacant for over a year, their consent is needed if the administrator wishes to excardinate or incardinate a cleric, or grant a diocesan cleric permission to migrate to another diocese (c. 272). Their consent is also needed if the administrator wants to remove the chancellor or notaries *sede vacante* (c. 485).

Finally, for a new bishop to assume his office as diocesan bishop he must present the apostolic letters of his appointment to the college of consultors (c. 383, §3).

IV. OTHER ISSUES

The review of statutes submitted as part of this study raises some additional issues. For the moment, let me signal three: statutes for consultors, the role of the bishop, and the spirit which these documents reflect.

A. *Statutes for College of Consultors*

The code does not mention statutes for the consultors. If none are adopted, the consultors are bound by the general law of the code. Under this law, the college of consultors is a *collegium,* and must observe all the code's provisions on collegiate bodies. These include canons 124-128 on juridic acts, and 164-179 on elections. Many of these provisions are for validity, including the procedure to be followed in consulting and obtaining consent (c. 127, §1). Given the seriousness of the items involved financially, it is important they be observed.

Thus before performing more important acts of administration in the diocese (c. 1277), the bishop must convene the consultors according to the norm of canon 166, they must be given adequate information, and he must listen to each of the consultors at the meeting.[24] The college can have its own statutes, however, and in these some specifics could be added to ease the situation of consulting on more important acts of administration.[25]

---

[24] See cc. 126; 127, §1. For validity, the consultors must be informed about what constitutes the substance or amounts to a condition *sine qua non* of the act about which they are advising; if they are not informed or in error about other aspects of the act, it would be valid but rescissory action could be taken—cf. c. 126.

[25] Thus the statutes for the college of consultors in the diocese or Peoria utilize a provision of c. 127, §1 ("unless particular or proper law provides otherwise when counsel only is to be sought") and permit advice to be sought in special circumstances through a conference call, or even by mail. Note this does not apply when consent is needed, for then the group must be convoked.

B. *The Role of the Bishop*

The presbyteral council is an expression of the *presbyterium* of the diocese. In Vatican II there are two approaches to the role of the bishop in regard to the presbyterium. In *Lumen gentium* the bishop is included with the priests in forming one presbyterium (*LG* 28). In other conciliar documents, the presbyterium acts "with the bishop," so the bishop is considered as standing apart from the body of presbyters in the diocese (*CD* 11, 28; *PO* 7; *AG* 19). In sixty-five dioceses the *Lumen gentium* approach is followed, the bishop being listed as a member of the presbyteral council.

The code calls for the bishop to "preside over" the presbyteral council (c. 500, §1) and the college of consultors (c. 502, §2). This is taken as chairing and serving as chief executive officer in the statutes concerning consultors, and in twenty-six presbyteral council statutes. In these latter, sometimes the body may elect a secretary and even an assistant to the bishop, but the diocesan bishop is still clearly in a chief management role as well as presider over the presbyteral council.

In ninety-one dioceses the bishop "presides" but the members elect officers, usually called chairman, vice-chairman, and secretary. These latter actually run the organization, under the authority of the bishop. Five dioceses make no mention of the bishop presiding, and elect their own officers.

Finally, the question has come up concerning a tie vote when consent is being sought. In current law this applies only to the consultors. If the consultors are deadlocked, can the bishop break the tie? Since the bishop is the presiding officer, it seemed at first that he could break a tie in keeping with canon 119, 2°. However, the Commission for the Authoritative Interpretation of the Code has responded that as a superior, the bishop cannot break the tie when it is a question of obtaining the consent of a body of persons.[26] He is not counted as a member of the consultors for this purpose, so consent is not given if there is a tie vote.

C. *Spirit of the Statutes*

Most of the presbyteral council statutes were rewritten after 1983. They provide an initial indication of how much reception has been given the *novus habitus mentis* Paul VI and John Paul II describe as characteristic of the new code. This way of thinking is to reflect the Second Vatican Council, which sets the standard for interpreting the code.

There is a strikingly heavy canonical tone to many of the statutes. While the preamble in some continues to present quotations from Vatican II, in many others

---

[26]Commission for the Authoritative Interpretation of the Code, response of May 14, 1985: *AAS* 77 (1985) 771.

even the introductory material consists in citations from canons. The content of the statutes is sometimes merely a direct quotation from the canons, with little adaptation to the local situation.

Some dioceses properly understood "statutes" in the American context to permit a constitution, which is a fairly lean document setting forth the essentials, and by-laws which provide greater detail, for example in regard to election procedures. Other dioceses have combined all detail into one document, and may spend several pages describing an election process but indicate very little about the actual functioning of the body.

In a few cases, the documents seem to betray a sense of distrust—of the bishop, or of the members. They lack the tone of collaboration and mutual support which the documents of Vatican II attempt to set in the Church.

In a very few instances, the drafters of the statutes apparently did not understand what statutes are supposed to do. They repeat verbatim provisions of the code which state that the statutes are to determine something, and fail to make any further determination!

Finally, some presbyteral council statutes are so vague that it is impossible to determine something so fundamental to the body as its membership. In these situations the document would not be usable in resolving a dispute about membership, quorum, or the majority needed for certain actions. Yet membership is a key element to any "body" such as a presbyteral council. However, there is neither time nor space to explore these issues at greater depth; they remain an interesting item on the canonical agenda.

CONCLUDING REMARKS

Bishops and presbyters share a responsibility for the welfare of the people of God they serve. This responsibility differs in keeping with their respective offices, but neither can serve in isolation from the other. Vatican II desired to provide a more effective structure to facilitate their cooperation, and focused on the consultative body which serves as the *senatus* of priests who aid the bishop in the governance of the diocese.

Subsequent developments have retained two bodies, the presbyteral council and the college of consultors. Under the new code dioceses are required to have both bodies. Diocesan bishops and presbyters are faced with the task of making both bodies work in such a way that they do not interfere with one another, but provide realistic assistance in the governance of the diocese.

Some dioceses have attempted to do this by combining the two bodies into one. Others have provided for consultors to be fully informed of presbyteral council activities through a system of ex-officio or appointed membership to retain consultors on the council for the duration of their term on the college. Still others have not addressed the issue, at least in their documents.

It has not been possible to evaluate the effectiveness of the various systems studies. That would take a more in-depth, sociologically validated study. Given the importance assigned by the council and the code to the working together of bishops and presbyters, such a study may be desirable now that there has been some experience with the code's system. Further canonical evaluation of the statutes would also seem advisable.

Finally, dioceses may wish to consider adopting statutes for the college of consultors as well as for the presbyteral council. While not demanded by the code, such statutes would provide an important support to those priests who serve on the consultors. The process of developing them could also aid in clarifying for the bishop and the consultors some of the norms which must be observed by such bodies.

APPENDIX:
SAMPLE STATUTES FOR COLLEGE OF CONSULTORS[27]

I. *Nature of the College of Consultors*

The College of Consultors is a group of priests who act as official advisors to the Bishop in certain matters pertaining to the administration of the diocese, and as a governing board of the diocese when the see is vacant or impeded through the inability of the Bishop to communicate with the diocese. (c. 502, §1)

II. *Membership and Terms of Office*

A. Number (specify how many consultors—c. 502, §1 states the number must be between 6 and 12).
B. Selection (specify how the bishop will select members; it could be the whole presbyteral council, if it numbers 12 or less and serves for a five year term, is selected; it could be that some are always to be selected from among the elected members; etc.).
C. Term
   1. Consultors serve as a body for a five (5) year term. The College remains in office until a new college is named. (c. 502, §1)
   2. If any consultor retires from the College for any reason before the expiration of the five year term, the Bishop shall appoint from among the members of the Presbyteral Council another in his place to fill the unexpired term.

---

[27]This sample is an adaptation of the statutes adopted by the diocese of Wilmington, with some elements from those of the diocese of Peoria. Canon numbers are provided as references; a determination should be made whether to include them in the actual statutes.

3. If the five year term of the College expires during the vacancy of the diocese, the consultors remain in office until the new Bishop takes possession of the diocese and subsequently constitutes a new College of Consultors.

III. *Officers*

A. The Diocesan Bishop is the President of the College of Consultors. (c. 502, §2. Provision could be made for a chairman to be selected to manage the operations of the college.)
B. If the diocese is an impeded see, the priest selected to govern *sede impedita* presides over the College of Consultors in the place of the bishop. (c. 502, §2)
C. If the diocese becomes vacant and there is no auxiliary bishop, the priest who is oldest in ordination in the College of Consultors presides until an Administrator is elected, after which the Administrator presides during the vacancy. (c. 502, §2)
D. There shall be a secretary of the College of Consultors who shall be selected from among the members of the College. (Determine manner of selection: appointment by the bishop, election, seniority, etc.; also determine how to replace a vacancy in the office of secretary when the diocese is vacant.)

IV. *Meetings*

A. The College of Consultors meets (specify how frequently, or "on call of the Bishop or, when the diocese is vacant, the Administrator").
B. For the election of an Administrator, the norms of canon law are to be followed (cc. 119, 1°; 164-179).
C. If canon law requires the consent of the College of Consultors for an action to be valid, the matter is to be considered formally at a meeting of the College (c. 127, §1); the bishop is not able to break a tie when consent is required.
D. If canon law requires the advice of the College of Consultors, an actual meeting is desirable. If this is not possible, consultation by a conference call is permitted so as to maintain the collegial nature of the consultation. If this also is not possible, necessity may require that consultation be by mail; but if at least (determine a number of percentage of members) of the College desire a meeting to discuss the matter, the meeting will be called as soon as possible. (c. 127, §1)

V. *Competence*

A. As advisors to the Bishop, the College is to be consulted:

1. to give advice:
   a. in more important acts of administration; (c. 1277)
   b. in the hiring and firing of the finance office; (c. 494, §§1-2)
2. to give consent:
   a. for acts of extraordinary administration; (c. 1277)
   b. for the alienation of diocesan property, within limits set by the N.C.C.B. (c. 1292, §1)

B. As a governing board the College has the following functions:
   1. When the diocese is occupied by the Diocesan Bishop, to receive the Apostolic Letters of appointment of a Coadjutor Bishop; (c. 404, §1)
   2. When the diocese is an impeded see:
      a. if no other provisions have been made in accord with canon law, to elect a priest to govern the diocese (c. 413);
      b. to receive the Apostolic Letters of appointment from a Coadjutor or Auxiliary Bishop (c. 404, §3);
   3. When the diocese is vacant:
      a. if there is no auxiliary bishop, to notify the Apostolic See of the vacancy; (c. 422)
      b. if there is no auxiliary bishop, to govern the diocese collegially until an Administrator is elected; (c. 419)
      c. to elect an Administrator within eight days of vacancy; (c. 421, §1)
      d. to fulfill the role of the Presbyteral Council during the vacancy; (c. 501, §2)
      e. to consent for the Administrator to remove the Chancellor or other notaries; (c. 485)
      f. after a year of vacancy, to consent for the Administrator to permit excardination, incardination or migration of clergy; (c. 272)
      g. to receive the Apostolic Letters of appointment of a new Bishop (c. 382, §3).

VI. *Adoption and Amendment*

A. These statutes shall be adopted (specify how: e.g., by vote of the College and approval of the bishop; or by action of the bishop).
B. These statutes may be amended (specify how: e.g., by vote of the College and approval of the bishop; or by action of the bishop).

SYNODAL GOVERNANCE IN THE EASTERN CATHOLIC CHURCHES

John D. Faris

Synodal governance in the Church, although a time-honored institution, has not been without its critics. Bishop Gregory of Nazianzus (+390) had this to say about the assemblies of bishops:

> If it is necessary to write the truth, I intend to avoid every assembly of bishops, inasmuch as I saw no council with a successful and favorable end, nor one which averted problems instead of causing and increasing them. There are always arguments and struggles for power. (I ask you not to think of me as troublesome and annoying in writing this way.) Nor can the bishops be corrected: if someone should accuse them of unscrupulousness, he himself would be brought to judgment quicker than he could suppress their evil ways.[1]

Bishop Gregory made these remarks after his unfortunate experience at the Second Ecumenical Council at Constantinople in 381. It is surprising that an institution so severely criticized in the fourth century still prevails today as the ordinary form of governance in the churches of the East. It is our task to examine the nature of synodal governance and its various expressions in the discipline of the eastern Catholic churches.

A COMMUNION OF CHURCHES

In order to understand the system of governance in the eastern Catholic churches, it is necessary to discuss briefly the status and nature of the churches themselves. To do so it is necessary to modify our understanding of the universal Church. Too often, the Catholic Church is inaccurately identified with the Latin Church and the eastern Catholic churches are regarded as parts of the Church in the same juridic category as parts of the Roman Church, such as the Catholic Church of the United States, France, or Europe. At times, the eastern Catholic churches are seen as subordinate appendages of the Church, belonging to the Church in the same manner as certain territories belong to the United States but do not enjoy the status of a state.

With the Second Vatican Council, the 1983 *Code of Canon Law,* and the ongoing codification of the law for the eastern Catholic churches, these views have been modified. A more accurate description of the Catholic Church is that it is

---

[1] *PG*, Letter 130, vol. 37, col. 226.

a *communion of churches,* which are in communion with the Bishop of Rome. The Second Vatican Council took this approach and described the Church as follows:

> The holy Catholic Church, which is the Mystical Body of Christ, is made up of the faithful who are organically united in the Holy Spirit by the same faith, the same sacraments and the same government. They combine into different groups, which are held together by their hierarchy and so form particular churches or rites.[2]

Let us briefly examine this passage: it identifies the Church with the Mystical Body of Christ and states that it is constituted by members of the Christian faithful united in the Holy Spirit sharing the same faith, sacraments and government. However, this community is not one monolithic structure; it would be difficult for an individual member of the Christian faithful to perceive a sense of community from such a large entity. Rather, the Christian faithful coalesce to form different groups because of a shared cultural, spiritual, theological, liturgical and disciplinary tradition.[3] These groups are bound together by a hierarchy, all of whom are in communion with the Roman Pontiff and with each other. Certain conciliar documents refer to these ecclesial groupings as "particular churches or rites."[4]

CHURCH VS. RITE

In the past, the term "rite" has been employed to designate both the *corpus* of spirituality, liturgy, theology, and discipline of a community and the community itself. For example, a community observed the Melkite Rite in living the faith and a person was a member of the Melkite Rite. This equivocal usage of the term rite has been found to be inadequate. The term "rite" is correctly employed to designate the *corpus* of tradition observed by a community; when we refer to the ecclesial community itself, i.e., the church, it is appropriate to employ the term "church."

A Catholic is properly designated not as a member of a "rite," but as a member of a specific church, which follows a certain rite. Thus, we must become accustomed not to refer to the community as the Melkite "Rite," or Armenian

---

[2] *Orientalium Ecclesiarum,* n. 2. All English translations of conciliar texts are taken from Austin Flannery, gen. ed., *Vatican Council II,* (Northport, New York: Costello Publishing Co., 1975).

[3] See also *Lumen Gentium,* n. 23: "It has come about through divine providence that, in the course of time, different Churches set up in various places by the apostles and their successors joined together in a multiplicity of organizally united groups which, whilst safeguarding the unity of the faith and the unique divine structure of the universal Church, have their own discipline, enjoy their own liturgical usage and inherit a theological and spiritual patrimony. . . This multiplicity of local Churches, unified in a common effort, shows all the more resplendently the catholicity of the undivided Church."

[4] *Lumen Gentium,* n. 13; *Orientalium Ecclesiarum,* n. 2 et passim.

"Rite," but to the Melkite Church or the Armenian Church.[5]

The distinguishing factor of the various churches is not the rite, i.e., form of divine worship which is observed. Indeed many churches observe the same rite: the Ukrainian, Greek, and Melkite Churches all observe the same rite which originated in Constantinople.[6] Instead, the crucial factor which distinguishes the eastern Catholic churches from each other is that each church has its own ecclesial structure, a hierarchy of its own.

AUTONOMOUS CHURCHES

Churches with their own hierarchical structure are referred to in canon law as *ecclesiae sui iuris* ("churches in their own right"), a term which indicates their legal status with regard to the universal Catholic Church. Of course, the Latin Church is also an *ecclesia sui iuris,* even though its head is also the head of the entire Catholic Church.

Although every comparison fails in some way,[7] one might conceive the relationship between the eastern churches and the universal Church in the Catholic communion to that of the individual states in the United States and the federal government. These states rule themselves independently except in those matters which are reserved to the federal government. Similarly, the future Eastern Code will assign to the eastern catholic churches certain rights and will also establish what matters are to be reserved to the "federal" authority of the Roman Pontiff.

The term *"sui iuris"* can be translated as "autonomous" and the churches themselves are referred to as autonomous churches.[8] It must be emphasized that the autonomous churches are not the juridical equivalents of the subdivisions of the Church such as the American Church, the South American Church or the African Church. None of these subdivisions enjoy a juridical status in canon law.[9]

---

[5] There are still some vestiges of improper usage; we still refer to a "transfer of rite," which is precisely a transfer from one autonomous church to another.

[6] In the future, certain hierarchies of the Latin Church might be granted a juridical status comparable to that of the eastern churches. These churches would still share in the common tradition of the Latin Church.

[7] It would be misleading from the perspective of ecclesiology and canonistics to carry this comparison too far and to qualify the Catholic Church as a "federation" of churches.

[8] This is the translation employed in *The Code of Canon Law,* ed. The Canon Law Society of Great Britain and Ireland (London: Collins Liturgical Publications, 1983). See C. 112. The 1983 *Code of Canon Law* refers to the various churches in Catholic communion as "autonomous *ritual* churches" *(ecclesia ritualis sui iuris).* However, the term "ritualis" is unnecessary.

The term "autonomous church" is not without its detractors. The Preparatory Commission for the Vatican II *Decree on the Eastern Catholic Churches* rejected the use of the term "canonical autonomy" because it felt that the term could easily give rise to misinterpretation. See Ivan Zuzek, "Animadversiones Quaedam in Decretum de Ecclesiis Orientalibus Catholicis Concilii Vaticani II," *Periodica* 65 (1966): 278. The Commission responsible for the revision of the Eastern Code also had difficulties with the term. See *Nuntia* 3 (1976), p. 46.

[9] It is also opportune to note that subdivisions such as the American Church are no longer a purely Latin ecclesial communion, but are comprised of hierarchies representing a variety of autonomous churches.

There are several factors which must be mentioned regarding the autonomy of these churches:

1. Ecclesial *autonomy* is not to be construed as absolute independence from any hierarchical superior, which, in canonical terms is designated as *autocephalous*. The two terms can be distinguished as follows: Autonomy is the right to self-governance while remaining submitted to a superior authority in certain matters. Autocephaly is independence from any superior authority in matters of governance.[10] Naturally, although patriarchs have been designated as *pater et caput* of their respective churches,[11] no church within the Catholic communion can be autocephalous since every Catholic must recognize the supreme authority of the Roman Pontiff.

2. These autonomous churches can be of various hierarchical rank, depending upon the hierarch who heads it and its constitutional setup:

    a. *Patriarchal Churches:* Armenian, Chaldean, Coptic, Maronite, Melkite, Roman, Syriac.

    b. *Major Archiepiscopal Churches:* Ukranian.

    c. *Metropolitan Churches:* Ethiopian, Malabarian (with two metropolitan sees), Malankarian, Romanian, Ruthenian (Byzantine Catholic dioceses in the United States), Hungarian.

    d. *Other Churches:* There are several small groups of eastern churches which have no eparchial structure at this time: Albanians, Byelorussians and Russians.

The degree of autonomy is not identical in all the autonomous churches: it is a *gradated* autonomy determined by the status of the hierarchal head of the autonomous church. An autonomous church which has a patriarch as its hierarchical superior enjoys a greater independence in governance than the major archiepiscopal churches, which, in turn, have a great ability to self-govern than do the metropolitan and other autonomous churches.

3. The canonical status of *sui iuris* cannot be self-proclaimed by the ecclesial communion itself; such a status of canonical independence must be either expressly or tacitly granted by the Supreme Authority of the Church, i.e., an ecumenical council or the Roman Pontiff.[12] At this time,

---

[10]"*Autonomy* in general is the exercise of the right to freedom and self-determination enjoyed by individuals and groups within and vis-a-vis a higher group or authority. When a Particular Church is the titular of such autonomy within and vis-a-vis an autocephalous church (or rarely simply the universal church), we have ecclesiastical autonomy. The fact of still being *within* or still belonging to the autocephalous church (often called the Mother Church) is expressed canonically above all by having the election of the head of the daughter church confirmed by the Mother Church, obtaining holy myron from the latter, and its head being commemorated in the dyptics of the former, etc.

"*Autocephaly* represents the fullness of ecclesiastical self-determination of a Particular Church within the church universal, including the right to elect its own head without needing to have the election confirmed by any superior ecclesiastical authority." George Nedungatt, "Autonomy, Autocephaly, and the Problem of Jurisdiction Today," *Kanon* 5 (1981), p. 22.

[11]*Orientalium Ecclesiarum*, n. 9.

[12]*Postquam Apostolicis* c. 303, §1, 1° and *Orientalium Ecclesiarum*, n. 11.

there are twenty-one churches of East and West which enjoy the status of being *sui iuris*.[13]

Thus far, we have examined the legal stature of the autonomous Catholic churches. Let us now address ourselves to their mode of governance. The eastern catholic churches are governed by a *hierarchical head* (either a patriarch, major archbishop, metropolitan or other hierarch) and *collegial body* (either a synod or a council of hierarchs) which cooperate in the governance of the autonomous church.

SYNODAL GOVERNANCE

The institutions of synods and councils are well-known in eastern Catholic canon law. The terms themselves have been used interchangeably: *synodos* (Greek) and *concilium (con-calo)* "to summon together" (Latin). However, as juridical institutions, the future Eastern Code of Canon Law will make some distinctions. The patriarchal and archiepiscopal churches have a synod of bishops *(synodus episcoporum)* which is composed of all the ordained bishops of the respective church. There is also the permanent synod *(synodus permanens)* which is composed of the patriarch/major archbishop and four bishops and functions in a manner comparable to a cabinet body. We shall discuss the nature and role of each of these at length.

The bishops of a metropolitan church do not form synods, but have a council of hierarchs, whose competency is much more restricted than that of a synod.

A synod is an assembly of bishops of the entire church or a certain part of the church for deliberating and deciding upon ecclesiastical matters.[14] It is important to note that a synod or council is an assembly of bishops. While others can be invited to attend in the capacity of experts or guests, only the bishops (and sometimes not all of them) enjoy a deliberative vote. This episcopal assembly collegially exercises a jurisdiction distinct from the jurisdiction of the individual bishops. Thus, bishops who are gathered only for consultation or who are not acting in a collegial manner with an authority which will bind everyone, are not, according to eastern canon law, functioning as a synod.[15]

Given this definition of synodal activity, the synodal institution, in its true and proper sense, has fallen into disuse in the Latin Church. Let us examine a few institutions of the Latin Church which are cited as examples of synodal governance:

---

[13]Ronald G. Roberson, *The Eastern Christian Churches* (Rome: Editrice Pontificia Universita Gregoriana, 1986), pp. 27-37.

[14]". . . conventus Episcoporum totius Ecclesiae vel partis alicuius ad deliberandum et decernendum de rebus ecclesiasticis." Stephanus Sipos, *Enchiridion Iuris Canonici* ed. Ladislaus Galos, 7th rev. ed. (Rome: Herder, 1960), p. 156.

[15]Sipos, *Enchiridion*, p. 156.

The diocesan synod, which is treated in CIC cc. 460-468 does not fulfill the requirements of being a synodal activity for two reasons: It is not a gathering of bishops and the participants do not enjoy a deliberative authority since the diocesan bishop remains the sole legislator and promulgates the acts of the synod (CIC c. 466).[16]

Another institution which is compared with a synod is the conference of bishops, treated in CIC cc. 447-459.[17] These conferences which are established either on a national or territorial basis (CIC c. 448, §1-2) are a limited expression of synodal activity since there are only twenty-nine cases in which the conference can issue decrees.[18] Such decrees have binding authority only if two-thirds of the members enjoying a deliberative voice approve, the decree has been legitimately promulgated and it has been reviewed by the Apostolic See. (CIC c. 455, §1-2) In other cases, wherein the bishops are acting unanimously on a matter which is within their competency, the binding force does not come from the authority of the episcopal conference, but from the individual bishops insofar as they have made a law for their respective dioceses.[19]

The universal synod of bishops (CIC cc. 342-348) is also cited as an example of collegial governance in the Catholic Church.[20] However, this institution enjoys only a consultative role unless in a specific case the Roman Pontiff endows it with a deliberative authority which is restricted insofar as any decisions taken by the synod must be ratified by the Roman Pontiff (CIC c. 343).

It is possible to analyze synodal governance in the eastern Catholic churches from various perspectives. We could examine it from a theological perspective and demonstrate how such activity is an ecclesial expression of the *communio* relationship within the Trinity.[21] We could also analyze synodal governance from an historical perspective, beginning with the collegial activity described in the

---

[16]The future Eastern Code refrains from using the term "synod" in this context and refers to this assembly as a convocation *(conventus)*, which is comprised of the bishop and representative of the clergy, religious and laity. See cc. 233-240 of the 1986 *Schema Codicis Iuris Canonici Orientalis*.

[17]The Second Vatican Council even makes a comparison between the episcopal conferences and the patriarchal churches: "Some of these, notably the ancient patriarchal Churches as mothers of the faith, gave birth to other daughter-Churches, as it were, and down to our own days they are linked with these by bonds of a more intimate charity in what pertains to the sacramental life and in a mutual respect for rights and obligations. This multiplicity of local Churches, unified in a common effort, shows all the more resplendently the catholicity of the undivided Church. In a like fashion the episcopal conferences at the present time are in a position to contribute in many and fruitful ways to the concrete realization of the collegiate spirit." *Lumen Gentium*, n. 23. Perhaps these episcopal conferences will eventually contribute to a national church being granted the canonical status of *sui iuris*.

[18]James A. Coriden, et. al., *The Code of Canon Law: A Text and Commentary*, (New York: Paulist Press, 1985), p. 370.

[19]Coriden, opcit. p. 373.

[20]While admitting that this institution is one in which the universal Church is represented and the needs of the eastern Catholic churches are also addressed, it is treated herein as an institution of the Latin Church, since it is not even mentioned in the 1986 *Schema Codicis Iuris Canonici Orientalis*.

[21]See Pierre Duprey, "The Synodical Structure of the Church in Eastern Theology," *One in Christ* 7 (1971), pp. 152-182; Rene Metz, "L'institution synodale d'apres les canons des synodes locaux (topiques)." *Kanon* 2 (1974), pp. 154-176.

New Testament community at Jerusalem, continuing throughout the centuries in various institutions in both the Latin and eastern churches (both catholic and orthodox) and culminating in the documents of the Second Vatican Council.[22]

Our approach, of course, will be canonical: we shall examine how synodal governance is articulated in the 1986 *Schema Codicis Iuris Canonici Orientalis* (hereinafter referred to as the *"Schema"* or *"SCICO"*), which is the first draft of the entire future Eastern Code issued by the Pontifical Commission for the Revision of the Eastern Code of Canon Law.[23]

PATRIARCHAL CHURCHES

The *Schema* refers to two institutions with the title of "synod:" the synod of bishops *(synodus episcoporum Ecclesiae partriarchalis vel Ecclesiae majoris archiepiscopalis)* and the permanent synod *(synodus permanens)*.

SYNOD OF BISHOPS

Together with the patriarch, the synod of bishops constitutes the highest authority in the patriarchal church. The *Schema* does not determine explicitly which of these institutions is superior to the other, but rather, the Commission took the approach that the future Code will apportion in a pragmatic manner the respective competency of the patriarch and the synod of bishops.[24] Although there is some degree of overlapping, in general, the competency is circumscribed as follows: There are three facets of the power of governance in the Church: executive, legislative and judicial (SCICO c. 981, §1). The patriarch enjoys executive authority and the synod of bishops enjoys the legislative and judicial authority in the autonomous church according to the norm of law.[25]

Territorial Restriction of Authority

The *Schema* imposes a restriction on the authority of both the patriarch and the synod of bishops according to territorial circumscriptions. With certain ex-

---

[22] See Joseph Hajjar, "Les synodes des Eglises Orientales Catholicques et l'eveque de Rome," *Kanon* 2 (1974), pp. 53-99; Daniel Faltin, "L'institution synodale dans le Concile Vatican II," *Kanon* 2 (1974), pp. 39-52.

[23] Rome, 1986.

[24] See *Nuntia* 2 (1976), p. 50. This relative parity of the patriarch and the synod was also expressed in the Second Vatican Council: "The patriarchs with their synods are the highest authority for all business of the patriarchates, not excepting the right of setting up new eparchies and appointing bishops of their rite within the patriarchal territory, without prejudice to the alienable right of the Roman Pontiff to intervene in any particular case."

[25] While administrative acts are ordinarily not within the competency of the synod of bishops, the *Schema* stipulates that the patriarch and the common law can establish a different arrangement in certain cases. See SCICI c. 110, §4.

ceptions which will be noted later, the authority of both of these institutions is restricted to the territory of the patriarchal church (SCICO cc. 54, 55, 146). Nearly all the patriarchal churches have become world-wide communities with faithful on all the continents. At times, the majority of the faithful resides outside the territorial limits of the patriarchal church. Consequently, this territorial restriction of the patriarchal/synodal authority has been greatly discussed during the revision process.

If one considers the doctrinal right of the Roman Pontiff to intervene in any manner he deems necessary (SCICO c. 42), the need for codified territorial restrictions on patriarchal/synodal authority takes on the appearance of being a superfluous issue. There have been recent cases wherein the Roman Pontiff intervened directly in matters within the competency of the synod of bishops and within the territory of the patriarchal church.

Canonical Counterparts

The synod of bishops is treated SCICO cc. 102-113.[26] Its counterpart in the current Eastern Code is the "electoral synod" *(synodus electionum)* which is responsible for the election of the patriarch and the election and proposal of bishops.[27] The patriarchal or national synod (*Cleri Sanctitati* cc. 340-342) which is similar to a plenary or provincial synod in the Latin Church (CIC cc. 439-446), has been eliminated in the *Schema*. Instead, the law provides for a convocation *(conventus)* of the entire patriarchal church, which is to be convoked at least every five years and is to be composed of bishops, and representatives of the clergy, religious and laity. This convocation has only consultative authority. (See SCICO cc. 140-145.)

Composition

The synod of bishops is exclusively comprised of all the ordained bishops of the patriarchal church constituted anywhere in the world (SCICO c. 102, §1).[28] While all the bishops of the patriarchal church are members of the synod, the *Schema* provides for the particular law of the patriarchal church to make a distinc-

---

[26] Title 4: "De Ecclesiis patriarchalibus," Chapter 3: "De Synodo Episcoporum Ecclesiae patriarchalis."
[27] See *Cleri Sanctitati* cc. 221-239; 251-256.
[28] It is interesting to note that *Cleri Sanctitati* c. 224, §1 permitted nominated but not yet ordained bishops to participate in the synod. One eastern canonist, Acacius Coussa, stated that this arrangement was inconsistent with the eastern discipline since prior to ordination the bishop-elect cannot exercise jurisdiction. See Acacius Coussa, *Epitome Praelectionum de Iure Ecclesiastico*, vol. 1, (Grottaferrata: Typis Monasterii Exarchi Cryptoferratensis, 1948), p. 232.

tion regarding the voting power of the members. The eparchial bishops who are constituted within the territory of the patriarchal church have a deliberative vote in all matters and the *Schema* does not provide for a restriction of this power. Regarding the bishops constituted outside the territory of the patriarchal church and titular bishops, particular law can restrict their deliberative vote in any matter except those regarding the election of the patriarch, the election of bishops and candidates for office outside the patriarchal church.[29] A major concern underlying this canon is that the bishops constituted outside the territory of the patriarchal church not be permitted to vote on matters which will have no binding authority on them. If one accepts the territorial restrictions on the authority of the patriarch and synods, this restriction on the deliberative voting power is understandable.

Electoral College

An important function of the synod of bishops is the election of the patriarch, the election of bishops and the election of candidates for episcopal office outside the territory of the patriarchal church.

We have already noted that all the ordained bishops of the patriarchal church enjoy a deliberative vote in the elections. The common law makes no distinction between eparchial, titular or retired bishops (SCICO c. 65, §1). One is elected patriarch who receives two-thirds of the votes. Particular law can stipulate that after at least three ballots, a simple majority suffices (SCICO c. 71, §1).

This right of the synod of bishops to elect the patriarch is not absolute: it is restricted to fifteen days. If no one is elected within fifteen days, the matter is deferred to the Roman Pontiff who can decide how to resolve the matter. In such a case the Roman Pontiff could either appoint the patriarch or remit the matter to the synod for resolution.

After the election (if the one who is elected is already an ordained bishop), the candidate is proclaimed and enthroned (SCICO c. 74). The synod of bishops notifies the Roman Pontiff of the canonical election, enthronement, profession of faith, and promise to fulfill his duty made by the patriarch. The patriarch then is to request ecclesiastical communion from the Roman Pontiff (SCICO c. 75). Even though the patriarch obtains the rights of his office upon enthronement (SCICO c. 76, §1), he must receive ecclesiastical communion from the Roman Pontiff before he can convoke the synod of bishops or ordain bishops (SCICO c. 76, §2).

The election of bishops for offices within the territory of the patriarchal church is conducted as follows: Members of the synod of bishops propose to the synod candidates they deem worthy of the episcopate. The synod then is to compile

---

[29]See SCICO c. 149.

a list of candidates by secret ballot and the patriarch submits the list to the Roman Pontiff for approval. Once this approval of a candidate is given by the Roman Pontiff, it remains in effect until it is explicitly revoked (SCICO c. 180). The synod then proceeds with the election according to the norm of law. If the one who is elected is already on a list approved by the Roman Pontiff, he is to be notified secretly by the patriarch. If he accepts the election, the patriarch is to notify the Apostolic See of the acceptance, proclamation and ordination of the new bishop. If the one who is elected is not on a list approved by the Roman Pontiff, his name must be submitted to the Roman Pontiff and absolute secrecy must be maintained until approval is granted (SCICO c. 183).

Regarding bishops constituted outside the territory of the patriarchal church, the synod elects at least three *candidates* for a particular office and the patriarch submits the list to the Roman Pontiff, who will make the appointment (SCICO c. 149). It should be noted that the Roman Pontiff is not restricted to choose from the list of candidates.

Legislative Competency

SCICO c. 110, §1 states: "The synod of bishops is exclusively competent to pass laws *(leges ferre)* for the entire patriarchal church, which acquire force according to c. 150, §2-3." The canon accords much authority to the synod of bishops. Whereas the CIC is both the common and particular law of the Latin Church, the future Eastern Code will be much more restricted insofar as it will provide only the law common to all of the eastern Catholic churches and allow for each autonomous church to "complete" its own legislative *corpus* with particular law. Such an arrangement is necessary since the Eastern Code is attempting to provide legislation for twenty-one different communities, each with its unique characteristics in discipline.[30]

A few examples of where the synod of bishops is competent to make particular law are the determination of when the patriarch can make canonical visitations (SCICO 82, §1), the determination of when the sacraments of initiation must be administered (SCICO c. 694), the establishment of marriage impediments (SCICO c. 787), the determination of the roles of minor ministers (SCICO c. 325). A taxative list of matters remanded to particular law will be quite extensive.

The phrase "which acquire force of law according to SCICO c. 150, §2-3" is important because it refers to the territorial limitations of the authority of the synod. Paragraph 2 delineates the limitations of the synodal authority:

Laws enacted by the synod and promulgated by the patriarch, if they are liturgical, have force everywhere in the world; however, if they are

---

[30]See the unpublished license dissertation by Benedict A. De Socio, *The Infra-Universal Legislation of Churches "Sui Iuris" in the Proposed Code of Eastern Canon Law,* (Washington: The Catholic University of America, 1987).

disciplinary or treat other decisions of the synod, they have force only within the territorial boundaries of the patriarchal church.

Thus, the authority of the synod of bishops is circumscribed territorially according to the matter treated in the legislation: if the legislation concerns liturgical matters, it binds everyone in the patriarchal church. If it is a disciplinary or other matter, the force of the legislation *per se* is restricted to the territory of the patriarchal church. There is a way, however, for the legislation of the synod of bishops to acquire force of law beyond the patriarchal territory. This arrangement is formulated in paragraph three:

If the eparchial bishops constituted outside the territory of the patriarchal church desire to give the force of law to the disciplinary laws and other synodal decisions which do not exceed their competency, they can attribute to them the force of law in their own eparchies; if however these laws and decisions are approved by the Apostolic See, they have the force of law everywhere in the world.

The disciplinary decisions do not acquire the force of law in virtue of the authority of the patriarch or the synod, but in virtue of the authority of the eparchial bishop within his own eparchy or the universal authority of the Apostolic See.

Judicial Competency

Another area of responsibility of the synod of bishops is its judicial role. The judicial system formulated in the *Schema* provides for eparchial tribunals (SCICO cc. 1081-1083), an ordinary patriarchal tribunal (SCICO c. 1078),[31] the tribunal of the synod of bishops (SCICO c. 1077) and, of course, the tribunals of the Roman Pontiff (SCICO cc. 1073-1075).

Within the territory of the patriarchial church, the tribunal of the synod of bishops constitutes the supreme tribunal for all cases of the patriarchal church, especially the contentious cases involving eparchies and bishops, except those which are reserved to the Roman Pontiff (SCICO c. 1075, §1). The tribunal is composed of three bishops elected by the synod of bishops for a five-year term. One of the three serves as a general moderator for the administration of justice in the patriarchal church. This tribunal is the final instance of appeal in the patriarchal church excepting, of course, the right of appeal to the Roman Pontiff (SCICO c. 1077).

---

[31]This tribunal will serve as the appellate court of the second and later instances for cases already tried in inferior tribunals and also will serve as the tribunal of the first instance for certain specified cases such as those involving exarchs and delegates of the patriarch who are not bishops and physical or juridical persons immediately subject to the patriarch.

Role of Advise and Consent

There are certain actions which are within the exclusive competency of the patriarch and do not require the prior consultation or approval of any other hierarch or body. For example, the patriarch can issue encyclicals related to his own church or rite to the entire patriarchal church (SCICO c. 81, §1, 3°); he can publish instructions concerning doctrine, piety or spiritual exercises (SCICO c. 81, §1, 1°); he fulfills the functions of a metropolitan in the case of a *sede vacante*, negligence or in those places where no province is established (SCICO c. 79).

There are other actions which require either the consultation or the consent of the synod of bishops. The *Schema* instructs the patriarch to *consult* with the synod in more grave matters or in matters which concern the entire patriarchal church (SCICO c. 81, §3).

Other actions require the *consent* of the synod of bishops. Only with this consent can the patriarch establish eparchies and provinces within the territory of the patriarchal church (SCICO c. 84, §1);[32] appoint auxiliary or coadjutor bishops (SCICO c, 84, §2, 1°); transfer a metropolitan, eparchial bishop or titular bishop to another see (SCICO c. 84, §2, 2); publish liturgical texts (SCICO c. 654, §1);[33] remove the patriarchal finance office (SCICO c. 122, §2); enter into accords with the civil authorities (SCICO c. 97).[34]

PERMANENT SYNOD

The permanent synod is a part of the patriarchal curia[35] and is comparable to a cabinet body in civil government. The permanent synod is composed of the patriarch and four bishops who are designated for a five-year term. Three of the bishops (two of whom must be eparchial bishops) are elected by the synod of bishops and one is nominated by the patriarch (SCICO c. 115). The permanent synod is to be convoked at least twice a year, and whenever the patriarch deems it opportune or common law requires the consultation or consent of this body (SCICO c. 120).

The *Schema* stipulates that certain actions by the patriarch require the consultation or the consent of the permanent synod.

For example, the *Schema* requires that the patriarch *consult* the permanent synod in more grave matters or in affairs involving the entire patriarchal church (SCICO c. 81, §3); prior to admonishing a bishop if there is no danger in delay (SCICO

---

[32] It should be noted that this action requires consultation with the Apostolic See.
[33] This action requires the approval of the Apostolic See.
[34] This action also requires the prior permission and subsequent approval of the Roman Pontiff before the accord can be put into effect.
[35] This institution is treated in Chapter 4: "The Patriarchal Curia" cc. 114-121.

c. 94, §2); prior to giving an interpretation of the law (SCICO c. 112, §2).

Examples of actions requiring the *consent* of the permanent synod are: the transfer of place of the election of the patriarch (SCICO 64, §1); the establishment or modification of an exarchy (SCICO c. 84, §3); the granting of exemption to a place or juridical person (SCICO c. 89); the nomination of a patriarchal finance officer (SCICO c. 122, §1).

It should be noted that matters which require the consultation or consent of the permanent synod remain within the competency of that body even during the convocation of a synod of bishops. The patriarch can only commit the matter to the synod of bishops with the consent of the permanent synod (SCICO c. 119).

MAJOR ARCHIEPISCOPAL CHURCHES

The *Schema* makes the general provision that what is stated about the patriarchal churches and patriarchs is also applicable to the major archiepiscopal churches and major archbishops unless the law expressly provides otherwise or it is evident from the nature of the matter (SCICO c. 152). As indicated above, there is only one Catholic major archiepiscopal church, the Ukranian Church.

One significant difference between the patriarch and the major archbishop is that after the synod of bishops has elected the major archbishop, the one who is elected must request confirmation from the Roman Pontiff. Only after the Roman Pontiff has confirmed the election can the proclamation and enthronement proceed. If the confirmation is denied, the synod of bishops is to conduct a new election within the time determined by the Roman Pontiff (SCICO c. 153).

METROPOLITAN AND OTHER AUTONOMOUS CHURCHES

Governance of the metropolitan and other autonomous churches is quite different from that of the patriarchal or major archiepiscopal churches; it can be characterized as "synodal governance" only in a very broad sense of the term. It will be shown that the rights of the heads of the metropolitan and other autonomous churches are much more restricted than their counterparts in the patriarchal or major archiepiscopal churches.

The head of a metropolitan autonomous church is not elected, but is appointed by the Roman Pontiff and assisted by a council of hierarchs according to the norm of law (SCICO c. 155, §1). In addition to areas of competency accorded to the metropolitan by common law or particular law established by the Roman Pontiff, the metropolitan can ordain and enthrone bishops appointed by the Roman Pontiff, establish a metropolitan tribunal, oversee the faith and discipline of his church, conduct canonical visitations in eparchies if the eparchial bishop neglects to do so, assign an eparchial administrator if the eparchial consultors fail to elect a qualified candidate after eight days, communicate the acts of the Roman Pontiff to the eparchial bishops and others to whom the matter is addressed, unless the Apostolic See has provided otherwise (SCICO c. 159). The metropolitan also has the right to perform all those other administrative acts which by common law are committed to the superior administrative authority of an autonomous church, however, only with the consent of the council of hierarchs (SCICO c. 165, § 3).

As stated in SCICO c. 155, the metropolitan is assisted in the governance of the autonomous church by the council of hierarchs.[36] All the eparchical bishops of the metropolitan church exclusively comprise the council of hierarchs and each has a deliberative vote. The majority of the council can determine if other bishops of the same church or another autonomous church can be invited, but then only as guests (SCICO c. 163, §1).

The *Schema* stipulates that the metropolitan and the council of hierarchs are to consult reciprocally on any extraordinary matter or any matter entailing a special difficulty (SCICO c. 160). As an electoral college, the council of hierarchs cannot directly elect bishops. The arrangement formulated in the *Schema* is similar to that for the nomination of bishops outside the territorial boundaries of the patriarchal church: the council of hierarchs is to draw up a list of at least three suitable candidates for a position and this list is to be sent to the Apostolic See, which will consequently make the nomination (SCICO c. 166).

Regarding the legislative competency of the council of hierarchs, the *Schema* is also more restricted. The *Schema* accords the council hierarchs the power to legislate in those cases which common law allocates to the particular law of an autonomous church (SCICO c. 165, §1), but this legislation does not automatically acquire the force of law. The metropolitan must notify the Apostolic See of any such norms, which can be validly promulgated only after the Apostolic See has notified the metropolitan of the reception of the acts (SCICO c. 165, §3).

There are other autonomous churches which are neither patriarchal, major archiepiscopal nor metropolitan. The *Schema* provides for these churches in cc. 172-174. These communities are examples of a case of "diminished autonomy." These churches are immediately dependent upon the Apostolic See (SCICO c. 173).

The head of these churches is appointed according to the norms of common and particular law established by the Roman Pontiff (SCICO c. 172). As a delegate of the Apostolic See, this hierarchical head enjoys the right to perform certain administrative actions such as the establishment of a tribunal, oversight of the faith and ecclesiastical discipline of the autonomous church, and conduct canonical visitations in eparchies if the eparchial bishop fails to do so (SCICO c. 159, 3°-8°). In all other cases, if common law remits a matter to the particular law or the superior administrative authority of an autonomous church, the competent authority

---

[36]Notice that there is no mention of the two sharing the position of highest authority as was the case with the patriarchs and the synod of bishops.

in these churches is the eparchial bishop with the consent of the Apostolic See, unless it is otherwise expressly stated (SCICO c. 174).

CONCLUSION

In a cursory manner we have examined the synodal institutions of the eastern Catholic churches. History has shown us that the system itself is filled with obstacles. Those aspects of synodal governance which were criticized by Gregory Nazianzus in the fourth century have not disappeared. Yet we must realize that these problems exist not because of the synodal institutions, but because of our own human frailties.

Synodal governance reminds us that God entrusted the Gospel to a collective body, the Church; it is a treasure too valuable to be entrusted to any individual. Therefore, from the very beginning, it has been as a collective body that the authorities in the Church made decisions about how the Gospel should be lived. We can only marvel at the way the Holy Spirit has guided us to the door of the third millenium in spite of ourselves.

CLERICAL MISCONDUCT:
CANONICAL AND PRACTICAL CONSEQUENCES

JOHN G. PROCTOR

The timeliness of this presentation can hardly be denied. For the past two or three years, it seems as if we have been bombarded with stories—horror stories—of evil and perverted deeds, perpetrated by Catholic priests on unsuspecting and helpless victims. Newspapers all over the country have run "exposes," and various Catholic journals of both the left and right have unhesitatingly editorialized about possible solutions to what is perceived as a very serious problem.

Although most of the stories have involved allegations of sexual misconduct, there also have been references to other types of alleged misconduct, for example, professional and financial priestly malfeasance. The situation has become serious enough to warrant many dioceses presenting special workshops for their priests. These workshops not only attempt to establish particular policy for the handling of misconduct cases, they also serve as stern lecture sessions, warning priests of the dire consequences which will befall them if they are accused of or are found to have been guilty of clerical misconduct.

So here we are. Clerical misconduct is perceived as a real and present problem. Consequently, policies are being formulated and enacted. Considerable media interest has been generated. Some people's lives can be dramatically and drastically affected by this, especially the accused cleric and the alleged victim.

Initially, I think it is necessary to offer a context for my remarks and to clarify some definitions. In this way, I hope to limit the scope of my presentation, while at the same time attempt to better focus it. I am not qualified to discuss the concepts or the practice of civil law.[1] Rather, this paper deals with the canonical

---

[1] There are some articles which the reader might find helpful in learning about these concepts. I refer especially to C. Eric Funston's "Made Out of Whole Cloth? A Constitutional Analysis of the Clergy Malpractice Concept," *California Western Law Review* (Volume 19, 1982-83), pp. 507-544; Ben Zion Bergman's "Is the Cloth Unraveling? A First Look at Clergy Malpractice," *San Fernando Valley Law Review* (Volume 9, 1981), pp. 47-66; and Jacob M. Yellin's "The History and Current Status of the Clergy-Penitent Privilege," *Santa Clara Law Review* (Volume 23, 1983, No. 1), pp. 95-156. Other articles include: "American Briefing (New Causes of Action in the U.S.)," *Solicitor's Journal* (Vol. 129, July 12, 1985), p. 474; Bill Girdner, "To Err Is Human," *California Lawyer* (Vol. 5, August, 1985), p. 21; Robert McMenamin, "Clergy Malpractice," *Case and Comment* (Vol. 90, September/October, 1985), p. 3; Kimberly Anne Klee, "Clergy Malpractice: Bad News for the Good Samaritan or a Blessing in Disguise?" *University of Toledo Law Review* (Vol. 17, Fall, 1985), pp. 209-253; Cassandra Butler, "Church Tort Liability in Spite of First Amendment Protection," *Southern University Law Review* (Vol. 12, Fall, 1985), pp. 36-46; Christopher Brauchli, "From the Wool-Sack," *Colorado Lawyer* (Vol. 14, November, 1985), p. 2005; Claudia Postell, "Clergy Malpractice," *Trial* (Vol. 21, December, 1985), p. 91 (2); Helena Sunny Wise, "Clergy Malpractice Suits," *Los Angeles Lawyer* (Vol. 8, December, 1985), pp. 20-21; William Rehwald, "Clergy Malpractice, A Letter to the Editor," *Trial* (Vol. 22, March, 1986), p. 6 (2); Thomas Paprocki, "Malpractice in the Ministry," *Compleat Lawyer* (Volume 3, Spring, 1986), p. 18 (3); Lee Brooks, "Intentional Infliction of Emotional Distress by Spiritual Counsellors," *Michigan Law Review* (Vol. 84, May, 1986), pp. 1296-1325; Edward Barker, "Clergy Malpractice," *Trial* (Vol. 22, May, 1986), p. 12 (2); Edward Barker, "Clergy Negligence; Are Juries Ready To Sit In Judgment?" *Trial* (Vol. 22, July, 1986), p. 56 (4); and Carl Esbeck, "Tort Claims Against Churches and Ecclesiastical Officers," *West Virginia Law Review* (Vol. 89, Fall, 1986), pp. 1-114. A whole monograph has been written on this subject: *Clergy Malpractice* by Malony, Needham, and Southard (Philadelphia: The Westminster Press), 1986.

consequences of both the accusation and fact of clerical misconduct. Specifically, I intend to include the following elements: a working definition of "clerical misconduct"; the acusation itself; the rights of the accused and the accuser; the process of handling the accusation (the investigation), with particular emphasis on the consequences of a true accusation (that is, the application of penalties); the disposition of a cleric truthfully accused; the reparation owed a cleric untruthfully accused; rehabilitation and reinstatement and the permanently dysfunctional cleric.

A Statement of Principle

Prior to initiating a specifically canonical discussion on clerical misconduct, it seems wise to articulate a philosophical foundation for the application of the particular canons. The application of Church law comes from both experience and insight. Before law can be applied justly, the Church must experience its own moral integrity. Such integrity is based on the protection of the rights of both community and individual, institution and person. Good law requires an assessment of the community's values. Those values having been discerned, law can then be applied.

Most, if not all, so-called misconduct cases involve two sets of conflicts: the conflict between the rights of the accuser (to have a grievance heard and resolved) and the rights of the accused (to be shielded from malice and protected from caprice); and the conflict between institutional goals (usually financial) and personal well-being (health, reputation, career, security). Unless a philosophy for resolving these conflicts is achieved prior to the application of law, the fate of the accuser and of the accused and the welfare of the community are nothing more than the consequences of expediency.

It is my contention, with specific reference to Church law, that the resolution of clerical misconduct cases must depend on values higher and deeper than the mere avoidance of economic loss. In Church law, the welfare of people becomes a primary goal. Unjust procedures, cavalier dismissals, self-exculpatory denials and similar behavior harm the Church far more significantly than financial loss. On the contrary, a fair application of Church law (where, for example, the Church might find itself at fault to some extent) can only enhance respect for Church law and for the Church itself.[2]

---

[2]Cc. 220, 221, and 223, §1 are particularly instructive in this matter. Father James Provost argues that the limitation of rights in Church law is permitted "not because of the Church's convenience, but only because such an exercise would harm the conditions within which Christians seek their perfection in the life of the Church." James H. Provost, "Book II: The People of God," in *The Code of Canon Law: A Text and Commentary,* eds. Coriden, Green, Heintschel (New York: Paulist Press, 1985), p. 158 *(henceforth CLSA Commentary).* Such an interpretation of rights heavily favors a personalistic application of Church law.

It is my further contention, moreover, that real respect for the welfare of individuals in cases of alleged clerical misconduct must be the primary philosophical principle governing the application of law in these matters.[3] Thus, the resolution of these cases requires a real and concrete sensitivity on the part of Church authorities for both the accuser and the accused, for any victims and for any perpetrators. The financial welfare of the Church or the protection of its patrimony cannot be lightly ignored. However, when protection of the financial status of the Church finds itself in conflict with the personal welfare of its members, then financial considerations must take a secondary role in resolving very serious issues.

If this principle of personalism (that is, the priority of individual Church members' welfare over purely financial protection for the institution) is observed in cases of clerical misconduct, I believe many benefits will result. The Church will be perceived as following the will of her Master in a concrete situation; the anger of the parties involved in these cases will be diminished because they will feel that caring sensitivity is really being offered them; the potential scandal of such situations will be diminished, if not offset, by the visible practice of ecclesial charity; the Gospel will be vindicated.

In summary, then, clerical misconduct cases require the protection of values higher than merely financial interests. The misapplication of institutional concern harms the Church far more significantly than a simple financial loss. On the other hand, the perception of a Church, guided by the Gospel in caring for all the members, does a great deal to alleviate the ugliness and scandal attached to these kinds of cases.

A Definition of Clerical Misconduct

The phrase "clerical misconduct" is fairly ambiguous. To the public, it generally means some kind of behavior that is "unpriestly", that is, a behavior which offends the average person's notion of what a priest should or shouldn't do. Thus, "clerical misconduct" can mean something as petty as "I don't like Father's language," to something far more serious: "Father has molested my son or daughter", "Father has stolen money from me", " Father has made improper suggestions to me in the reconciliation room." Because the phrase "clerical misconduct" is misunderstood and imprecisely applied, it is necessary to achieve some canonical accuracy about the nature of this misconduct.

---

[3]It is important to recall the words of Pope John Paul II in the Apostolic Constitution *Sacrae Disciplinae Leges:*" . . . the Code is in no way intended as a substitute for faith, grace, charisms, and especially charity in the life of the Church and of the faithful. On the contrary, its purpose is rather to create such an order in the ecclesial society that, while assigning the primacy to love, grace, and charisms, it at the same time renders their organic development easier in the life of both the ecclesial society and the individual persons who belong to it." *CLSA Commentary, op. cit.*, p. xxv.

The type of misconduct we are dealing with is specifically "clerical." "Clerical misconduct" would, then, be that misconduct engaged in by a cleric: a person who has been ordained at least to the diaconate.[4]

We must now refine the term "misconduct." When the Board of Governors asked me to address this topic, they thoughtfully included three specific canons which they felt I should address: cc. 1389, 1395, and 1396. It only makes sense, then, to define "clerical misconduct" in terms of the mandate which originally prompted this presentation.

In this presentation the definition of clerical misconduct includes three areas of concern: the abuse of clerical authority or clerical negligence; various violations of clerical chastity; and violation of one's residence obligations.

Canon 1389 establishes a penalty for "one who abuses ecclesiastical power or function." Also to be punished is "one who through culpable negligence illegitimately places or omits an act of ecclesiastical power, ministry or function which damages another person."[5] Green, in his commentary on this canon,[6] speaks of "two significant values." A principal value behind the theory of misconduct articulated in this canon is accountability. Church members have a right to expect that their ministers will be accountable and responsible for the positions of public trust they enjoy.

Another value protected by the application of this canon is a clearer understanding of the responsibilities commensurate with one's office. Clerics have the right to a clear description of what is expected of them, their responsibilities, so that any confusion about irresponsibility or malfeasance can be avoided. Moreover, certainly included in the scope of this canon is the notion of misconduct through omission. Serious harm can result not only from some wrong conduct on the part of a cleric, but also from his inaction or his culpable ignorance about some action he should perform. If both Church members and clerics are thoroughly familiar with what is expected from clerics in the exercise of their public office in the Church, then clerical misconduct can be minimized and the reparation of damages will be accomplished more easily.

A final comment on this canon seems germane. One of the responsibilities attached to clerical power or function is that of continuing education about one's public office.[7] Culpable ignorance in the performance of one's office is necessarily included in the scope of this canon.

In summary, clerical misconduct as defined by this canon would include abuse of power or function through commission or omission and culpable negligence and ignorance causing harm to another.

---

[4]Cf. c. 266, §1.

[5]Cf. *CLSA Commentary, op. cit.*, p. 927.

[6]*Ibid.*, p. 926. Actually, Green is commenting on c. 1384, a similar canon which, *mutatis mutandis*, has relevancy for c. 1389.

[7]Cf. c. 279.

Canon 1395 deals with the area of violations against chastity (not, strictly speaking, celibacy).[8] Various actions are proscribed for the cleric. Such actions include: *concubinage,* or a continuing non-marital sexual relationship between a cleric and a woman; habitual sexual conduct on the part of a cleric that results in scandal, even if this conduct does not involve an on-going relationship; and non-habitual sexual conduct on the part of a cleric if such conduct involves any one of three elements: the use of threats or force; public perpetration; or the involvement of a person of either sex under sixteen years of age. In each of these areas of sexual misconduct, obstinacy of action or recidivism makes the misconduct more serious.[9]

A word or two needs to be said here about the notion of being "public." In canonical tradition, something is "public" in one of two ways: either there is irrefutable evidence of it through accessible ecclesiastical or civil documents or there are witnesses willing to come forward to testify to it in the external forum. However, there are two other ways of thinking about being "public" for the cleric. The first consideration is the public nature of the ministry itself. Ministry requires a special accountability because of its public nature. Thus, although some activity might be "private" in the cultural sense of the word, it nonetheless takes on a public context because of the public status of the minister. In this sense, all clerical misconduct cases are public good cases. Secondly, it is important to observe in a society of great technology and even greater litigation, that very few actions are truly "private" in the canonical sense. People tend to conduct themselves in traceable ways. For clerics, then, this double exposure to publicity becomes an important factor in the prosecution of misconduct cases.

Canon 1396 deals with violations of clerical residence requirements. Certain offices require obligatory residence.[10] The canon deals with the right of the People of God to have access to their ministers, the right to have an assured ministerial presence.

Reference should be made here also to cc. 273-289. These canons describe the kind of lifestyle that should be led by clerics, although many requirements are dispensed for deacons. In addition to various elements of the clerical lifestyle with which we are all familiar, celibacy for example, these canons also outline an approach to clerical behavior that is logically connected to our present discussion. Simplicity of life style, propriety in all sexual matters, the avoidance of

---

[8]The distinction here is, I think, important. One frequently hears that a cleric's life should be protected from investigation into what is characterized as "matters of the internal form." Celibacy is manifestly a matter of the external form. But this canon's reference to chastity specifically takes into account certain matters which normally are internal form matters. Thus, it would seem that the cleric's public status in the Church makes him accountable in a unique way not only for his celibacy but also for significant matters dealing with sexual behavior.

[9]It is clear from the context of the canon itself that deliberate ignorance of the offense or studied avoidance of the offender does little to remedy the problem.

[10]Cf. c. 395 for the residence obligations of residential bishops; c. 410 for the residence obligations of coadjutor and auxiliary bishops. Cf. also c. 533 dealing with pastors; c. 543, §2, 1 for team ministers; c. 550 for associate pastors.

behavior unbecoming and alien to clerical life, and even continuing education are all to be considered in the avoidance of clerical misconduct.

The Code prescribes various penalties for misconduct. These penalties range from the very unspecific "just penalty" to the very specific "dismissal from the clerical state." The law, then, urges a very flexible response to misconduct, depending on a variety of circumstances.

In summary, clerical misconduct, at least for the purposes of this presentation, denotes three areas of concern: the culpable abuse of ecclesiastical power or function, along with negligent or ignorant use of the same; certain sexual misconduct, with special emphasis on continuing impropriety, the use of force or threat, or the involvement of minors; and finally, infractions against the Code's requirements of residence attached to clerical office. In general, also, clerical misconduct must be contextualized in terms of clerics' pastoral/legal obligations to live an appropriate life style.

The Accusation

Most clerical misconduct cases begin with an accusation. It would make circumstances a lot easier if accusations were always clear and detailed. But such is not the case. Some accusations are muddled; some are ill-focused; some are incredible. It becomes necessary, therefore, to make a few clarifying comments about the accusation itself and its context.

Canon 1390 deals with the crime of falsehood, specifically as a violation of one's right to a good reputation.[11] Along with the law's concern that a confessor not be falsely accused of solicitation within the process of reconciliation,[12] this canon deals with any deliberately false accusation against any person to an ecclesiastical superior. The canon specifically includes a provision allowing for forced collection of damages from the calumniator.

I believe the inclusion and retention of c. 1390 in the present Code,[13] merits serious consideration. One of the clear purposes of the revision of the Code was to make it as responsive as possible to real situations in the Church. In that context, obvious anachronisms and clear irrelevancies were deleted. Thus, the deliberate retention of this canon seems to underline that the possibility of false accusation remains a realistic concern in the Church.

---

[11] The right to a good reputation is explicitly stated in c. 220. Aside from its status as a basic human right, a good reputation can have juridic effects, and conversely, its loss can have negative juridic effects. (Cf. c. 1741, for example, which has specific application in this discussion.) C. 220 also stipulates the right to privacy, a not inconsequential consideration when discussing an accusation against a cleric. Further complicating this right to privacy which, as Provost says, "will be a source of debate and development over the coming years," (*CLSA Commentary, op. cit.*, p. 153) is the tension that may arise between the articulated right and the necessarily public status of the cleric.

[12] Cf. C. 982 also on this matter.

[13] Cf. c. 2355 in CIC (1917).

In light of c. 1390, it is the responsibility of the person who receives an accusation against a cleric at least to ascertain initially that there is not a malicious or nefarious motivation attached to the accusation. In other words, all accusations are not created equal. Dealing specifically with the accusation, juridic logic requires that any obvious taint be ferreted out immediately and should assure that such ill-founded accusations do not further see the light of day.

This is not to argue for a dismissive approach to the report of an accusation. It is, however, to argue against policies or dispositions which presume clerical guilt or which fail to acknowledge human weakness and frailty even in the very serious circumstance of accusing a cleric of misconduct. Perhaps, to borrow a time-honored canonical phrase, it should be the duty of the recipient of an accusation to ascertain that the accusation has a *fumus boni juris*.

Another important issue concerning the accusation of clerical misconduct deals with the accusation's content. It would be most inappropriate (and ultimately self-defeating) to argue that one who accuses a cleric of misconduct must be canonically conversant. On the other hand, as serious a charge as an accusation of clerical misconduct clearly must have some substance, what I suppose could be characterized as "probable cause." At the very least, an accusation has to have at least three elements: a generally identifiable accuser, a specified accused, and the particularization of a charge.

Although the law does not specifically treat of what requirements are essential to make a legitimate accusation in cases of clerical misconduct, some indication can nonetheless be discovered. Canon 1504 deals with the essential minimal elements for the introduction of a *libellus* in a contentious case. "At least . . . general facts and proofs"[14] must be indicated by the accuser. Without such an indication, the basis for evaluating an accusation is missing. A guiding principle for assessing these accusations would include specificity and believability: specifically with regard to the facts and proofs, believability on the part of the accuser.

One final comment needs to be made on this issue. Canon 221 contains a series of elements necessary for protecting rights in the Church through due process of law. This canon has specific application for the discussion of an accusation against a cleric. The good-faith accuser enjoys the protection of this canon. In other words, the serious accuser has the right to vindicate his complaint through due process of law. Thus, it is self-evident that any automatically dismissive approach to all accusations is a violation of basic rights. The right to legal process must be considered in the reception of an accusation.

In summary, then, three comments about the accusation of clerical misconduct seem germane: there is always the possibility of false accusation and this possibility must be taken into consideration when such an accusation is made; there must be some semblance of substance to an accusation; accusations must not be dismissively treated as a matter of course.

---

[14]*CLSA Commentary*, p. 971.

The Rights of the Accuser and of the Accused

The person making an accusation of clerical misconduct is basically seeking to vindicate the rights articulated in c. 221. These rights include the right to be heard, the right to legal process, and the right to the resolution of a grievance. These rights have been discussed above.

However, there are other rights being asserted by the accuser in cases of clerical misconduct. These might be characterized as derivative rights. Although these so-called derivative rights many times receive secondary attention in canonical discussion, nonetheless they many times represent the chief grievance or complaint being lodged by the accuser. These rights include, but are not limited to,[15] the following: the right to be free from bizarre, disturbing, or detrimental clerical behavior; the right to be free from clerical incompetence, malfeasance, or negligence; the right to be free from clerics afflicted by mental illness or bodily infirmity to the extent that they are incapable of performing their duties in an acceptable fashion; the right to be free from clerics who have bad or scandalous reputations or personal histories; the right to be free from clerics who squander or misappropriate church funds, either for nefarious or immoral purposes or simply for their own self-advantage.

To articulate these rights enjoyed by the accuser in clerical misconduct cases may seem excessively legalistic. However, to underestimate the importance of these rights is to make a double mistake: it places the machinery for dispensing ecclesial justice outside the reach of the faithful; at the same time, underestimating these rights causes well meaning people to seek redress and resolution of their grievances in the civil system, thus creating even more serious problems for the Church.

The accused cleric also has rights, even (or, perhaps, *especially*) if the circumstances of the accusation turn out to be accurate and truthful. The accused cleric has the same access to c. 221 as his accuser. Thus, the accused cleric can vindicate and defend his rights, specifically, the right to due process of law and the right to be penalized only in accord with the law.

The accused cleric also has a series of rights which can appear secondary in cases of alleged misconduct but which are extremely important to one's personal, professional, spiritual, and economic well-being. The right to a good reputation and privacy has already been mentioned.[16] There are other rights that should be kept in mind: the right to support,[17] the right to spiritual guidance, the right to

---

[15]Cf. c. 1741. For a better specification of these rights, see Parizek's treatment in *CLSA Commentary, op. cit.*, 1037-1040. See also Robert Ombres, "The Removal of Parish Priests," *Priests and People* (Vol. 1, No. 1, April, 1987), pp. 9-12.

[16]On the issue of privacy rights and their occasional limits, see Edward Dillon, "Confidentiality of Ecclesiastical Records," *The Catholic Lawyer* (Volume 30, No. 3, Autumn, 1986), pp. 177-197.

[17]There is both a cleric's generalized right to support (cc. 222, 265, 269, 281, 384, 455, 531, 1274) and also his right to support with specific reference to the penal process (c. 195 and c. 1350).

expert canonical help, and the right not to incriminate one's self, to name just a few.

If we are truly conscious of people's rights, our legal practice will be the better. On the one hand, we will not treat accusations and accusers with contempt or dismissive arrogance. We will take seriously the faithful's right to professional and accountable ministry. On the other hand, we will not automatically presume clerical guilt in the midst of a hostile atmosphere. Nor will we abandon the very colleagues to whom we owe a fundamental charitable and ecclesial concern. The protection of rights makes all of us more decent people.

One further point needs to be made. Generally speaking, rights are not absolute. Rights are conditioned. To assert the existence of rights is not to claim such an absolute inviolability of those rights that the Church's ability to minister effectively would suffer. This is a particularly critical insight for clerics. It is generally agreed that there is no fundamental right to ordained ministry, rather simply a right to present one's self for such ministry. It is also generally recognized that ministry is, of its very nature, vicarious, that is, performed in another's name, here, in the name of the Church. Thus, a cleric's rights can be limited in some circumstances. The Code gives us two such circumstances: the common good can condition rights, as can one's own duties or the rights of others.[18]

There are other circumstances which can condition rights. In the particular case of clerical misconduct, any criminal action, grave sin, or significantly untoward behavior which continues even after admonition from Church authority conditions one's rights. Also to be included in this list are: obstinacy in wrongful activity, recidivism, and deliberate malice in the commission of misconduct.

The Investigation and Its Consequences

When an accusation of clerical misconduct has been made, there must be a response on the part of Church authority. The most obvious response to an accusation is to initiate an investigation. Such questions as how the investigation is to take place, who the investigator is to be, and what action(s) should be taken after the investigation are particularly difficult.

General experience seems to indicate that most canonists refer to the sixth and seventh books of the Code in answer to questions concerning investigations of clerical misconduct. However, it might be better to initiate such investigations, not with a penal model, but rather with a therapeutic one. For example, Green states: "Frequently the most beneficial approach is a therapeutic rather than a penal one, especially if there is diminished imputability on the part of the cleric."[19]

---

[18] Cf. c. 223.
[19] *CLSA Commentary, op. cit.*, p. 929.

Provost echoes the same thought: "Book VI provides a number of norms that must be observed in imposing sanctions in the Church. No sanction can be imposed unless a person has externally violated a law or precept, has done so gravely, and is personally imputable for the act (c. 1321, §1). A sanction can be applied by using either a judicial procedure or an administrative one—only, however, after it is clear that nothing else (e.g. fraternal correction, warning, or pastoral solicitude) will repair scandal, restore justice, or lead to a change in the problematic way of acting (c. 1341)."[20]

However, in cases of alleged clerical misconduct before a decision can be made about the modality of intervention, the accusation itself must first be investigated. This brings us to cc. 1717-1719.

The Code allows maximum flexibility in initiating and executing an investigation. The investigating responsibility falls to the ordinary (here, the diocesan bishop). Although the diocesan bishop may delegate investigatory powers to another suitable person, the delicacy of a misconduct allegation would seem to require the bishop's personal intervention.[21]

The investigation has three objects for its focus: the facts of the case, any relevant circumstances, and the issue of imputability. In other words, the investigation has as its purpose to ascertain whether there is a real possibility of truthfulness to the accusation. The flexibility allowed in this investigation is even carried to the point of making the formal investigation superfluous if the strength of the accusation stands on its own merits. Furthermore, it is during the investigation that the bishop may determine to assess or pay damages if warranted.[22]

There is one further value to be upheld during the investigation. It is imperative that the good name of the accused or of the accuser not be placed in jeopardy. Thus, the investigation is confidential, even to the point of placing any *acta* in the secret archive of the chancery.

Having completed the investigation (or having decided that it is superfluous), the bishop must make three determinations: should anything further be done? (Sometimes the investigation will establish that the accusation is without merit.) If something further should be done,[23] should the penal process be employed? If the penal process is seen as an adequate response to the situation, should the bishop then proceed administratively or judicially?

It is the second determination that many times proves to be the most difficult. To guide the bishop in making this determination, reference should be made to cc. 1341-42.

---

[20]*CLSA Commentary, op. cit.*, p. 155.

[21]For purposes of this paper, because I believe the bishop to be the proper investigating officer, I shall refer simply to "the bishop" rather than to "the ordinary."

[22]Cf. c. 1718, §4.

[23]It is here that the search for moral certitude begins. Until the decision is made to continue with the process, the only purpose of the investigation is to ascertain the credibility of the accusation.

Both the pastoral nature of Church law and its requirements for establishing full imputability in the penal process argue at least implicitly (if not explicitly) for the desirability of non-penal models when misconduct accusations are found to have some merit. Penal solutions are definitely last-resort solutions.

In guiding the bishop's decision on this matter, c. 1341 lists, non-taxatively, some conditions to be considered. Penal procedure is to be used *only* when scandal cannot be sufficiently repaired, when justice cannot be sufficiently restored, and when a miscreant cannot be reformed in any other way. Specifically, penal procedure is to be used when fraternal correction, rebuke, or "other ways of pastoral care" have been ineffective. It is hard to imagine all these techniques being ineffective with any given offender (particularly with reference to accusations of misconduct under c. 1395) and yet full imputability still being attributed to him, not to speak of being judicially maintained.

The issue of imputability cannot be taken too lightly. Although it is not the purpose of this paper to present a detailed treatment of imputability, it might nonetheless be of some use to make at least a passing reference to specific conditions and/or factors which either remove imputability or significantly diminish it.

A variety of conditions and/or factors affect imputability. Most of these conditions/factors would be recognizable by modern medical practice as psychological problems. The list would include: insanity, fear, ignorance, psychological impairment, alcoholism and drunkenness (even if drukenness is deliberate), drug use or addiction, senility, affective or psychosexual disorders, provocation, judicial invention, and cultural or local circumstances. Although the law presumes imputability in the occurrence of an external violation, this presumption can be overturned, something which will frequently happen in these circumstances.

In summary, it is hard to imagine the desirability of the penal process in matters of alleged clerical misconduct. The law itself seems to have a reluctance to use the penal process. Furthermore, because of the almost certain presence of diminished (if not totally mitigated) imputability, it is difficult to envision the usefulness of the penal process. A therapeutic model is definitely to be preferred.

To argue for a therapeutic disposition of clerical misconduct cases, however, does not mean to deny a bishop the tools he needs to take decisive action during the actual course of canonical process. The therapeutic model needs the accused's cooperation. In the face of the accused's refusal to cooperate, or if the accused reasonably demands access to the full penal process, there are certain actions available to the bishop. When an investigation reveals that an accusation of clerical misconduct has merit, the bishop has a variety of options. These options not only safeguard the good of the Church, they can also protect the cleric.

Canon 1722 outlines a series of actions available to the bishop at any time after the initial investigation establishes that the accusation has merit. The bishop may be motivated by different considerations: the avoidance of scandal, the protection of witnesses, or the protection of the judicial process itself or the course of justice. Having heard the Promoter of Justice and having cited the accused (a requirement not to be minimized), the bishop may: remove the accused from the sacred ministry or from any ecclesiastical office or function,[24] impose or prohibit residence in a given place or territory, or prohibit public participation in eucharistic worship.

Several factors are self-evident in the application of this canon. Most importantly, there must be a real legal reason for the utilization of these measures. The utilization of these measures is not something automatic: the Promoter of Justice has definite input. These measures cannot be imposed whimsically or capriciously: the accused must be cited (and should be heard). Finally, these measures must be withdrawn when the reason for their imposition ceases. When the case has been decided, these measures cease automatically.

In all honesty, however, it must be admitted that there will be some times when the penal process will have to be used. The final determination then left to the bishop, with some conditions, is the choice of either administrative penal procedure or judicial penal procedure.

If the bishop chooses administrative procedure, there are certain legal requirements to be observed.[25] The bishop must inform the accused cleric about the specific accusation and the evidence which sustains it. Moreover, the bishop is not to proceed administratively unless he has heard the advice of two assessors to whom the evidence in its entirety should be available. Although the bishop is not bound by the assessors' advice, they nonetheless have an important consultative role.

The accused has the right to self-defense. Such a right encompasses the availability of retaining competent canonical counsel, access to all the accusations and the relevant documents employed to sustain them (evidence), and information about one's procedural and appellate rights.

Finally, in the imposition of any penalty, the bishop is to follow the norms (cc. 1342-50) concerning the application of penalties. There are three considerations to be remembered. Certain penalties (e.g. perpetual penalties like dismissal from the clerical state) can only be imposed judicially (or by action of the Holy See). Furthermore, censures (as distinguished from expiatory penalties) can only be imposed if there has been a prior warning and a reasonable time has been given for reformation. Finally, an appeal or recourse of any penalty (censure or expiatory penalty), administratively or judicially inflicted, automatically suspends the execution of the penalty.

Certain other conditions are attached to the administrative infliction of penalties.

---

[24]This is not a suspension. It is not penal, but protective. It is temporary, its duration decided by specific circumstances and not by unbridled judicial discretion; although this action is subject to recourse, it does not seem to be susceptible to the provisions of c. 1353. Finally, it does not condition or jeopardize any vested rights of the cleric. An administrative act, it does not have (canonically) penal consequences.

[25]Cf. c. 1720.

When the bishop has reached moral certitude,[26] he is to issue a decree explaining legally and factually why the penalty has been imposed. This decree is a kind of clarification of the penal and procedural law relevant to the case, as well as of the facts which compelled the decision.

If the bishop chooses a judicial procedure, or if the law itself dictates such a procedure, the relevant canons are to be found in the first part of the seventh book of the Code.[27]

There are also some stipulations unique to the judicial penal process.[28] Two of these special procedures are noteworthy. The accused cleric has the right to be the last to be heard. Not only is the accused thus given the chance to answer each and every component of the accusation, he is able also to give his response the broadest possible foundation. The accused cleric is also protected against self-incrimination. He cannot be compelled to confess to an accusation nor can he be forced to take an oath. Thus, the accused cannot be coerced into confessing under the threat of a heavier penalty for failure to confess.

I have tried to outline information pertinent to the investigation and consequent prosecution of a case of alleged clerical misconduct. Three main themes have emerged: first, the accuation must have a factual basis, a finding arrived at through a properly conducted investigation; second, it is preferable to deal with cases of clerical misconduct therapeutically and not penally; finally, if the penal process is chosen as the proper resolution, proper procedure must be followed.

The Disposition of a Cleric Truthfully Accused

Sadly, some accusations of clerical misconduct are true. Having arrived at this conclusion in an honest and fair manner (i.e. having respected the integrity of penal and/or procedural law), it is the responsibility of the bishop or of the court to take the appropriate steps with the guilty cleric.

There can be no doubt that simple transfer or removal of an offender is no longer an adequate response to these situations, either in terms of civil law, nor in terms of ecclesial concern.[29] On the other hand, simply abandoning a guilty

---

[26]Pius XII stated that moral certitude is "characterized on the positive side by the exclusion of well-founded or reasonable doubt, and in this respect it is essentially distinguished from the quasi-certainty which has been mentioned; on the negative side it does admit the absolute possiblity of the contrary, and in this it differs from absolute certainty. The certainty of which we are now speaking is necessary and sufficient for the rendering of a judgment, even though in the particular case it would be possible eiher directly or indirectly to reach absolute certainty. Only thus is it possible to have a regular and orderly administration of justice, going forward without useless delays and without laying excessive burdens on the tribunal as well as on the parties." *CLSA Commentary, op. cit.*, p. 994.

[27]Cf. cc. 1400-1670.

[28]Cf. cc. 1720-1728.

[29]With regard to the transfer of pastors, see James F. Parizek, "Pastors on the Go: The Pastor's Rights in the Removal Process," *CLSA Proceedings, 48th Annual Convention* (Washington, D.C.: 1986), pp. 126-138; see also J. Stanley Teixeira, "Clergy Personnel: Policy and Canonical Issues," *The Jurist* (Vol. 45:2, 1985), pp. 502-520.

cleric cannot be countenanced either in canonical practice nor in simple human charity.

In the therapeutic model, there is much less difficulty in deciding the cleric's disposition. Psychiatric intervention combined with a rehabilitative atmosphere and a proven regimen of counselling seems to be the common approach. However, certain questions arise if the penal process has been used.

In light of the previous discussion on imputability, it is difficult to understand how one of the censures could be imposed. Such draconian measures against manifestly mentally unstable persons seem unfair. Therefore it seems that the imposition of some form of expiatory penalty will be the ultimate disposition for the guilty cleric. Penal remedies and/or penances by themselves do not seem an adequate response.

There are some considerations which merit serious discussion in dealing with clerics guilty of misconduct. Can such clerics be financially abandoned by their bishops, as a way of disassociating the local church from the misconduct? Can the bishop order such interventions as mandatory commitment in a penal institution or narcoleptic chemotherapy or chemical castration as a response to a true finding of clerical misconduct? The answer to both questions is in the negative.

Canon 1337 would seem to allow for a mandatory commitment of a cleric. However, practical consequences argue against such a penalty. In the first place, mandatory commitment does not achieve the result of rehabilitation or expiation unless the cleric cooperates with the residential placement. Furthermore, the mobility of our present society and the protection of individual liberty imposed by civil law make such a penalty unreliable. As Green states: "The . . . penalty, which involves a prohibited or prescribed residence, has had a lengthy history, but it has been significantly modified in modern times due to the notable changes in Church-State relationships and the diminished ability of church authorities to control the movements of clerics and religious. Accordingly, it is questionable how realistic this penalty is for clerics and religious today."[30]

Can a cleric legally be coerced into accepting narcoleptic chemotherapy or some other chemical or surgical treatment? The law draws a careful correlation between penalties and the supernatural end of the Church.[31] Such a correlation seems particularly germane in misconduct cases. The imposition of such a personally invasive penalty on a person does not correspond to the supernatural end of the Church. Such a penalty offends the supernatural end of the Church, precisely because of the fact of coercion. Furthermore, such a penalty rather egregiously offends against the traditional norm "nulla poena sine lege,"[32] Finally, such a penalty would seem to abuse the traditional understanding of clerical obedience as "restricted to those matters that are prescribed by canon law . . . The bishop

---

[30] *CLSA Commentary, op. cit.*, pp. 909-910.
[31] C. 1312, §2.
[32] Cf. c. 221, §3.

is empowered to enforce the universal law that regulates the clerical state, and the clergy are bound to obey in whatever pertains to their state as such."[33]

In summary, it seems that either a therapeutic model or the imposition of expiatory penalties in some form is the resolution available in cases of a cleric guilty of misconduct.

The Reparation Owed a Cleric Untruthfully Accused

Some accusations of clerical misconduct are not true. The falsity of an accusation can be determined in a number of ways: on merit itself (due to malice, for example, on the part of the accuser); due to lack of evidence or an inadequate foundation; due to a finding of innocence after a therapeutic or penal procedure. In these circumstances, it would seem fair that the falsely accused cleric receive some reparation, at least to the extent that his reputation has been damaged.

Common sense would seem to dictate that a cleric's reputation be restored in proportion to the publicity surrounding the accusation. Furthermore, if quantifiable damages have been sustained by the cleric due to a deliberately false accusation, the cleric has access to the canonical procedures for indemnification. Finally, the law itself deals with certain special circumstances, most of which are punishable by a canonical penalty: false denunciation (c. 982), perjury (c. 1368), or deliberate falsehood (cc. 1390-91).

Any administrative deprivations imposed upon a cleric as a consequence of a false accusation or a good-faith investigation immediately cease upon his exoneration or acquittal. Common sense would also seem to indicate that a cleric's personnel file be adjusted to indicate not only the simple fact of innocence or exoneration, but also a record of the restoration of his office and status. Any records of the investigation, as noted above, are to be stored in the secret archives of the diocese.

Occasionally, there are situations where exoneration of the cleric rests on no particular merit of his own. Sometimes acquittal may be due to the simple fact of lack of evidence; sometimes a penalty may be waived due to seriously diminished imputability; sometimes defects in canonical competence or skill may force an acquittal. Nonetheless, it may still be rather obvious that something is amiss in the cleric's lifestyle, behavior, or motivation.

Canon 1348 addresses this situation. The fact that an acquittal is achieved or that no penalty has been imposed does not necessarily mean that a cleric should be morally or personally exonerated. In this circumstance, the bishop can "provide for the public good any for the person's own good by means of appropriate admonitions and other ways of pastoral care or even through penal remedies, if circumstances warrant it."

---

[33]*CLSA Commentary, op. cit.*, p. 201.

There are also those unfortunate circumstances where damages are unavoidably sustained through lawfully placed juridic acts. Sometimes damages are sustained through the good-faith actions of others who mean no harm. Sometimes damages arise accidentally or unintentionally. There is no canonical redress for such actions.[34] However, there is no canon which forbids equitable and charitable compensation, indemnification, or redress in these matters.

Rehabilitation, Reinstatement, and the Permanently Dysfunctional Cleric

Perpetual penalties are rarely inflicted and when they are, certain conditions strictly apply.[35] Penalties may also be remitted; sometimes they cease. There is even the possibility of penal or criminal prescription ("statute of limitations").[36] Thus, the law itself implies that rehabilitation and reinstatement are possible in cases of clerical misconduct.

Whether or not there is hope for rehabilitation or reinstatement, the law provides for the on-going support of the penalized cleric. Canon 1359 provides for the "decent support" of the penalized cleric. The cleric's right to support (c. 281) can be abridged only in the most exceptional circumstances. Canon 1746 provides for involuntary retirement. Only in the case of dismissal from the clerical state is the provision for support waived, and even in this situation, the bishop is still encouraged to care for such a person "in the best manner possible" when the person is "truly in need due to the penalty." The issue of rehabilitation or reinstatement of a cleric, particularly when the offense involves the misconduct mentioned in c. 1395, is not a specifically legal one. Penalties themselves are many times meant to produce behavior modifications. However, the case of misconduct stemming from mental or psychological factors probably will not be resolved by the imposition of penalties. Once again we must defer to the therapeutic model.

The law does, however, offer some direction. Canon 1044, §2, 2°grants the bishop a discretionary right to prohibit a cleric the exercise of orders when that exercise has been impeded by insanity or some other psychological defect. The bishop's discretion is conditioned by the fact that he is to consult with an expert.

The reinstatement of a rehabilitated cleric is possible, but great caution must be used. There must be consultation, evaluation, and discretion exercised in such a decision. The decision belongs to the bishop who must give careful attention to the good of the community and to public knowledge of the cleric's status. Although a cleric enjoys the right to support, it does not necessarily follow that

---

[34]Cf. c. 128. Special note should be made, however, that compensation is obligatory for *any* act placed with malice or culpability.

[35]For example, perpetual penalties cannot be imposed by administrative decree (c. 1342, §2), when a penalty is indeterminate, the judge may not impose a perpetual penalty (c. 1349).

[36]Cf. cc. 1354-1363.

he may continue with the public exercise of ordained ministry. In this case, any right to minister must be conditioned by three factors: the vicarious nature of the ministry itself; the psychological condition of the minister; the possible harm or scandal caused to the community. In some cases, the cleric will be permanently dysfunctional. In such cases, aside from the obligation of support, other considerations flow from charity and pastoral sensitivity, not specifically from law.

Practical Considerations

In light of the above presentation, some practical considerations are called for.

1) Each diocese should draft a clear and workable policy concerning the accusation and fact of clerical misconduct. This policy should include a detailed and canonically correct description of procedures to be employed, as well as a frank statement of the consequences of a truthful accusation. Credible reporting mechanisms should be provided and used. Mention should be made of the possibility of exoneration or aquittal. The policy has to be a collaborative effort between the presbyterate and the diocesan bishop, perhaps with the assistance of the presbyteral and diocesan pastoral councils. Furthermore, the policy has to be explained and clarified so that it will be understood and received by the presbyterate and the faithful. Wise episcopal assessors are to be chosen. There has to be access to the process guaranteed by the policy. Finally, both the policy and the process have to be perceived as just by both the faithful and the clergy. Above all, the policy should reflect the sensitivity and concern that must be demonstrated in a specifically ecclesial environment.

2) In connection with such a policy, the local church must provide a network of support services that are available to the parties involved in a complaint of clerical misconduct. Such a network would include psychologists/psychiatrists, spiritual counsellors, legal experts (both canonical and civil), media counsultants, and health experts. Every diocese must have a credible ministry-to-priests program. It should be known and understood that diocesan authorities will be diligent in their efforts to repair damages and prevent, as far as possible, those damages from occurring in the future.

3) There must be a greater atmosphere of trust among the clergy of the local churches. There must be a greater atmosphere of trust between the clergy and their bishop. This increased trust will result in two benefits. First, the clergy will be more attentive to their colleagues and will be in a better position to help them. Secondly, there will be less fear of capricious and whimsical treatment at any level of the process. In a trusting atmosphere, many of the canonical problems can be resolved before they occur. Moreover, greater trust will result in greater

understanding and insight. In such an atmosphere, the impact of these problems will hopefully diminish.

PRESIDENTIAL REPORT

RICHARD G. CUNNINGHAM

INTRODUCTION

On the ground floor of the Supreme Court of the United States in Washington, DC, there is a sculpture of Themis, the Greek goddess of Justice, holding her scales and riding on the back of a turtle. The work, by Phillip Ratner, is entitled "Slow but Sure." It is an adequate description of my year as president of the Canon Law Society of America.

After our successful 1986 convention, I returned to Boston to begin one of the presidential responsibilities, the work of correspondence. Letters of gratitude were sent to the men and women who gave us that fine meeting in Denver, the nominees for various offices (those elected and those not), and all of the outgoing officers, committee chairpersons and committee members.

COMMITTEES

A number of requests to new persons to serve on our many committees eventually resulted in bringing into place our 4 Standing, 7 On-Going, 15 Ad Hoc and 7 BOG committees. During this time *Committees on Religious Affairs, Liturgies* and *Marriage Theology* were reconstructed. Three new committees, growing out of the Denver Convention, were established and a new committee was formed more recently to undertake *A Study of Procedures for the Protection of the Rights of Persons in the Church.*

The good work of our committees may be reviewed in the individual reports which are found in this book.

CONVENTION RESOLUTIONS

The resolutions adopted by the majority of voting members during the annual business meeting in Denver have been implemented in the following manner:

1) *The CLSA Investment Policy* was discussed more in detail by the BOG. Following a study on the monitoring of investments by the *BOG Nudget Committee* (Leonard Scott, John Myers & Rick Thomas), the BOG determined our policy would apply to all CLSA funds and directed the Treasurer and Executive Coordinator to transfer CLSA funds to the Christian Brothers Investment Services.

The same policy has been established also in our *CLSA Policy Manual*.

(Note: 2) *The Survey of Educational Opportunities in Dioceses* was defeated at the annual business meeting.)

3) The *Commendation to Father James I. O'Connor, SJ*, on his retirement as compiler and editor of *The Canon Law Digest* since 1953, was forwarded to him and he has expressed to all our members his gratitude for the resolution and "the affection and esteem manifested to me."

4) The possibility of continuing the publication of *The Canon Law Digest* is being pursued by Ed Pfnausch.

5) The resolution of *Appreciation to Father James Provost* for his 6 years as Executive Coordinator and for his contributions as a teacher of canonists, together with a hand-lettered certificate of appreciation, were forwarded to him and gratefully acknowledged by Jim as, "a graphic reminder of the rich experience I have enjoyed with the CLSA and the importance of the people who are the Society."

6) A *Committee on the Selection of Bishops* has been established to undertake an essential review and study of the material gathered by past Committees on the Selection of Bishops during the years 1969-1981.

7) An *Expression of Support for Archbishop Hunthausen*, in his efforts to restore peace and unity within the Church of Seattle, and an *Expression of the CLSA's concerns* over serious canonical issues and their possible effects addressed to the *Apostolic Pro-Nuncio* and the *President of the National Conference of Catholic Bishops*, together with a *Study to Address Such Canonical Issues;*

and

8) A *Study of Apostolic Visitation*, have been implemented in the following manner:

(a) the BOG determined that the two resolutions, nos. 7 & 8 should be combined;

(b) the 2 resolutions were conveyed to Archbishop Hunthausen who gratefully acknowledged them and asked me "to convey to the members of the Society my profound appreciation for these expressions of support;"

(c) the 2 resolutions were hand delivered to the Apostolic Pro-Nuncio at a meeting he graciously arranged for the officers of the CLSA. He expressed his concerns regarding how such a study would be construed and its timing, along with his appreciation for the opportunity to discuss our resolutions.

The officers brought his concerns to the January BOG meeting and a report on our discussion and decision to undertake the study was sent to the Apostolic Pro-Nuncio who acknowledged it, writing, "The courtesy of sharing this information with me is appreciated." (See under *MEETINGS*, Archbishop Laghi);

(d) the 2 resolutions were forwarded to the President of the

National Conference of Catholic Bishops and Archbishop May acknowledged them, noting "with interest the intention of the Canon Law Society of America to research in greater depth the canonical and theological issues involving the relationship of local churches and the Holy See;"

e) there has been formed a *Committee for the Study of Apostolic Visitation and the Limitation of Powers of a Diocesan Bishop* and the study has begun.

9) A resolution seeking the assistance of the NCCB in petitioning the Holy See for an *Indult Permitting Degreed Laity to Function as Single Judges* in U.S. tribunals in formal marriage cases was forwarded to the NCCB. Archbishop May transmitted the resolution to their Committee on Canonical Affairs who, at a meeting in June, rejected this resolution, "since it would involve granting jurisdiction to a lay person."

10) A *Task Force for a Study of the Procedures of the Congregation for the Doctrine of the Faith* has been established recently and a study is now underway.

11) A resolution urging the NCCB to request a *Modification of the Norms of the Congregation for the Doctrine of the Faith in Privilege of the Faith Cases to Allow Competent Non-ordained Persons to Serve as Judge-Instructors* in such cases was forwarded to the NCCB. Archbishop May transmitted the resolution to their Committee on Canonical Affairs, who, at a meeting in June, accepted the merits of the resolution and recommended that the NCCB seek this modification.

12) Our policy of *Affirmative Action* has been incorporated into the final draft of our *Canonical Standard for Labor-Management Relations*.

13) The posthumous *Commendation of Father James J. Young, CP,* for his dedicated ministry to the separated and divorced and our appreciation of the contributions he made, was forwarded to Father Joseph Gallagher, President of the Paulists, who gratefully acknowledged our testimony to a "person, a Paulist, and a priest who very clearly made a difference," and to Mrs. Norah Young, Father Jim Young's mother who expressed her profound appreciation for our thoughtful resolution, writing, "I find comfort in all that it conveys."

MEETINGS

THE BOARD OF GOVERNORS—Essential to the harmonious coordination of the many activities of the CLSA is the BOG.

Meetings were held in Denver, following the annual convention, at the Marriott Hotel, in Delray in January at the Duncan Retreat Center, in Mundelein in April at St. Mary of the Lake Seminary, and in Nashville prior to the annual convention at the Hyatt Regency Hotel.

In addition to the ordinary business of the Society pertaining to budget and expenses, committee work and future convention planning, the BOG addressed, among many topics calling for discussion and direction, membership services, membership qualifications, on-going canonical education, workshops, convention voting procedures, convention liturgies, convention sites, ecumenical matters, the Scholarship Fund and future planning.

Special attention has been given to the celebration of the CLSA's Golden Anniversary in Baltimore, October 10-13, 1988. A *Blue Ribbon Committee* (Leonard Scott, Jeremiah Kenney, Michael Schleupner, William Varvaro & Edward Pfnausch) has been working with our *R&D Committee* (Raymond Burke, James Parizek & Thomas Stocker) and our *General Convention Chairperson* (Stanley Teixeira) to insure that our 50th annual convention will be a memorable event and a golden experience.

During this past year a total of 12 days has been given to meetings of the BOG.

Heartfelt congratulations to our retiring BOG member, John Myers, who has been appointed Coadjutor Bishop of Peoria, Illinois.

REGIONAL MEETINGS—I had the extraordinary opportunity to attend and speak with our members at all the regional meetings this past year. These were excellent experiences.

In past issues of our *Newsletter* I have attempted to describe in some detail the hospitality and education received by me in New Orleans, Las Vegas, San Antonio, Peoria, Helena and Charleston. The manifest richness of the gifted and talented canonists with which the Church in America is blessed is strongly evident. From you I have learned so much Canon Law.

ARCHBISHOP LAGHI—On Nov. 17, 1986. Leonard Scott, Ed Pfnausch and I met at the Apostolic Nunciature in Washington with Archbishop Pio Laghi.

We discussed the visit to Pope John Paul II to the United States in September, the CLSA's officers' visit in 1986 to the Roman congregations and our attempts to persuade the Apostolic Signatura officials to recognize the Summer Institute at C.U. as a certification program for individuals to continue on with their customary work in our tribunals.

Archbishop Laghi recommended the Signatura's Bishop Grocholewski be invited to attend the C.U. Institute and the Archbishop expressed his own willingness to assist us in this invitation.

We presented Archbishop Laghi with copies of our *Newsletter, Proceedings & Roman Replies* and he encouraged us to contact Fr. Dennis Schnurr of his office who would assist us in obtaining for publication copies of certain documents that would be of interest to canonists.

The subjects of Apostolic Visitation in general and the action in Seattle in particular were discussed at length. We explained that the object of our Denver Convention resolutions was our hope to study and clarify the canonical issues pertinent to the Seattle action and the matter of Apostolic Visitation and attempt to eliminate some of the confusion and even anger engendered by these through some responsible canonical education. At the time the Archbishop gave every indication of interest in our proposed study and the meeting ended with mutual expressions of appreciation for the visit and the dialogue.

Following a further study of our resolutions, the Archbishop wrote me expressing his concern that our decision might be construed at this time as an effort to scrutinize the specific case involving the Archdiocese of Seattle. He emphasized the primary importance of the well-being of the local Church in Seattle and asked we weigh the good of our initiative against its effect upon the unity and peace of the Church of Seattle.

In January, at our BOG meeting, a lengthy discussion was held to take into consideration the Archbishop's concerns. A consensus statement was unanimously agreed upon to the effect that we would not abandon the resolutions because of the difficulties they may present but rather would commit ourselves to undertake the studies called for in the resolutions.

While we recognized that such a study would neither hurt nor help what had already taken place in Seattle, we, nevertheless, believe that a professional study of this subject matter is called for and is consistent with the history of our Society as a professional association, as well as with our *Constitution:*

"We accept our responsibility as Christians trained in Canon Law to continue research and study . . ."

and with our *Code of Professional Responsibility:*

"Canonists bear a special responsibility for the education of all the Christian faithful concerning their rights and responsibilities in the life and mission of the Church."

We established a *Committee for the Study of Apostolic Visitation and the Limitation of Powers of a Diocesan Bishop* and forwarded a copy of our discussion, decision and plan to Archbishop Laghi.

He acknowledged our letter and expressed his appreciation for our courtesy in sharing this information with him.

ARCHBISHOP MAY—On June 11, 1987, Ed Pfnausch and I met with Archbishop John May in Washington at the headquarters of the National Conference of Catholic Bishops for an hour. On our arrival we were warmly welcomed by Msgr. Dan Hoye and Fr. Don Heintschel.

The Archbishop was most cordial expressing his appreciation for the work of the CLSA and recalling the great service our Society has rendered to the American bishops in the past. We once again expressed our readiness and willingness to serve in any way we could.

We discussed a potential CLSA Workshop in the area of "canonical penalties" and he agreed it was important to develop the canonical parameters in this area. We discussed the need for more realistic and credible due process mechanisms in dioceses and he recalled all the good work done in the past by the CLSA in the area of due process as well as arbitration and conciliation procedures.

We spoke of the possibilities of alternatives to JCL programs and their sponsorship by C.U., especially now as the problem of staffing our tribunals becomes more crucial as does the need for officially approved certification programs.

Don Heintschel joined us for some of the hour and he emphasized the substantial assistance members of the CLSA have given to the Committee on Canonical Affairs.

The Archbishop thanked us for our good work and welcomed our on-going consultative services.

CATHOLIC UNIVERSITY, DEPARTMENT OF CANON LAW—On Nov. 17, 1986, Leonard Scott, Ed Pfnausch and I met with Fr. Tom Green as chairperson of C.U.'s Canon Law Department, for the purpose of discussing alternative program possibilities in the area of degreed canonical education.

Our request for consideration of this matter was brought to the Faculty of the Department of Canon Law who examined our proposals and requested from the BOG more detail on the potential scope of an alternative JCL program and the realistic potential of a market for such an undertaking.

Following a lengthy discussion at the April BOG meeting the thoughts of the BOG were sent to the Department of Canon Law. We agreed there is interest already expressed in this proposal and that a feasibility or market study would be useful in helping to reach a decision in this matter. We explained that the CLSA is open to cooperating with the Canon Law Department in a market study. However, we believe the program needs to be spelled out first before soliciting any expression of interest or commitment. The program would need to be a core JCL course but the BOG wishes to leave the Canon Law Department free to use its own expertise in the development and design of a model program.

The BOG also directed me to consult with the Department of Canon Law at Ottawa's St. Paul's University on this subject.

The matter is pending.

SYMPOSIA & WORKSHOPS

An April *Symposium on Lay Ministry* in Chicago proved to be a success. Copies of the papers prepared for this occasion were sent to the delegates and experts participating in the October Synod on the Laity. These papers may be found in the 1987:1 copy of *The Jurist*. At a later date the CLSA will prepare a book containing the papers for sale to interested persons.

Our *Symposium on Diocesan Governance* is available in our new book, *The Ministry of Governance,* and later this year a companion handbook will appear entitled, *The Governance of Ministry.* Both of these works are available from our Executive Coordinator's Office.

The *Permanent Seminar on the Protection of Rights* has published the results of its work in *The Jurist,* 1986: 1.

The *Survey of Due Process Experience,* after a successful March meeting in Chicago, finalized its report which is available from our Executive Coordinator's Office.

A *Joint Committee of the Canon Law Society of America* and the *Canadian*

Canon Law Society has completed its work on a study of *Imprimatur.* The final report will be published at a later date.

Successful workshops at Marriotsville, on *Religious Governance in the New Code,* and at Convent Station, NJ and Evansville, IN on *Sacramental Law,* were sponsored by the CLSA. Our members also taught in and participated in the two summer institutes at C.U. A similar institute is to be held this month in Mundelein, IL at St. Mary of the Lake Seminary under the sponsorship of the Chicago Province and the Pacific Northwest Region is seriously considering sponsoring one in their area.

OUR SCHOLARSHIP FUND

It is a delight to be able to report on our most special project. This was a vast undertaking under the skilled and dedicated direction of Bill Schumacher. He, together with many other volunteers, who contributed so much energy, time and talent, coordinated a marketing advisor, photographer, typesetter, key liner and tape man while lining up the area coordinators who in turn lined up the volunteer telephone callers. At the same time, Bill, with the able assistance of his own staff and of Ed Pfnausch and the Executive Office staff, arranged for all the necessary lists, names, addresses and mailings of letters, brochures and pledge cards. Sales kits, audio training cassettes, time-lines and report sheets went from Bill to the Area Coordinators. The telephone calls were made and the response of the membership was heartwarming. In fact, the professional fund raisers tell us our response was excellent, both on the part of all who volunteered to help and all who contributed. The extensive efforts of so many men and women over the months, weeks, days and hours consumed by this project made it possible for us to achieve our goal of $50,000.00.

An Ad Hoc Planning Committee for the Establishment of a Board of Trustees for the Scholarship Fund (Bill Schumacher, Michael Connolly, Donald Fruge, John Folmer, Rick Thomas and Ed Pfnausch) promptly completed its work and reported to the BOG in April.

We have already begun the next phase of our Fund raising, a *Project* under the capable co-direction of Jim Coriden and Bill Varvaro, together with a network of Area Coordinators. They will solicit contributions from foundations and other sources. Our goal in this phase is $500,000.00.

A *Scholarship Criteria Committee* (Paul Golden, Cecilia Bennett, Sharon Holland) has researched the criteria of need, methods of application, screening of applicants and other matters pertaining to the awarding of the CLSA Scholarships.

A sub-committee of the *BOG* (Leonard Scott, John Folmer, Lynn Jarrell) has formulated articles of incorporation for the Board of Trustees to administer the Scholarship Fund and to bring to this convention any necessary enabling resolutions.

I believe each one of us can be proud of the contribution our Society is about to make to canonical education in the service of the Church of America. I invite all to the hearing to be held at this convention on the Scholarship Fund.

I tip my hat to Bill Schumacher and all who have supported this good work. As I said in my letter to the membership last December:

"Here's to those CLSA members in 1986 who cared enough to see their apostolate continue into the Church's twenty-first century."

Health and benediction!

SOME IMPORTANT ADDITIONAL MATTERS

With enthusiastic gratitude and in the name of all the members of the CLSA, I want to acknowledge with deep appreciation the most recent contribution of Larry Wrenn. His newest work *Procedures* will take an important place on our library shelves under "active reference" right next to the well worn volumes of *Annulments* and *Decisions*.

Thank you, Larry. As usual your dependable harmonizing of expertise and excellence has served us well.

Proceedings, 1986 has finally been published. Our apologies to all the members for the delay in the final printing of this massive volume. Several dozen tales of woe, disappointment and frustration, together with legions of noon-day devils are the culprits responsible for slowing down the task of getting this volume to you. The whole process is being re-evaluated.

During this past year I have been in contact with the *Association for the Rights of Catholics in the Church* and the *National Association of Church Personnel Administrators*. (Ed Pfnausch, Lynn Jarrell and I attended the latter association's meeting in April which preceded our own BOG meeting at St. Mary of the Lake Seminary in Mundelein.)

Responsibilities at out Boston seminary prevented me from attending the annual meeting of the Canon Law Society of Great Britain and Ireland this past May, but I have been in correspondence with its president as well as the presidents of the Canadian Canon Law Society and the Canon Law Society of Australia and New Zealand. All three groups hope to be represented at our Golden Anniversary Convention in Baltimore. (Ed Pfnausch represented us this year at the meeting of the CLS—GBI held just outside of London.)

George Wythe of Virginia, a signer of the Declaration of Independence, was the first teacher of law in the United States. In 1806 he died suddenly and tragically after drinking a cup of coffee that had been poisoned. Being a teacher of canon law myself I am all too aware of the kind of feeling of professional isolationism a canon law professor at a seminary can sense finding himself in the midst of a strong theological faculty. Therefore I have written to as many canon law professors at seminaries as I could find to discuss ways in which the CLSA might be of a better service to us veteran warhorses holding the lines singlehandedly out in the satrapies.

The Dean of the Faculty of Canon Law at St. Paul University in Ottawa, Fr. Jean Thorn, invited me to present a lecture there last March. This provided a splendid opportunity for me to meet with the 51 American students enrolled in that fine institution and to talk with them about the CLSA.

Canon Law and canonical education were the subjects of an hour long interview this past April when I was invited to be the guest on "Mother Angelica Live" originating from their awesome cable television studios in Birmingham, Alabama. Mother Angelica is quite a remarkable woman, directing a TV ministry that presently has the potential to reach 20 million American homes each night.

While on the subject of television I produced and presented 13 half hour television programs for cable television. They were an attempt to bring to people a popular(?) presentation and understanding of canon law in the Catholic Church. No emmys yet!

CONCLUDING OBSERVATIONS

I cannot speak highly enough of the kindnesses and cooperation of our elected Board of Governors and our elected officers. Special thanks to Lynn and Rick and Scotty with congratulations and every good wish to Leonard Scott as he begins his year as president of the CLSA. It promises to be a fine one under his capable leadership.

Our choice of an Executive Coordinator—Ed Pfnausch—has proven to be a wise and excellent one. A delight to work with, Ed brings so many talents and insights to the task, that already within a year we are much richer for his good works. Thank you, Ed.

And thank you to all our committee chairpersons and members, and to all the men and women of our Society who have supported and cooperated in our efforts and manifested so much generous interest in our works and aims.

I wish to acknowledge a debt of gratitude to the rectors and faculties of St. John's Seminary, Brighton, and Pope John XXIII National Seminary, Weston, for their on-going encouragement and enthusiastic support. Their thoughtful patience and perseverance with their sojourning professor of canon law represents a major contribution to the work of the CLSA.

"Slow but Sure" was my goal but the year proved to be busy and hectic while at the same time exciting and challenging.

"Slow but Sure" was my hope but there almost certainly have been some inadvertant errors, oversights or omissions. I own them and apologize for them.

Thank you for giving me the opportunity to serve you as your president. Surely the salt that keeps a president afloat is the membership of our distinguished Society. You ladies and gentlemen have been so encouraging, cooperative and willing always to help.

I am proud of the CLSA. We are indeed blessed by our membership within such a wide community of devoted persons who give constant witness to their faith by their work.

May our knowledge, interpretation and practice of the law continue to rise each day as our prayer.

CANON LAW SOCIETY OF AMERICA
TREASURER'S REPORT

October 1987

It is once again my honor as well as my duty to present the Treasurer's report for the fiscal year ending September 30, 1987.

The format of the report remains the same as in previous years and by now you have become familiar with it.

During the past fiscal year we have completed the implementation of the general ledger software on the IBM 36 at the Executive Coordinator's office. This will allow us in the future to do account analysis and thus enable us to analyze cash flow and do more accurate budgeting.

The membership voted last year to invest its monies based on a socially conscious policy. The Board of Governors studied this under the leadership of the Vice President. The Board has decided to place the investments of the Society under the management of the Christian Brothers Investment Services. The transfer of funds from Merrill Lynch to Christian Brothers is now in process.
to Christian Brothers is now in process.

As you remember, we did budget a deficit for the fiscal year. The Society did indeed incur a deficit even though a substantial number of savings was effected. The deficit was not as large as projected. That there was a deficit at all was due largely to our misjudgment of the projected attendance at workshops.

Although a deficit is again projected for the coming year, I believe that a continuation of our present cost-conscious attitudes and behavior will keep it to a minimum.

I appreciate your generosity in giving to the Scholarship Fund. It is in need of still more funds and would willingly accept them. I encourage you to support the work of the Society by attendance at workshops, purchasing publications, recruiting new members and your prayers.

Thank you for your support.

Assets and Liabilities

	September 30, 1987	*September 30, 1986*
Assets		
Cash		
Madison National	84,930.89	83,933.63
Merrill Lynch	13,123.13	.32
Total Cash	98,054.02	83,933.95
Receivables		
Books	6,200.00	
Dues	21,732.46	
Total Receivables	27,932.46	
Inventories		
Publications	67,317.32	74,675.38
Postage	510.88	810.89
Total Inventories	67,828.20	75,486.27
Sub-Total	193,814.68	159,420.22
Quasi-Endowment	81,595.00	66,333.00
Total Assets	275,409.68	225,753.22
Liabilities		
Deferred Revenues		
Deferred Dues	86,650.00	72,073.66
Deferred Convention Reg.	24,111.92	23,070.50
Deferred Commentary	349.80	3.52
Deferred Wksp Fees	4,710.00	
Total Deferred	115,468.40	98,893.96
Accounts Payable		
General Operations	14,400.00	
Royalties Payable	2,450.12	1,196.78
Payable to Scholarship Fund	52,074.71	22,053.74
Total Accounts Payable	68,924.83	23,250.52
Restricted Funds		
JCCLSS	94.82	94.82
Sub-Total	184,488.05	125,239.30
Quasi-Endowment	81,595.00	66,333.00
Total Liabilities	266,083.05	191,572.30
Fund Balance	9,326.63	34,180.92
Total Liabilities and Fund Balance	275,409.68	225,753.22

STATEMENT OF INCOME AND EXPENSES

	September 30, 1987	*September 30, 1986*
General Operations		
Income		
Interest	665.28	1,493.63
Membership Dues	87,908.88	63,511.13
Royalties	22,030.22	76,955.85
Donations	25.00	15.00
Miscellaneous Income	253.06	
Total Income	110,882.44	155,936.90
Expenses		
Board of Governors	15,868.70	20,573.76
President	4,607.56	5,677.67
Vice-President	434.35	151.60
Treasurer		1,358.42
Executive Coordinator Office		
Coordinator	23,901.40	6,249.00
Staff	18,680.01	24,305.83
Purchased Service	19,930.46	18,765.30
Materials/Supply	3,325.67	3,430.93
Capital	900.00	3,145.00
Sub-Total, Exec. Coord.	66,737.54	55,896.06
Membership Services	27,419.70	32,705.12
Convention Planning	1,451.01	2,843.78
Scholarship Maintenance	2,638.86	5,382.58
Committees		
Membership	714.51	1,523.42
Professional Responsibility		
Research & Discussion	178.25	1,728.88
Resolutions		
Civil Law/Canon Law	67.94	20.00
Advisory Opinions	380.85	
Marriage Research	733.45	
Religious Affairs		
Women in the Church	1,276.57	743.36
Apostolic Visitation	1,328.40	
Sub-Total, Committees	4,679.97	5,662.97
Projects		
Permanent Seminar/Rights	328.00	4,456.25
Due Process Survey	2,127.86	1,042.84
Visit-Apostolic See	2,000.00	5,979.06
Doctrinal Responsibility	201.00	625.40

Sub-Total, Projects	4,656.86	12,555.44
Total Expenses	128,494.55	142,807.40
Net Gain/-Loss	-17,612.11	13,129.50

Publications

Income		
Sales Income	48,548.91	
Cost of Sales	15,636.19	
Adjusted Income	32,912.72	44,237.38
Expenses		
Staff	20,406.58	21,987.66
Postage	9,074.21	
Materials/Supply	180.14	2,543.91
Total Expenses	29,660.93	65,166.67
Net Gain/-Loss	3,251.79	-20,929.29

Conventions

Income		
Registration	31,095.10	31,864.00
Donations	2,093.93	
Miscellaneous		318.90
Total Income	33,189.03	32,182.90
Expenses		
Honoraria	4,200.00	2,250.00
Food Service	19,941.30	18,181.14
Other Purchased Services	7,289.35	12,128.52
Materials	335.10	3,810.30
Total Expense	31,765.75	36,369.96
Net Gain/-Loss	1,423.28	-4,187.06

Workshops

Income (Registration)	31,422.00	71,790.00
Expenses		
Honoraria	6,500.00	8,100.00
Purchased Services	21,759.01	38,375.57
Materials/Supplies	502.50	1,774.36
Total Expenses	28,761.51	48,249.93
Net Gain/-Loss	2,660.49	23,540.07

Grants (Laity Symposium)

Income	7,000.00	
Expenses		
Purchased Services	6,449.68	
Materials/Supply	76.06	
Total Expenses	6,525.74	
Net Gain/-Loss	474.26	
Gain/-Loss for FY	-9,802.29	1,551.22

REPORT OF THE EXECUTIVE COORDINATOR

EDWARD G. PFNAUSCH

1986-1987

My first full year as Executive Coordinator has been an interesting and rewarding one. The many aspects of the office have provided a constant challenge. The support of the Board of Governors and so many of the members of the Society has made that challenge a joy. I report on the Constitutional responsibilities of the Executive Coordinator.

I. OFFICE

The office continues, through the generosity of The Catholic University, to be housed at 431 Caldwell Hall. Shortly after the Denver convention, Mrs. Debra Johnson resigned as office manager. During the past year, Mrs. Margaret Jones has assumed responsibility for general office procedures and Mr. Les Gadson continues to be responsible for the publications department. Both of them have generously taken on added responsibilities during the year. Two canon law students have provided part-time assistance: Mr. Ed Peters for the first semester and Ms. Siobhan O'Toole since last January. Another university student, Ms. Jane Lawler was in the office part-time last spring.

Significant progress has been made in correcting and updating the various mailing lists and the membership information. That process was helped by the major scholarship fund drive, directed by Bill Schumacher, that took place last winter. The printing of materials and the mailing, as well as recording the returns were handled by the office staff. Over a hundred new members were added in the past year. As a service to the Committee on Membership and Nominations, the office handles routine applications and prepares materials for the committee for more complex applications. The management of financial operations on the IBM System/36 was accomplished early in 1987 so that regular reports can be sent to the Treasurer for analysis and correction. On behalf of the Treasurer, bills for annual dues were sent and collection recorded in the office.

The CLSA has obtained a ruling granting independent tax status from the IRS. As a result, we are no longer included under the group ruling in the *Catholic Directory* but will appear, beginning with the 1988 edition, under the heading of those groups who have an independent ruling.

Three *Newsletters* were produced and distributed to members. The schedule for these publications will remain the same. The first will be produced as quickly as possible after the annual meeting since three quarters of the members are not able to attend that meeting. A second will appear in the Spring to provide an update on activities of the Board of Governors and committees and a third, focusing on the annual convention, will appear in August. Members who have items of interest or news for the *Newsletter* are urged to send them to the executive coordinator.

At the April Board of Governors meeting, it was decided to provide the Bulletin of Issues of Religious Law to all members. The first of these issues was sent with the convention mailing. Another is ready for mailing and will be included with the next general mailing to the membership.

Information about the annual meeting in Nashville was mailed early this year. Additional resolutions were included in the August *Newsletter* and others are included in the convention packet. The office also provided basic services for six workshops during the year and has planned for others in the future. Two workshops were held in conjunction with the annual meeting in Denver. A workshop for secretaries was held in October, one on religious governance in the Spring and two on sacramental law. It was, unfortunately, necessary to cancel the workshop on jurisprudence and one of the sacramental law workshops. The pre-convention workshops for Nashville have been well received and the workshop on religious governance will be scheduled again on the west coast. Plans for a workshop on sanctions will be announced in the next *Newsletter*. The services for workshops provided by the office include the preparation and distribution of brochures, local arrangements, reservations, preparation of materials and follow up services to the presenters.

II. PUBLICATIONS

Sales continue to be steady and new publications have been added to our inventory. *The Ministry of Governance* is the first result of the symposium on diocesan governance. A handbook, to be called *The Governance of Ministry,* is still in preparation and will appear in the next year. A new work by Larry Wrenn, *Procedures,* was distributed to all members as a membership service. Additional copies of both of these books can be ordered from the Office of the Executive Coordinator.

Two CLSA works appeared this year in *The Jurist.* The results of the permanent seminar on "Protecting and Promoting Rights in the Church" appeared in 1986: 1 issue and the papers from the CLSA symposium on the laity and church law appeared, with a consensus statement, in the 1987: 1 issue. Additional copies of these resources are available from *The Jurist,* Catholic University, Washington, D.C., 20064. A companion volume to the papers on rights is available from the CLSA Office: *Due Process in Diocese in the United States, 1970-1985.* All three of these publications were brought to completion by the diligent and generous efforts of Jim Provost.

The 1986 *Proceedings* were delayed for a number of reasons, but have been distributed to all members. Any member who has not received a copy should contact the Office of the Executive Coordinator as soon as possible.

Roman Replies and CLSA Advisory Opinions, again prepared by Bill Schumacher and Jim Cuneo, has been distributed as a benefit to those attending the annual meeting. Additional copies may be obtained from the office.

III. LIAISON

The executive coordinator is charged with maintaining liaison with other Catholic organizations and other canon law societies.

During the year there has been regular and substantial communication with both the Pro-Nuncio and his staff and the NCCB. I participated, with Dick Cunningham and Leonard Scott, in a cordial and helpful meeting with the Pro-Nuncio last November. The wide range of topics of this meeting are discussed in the President's report, but the continued assistance of Father Dennis Schnurr of the Pro-Nuncio's office has been especially helpful in obtaining materials for *Roman Replies*. There were also several meetings and discussions with members of the NCCB staff. Members of the Society provided two translations and one mailing was sent from the office. President Cunningham also reports on the informative and encouraging meeting last June with Archbishop May.

Communication with other Catholic organizations is maintained by shared mailings and direct collaboration. The production of the Bulletin on Issues of Religious Law is a fruitful result of the collaboration between the CLSA Committee on Religious Affairs, the LCWR and CMSM.

Shared information is also characteristic of the relationships with other canon law societies. I was honored to attend the annual meeting of the Canon Law Society of Great Britain and Ireland last May. The informative papers, lively discussion and the renewal of personal friendships and collaboration resulted from that trip. The warm hospitality of the members of the society, their interest in the work of the CLSA and their own significant projects and papers provide encouragement in continuing our own implementation of the 1983 Code. Last month I attended the meeting of the Consociatio Internationalis Studio Iuris Canonici Promovendo in Munich. More than 300 canonists, primarily teachers of canon law, focused on associations in Church. Correspondence has been maintained with the Canon Law Society of Australia and New Zealand and the Canadian Canon Law Society.

IV. PUBLIC RELATIONS

Most press inquiries focused on annulment statistics and procedures. There were several more general inquiries in conjunction with the Holy Father's visit to the United States.

V. VARIA

This past year has been an interesting learning experience for me. The office is a busy place with a variety of aspects. A major challenge in the past year has been beginning a familiarity with the CLSA computer system. Progress has been made, but some things did not get done. Efforts to transfer the text of the code to smaller diskettes and development of the data base have been "on hold." A new membership directory did not appear as expected. Its format has been authorized by the Board of Governors and is on the "front burner" for the new fiscal year. A positive result of the year has been a clarification of office procedures and accountability. There are at least five different "departments" in the CLSA office—membership services, publications, workshops and meetings, financial and public relations liaison. In each of these, the contribution of the Board of Governors and the committees provides the executive coordinator with opportunities to indeed "coordinate" activities in addition to overseeing the smooth operation of the departments. My sincere thanks to the officers and the Board for their support and direction; my thanks to the members for their encouragement and generosity.

COMMITTEE REPORTS

Committee: **Membership and Nominations**
Constituted: CLSA Constitution, Article X
Charge: The functions of the Committee on Membership and Nominations are:
    a. To submit to the active members, at least one month prior to the date of election, the names of nominees as provided for in Article IX of the Constitution;
    b. to propose for approval of the Board of Governors applicants for active membership under the exceptive clause of Article III, n. 1 of the Constitution, and to propose for honorary membership in the Society those who, in its opinion, qualify according to Article III;
    c. to formulate and recommend to the Board of Governors plans for maintaining and increasing the membership of the Society.
Membership: Patricia McGreevy, O.S.B., Chairperson
James Baker
Lucy Vazquez O.P.
Royce Thomas, Treasurer, ex-officio non-voting member

Annual Report

The Committee met on January 21-24, 1987, in Orlando, Florida. The following action was taken on each of the constitutional mandates:
1. The nominees to be presented for office in the CLSA are as follows.
Vice President: Paul Golden, C.M.
Sidney Marceaux
Secretary: Lynn Jarrell, O.S.U.
John Bell
Treasurer: Rick Thomas
Consultors: John Amos
Ray Burke
Jim Cuneo
Barbara Ann Cusack
Daniel Ward, O.S.B.
Frank Wallace
2. The committee was advised by the Board of Governors that a proposed constitutional amendment to Article III, No. 1, was under consideration. The amendment will delete the exceptive clause from the Constitution:
    ". . . unless an applicant shall, in the opinion of the Membership and

Nominations Committee, have gained a broadly based competence in canonical issues through work in canonical affairs and/or the projects of the Canon Law Society of America for a significant period of time or who, while being a practitioner of the law in one or more areas for over a year, is sponsored by an active member; application for active status on this latter basis shall in each instance be proposed by the Committee on Membership and Nominations to the Board of Governors for approval of active status.''

The committee concurred unanimously with the BOG proposal and agreed to co-sponsor it.
3. Applications for active and associate membership will be dealt with by the Committee in the manner currently prescribed by the Constitution.
4. The Committee reaffirmed the recommendation reported in the 1986 annual report of the committee regarding increased membership in the CLSA. It further recommended that the BOG contact the Women's Caucus and the Black-Hispanic Caucus to surface names of potential nominees for office and committee assignment. The matter was considered by the BOG at its spring meeting. As a result, the committee was charged with the task of securing these names from the Women's Caucus and the Black-Hispanic Caucus. These names will be referred to Monsignor Leonard Scott, CLSA Vice-President, by August 1, 1987.

The following action was taken on the unfinished business pending before the committee:
1. The proposed revision of the CLSA application for membership form and the sponsor's letter was tabled pending the decision on the proposed constitutional amendment, Article II, No. 1.
2. The committee agreed to the inclusion of a form for nomination of officers for the CLSA in the convention packet.
3. Reverend James Baker, Chancellor, Dodge City, Kansas, will complete the unexpired term of Reverend Robert Cunningham who resigned from this committee. Baker will assume the chair of the committee following the Nashville Convention.
4. The committee is currently collecting data for job descriptions for the officers of the CLSA.

Committee: **Professional Responsibility**
Constituted: Code of Professional Responsibility, canon 9c(i), d(i)
Charge: The three senior consultors of the Canon Law Society of America's Board of Governors constitute a standing Committee on Professional Responsibility. The functions of any party aggrieved with respect to provisions of the Code of Professional Responsibility, to make an initial finding that the complaint is not frivolous; and in the event the complaint to be serious in

	character, to refer the matter to the Hearing Officers.
Membership:	Marie Breitenbeck, O.P.
	Jordan Hite, T.O.R.
	John J. Myers

Annual Report

No complaints have been received during the 1986-1987 CLSA year by the Committee.

Committee:	**Research and Discussion**
Constituted:	CLSA Constitution, Article X
Charge:	The functions of the Committee on Research Discussion are:

1. Above all to work for the attainment of the purposes of the Society set forth in Article II of the Constitution;
2. To submit to the Board of Governors for approval the names of speakers and topics for discussion at the annual general meeting;
3. To initiate or cooperate in all research projects of the Society such as seminars, symposia and special studies relative to research and discussion and to recommend to the Board of Governors honoraria for participants in these studies as well as for speakers at the annual general meeting;
4. To cooperate with the executive coordinator in arranging for all publications of the Society.

Membership:	Raymond L. Burke, Chairperson
	James F. Parizek
	Thomas R. Stocker

Annual Report

Convention Program Planning

The Committee finalized the program for the Nashville Convention.

The program for the Baltimore Convention in 1988 has been approved. The Committee is in the process of contacting the suggested presenters. The Committee has worked in conjunction with the Blue Ribbon Committee of the Board of Governors.

Preliminary suggestions for the 1989 Convention in Seattle have been presented to the Board of Governors. The Board of Governors has given the Committee additional direction in planning the program for Seattle.

Research Requests

The Committee received two research requests. Sister Ellen O'Hara, C.S.J. proposed a study of the human and legal processes involved in the discernment of the future viability of an institute of consecrated life. The Committee recommended the study to the Board of Governors who referred it to the Religious Affairs Committee for further recommendation.

The second request, made by Father Daniel Murray, was for a study of the canonical matters to be considered by vocation directors and seminary authorities prior to the acceptance of a candidate for the priesthood. The study was recommended to the Board of Governors as an article for *The Jurist*.

Convention Evaluation Form

The Committee studied the evaluation form used at conventions in comparison with the form used by the Catholic Health Association. The Board of Governors encouraged the Committee to make suggested changes in the form. Father James Parizek is in charge of the work of revision.

Committee:	**Resolutions**
Constituted:	CLSA Constitution, Article X
Charge:	The functions of the Committee on Resolutions are:
	1. To solicit, develop and draft proposed resolutions which will express the concerns of the Canon Law Society of America;
	2. To consult with the membership at large and, in particular with the Board of Governors, the standing and ad hoc committees of the Society, and the organizers of the convention;
	3. To formulate resolutions on given points in response to requests of the members of the Society;
	4. To compose differences in the formulation of similar proposals and to revise all proposals so that the meaning of each is clear;
	5. To encourage resolutions which authentically express in a positive way the activities and concerns of the Society.
Membership:	John A. Renken, Chairperson
	M. Patricia Green, O.P.
	Leonard Pivonka

Annual Report

General requests for resolutions were included in the convention mailing in June. The members of the Board of Governors and the chairs of the committees were contacted personally in June with an invitation to offer resolutions. All proposed resolutions received by August 1, 1987, were published in the society's

Newsletter. Any resolutions received after that date will be included in the convention packet. Resolutions submitted immediately prior to the resolutions hearing will be distributed to the convention participants for consideration.

The resolutions hearing will be held on Tuesday of the convention week when the membership may discuss resolutions submitted. The resolutions will then be put into final form by the Committee for presentation and vote at the Business Meeting on Wednesday.

Committee: **Advisory Opinions**
Constituted: 44th Annual Meeting, 1982
Charge: To issue advisory opinions on the meaning of the canons of the revised code after its promulgation. Such opinions are to provide non-official interpretations in response to requests for them.
Membership: J. James Cuneo, Chairperson

Annual Report

The results of the Committee's work are published in the booklet, *Roman Replies and CLSA Advisory Opinions 1987.*

The Committee on Advisory Opinions continues fulfilling its original plan, namely to make itself available for responses to canonical questions. Secondly, we continue to gather opinions which may be given in local churches that could be of interest for publication in Advisory Opinions, even though the opinions and questions were not generated directly through the Committee. In this year's publication we have addressed several interesting questions. They include the following topics: The right of Catholic clergy to officiate at the marriage of parties who are not obliged to canonical form; canonical procedures for arranging marriage involving a "traditionalist" Catholic; canonical issues in the suppression and merger of Catholic parishes; the jurisdiction of non-ordained persons exercising parochial ministry; and others.

Although this year's publication once again contains a good deal of interesting material from various sources, nevertheless it is always surprising to me that there is not available to us a greater exchange of written opinions. Earlier in the year letters were sent to Chancellors and Judicial Vicars, as well as to members of the Committee on Advisory Opinions in order to see if they had any materials in their files that would be worth sharing with the membership of the Society. Only a very limited number of responses to that request have been received. Some people have indicated that they regularly provide canonical opinions in the course of fulfilling their various functions in dioceses, congregations, universities, etc., but that these are not formally written, and therefore they do not have anything on file to provide us. It has been our hope that the members of the Canon Law Society would feel more free to share their opinions with the Committee. It is on the level of local ministry that canonical questions are raised and then answered by our brother and sister canonists. It is on that level that jurisprudence is developed. Over the years we have been able to circulate tribunal jurispurdence. It would be good if we could also circulate more readily our administrative jurisprudence. Perhaps it is simply a matter of time before we can generate a greater exchange in this area. In the meantime the questions and the opinions which are presently available to us are very interesting and hopefully the opinions will be helpful to many.

Therefore the Committee is interested in receiving opinions which CLSA members have formulated in response to direct inquiries for inclusion in future collections of CLSA *Advisory Opinions.*

The Committee is also prepared to receive inquiries requesting an opinion. These requests are handled as follows;
1. Some are handled directly by the chairperson, with a response to the individual submitting the inquiry.
2. Others may require work by a canonist with special expertise or are of such a nature that several opinions would be appropriate. The chairperson will locate the appropriate person(s) and obtain an opinion in response to the inquiry.
3. Finally, some may be quite complicated issues which call for more lengthy research. These will be forwarded to the CLSA Research and Development Committee for their attention through such means as convention papers, research requests, etc. The person inquiring will be advised that this has been done.

Members who wish to share with the Committee any opinions they have developed or persons who wish to make canonical inquiries for the Committee are encouraged to forward them to the Committee Chairperson: Rev. Msgr. J. James Cuneo, The Catholic Center, 238 Jewett Avenue, Bridgeport, CT 06606-2892.

Committee:	**Eastern Canon Law and Interritual Matters**
Constituted:	46th Annual Meeting, 1984
Charge:	To serve the Canon Law Society of America as a resource body in the area of Eastern canon law and interritual matters, and to aid the CLSA membership in understanding the Eastern Catholic Churches.
Membership:	John D. Faris, Chairperson
	John T. Sekellick
	William P. Wolfe

Annual Report

In October 1986, the *Pontificia Commissio Codici Iuris Canonici Orientalis Recognoscendo* distributed a complete draft of the future Code of Eastern Canon Law to all of its members. In keeping with the charge given to the Committee a report comprised of select observations on the Draft was prepared by the Committee. This report is available through the office of the Executive Coordinator and will be published in *Proceedings, 1987.*

Committee: **Religious Affairs**
Constituted: On-going committee
Charge: To serve the Canon Law Society of America as a competent resource body in the area of law for religious; to help raise consciousness in CLSA on religious life and law among its members:
1. To assist the planning of the annual meetings of the CLSA in the areas affecting law for religious;
2. To maintain a level of professional competence in the area of law for religious among its members.
Membership: Sharon Holland, I.H.M., Chairperson
Arthur J. Espelage, O.F.M.
Joseph J. Koury, S.J.
Elissa Rinere, C.P.

Annual Report

Through correspondence, the newly appointed committee surfaced topics to be presented to R&D for further research and presentation at future conventions. Areas of canonical concern included: the approval of new groups (criteria), assistance to contemplatives, religious dissent, secular institutes in the U.S., lay preaching, and mergers of existing institutes.

Through the chair, the committee continued involvement in the planning and publication of the *Bulletin on Issues of Religious Law,* sponsored jointly by CLSA, LCWR, CMSM and NCVR. In order to provide wider circulation of the *Bulletin* among CLSA members, alternatives to distribution through the convention packet are under consideration.

Committee: **Roman Replies**
Constituted: BOG, October 1980
Charge: To collect and publish recent responses from various Roman dicasteries which would be of wide interest to CLSA members.
Editor: William A. Schumacher

Annual Report

The results of the committee's work are published in the separate booklet, *Roman Replies and CLSA Advisory Opinions 1987.*

Early each year the chancellors, judicial vicars and vicars for the religious of American sees are asked to submit for possible publication any recent replies from the various Roman dicasteries which might be of wider interest to the members of the Society. Similar requests are made of all major superiors of religious institutes in the United States.

To encourage a wider participation in this annual project, all members are asked to be alert for such materials that may come to their attention. In all cases, it is desirable to submit also the initial inquiry or request which prompted the reply from the dicastery to provide a better understanding of the meaning of the response. Materials may be submitted through the office of the Executive Coordinator or directly to the editor: Rev. William A. Schumacher, 155 E. Superior Street, Suite 319, Chicago, IL 60611.

Committee:	**Women in the Church**
Constituted:	35th Annual Meeting, 1973
Charge:	To continue the study of the status of women and to address itself to the achievement of an equality for women in the Church's law.
Membership:	Lynn Jarrell, O.S.U., Chairperson
	Jay Maddock
	Nancy Reynolds, S.P.
	Harmon Skillin

Annual Report

The Committee met on two different occasions during the course of 1986-87. During these meetings, the following items were addressed and plans made.

I. *Items Addressed*

The Committee put into action and responded to three different projects that surfaced from the membership over the last two years. The first of these projects was whether to sponsor a permanent seminar on lay jurisdiction in the Church. The Committee proposed this topic of lay jurisdiction be addressed, but through the format of an in-depth workshop sponsored by the Canon Law Society. Through this format, the topic would reach a broader audience and would allow for more interaction between the presenters and the participants. The proposal for the workshop on lay jurisdiction was formally presented to the Board of Governors in October, 1987, with the intention of the workshop being presented sometime during the Spring of 1989. Hopefully, the papers given at the workshop will be published in a CLSA publication.

The next project addressed was the issue of just hiring procedures and salary scales for those who work for the Church. It was decided that the recently approved CLSA paper entitled, "Canonical Standards in Labor-Management Relations: A Report," addressed these issues. In addition, the Committee gave written and verbal support to the efforts of the National Association of Church Personnel Administrators who are attempting to address the topic of just treatment for those who work for the Church. No further proposal by the Committee itself is envisioned at this time.

A third project, which was brought to the attention of the Committee, was the need for proposing guidelines for the use of inclusive language in all CLSA publications. The Committee drafted a set of guidelines and presented these guidelines to the Board of Governors in October, 1987.

II. *Plans Made for the Future of the Committee*
The Committee drew up a list of its various ongoing responsibilities. This list of seven duties will be given to the individuals who are appointed to serve on this Committee from October, 1987 to October 1990.

The current membership of this Committee strongly recommended that the Committee continue to exist in the Canon Law Society. The Committee's proposal to the BOG was that the membership be staggered over a three-year cycle and a female be named chairperson each year.

Committee: **Apostolic Visitation and the Limitation of Powers of a Diocesan Bishop**
Constituted: 48th Annual Meeting, 1986
Membership: John P. Beal, co-chair
Michael D. Place, co-chair
Dennis J. Burns
Frederick R. McManus
John W. Robertson

Annual Report

The committee met by conference call on May 22, 1987 and in Washington, August 25-26, 1987. At the August meeting the committee received a written report from Frederick McManus and an oral presentation by Patrick Granfield of The Catholic University. The committee has prepared a proposal for further work which has been presented to the Board of Governors.

Committee: **Civil and Canon Law**
Constituted: Forty-Seventh Annual Meeting, 1985
Charge: 1. Identify those norms of the Code which require the Church to defer to secular law.
2. Clarify the effects of secular law on canon law in various states and local jurisdictions.
3. Identify those issues, organizations, resources, publications and personnel to facilitate communications between canon law and secular law.
4. Identify possible areas of cooperations between canon and secular law.
Membership: James A. Coriden, Chairperson
Peter M. Shannon, Esq.
Jordon Hite, T.O.R.

Annual Report

The Committee has met three times, once at the end of the convention in Denver (10-16-88), and twice by conference call (3-9-87 and 3-30-87).

1. Our central preoccupation has been to sift through issues of mutual interest to canonists and civilists and try to come up with one or two which are not being explored by others and which we could fruitfully address.
2. We hope to have ready for publication soon the listing of canons which contain references to civil law, a brief study done by Jordon Hite.
3. Peter Shannon will present a major seminar at the Nashville Convention on the important topic of the two different theoretical grounds which American courts are employing in resolving church related issues, namely deference to the Church's own internal rules and hierarchy as over against the application of "neutral principles of law."

    We consider the regular presentation of such issues of mutual concern to be one of the committee's primary tasks.
4. We are in informal conversation with the Office of General Council of the NCCB about issues which they feel are in need of research and development. The General Council and one of his associates have raised some good issues. We'll talk again in early July.
5. Bill Schumacher has raised an intriguing matter of confidentiality for research and publication. We are presently considering whether and how we can pursue it.

Committee: **Continuation of Canon Law Digest**
Constituted: 48th Annual Meeting, 1986

Charge: To explore the possibilities of continuing the publication of *Canon Law Digest.*
Membership: Edward G. Pfnausch

Annual Report

Discussions continue with Father James O'Connor. Those discussions should produce enough information about the feasibility of the CLSA continuing this publication so that the Board of Governors can take action at the Nashville meeting.

Committee: **Joint Committee on "Doctrinal Responsibilities"**
Constituted: Board of Governors, 1980; reactivated by Board of Governors, 1985
Members: John A. Alesandro (CLSA)
John Beal (CLSA)
John Boyle (CTSA)
Patrick Granfield (CTSA)
Jon Nilson (CTSA)
Leo J. O'Donovan, S.J. (CTSA), Chairperson
James Provost (CLSA)

Annual Report

This joint committee's original charge was completed with the publication of *Cooperation Between Theologians and the Ecclesiastical Magisterium* (Washington: CLSA, 1982) and the adoption by the CLSA and CTSA at their respective 1983 annual meetings of the report, "Doctrinal Responsibilities" (*CLSA Proceedings* 45 (1983) 261-284). The Committee was reactivated in 1985 to respond to critiques which were raised concerning "Doctrinal Responsibilities" after it was submitted to the NCCB.

Committee members have been working with the NCCB Committee on Doctrine, which is reviewing "Doctrinal Responsibilities." As of the writing of this report, it appears the Committee on Doctrine has completed its action on the document, and will be reporting it to the NCCB Administrative Committee. Further action by the bishops will depend on the action taken by the Administrative Committee.

The joint CLSA-CTSA Committee remains committed to being of service to the bishops in evaluating the document, and will keep the two Societies informed when there is further progress to report.

Committee: **Joint Committee on the Imprimatur**
Constituted: Board of Governors, 1985
Charge: To explore the canonical issues related to the *imprimatur* as it is presented in current church law.
Membership: John A. Barry (CCLS), Chairperson
James A. Coriden (CLSA)
Denis Livernois (CCLS)
James H. Provost (CLSA)
Eric Reynolds (CCLS)

Annual Report

This committee was formed at the invitation of the Canadian Canon Law Society, who were asked by the Canadian Conference of Catholic Bishops to research seven questions related to the *imprimatur*.

After an initial meeting in Quebec in 1985, the committee conducted its work primarily through the mails.

Committee: **On Liturgies**
Constituted: Board of Governors, 1986
Charge: Establish guidelines for convention liturgies. Plan the convention liturgies.
Membership: Daniel Ward, O.S.B., Chairperson
Cora Billings, R.S.M.
Barbara Ann Cusack
Gregory Wielunski

Annual Report

The committee held several conference calls and subcommittee calls. The committee proposed draft guidelines for convention liturgies, which were approved by the BOG. In addition the committee has been preparing the liturgies for the Nashville Convention. The committee will continue to work on the guidelines and to plan future convention liturgies.

Committee: **Marriage Research**
Constituted: 35th Annual Meeting, 1973
Charge: The following mandate was approved at the 1984 CLSA convention:
—to identify specific areas of marriage research;

—to identify scholars who have done or will do research in those particular areas and who will produce manuscripts for publication;

—to facilitate the publication of this research either in the CLSA-sponsored publication *Marriage Studies* or in other scholarly or professional journals.

Membership: John A. Alesandro (chair)
Michael Place
William Varvaro

Annual Report

The first meeting of the newly-constituted committee was held on October 14, 1986, at the convention in Denver.

While not dismissing plans for the continued publication of the *Marriage Studies* the committee felt that it should begin its work by examining all of the means of publication at our disposal and different ways of fostering needed research. One of the practical points to be considered is the Society's method of compensating authors for their articles on marriage in Society publications.

One of the committee's first steps will be to survey the various marriage topics that have already been identified by the CLSA in the past as research questions and determine whether such questions have been addressed.

Another topic of interest to the committee is the development, if needed and feasible, of a computerized bibliography on the areas of marriage research in which the committee is specializing. Various sources can serve as a starting-point for such a study: Orsy's bibliographical sources and questions raised in his recent work; the index published by Strasbourg; the Louvain index. Encouraged by those consulted, the committee is continuing to pursue this idea.

The committee hopes to link its work with other activities in the field such as the recent symposium at Dayton University. Michael Place is planning to participate on August 11-12, 1987, in a follow up to the symposium held last year at the University of Dayton. This meeting may foster another symposium at Dayton on Christian marriage in the Spring or Fall of 1988. The committee hopes to work with ongoing conferences of this sort in a complementary fashion and to enlist the cooperation of the CLSA in such noteworthy projects relating to marriage research. It also hopes to tap for research projects many more members of the Society by searching the Society's membership database for those interested in the field.

The committee held its second meeting on February 13-14, 1987, at Bill Varvaro's residence in Brooklyn.

The pending file material relating to the publication of *Marriage Studies* was received from the former chair and will be examined to determine what might be helpful in furthering the committee's work.

The committee made the following survey of issues in the area of marriage that have already been studied by the CLSA:

Theological Topics
1. Understanding of Marriage in the New Testament
   —divorce and remarriage
   —indissolubility
   —mixed marriages
2. The Power to Dissolve Christian Marriage (Ursa's Case)
3. Faith and Marriage
   —focus on the baptized non-believer
   —sacramentality
4. Internal Forum Solutions
5. Second Marriage and the Eucharist
6. Contract/Sacrament
7. Indissolubility
8. *Oeconomia*

Canonical Topics
1. Psychological Issues
2. Competent Forum and the Rights of the Parties
3. *Ligamen*—Multiple Marriages
4. Relative Incapacity
5. Non-Inclusion of Essential Elements of Consent
6. U.S. Jurisprudence
7. Procedural Law
8. Marriage Preparation
9. Capacity for Marriage

Mandated but Never Completed
1. Alternatives to Tribunal
2. Canonical Institute of Dissolution
3. Canonical Form of Marriage

Since almost all of the topics mandated by the CLSA have been addressed, with greater or less success, the committee considered itself free to develop its own parameters of the research projects it will seek to initiate. Consequently, the committee decided to concentrate on *broader theological-canonical issues that deal with the substance of Christian marriage* (e.g., sacramentality and indissolubility). The committee will not address procedural topics or questions of moral or pastoral theology unless these impact on substantive issues.

Given this general thrust, the committee used the questions raised by Les Orsy in his work, *Marriage in Canon Law* (pp. 260-294), to map out specific areas of research and possible topics. It then submitted this primary list of issues to certain scholars in the field to criticize, comment on, and improve.

THE COMMITTEE'S PRIMARY LIST OF QUESTIONS AND ISSUES
(Numbers refer to Orsy's questions cited above.)

1-12. What is the right balance between protecting the institution and respecting the person? Is the tribunal system satisfactory?
—the presumption in favor of the bond in c. 1060
—the relationship between the internal and external fora in regard to marriage nullity and the right to remarry
—the delays in the ecclesiastical process of declaring nullity
—alternatives to the tribunal process; nullity as an object of contentious procedure; administrative decrees of freedom; the values of the current tribunal process (oftentimes healing for the participants)

2. Does *consortium* have one precise meaning applicable everywhere?
—cohabitation as an element of *consortium*
—the minimum requisites of *consortium* in a multi-cultural society
—Is the meaning of *consortium* geographical or personal?

3-4. How can consummation be the cause of absolute indissolubility? Is there a spiritual consummation of marriage?
—consummation *humano modo* and the spouse afflicted with AIDS
—condomistic consummation
—the use of *uno caro* by scripture, fathers and medieval theologians
—previous lengthy cohabitation and its effect on juridical consummation
—consummation as a joining of spirits, as the completion of interpersonality, as an affective union

5. Can the contract be separated from the sacrament?
—the impact of marriage as *foedus*
—sacramental marriage and the baptized non-believer
—the meaning of "faith" as a basis for sacramental marriage

6-7-9. What is the nature of the bond? How is marriage the sign of the union of Christ with his church? Can a marriage heal itself?
—the bond as the result of a formation process
—the bond as a *tertium quid*
—the essential elements of the bond
—the interaction of the bond as an ontological reality and the meaning of marriage as a relationship
—the nature of the "bond" of a canonically invalid marriage
—the nature of the "relationship" found in a canonically invalid marriage
—Can an invalid marriage *become* valid?

8. What is the power of the Church in relation to sacramental consummated marriages?
—the nature of the ecclesiastical authority exercised in each distinctive type of dissolution of the bond; the meaning of "dissolution"
—the notion of *dispensatio* in canon law and its applicability to the institute of dissolution

—Is *oeconomia* an ecclesial power affecting sacramental consummated marriages?
10. How is the law of consent likely to develop in the future?
—the object of consent
—intentionality
—the rights of marriage as distinct from the exercise of the rights
—the impact of cultural consciousness upon consent (e.g., divorce mentality)
—essential elements of consensual maturity
—juridical presumptions about consent
11. Should the law continue to impose the canonical form for validity?
—the special case of the marriage of a Catholic and an Orthodox
—Are DF cases the Church's form of "trial marriage?"
—Is canonical form a universal need, or only a local one?
—the impact on the Church of many non-canonical, valid, "sacramental" marriages if canonical form is not imposed for validity
13. Could persons living in irregular unions be admitted into Eucharistic communion?
—internal forum solutions
—*oeconomia*

The committee decided to initiate immediately two specific topics that seemed helpful:

a. An anthology of Rotal decisions from 1971 to 1986. This would be a preliminary study to prepare for a second study analyzing certain important decisions. The preliminary cataloguing would examine the most recent volumes of *Decisiones* and then canvass available decisions in the usual periodicals, with the following aim: to identify the decisions, point out their location, give a two-sentence *precis* of the content, organize the list by *caput nullitatis* (and within the *caput*, in chronological order). The committee is still searching for an author.

b. Ecumenical developments regarding Roman Catholic-Orthodox marriages. Ten recommendations from the New York-New Jersey Orthodox-Roman Catholic Dialogue were sent to Archbishop Weakland at the national level. The committee asked Monsignor Daniel Hamilton, a member of the regional dialogue, to consider its request to write an article on this topic.

The committee has adopted the strategy of regularly consulting with a group of approximately eighteen scholars in the field. As of the composition of this report the following have agreed to serve as "informal consultants" to the committee: Rev. Msgr. Kenneth Boccafola (Rota); Reverend Michael Buckley, S.J. (NCCB); Rev. Msgr. Thomas Doran (Rota); Reverend David Fellhauer (Dallas); Reverend Thomas Green (CUA); Reverend Robert Kennedy (CUA); Dr. Stephan Kuttner (Berkeley); Reverend Theodore Mackin, S.J. (Santa Clara University); Mr. Joseph Martos (Salesian Seminary, Allentown); Reverend Richard McCormick, S.J. (Notre Dame); Reverend Francis Morrisey (St. Paul's Ottawa); Reverend Ladislas

Orsy, S.J. (CUA); Prof. William Roberts (U. of Dayton); Reverend Robert Sanson (CUA); Reverend Lawrence Wrenn (Hartford).

Comments and suggestions for the committee should be addressed by CLSA members to: Reverend Msgr. John A. Alesandro; Rockville Centre Chancery; 50 North Park Avenue; Rockville Centre, New York 11570; 516-678-5800.

Committee: **Permanent Seminar: Protection of Rights in the Church**
Constituted: Board of Governors, 1984, implementing action of the 45th Annual Meeting, 1983
Charge: To investigate possible options for diocesan, regional and national procedures for the protection of rights of persons in the Church.
Co-directors: John Folmer and James Provost

Annual Report

The Seminar papers have been published in *The Jurist* 1986:1 issue, which was distributed in early 1987. Additional copies can be purchased through the office of the Executive Coordinator.

This completes the Permanent Seminar part of the project on protecting and promoting rights in the Church. The second portion of the first stage of the project, a survey on due process experience in the United States, is reported on separately by the task force which conducted the survey.

Committee: **CLSA Scholarship Criteria**
Membership: Paul L. Golden, C.M., Chair
Cecilia Bennett
Sharon Holland, I.H.M.

Annual Report

Introduction
(When the scholarship criteria are published, this introduction would contain the purpose and goals of the scholarship fund and some historical background. It would also explain the relationship of the fund to the CLSA, its Board of Governors and the Board of Trustees of the fund. Finally, it might explain the make up of the selection committee and the schedule of its meetings.)

Terms of the Scholarship
1. Scholarships are awarded for a one-year period. They are renewable once.

2. The Board of Trustees will announce the total amount of funding available for the next funding year. The size and number of awards is left to the judgment of the selection committee. Ordinarily, scholarships will defray only tuition costs, in whole or in part. The use of this money for other costs associated with a study program is left to the discretion of the selection committee.

3. Scholarships are awarded only to full-time students enrolled in a Licentiate of Canon Law program or in one-year program leading to the Licentiate. All pontifical faculties of Canon Law qualify. Theological studies, even as prerequisites to canonical studies, do not qualify for funding. Doctoral programs do not qualify for scholarships.

4. No applicant will be excluded by reason of age, race, sex or canonical status in the Church. Special consideration will be given to women and minority applicants.

5. Scholarships will not be awarded until the applicant has been formally accepted by a university into the Canon Law program.

6. Funds will be paid directly to a university upon presentation of bills, vouchers or other such documents.

Eligibility

1. Applicants must demonstrate a true need for scholarship funding, i.e., that they would not be able to pursue canonical studies without this financial assistance.

2. Applicants must be members of the Roman Catholic Church and be in good standing.

3. Applicants must demonstrate their intention of working in the canonical ministry in the Church of the United States upon completion of their studies. (Letters from Bishops, Judicial Vicars and/or Religious Superiors giving assurances of such future employment in a diocese or religious community are welcomed.)

4. Applicants must demonstrate appropriate scholastic aptitude for canonical studies. For the first year of study, the formal acceptance by a university is sufficient evidence. For the second year of study, the applicants must have a "B" average or its equivalent in their first year.

5. Applicants must demonstrate a level of professional competence and personal character compatible with the commonly accepted norms of canonical ministry.

Process of Application

All applicants must send the following to the CLSA Scholarship Selection Committee by March 15:
1. The completed application form
2. Their resume/curriculum vitae
3. Transcripts from undergraduate and graduate schools
4. A letter of recommendation
    From their Bishop, for priests and deacons
    From their Major Superior, for religious
    From their Bishop or a diocesan official (if applicable), for lay-

persons.
5. Three letters giving testimony concerning:
   Academic ability
   Professional competence
   Personal character
6. The letter of acceptance by the faculty or department of Canon Law.
7. A letter written by the applicant expressing the need for this scholarship and the intention to work as a canonist after graduation.

Committee: **Selection of Bishops**
Constituted: Board of Governors, 1987, implementing Resolution No. 6 of the 48th Annual Meeting, 1986
Charge: As a Committee of One to conduct a review and study of the work which has already been done in the area of the selection of bishops (particularly the work of the original 1969 CLSA committee), and to evaluate whether a future activation of this committee might be useful, and if so, to suggest ways such a committee might address contemporary concerns in this area.
Membership: Norman P. Bolduc

Annual Report

The work of this committee is proceeding in two stages.

It is presently in the process of gathering and organizing all materials relevant to the subject of the selection of bishops and is also conducting a search for any recent documents. These materials include the history and work of the CLSA's original 1969 committee on the subject (inactive since 1981), and the initial report submitted by the CLSA to the NCCB on the subject in 1974.

The second stage is an evaluation of these materials to determine whether or not the future activation of this committee would be useful. If so, this committee may then suggest whether such a committee should continue its original work or explore other directions in this area, as well as suggest ways the committee might address issues of contemporary concern.

The committee anticipates concluding its work within the coming CLSA activities year. A final report will be submitted to the society at the 50th Annual Meeting.

Committee: **Study of Procedures for the Protection of Rights of Persons in the Church**
Constituted: BOG, 1987
Membership: Ricardo E. Bass, Chairperson

Robert T. Kennedy
Joseph N. Perry

Annual Report

The committee has just begun its work.

Committee: **Symposium on Lay Ministry**
Constituted: Board of Governors, 1986
Charge: To conduct a symposium on lay ministry
Co-directors: James A. Coriden
James H. Provost

Annual Report

At its Spring 1985 meeting, the Board of Governors conducted a planning process to identify major concerns to be addressed by the Society in the 1985-1995 decade. The first priority it identified was the future of parish ministry, and in particular the involvement of more lay people in that ministry. The Board decided to implement this priority by authorizing research into the theoretical questions involved, followed by the development of practical steps such as the canon law needed in the formation and on-going education of lay ministers, as well as the canon law which governs the responsibilities and rights of lay ministers in the Church.

The Board decided to research into the theoretical questions conducted by a symposium. The Board subsequently asked that the symposium broaden its concern from lay ministry at the parish level, to set a broader context of lay persons in church law. The resulting papers would be useful not only for the CLSA's on-going concern about lay ministry and lay ministers at the parish level, but also for the participants at the 1987 Synod of Bishops.

In the Fall of 1986 ten authors agreed to submit studies as part of the symposium. Through the generosity of the Raskob Foundation, a challenge grant was received to fund a meeting of the authors with other consultants to discuss the papers. The Missional Servants of the Most Blessed Trinity and the Canon Law Society of America provided funds which the Raskob Foundation matched to enable the meeting of the symposium to be held at O'Hare Plaza Hotel in Chicago on April 4-6, 1987.

Sixteen persons participated in the symposium meeting (see attached list). In light of their discussion of this research, the participants developed a statement of general observations, specific recommendations to the bishop and *periti* attending the Synod of Bishops, and further research topics for the CLSA to address.

The papers of the symposium together with an introduction and the final statement were published in the 1987:1 issue of *The Jurist*. The Board of Governors directed that the seminar papers and the final statement from the seminar meeting be distributed to the delegates and *periti* named to attend the 1987 Synod of Bishops meeting.

This completes the symposium project itself, although a number of related questions remain to be researched as recommended in the attached final statement.

LAITY IN THE RENEWING CHURCH: VISION AND OPPORTUNITIES
Statement from the C.L.S.A. Symposium
On Laity in Church Law

1. The Second Vatican Council stimulated renewed attention to lay persons in the Church. The revised Code of Canon Law, which is itself intended as an implementation of the council, reflects this heightened awareness of lay persons in the mission of the Church. At the invitation of the Canon Law Society of America, a group of sixteen women and men met in Chicago April 4-6, 1987 to reflect on ten background papers and to explore laity in the renewing Church in light of the vision and opportunities of church law today. This group of lay persons, vowed religious, and clergy included theologians and canon lawyers, church professionals and persons engaged in secular activities. We present the following remarks at the conclusion of our study together.

2. Through incorporation in Christ by baptism, men and women become *christifideles*, Christian faithful. They are constituted as the people of God. Within this common fundamental condition of all the baptized, some are termed "lay." As Vatican II observed, lay persons are not sacred ministers or vowed religious. The council characterized the condition of lay persons as typically "secular." That is, lay persons are those who are engaged in the activities of the world, although the council recognized a proper role for the laity in the Church as well as in the world.

3. The concepts of "world" and "Church" are central to understanding "laity." Yet these concepts have various meanings, as is evident for "world" and "Church" in the Bible and Christian tradition, and even for "laity" in the documents of Vatican II. In our discussions it has been evident that there are various theologies which attempt to relate "laity," "Church" and "world." These terms continue to reflect different languages or meanings. Thus it is difficult to achieve mutual understanding when addressing laity in church law. We therefore approach this topic cautiously, recognizing how limited any statement will be, especially in these times of rapid change.

4. For example, here are three approaches to the context of our study, attempting to relate "laity," Church," and "world."
   a. Mission is the raison d'etre, the reason for being of the Church. The Church exists in and from particular churches. Therefore mission must

be seen first of all in the context of the particular church. This mission includes three dimensions: *martyria,* a prophetic dimension; *koinonia,* the communion of believers with one another and with God; *diakonia,* or service for the life of the community and the humanization of the world. Organized service, or ministry, relates to all these dimensions of mission but presupposes a community mature enough for each of its members to assume a proper role in this mission.

b. The primary reality is the people of God, the community of *christifideles.* This people is constituted through baptism for carrying out Christ's mission. The mission of the Church is thus the context for all ministry and apostolates. Through charisms, which are widely distributed, the Spirit is acting in the community. Some charisms receive recognition through sacramental ordination as deacons, presbyters, or bishops. There are other charisms which need encouragement and recognition in the Church and in the world.

c. "Laity," "Church" and "world" are interrelated concepts which mediate the experience of everyday life. It is a key value that lay persons understand themselves as "Church," that they see themselves as included in what it means to be Church. Those who serve in the Church have the responsibility of helping all the people of God understand that they are the Church, and helping them relate faith to everyday life. This service is a collaboration of clergy, vowed religious, and laity.

5. All the people of God are the Church. There is a special need to acknowledge and affirm that as a fruit of their baptism, lay persons are actively engaged in both the Church and the world. Therefore we address the following remarks to the members and *periti* participating in the 1987 Synod of Bishops and to the Canon Law Society of America.

To the Synod

6. In promulgating the new code and in subsequent references, Pope John Paul II has repeatedly insisted that the council provides the means to interpret the code. Therefore the works and spirit of Vatican II provide the primary pattern for addressing issues in the Church today, including the vocation and mission of the laity. The Code of Canon Law should not be alleged as a reason to restrict that vocation and mission.

7. *Christus Dominus* admonishes the bishops to approach people, searching and fostering dialogue (CD 13). Attentive listening to the experience of lay persons living out their faith in the world and in the Church provides an indispensable perspective on "the vocation and mission of the laity in the Church and in the world." Therefore it is necessary that the pastors of the Church engage in this dialogue not only in preparation for the 1987 Synod of Bishops, but as a continuing pastoral practice.

8. More fundamental and important than any distinctions in the Church is the common condition arising from baptism. Any language, including any attempt

at a special definition of "lay," which would increase the distance between clergy and laity should be avoided. Rather, that interrelatedness and interdependence emphasized by Vatican II (LG 10) should be fostered.

9. The laity, with growing urgency, seek a deeper and more vigorous spiritual life than has often been available to them. It is crucial that the Synod address this thirst of lay persons for a gospel-centered spirituality nourished by the Word and sacraments, and rooted in their daily experiences of living in the world. The Synod would do well to recall that *all* Christians are called to discipleship. Moreover, pastors, teachers, spiritual directors, and other ministers in the Church should nurture and support the laity as they struggle to respond to the radical call to follow Jesus.

10. There is currently a serious crisis in ordained ministry which is having deleterious effects on nurturing the faith of the people of God. Evidence of this crisis is manifold: parishes denied the regular ministry of an ordained priest, communities which are denied regular participation in sacramental celebrations which should characterize the Catholic Church, a malaise and "burn out" among priests, the danger of a growing midunderstanding of sacramental ministry. Responses to this crisis have been inadequate and patch work, and there is the danger of becoming a non-sacramental Church. This crisis in ordained ministry must also be addressed if there is to be an adequate approach to the vocation and mission of lay persons.

11. The question of "lay ministry" provides a special application of the principle that the Code of Canon Law is to be interpreted in light of the teaching of the council. Vatican II applied the term "ministry" to a wide variety of activities by lay persons, a usage continued in the fruits of previous Synods of Bishops (for example, *Evangelii nuntiandi,* n. 73, and *Familiaris consortio,* nn. 28, 32, 38, and 39). The narrower use of "ministry" and "service" in the Code of Canon Law must be balanced by the broader use of these terms in the Church's Magisterium.

12. The rights and duties which arise from charisms are critical for building up the life of the community; they demand that lay ministry be taken seriously. We encourage the pastors of the Church to recognize and foster these charisms, providing the adequate preparation and support that is required by the law of the Church (c. 231).

13. Lay involvement in what was formerly done by clergy is not always an exceptional service, but actually an example of the proper collaboration and cooperation of clergy and laity in the Church and in the world. It is important that this be given official recognition. One method for providing ongoing collaboration between clergy and laity is to provide from the start a common preparation of clergy and laity for ministry.

14. The exclusion of *lay* women from installed *lay* ministries should be abandoned. The distinctions in church ministry are on the basis of sacramental orders, and ought not be the result of discrimination based on gender.

15. Any talk about collaboration of the laity in the life and mission of the Church

rings hollow if there are no structures in a diocese to assure this in practice. Yet the new Code of Canon Law does not require any collaborative or consultative structures necessarily involving lay persons. It is critical that this lacuna be addressed, for example by making diocesan and parish pastoral councils mandatory.

16. In the present pastoral needs of the Church, and in the present state of development of the Church's mission, there is a special need to protect the proper autonomy of lay activity in the Church and in the world so as to prevent unjust, arbitrary, and inequitable treatment. This applies to the whole range of lay involvement in social, political and cultural activities. In a particular way it applies to the wide range of specialized involvement in the Church's mission, including associations, church programs, services, and offices.

17. In addressing the vocation and mission of the laity, it is necessary that the language in which the results of the Synod are expressed be understandable to all the Christian faithful.

To the Canon Law Society of America

18. In the course of our research and study together, we have identified a number of issues which need further research:
   a. Study and practical steps are needed to address the protection of the proper autonomy of lay activity discussed in n. 16, above.
   b. Further research is needed on questions relating to rights and duties in the Church; for example:
      1) The relationship between the promulgated text of the canons with the Principles for the Revision of the Code of Canon Law, approved by the 1967 Synod of Bishops, which were explicit on the need to state basic rights and to provide adequate protection for them in the Church;
      2) The meaning of "rights" in the new code—are they "constitutional," or merely "functional" derivations from obligations and responsibilities;
      3) The interrelationship of obligations and rights;
      4) The meaning of "acquired rights" in church law, and are they truly protected by the provisions of the code;
      5) Structures and procedures for vindicating rights in the Church.
   c. Research and practical proposals are needed concerning the appointment, qualifications, evaluation and removal of persons in official ministry. This applies to:
      1) Clergy, vowed religious, and lay persons;
      2) Procedures, structures, and criteria;
      3) The special situation of professional lay ministers.
   d. Research is needed into the meaning and relationship of the priesthood of all the faithful and the ordained priesthood.
   e. Research and practical proposals are needed into vehicles for collaboration and cooperation of clergy and laity at all levels of church life; for example:

1) Various kinds of bodies involving clergy and laity;
  2) Collaboration of lay persons involved in parish ministry with one another, and with clergy;
  3) Ministry preparation.
 f. Special attention needs to be given to the use of the term "Church," in terms of its use in referring to an official, agency or institution, and its use implying all the people of God.
 g. Research is needed into the meaning of the "secular" or "wordly" quality of laity.

PARTICIPANTS IN THE SYMPOSIUM ON LAITY IN CHURCH LAW

Rev. James A. Coriden - Academic Dean, Washington Theological Union; co-director of symposium
Dr. Keith J. Egan - Director, Program on Spirituality, St. Mary's College, Notre Dame; author: "Legal Elements Toward a Lay Spirituality"
Ms. Suzanne E. Elsesser - Consultant; Co-author of NCCB survey on lay ministry training program; discussant
Sr. Sharon Holland, I.H.M. - Assistant Professor of Canon Law, Catholic University; author: "Equality, Dignity and Rights of Laity."
Mr. Ed. Marciniak - Director, Institute for Urban Life; discussant
Rev. Msgr. Frederick R. McManus - Professor of Canon Law, Catholic University; author: "New Code, New Focus"
Dr. Jon Nilson - Chairman, Department of Theology, Loyola University of Chicago: discussant
Dr. David Nowak - Director, Archdiocese of Milwaukee Lay Ministry Training program; Chair, National Association of Lay Ministers committee on lay ministry training: discussant
Rev. Roch Page - Professor of Canon Law, St. Paul University; author: "Lay Associations of the Faithful"
Rev. Edward G. Pfnausch - CLSA Executive Coordinator; discussant
Rev. Michael Place - Theological Consultant to Archbishop of Chicago; author: "Laity and the Secular Mission of the Church"
Ms. Ann Prew-Winters - Tribunal Judge, Cincinnati; author: "Who is a Lay Person?"
Rev. Normand Provencher, O.M.I. - Professor of Theology, St. Paul University; author: "Church and World"
Rev. James H. Provost - Associate Professor of Canon Law, Catholic University; director of symposium
Sr. Elissa Rinere, C.P. - Tribunal Judge, Hartford; author: "The Term 'Lay Ministry'"
Sr. Lea Woll, S.L.W. - Director of Lay Ministry Placement, Archdiocese of Chicago; discussant
Not able to be present:
Sr. Elizabeth McDonough, O.P. - Assistant Professor of Canon Law, Catholic University; author: "Laity and the Inner Working of the Church"
Rev. John Beal - Chancellor, Diocese of Erie; author: "Vindicating Rights and Responsibilities"

Committee: **Task Force to Study Procedures of the Congregation of the Doctrine of the Faith**
Constituted: 48th Annual Meeting, 1986
Membership: Robert P. Deeley, Chairperson
R. Daniel Conlon

Annual Report

The committee has just begun its work.

Committee: **Task Force on Scholarship Fund**
Constituted: 46th Annual Meeting, 1984
Charge: To initiate the internal fund-raising among CLSA membership in 1986; (2) to further research the questions raised by the report of the task force and come to definite determinations as regard the criteria of need, methods of application, screening of applications and any other unresolved issues; (3) to bring any necessary enabling resolutions before the 48th annual meeting in 1986.
Member: William A. Schumacher, Chairperson

Annual Report

FINAL REPORT TO THE BOARD OF GOVERNORS, CLSA

I. HISTORY OF THE PROJECT

At the Annual General Meeting in 1984, the Society vowed to establish a Task Force to determine the feasibility of the Society undertaking a program to sponsor scholarships so that members of the Christian faithful might be assisted in the professional study of canon law who otherwise would be unable to do so. The Task Force reported to the 1985 Annual General Meeting that such an undertaking would be within the reach of the Society and should have an initial capital goal of $500,000. An essential preliminary step would be the raising of 10% of this goal—$50,000—from among the membership. The body voted to accept this proposal and begin the undertaking.

Prior to the next Annual General Meeting in 1986, a mail solicitation campaign resulted in a partial fulfillment of this goal. (Figures regarding monies raised and members participating is given in tabular form at the end of this report for each stage of the campaign.)

Following the 1986 Annual General Meeting, President Richard Cunningham asked William A. Schumacher of Chicago to undertake this task. The latter accepted this task on October 28, 1986, and immediately undertook consultations with Mr. Robert F. Bobowski of Chicago, a nationally known expert in direct marketing. Working with the President and Executive Coordinator, they designed the two-stage campaign described below. Agreement in principle was reached in a three-way telephone conversation on November 12, 1986.

II. THE CAMPAIGN

A. The Mail Campaign.
The initial stage of the campaign was a direct mail solicitation of the entire US and overseas membership of the Society; institutional members were not in-

cluded. A package was developed consisting of a motivational letter from the President, an illustrated informational brochure, a pledge card and a return envelope. An added incentive was the offer of a souvenir personalized notepad for each donor. The typesetting and layout have been done in Chicago, the materials were printed in Washington and mailed to the membership by the CLSA office staff on December 7, 1986.

B. *The Telephone Campaign.*

The second stage of the fund raising drive would be a telephone sales campaign in which every member would be telephoned by a volunteer fellow-member about participation in this campaign. Overseas members were not solicited by telephone. To achieve this goal, the United States was divided into 16 areas, each with +100 members resident. These members volunteered to serve as Area Coordinators:

    Vince Tatarczuk (Portland ME)
    Bob Deeley (Boston)
    Tony Diacetis (Albany)
    Leonard Scott (Camden)
    Bill Sullivan (Richmond)
    Dennis Klemme (Venice FL)
    John Beal (Erie)
    Jim Ruef (Columbus)
    Rick Thomas (Little Rock)
    Mike Rosswurm (Fort Wayne)
    Charley McNamee (Rockford)
    Ellsworth Kneal (St. Paul)
    Mike Morrissey (Davenport)
    Sid Marceaux (Beaumont)
    John Hedderman (Salt Lake City)
    Harmon Skillin (Stockton)

Each Area Coordinator then recruited members in his area to make the telephone calls, on a ratio of roughly 1:10. 192 more members served as callers.

A sales kit was prepared for each caller consisting of the appropriate computer printout of the members, an audiocassette and instruction sheet on how to sell by telephone, report sheets, and extra mail kits. Each Area Coordinator put these sales kits together for his volunteers and received their weekly reports during the telephone campaign, which began on January 12, 1987, and lasted for three weeks.

The personalized notepads were sent to those requesting them on March 23, 1987, terminating the campaign.

III. RESULTS OF THE CAMPAIGN

In the first place, 209 members of the Society participated actively in the fundraising effort itself; this represents roughly 10% of the membership of the Society. In the aggregate, 565 members contributed to the campaign—about 25% of the membership. Professional fund raisers advise us that this participation is considered excellent for such a project.

Even the members who did not contribute have been made aware of the campaign on two occasions—receipt of the mail campaign and a call during the telephone campaign. The total amount raised (cf. table, next page) is seen by our consultants as a successful fulfillment of our goal.

Here are the results of our efforts:

DATES:	TOTAL MEMBERS PARTICIPATING	TOTAL CASH RECEIVED	TOTAL RECEIVED AND PLEDGED
10/85 thru 12/12/86 (Before Campaign)	183	$20,227	$23,183
1/10/87 (End of mail campaign)	+178=361	+$10,115 $30,392	+$11,155 $34,338
2/6/87 (Results of phone campaign)	+112=473	+$ 7,305 $37,697	+$ 8,435 $47,763
3/23/87 (Since campaign)	+ 92=565	+$ 4,990 $42,687	+$ 4,990 $47,763

Committee: **Task Force to Survey Due Process Experience**
Constituted: Board of Governors, 1984, implementing action of the 45th Annual Meeting, 1983
Charge: To survey the experience of "due process" in dioceses in the United States over the past fifteen years.
Membership: Ricardo Bass
John Folmer, Co-director
Joseph Perry
James Provost, Co-director

Annual Report

At the 1983 CLSA convention, the following resolution was adopted by the Society:
. . . that the Board of Governors eastablish a task force to investigate possible

options for diocesan, regional and national procedures for the protection of rights of persons in the Church and report to next year's annual convention.

The initial task force set up by the Board recommended a two stage approach. The first stage would do some background work on theory and practical experience; the second stage would then draw on the results of this work, and develop the "possible options" mentioned in the resolution.

The first stage of research included two projects. The first was the permanent seminar on the protection of rights, the results of which have now appeared in *The Jurist* (vol. 46, no. 1). The second project was a task force to survey the actual experience of "due process" in dioceses in the United States, in keeping with the NCCB publication *On Due Process* (Washington: NCCB, 1972).

The survey task force began working in September 1985. Members contacted most of the dioceses in the United States by personal phone call and/or letter. They reviewed the written materials from over forty percent of the dioceses in the United States as well as the written materials from seventy-four diocesan offices of education, sixty religious institutes of women, and eighteen religious institutes of men.

In keeping with an earlier suggestion from the BOG, the draft of the task force's report was subjected to an intense review at a meeting of twenty people, including the four members of the task force, held in Chicago on March 20-22 to review a draft of the task force's report. Invited participants were from dioceses with active "due process" systems, or dioceses which had developed materials in recent years even if they did not report a significant number of cases processed. Several suggestions were made for improving the report, and a set of recommendations were developed to complete the report.

The full report was published in the Spring of 1987 by the CLSA, entitled *Due Process in Dioceses in the United States 1970-1985,* and is available for purchase from the office of the Executive Coordinator. It consists of 251 pages of text, tables, and appendices, with detailed results of the survey. The following is a summary of the major results of the study.

The Findings
1. Over 57% of the dioceses in the United States have some experience with diocesan "due process," either in developing materials or in actually processing a case. It appears that the NCCB document *On Due Process* has found some reception in the Church in the United States. However, only about 25% of U.S. dioceses consider "due process" to be active in the diocese.
2. The policies now in effect in over 40% of the dioceses in the United States were studied in detail and compared with *On Due Process*. Several adaptations are noted in the full report.

    Moreover, seventy-seven dioceses (over 41%) report they have some experience in processing a "due process" case. Since 1970 over 900 cases have been submitted for "due process" consideration, and decisions have been reached in nearly 500 of these.

There is, therefore, some experience in U.S. dioceses on which to draw to evaluate "due process" as one of the options for the protection and promotion of rights in the Church.

3. The organization and operation of "due process" in U.S. dioceses evidences considerable variety, both in the type of operation and in some of the underlying concepts such as what kinds of cases will be allowed. Generally, the procedures presented in *On Due Process* have been followed, but there are some alternative systems based, for example, on courts of equity. The survey did not surface enough information to provide a basis for any comparison of the effectiveness of these various systems.

4. Those directly responsible for diocesan "due process" services report that in addition to managing the formal procedures they often serve as informal counselors to persons who have experienced some difficulty in the Church. At times they aid these persons to see their situation in a more appropriate light; sometimes they serve with various church officials; at times they serve as a sort of "ombudsman" within the diocesan structure.

From the statistics it is apparant that those dioceses which provide professional, full-time personnel for "due process" services report a larger number of cases. This is not an unexpected result. When greater resources become available for resolving disputes, people are more likely to take advantage of them, especially when disputes are related to employment.

5. People generally are not aware of the availability of "due process" where it does exist. This was identified as the most common obstacle to effective utilization of "due process" in the dioceses responding to the survey.

6. In addition to diocesan "due process" offices, there are other means for reconciling disputes being used in dioceses in the United States. Some of these are specialized, primarily through education offices; others are based on the pastoral structures in the diocese, such as the ministry of deans or various types of vicars.

During the course of the survey it became apparent that several dioceses are developing diocesan personnel policies which contain special grievance procedures. These are typically adopted first for personnel in the central diocesan administrative offices; a later step extends these provisions to other personnel employed in the diocese. The survey did not attempt to analyze these developments, as they are still new and are more restricted than diocesan "due process" experience as such, which is what the task force was charged to survey. They do, however, represent significant developments for the future of "due process" in American dioceses.

7. Religious institutes have developed their own "due process" policies. These are closer to the ecclesial approach on *On Due Process* than the policies adopted by diocesan education offices, which tend to reflect the secular parallels of public schools or the concerns of civil attorneys.

Diocesan "due process" can learn from the religious institutes a sensitivity toward evangelical values, and the recognition that not every difficulty can be addressed adequately through "due process" procedures. From the education offices a concern surfaces for more attention to the interaction of civil law and ecclesial concerns.

Recommendations

The task force submits the following recommendations, as contained in its final report.
1. "Due Process" Services

   The experience of several dioceses in the United States validates the worth of "due process" services; it is recommended such services be retained (even if only as a preventative measure), their availability be expanded, and they be integrated with other approaches to resolving difficulties, communications problems, and grievances.
   a. Each diocese is encouraged to conduct an audit of how complaints are handled, to see if they are addressed in a timely and appropriate manner. Included in such a review might be a meeting of all who are involved in appeal procedures of any type in the diocese, to see who is doing what.
   b. A "holistic" approach is recommended to difficulties, communications problems, and grievances. For example, the diocese could use the services of an "ombudsman"-type person skilled in communications, who can direct concerned people to the appropriate officials or agencies, and who can assist pastors, church administrators, boards, councils, etc., with making more explicit the expectations involved in various relationships such as employers and employees, pastors and councils, executives and boards.
   c. Where multiple grievance machinery exists, dioceses should examine whether it is advisable in their circumstances to consolidate them, or whether diversifying is appropriate. If it is appropriate to diversify, attention must be given to:
      1) the interrelationship of these systems, in keeping with the principle of subsidiarity;
      2) avoiding unnecessary duplication within the same case;
      3) the eventual culmination in arbitration, which is final and binding.
   d. Effective "due process" services require the development of procedures to deal with cases which cannot be handled by conciliation or arbitration, for example administrative tribunals or "delegated tribunals" (NCCB *On Due Process*). The task force members and those they consulted at the March 20-22, 1987 meeting recommend the CLSA prepare proposals in this regard for adoption by the NCCB.
2. Prior Process

   "Prior process" needs more direct attention in dioceses in keeping with *On Due Process*. For example:
   a. Policies and procedures should be evaluated with a view toward their adequacy from a "due process" point of view;
   b. The local "due process" system should be included in contracts for employ-

ment, etc., as the agreed means for resolving disputes;
   c. The CLSA should see to the development of a video-taped training program to acquaint church administrators with administrative and management procedures needed for effective prior process.
3. Publicity and Education

   There is a need to provide better publicity and education to the people of the Church about "due process" and its availability. Such efforts need to steer a middle course between drumming up business where there is none, and keeping the existence of "due process" a closely guarded secret. The following measures are recommended:
   a. Toward all in the Church:
      1) Education needs to be provided on rights of all the Christian faithful, and on the procedures available to vindicate those rights;
      2) To this end, the CLSA should see to the development of a video-taped program to teach the Christian aspects of dispute resolution, and to explain rights and "due process" procedures in a simple, non-threatening manner;
      3) Dioceses need to broaden the base of support and understanding for "due process" by involving more people in initiating, re-initiating, or seeing to the ongoing operation of "due process" procedures.
   b. Toward bishops, priests, and other church officials:
      1) Clarify that "due process" procedures are in conformity with canon (and civil) law.
      2) Emphasize that "due process" is a tool, not an enemy.
      3) The CLSA should develop a video-taped program for the benefit of bishops, to build their understanding and support of "due process."
      4) "Due process" services should be listed by dioceses in their entry in the *Official Catholic Directory.*
4. Training

   Training for "due process" personnel is a need felt in some dioceses. It is recommended that the CLSA see to the development of national resources, including video and written materials, for use in training conciliators and arbitrators in the skills and procedures needed to fulfill their tasks.
5. Procedures

   The procedures in *On Due Process* have been adapted in many ways. It is recommended that the procedures themselves be examined with a view to simplifying them, in light of the following elements.
   a. The enabling language should speak the Christian spirit behind the procedures.
   b. The term "due process" should be examined to see if a more appropriate term might be developed for the concerns, procedures and structures which are dealt with in *On Due Process* and diocesan "due process" services.
   c. In regard to the personnel involved:
      1) In light of the fact that most petitioners are lay persons, it is recommended

that a significant number of people staffing diocesan "due process" offices (clerks, etc.) and those actually conducting "due process" services be lay persons.
   2) Conciliators and arbitrators should be selected primarily on the basis of ability, rather than profession.
 d. In regard to the petititoner:
   1) Even if the violation of a right is not immediately evident, the allegation of a grievance is sufficient to give attention to a petition, at least at the entry level.
   2) The language explaining what is required of the petitioner should be simple and clear, for the petitioner's benefit.
   3) The statement of allowable and non-allowable cases should be clarified in each diocese's procedures.
 e. In regard to the process:
   1) Begin sessions with prayer.
   2) Establish clear and reasonable time lines.
   3) The policy should contain a glossary of terms in language which will be clear to the average Catholic in the diocese, and materials should be made available in the languages of the principal language groups in the diocese.

6. Future Action

The experience of the March 20-22 meeting illustrated the importance of the CLSA's involvement in "due process" concerns at this time. It is recommended that:

 a. The CLSA continue to pay attention to "due process" as part of its ongoing agenda, even by providing seminars or talks on the topic during its annual conventions.
 b. Other meetings of the type held March 20-22 be convened by the CLSA, even on an annual basis provided there is something substantial to discuss, and that these be separate from the CLSA convention and designed for personnel responsible for "due process" structures.
 c. Communications among "due process" offices be facilitated by a periodic newsletter, and that the CLSA take the initiative to get such a newsletter started.

TRIBUNAL STATISTICS SUMMARY FILE
LIST OF FIRST INSTANCE TRIBUNALS

Diocese	Year	Cases Presented	Cases Accepted	Decided by Sentence	Mixed-Marriage	Non-Catholic	Abandoned	Trib Abate	Ligamen	Other Dec	Lack of Form	Ratum Non-Consummatum
Albany	86	435	412	379			23	30	8		205	1
Alexandria	86											
Allentown	86	454	346	332	93	61	26	82	2	125	3	
Altoona	86	119	82	70	23	14	10	5	3	1		
Amarillo	86	40	40	58	16	21			3			
Anchorage	86	36	36	31	12	13	1	3	7		56	
Arch/Military Serv	86	325	325	237	104	105	14		17		216	
Arlington	86	255	232	206	68	54	4	27	17		178	
Atlanta	86	871	705	707	103	347	143	37	103		298	
Austin	86	294	294	235	65	118	6	12	16	1	182	
Baker Oregon	86	80	49	57	18	23	31		8		48	
Baltimore	86	567	567	502	175	160	1	5	25	1	360	
Baton Rouge	86	278	275	241	66	41			12		131	
Beaumont	86	180	155	155	62	41			28	2	110	
Belleville IL	86	203	203	108	32	34	1		4		56	
Biloxi	86	121	106	90			8	4	4		72	
Birmingham	86	62	62	75	22	42	11		9		34	
Bismark	86	95	95	101	29	19	4		2		34	
Boise	86	210	210	217	46	56	25		43	8	108	
Boston	86	1552	1552	919			212	371	7	11	712	
Bridgeport	86	312	176	165	43	12		10	2	1	153	
Brooklyn	86	1296	902	495	82	36	394		1	2	657	
Brownsville	86	160	48	47	7	3	5	96	5		74	
Buffalo	86	510	300	217	72	30	22		7	1	253	
Burlington	86		113	140	28	12	2		4	1		
Byelorussians	86											
Camden	86	241	135	156	42	39	7	98	8	3	195	
Charleston	86	143	136	109			4	88	9	3	53	
Charlotte	86	112	105	82	21	37	10	10	12	1	47	
Cheyenne	86	113	113	97	23	28		7	18	3	70	

297

TRIBUNAL STATISTICS SUMMARY FILE
LIST OF FIRST INSTANCE TRIBUNALS

Diocese	Year	Cases Presented	Cases Accepted	Decided by Sentence	Mixed-Marriage	Non-Catholic	Abandoned	Trib Abate	Ligamen	Other Dec	Lack of Form	Ratum Non-Consummatum
Chicago	86	1120	1128	1356	290	110	10	66	46	5	1003	
Cincinnati	86	508	508	344			83	110	27	1	274	
Cleveland	86	959		939	193	151	45	24	37	4	576	
Colorado Springs	86	72	56	57	15	10	4	20	14		46	
Columbus	86	256	301	178	63	75	13	25	7		50	
Corpus Christi	86	219	219	185	35	29	6	17	2		153	
Covington	86	206	204	195	42	79	6	14	18	4	101	
Crookston	86	63	62	67	22	16	1	5	2	23		
Dallas TX	86	366	364	319	77	131	11	45	38		299	
Davenport	86	174	174	155	45	38	3	11	22		73	
Denver	86	166	150	80			8		13	11	246	
Des Moines	86	132	132	115	35	34	3	2	15		49	
Detroit	86											
Dodge City	86	84	84	46	26	20	5	15	11		32	
Dubuque	86	557	557	376	90	102	131		15		77	
Duluth	86	78	78	61			8		2		51	
El Paso	86	97	88	86	9	6	9		5		87	
Erie	86	269	217	217	52	40	22		7		87	
Evansville	86	116	116	114	32	19	21		7		67	
Fairbanks	86	25	25	26	6	6	2	2	8		16	
Fall River	86	124	124	83			11	31			129	
Fargo	86	217	217	110	29	27	5	94	7	1	47	
Fort Wayne	86	299	200	180	42	49	61	18	12		86	
Fort Worth	86	232	226	138	54	85	1		33		152	
Fresno	86	233	184	165	48	30	1	2	12	3	195	
Gallup	86	32	20	19	6	5	3	3	1		39	
Galveston	86	670	614	567	131	198	11	20	77	4	425	
Gary	86	402	248	146	44	20	106	25	5		99	
Gaylord	86	124	111	103	31	30	1	7	12	1	57	

298

TRIBUNAL STATISTICS SUMMARY FILE
LIST OF FIRST INSTANCE TRIBUNALS

Diocese	Year	Cases Presented	Cases Accepted	Decided by Sentence	Mixed-Marriage	Non-Catholic	Abandoned	Trib Abate	Ligamen	Other Dec	Lack of Form	Ratum Non-Consummatum
Grand Island	86	82	77	92	28	27	6	7	13		41	
Grand Rapids	86	273	267	215	41	73	6	3	14	1	114	
Great Falls-Billings	86	80	80	65	24	14	12	4	13		64	
Green Bay	86	296	295	274			4	19	11	151		
Greensburg	86	197	196	167	39	42	14		4	2	103	
Harrisburg	86	495	333	208	65	59	7		22		126	
Hartford	86	510	388	413			3	9	3		355	
Helena	86	149	149	99	26	23	29		12		50	
Honolulu	86	127	127	114	29	22	3		4	1	109	
Houma-Thibodaux	86	115	115	120	13	7	1		3	1	66	
Hungarians	86											1
Indianapolis	86	139	138	170	90	27	7	26	24	1	1	
Jackson	86	94	94	110	52	48	19	3	15		32	
Jefferson City	86	162	97	97	27	34			21		47	
Joliet	86	613	617	372	124	62		90	7	2	211	
Juneau	86	19	19	19	3	8			5		6	
Kalamazoo	86	122	108	92	29	26	4	4	12	1	76	
Kansas City	86	350	289	251	50	100	30		32		105	
KS City/St. Joseph	86	220	220	128	49	92	3	20	45	1	89	
Lafayette	86	175	36	37	13	8	104		18		53	
Lake Charles	86	125	112	74			12		1		95	
Lansing	86	280	272	252	66	67	14	6	28	4	166	
Las Cruces	86	107	47	49	6	3	2	5		1	61	
LaCrosse	86	405	361	301	74	58	53	6	46		87	
Lincoln	86	67	63	117			5		4		37	
Little Rock	86	387	387	41	14	27	10		15		68	
Los Angeles	86	725	680	548	97	32	66	275	67	10	1021	
Louisville	86	264	264	183	48	34	7		8		163	
Lubbock	86	139	139	41	27	24	38				13	
Madison	86	293	216	135	37	89	10	102	26	5	69	

299

TRIBUNAL STATISTICS SUMMARY FILE
LIST OF FIRST INSTANCE TRIBUNALS

Diocese	Year	Cases Presented	Cases Accepted	Decided by Sentence	Mixed-Marriage	Non-Catholic	Abandoned	Trib Abate	Ligamen	Other Dec	Lack of Form	Ratum Non-Consummatum
Manchester	86	510	479	433	174	92	21	36	10		170	
Marquette	86	136	136	123	38	22	14		2		44	
Memphis	86	147	127	124	30	57	1	6	35		63	
Metuchen	86	180	266	254	67	20	64	18	1	2	146	
Miami	86	644	644	691	103	105	10		16	1	495	
Milwaukee	86	880	785	583	215	177	59	148	21	5	362	
Mobile	86	167	143	110	30	50	4	29	2		45	
Monterey	86	119	110	112	28	23	5	13	10		96	
Nashville	86	206	206	183	48	94	2	47	46	2	84	
New Orleans	86	361	348	348	60	50	3	18	3	4	305	
New Ulm	86	90	90	61	20	21		36	1		24	
New York	86	782	762	699			25		20	1	3	
Newark	86	584	437	386	57	38	5	4	7	2	410	
Newton-Melkites	86	10	8	5			2		2		8	
Norwich	86	259	202	198	53	19		3	2	1	99	
Oakland	86	241	214	234	106	86	27		2	2	261	
Ogdensburg	86	232	198	124	23	12	76	11	22		89	
Oklahoma City	86	330	319	266	60	172	57	6	11	1	109	
Omaha	86	205	200	197	45	43	14		4		128	
Orange	86	433	423	402	130	98	61	8	25	2	343	
Orlando	86	596	592	474	157	140	12	48	66		271	
Owensboro	86	184	184	169			15	27	17	1		
Palm Beach	86	314	311	238	54	65	15		23	12	131	
Parma	86	16	2	10	3	3			1		13	
Passaic (Byzantine)	86	23	23	11	4		13				10	
Paterson	86	187	185	155	54	20	30	2	4	192	192	
Pensacola	86	81	81	74	19	27		1	10		81	
Peoria	86	356	222	243	64	77	7	3	20	3	111	
Phila/Ukrainian	86	17	17	9	5					2	6	
Phoenix	86	453	453	308	85	62	17	148	31	1	258	

300

TRIBUNAL STATISTICS SUMMARY FILE
LIST OF FIRST INSTANCE TRIBUNALS

Diocese	Year	Cases Presented	Cases Accepted	Decided by Sentence	Mixed-Marriage	Non-Catholic	Abandoned	Trib Abate	Ligamen	Other Dec	Lack of Form	Ratum Non-Consummatum
Pittsburgh	86	1442	633	447	89	66	4	6	7	6	354	
Portland ME	86	444	372	499	56	111	22	50	8	1	204	
Portland OR	86		228	228	67	77	10		37		191	
Providence	86	401	296	284				25			214	
Pueblo	86	54	49	38	10	7	12	14	1		52	
Raleigh	86	227	135	106	25	50	1	13	15	1	88	
Rapid City	86	60	60	56	9	10	4		11	1	24	
Reno-Las Vegas	86	126	100	100	70	30	15	25	20	2	177	
Richmond	86	302	281	283	84	118	30	17	25		176	
Rochester	86	466	466	421	120	92		43	10		189	
Rockford	86	347	296	200	46	62	25	25	18	1	117	
Rockville Centre	86	750	750	446	93	30	116		1	6	438	
Sacramento	86	338	338	279	88	61	69		37		191	
Saginaw	86	302	145	117	33	86		4	7	1	79	
Salina	86	164	164	58	40	18	26		4		43	
Salt Lake City	86	77	75	48	10	18	2		9		58	
San Angelo	86	194	144	202	60	66		24	11		73	
San Antonio	86	510	400	415	71	95	12	8	14		12	
San Bernardino	86	247	185	139	26	31	11	51	7	173		
San Diego	86	327	293	260	56	67		24	12	7	332	
San Francisco	86											
Santa Fe	86	226	226	176	51	17	17		11		177	
Santa Rosa	86	145	80	72	22	19	5	68	5		95	
Savannah	86	149	89	71	16	26	1		12		50	
Scranton	86	799	788	595	287	146	11	2	2		158	
Seattle	86	550	545	423			5	100	89	238	2	
Shreveport	86	105	97	86	26	28	42	3	11	2	84	
Sioux City	86	151	146	166	44	41	2	14	1		55	
Sioux Falls	86	174	174	106	36	25		3	5		48	
Spokane	86	109	107	86	18	15	19		14		63	

301

TRIBUNAL STATISTICS SUMMARY FILE
LIST OF FIRST INSTANCE TRIBUNALS

Diocese	Year	Cases Presented	Cases Accepted	Decided by Sentence	Mixed-Marriage	Non-Catholic	Abandoned	Trib Abate	Ligamen	Other Dec	Lack of Form	Ratum Non-Consummatum
Springfield IL	86	339	339	290	93	93	4	15	15		142	
Springfield MA	86	482	441	455	84	43	2		11		234	
Springfield/Girar	86	195	192	125	25	62	90		20	2	38	
St. Augustine	86	180	180	153	38	69	9		21			
St. Cloud MN	86	209	166	145	37	20	13		9		62	
St. Maron	86	40	40	34	3	8			4		2	
St. Paul & Minn	86	671	515	672	201	108	156	44	3		298	
St. Petersburg	86	464	434	485			16	12	41		270	
Stamf/Ukrainians	86	3										
Steubenville OH	86											
Stockton	86	58	58	60	14	17	2	3	8	4	52	
Superior	86	100	100	111	31	26			2		60	
Syracuse	86	579	553	539	168	42	4	36	2		228	
Toledo	86	423	423	349	107	107	4	17	15		187	
Trenton	86	145	145	187	68	13	15	92	3	1	262	
Tucson	86	101	92	80			4	20	4		123	
Tulsa	86	156	135	145	31	28	9	7	34		76	
Van Nuys	86	4	4	2	2						3	
Venice/FL	86	311	278	316	81	102	3	26	32		134	
Washington	86	372	317	198			28	44	7		222	
Wichita	86	285	261	271	64	76	15	20	44		90	
Wilmington	86	153	153	105	38	29	20	3	15	2	42	
Winona	86	236	236	178	53	47	8	36	2		183	
Worcester	86	396	333	255			39	24	5			
Yakima	86	175	162	101	29	43	17	9	28		55	
Youngstown OH	86	346	265	271	103	83	20	31	18	5	161	

TRIBUNAL STATISTICS SUMMARY FILE
LIST OF FIRST INSTANCE TRIBUNALS

Diocese	Privilege of Faith	Pauline Privilege	Second Instance	Third Instance	Full-Time Personnel Professional	Full-Time Personnel Secretarial	Part-Time Personnel Professional	Part-Time Personnel Secretarial	Total Revenue	Fees Collected	Total Expenditures	Notes
Albany	8	3			4	3	7	3	143,693	56,500	159,757	
Alexandria					1	1			2,605	2,605	15,172	
Allentown					4	4	23	3	149,220	79,740	142,099	
Altoona	2	1			4	3	1	2	17,645	27,355	45,000	
Amarillo					1	1		1		9,684	329,079	
Anchorage		3			1	1	1		9,684	2,577	75,750	
Arch/Military Serv		4				4	1	1	94,009	94,009	133,370	
Arlington	17	6			1	2	28		79,307	29,687	79,307	
Atlanta	4	5			4	4	8	1	252,877	93,000	252,877	
Austin		2			1	1		1		45,000	104,000	
Baker Oregon	6	3			1	1	2		17,370	6,845	30,777	
Baltimore	3	3	10		7	4	47	1	278,904	164,586	284,027	
Baton Rouge	7	2			1	2	16	1	70,436	30,905	101,341	
Beaumont					1		1	3	42,000	27,000	65,500	
Belleville IL	1	2			3	1	3		55,309	15,808	55,309	
Biloxi					1	1	5		14,800	5,300	33,975	
Birmingham					2	1	7	1	44,663	15,426	44,663	
Bismark					3	1	24	1	65,000		65,000	
Boise	4	10			1	2			8,934	7,800	1,134	
Boston	2	2			4	6	2	2	186,000	167,000	196,000	
Bridgeport	2				8	3	8	2	200,000	65,307	164,753	
Brooklyn	7	3			12	9	12		569,103	484,103	534,648	
Brownsville					2	1	10		50,815	10,507	45,068	
Buffalo	7	4			4					61,030	99,164	
Burlington	4	1			4	1	5	3				
Byelorussians	17											
Camden					2	3		1	82,800	23,700	106,500	
Charleston		1			1	1		1				
Charlotte	1	1				2	3		17,772	17,772	16,698	
Cheyenne	1	2			2	1	9	3	22,631	22,631	55,119	

303

TRIBUNAL STATISTICS SUMMARY FILE
LIST OF FIRST INSTANCE TRIBUNALS

Diocese	Privilege of Faith	Pauline Privilege	Second Instance	Third Instance	Full-Time Personnel Professional	Full-Time Personnel Secretarial	Part-Time Personnel Professional	Part-Time Personnel Secretarial	Total Revenue	Fees Collected	Total Expenditures	Notes
Chicago	62	4			11	15	6	1	232,612	236,612	784,793	
Cincinnati	34	9			4	6	2		55,000		208,000	
Cleveland	1	2			5	5	11		197,000	197,000		
Colorado Springs	9				1	2			58,723		55,562	
Columbus	15	2			1	1	9	1	162,000	75,000	160,000	
Corpus Christi		4			1	3	2		44,791	44,791	82,353	
Covington	2	4	202		3	3	1		47,548	23,852	71,400	
Crookston					1		8		8,938	8,938	41,864	
Dallas TX	1	3			4	5	1	1	234,174	99,174	234,174	
Davenport	26	3			2	2	1	2	39,360	43,073	118,560	
Denver	21	6			2	7		1	58,385	58,385	214,320	
Des Moines	3	3			2	1	22		51,136	19,766	51,136	
Detroit												
Dodge City							1			3,055	14,308	
Dubuque	4				3	1			67,831	39,996	67,831	
Duluth	1				1		2	1		3,614	44,772	
El Paso		1			1	2	28		46,939	18,300	46,939	
Erie	25	2			5	2	3	1	187,500	30,000	187,500	
Evansville	18	2			4	2	6		98,925	19,054	98,925	
Fairbanks		2			1		3		26,692	3,685	30,377	
Fall River	6				2	1	18	1				0
Fargo		1			2	1	2	2	23,000	23,000	70,000	
Fort Wayne	18	2			3	3	16	2	173,360	50,851	170,350	
Fort Worth		3			2	1	2	1	58,201	58,201	120,000	
Fresno	2	7			2	1	12	2	101,900	33,900	101,900	
Gallup	2				1		3	1		4,705	11,500	
Galveston	11	12			3	1	4		159,114	90,320	147,478	
Gary	24	4				4	4	2		21,836	140,000	
Gaylord		1				1	7				67,334	

304

TRIBUNAL STATISTICS SUMMARY FILE
LIST OF FIRST INSTANCE TRIBUNALS

Diocese	Privilege of Faith	Pauline Privilege	Second Instance	Third Instance	Full-Time Personnel Professional	Full-Time Personnel Secretarial	Part-Time Personnel Professional	Part-Time Personnel Secretarial	Total Revenue	Fees Collected	Total Expenditures	Notes
Grand Island		1			2	1	3			4,780	73,046	
Grand Rapids		1	232		2	1	3	1	106,275	16,868	95,337	
Great Falls-Billings	1				1	1	9	1	51,781	4,305	52,226	
Green Bay			577		3	2	3	2	118,775	69,632	197,395	
Greensburg		1			1	2	6		12,450	12,450	78,000	
Harrisburg		2				5	10	2	167,000	27,000	167,000	
Hartford	1	2			6	2	6	1	100,000	100,000	250,000	
Helena		1				1	1	1	37,628	9,475	37,628	
Honolulu		1			2	2	5		34,066	19,923	64,071	
Houma-Thibodaux			202		13	1			16,321	16,863	33,184	
Hungarians												
Indianapolis	32	7			5	3	5	1	44,765	44,765	261,474	
Jackson					1	1	5				48,860	
Jefferson City	8	2			1		3	1			36,474	
Joliet	2	1			5	6	4		317,076	49,978	240,640	
Juneau					1		1	1	595	595	25,523	
Kalamazoo		12				1	5	2	11,000	11,000	11,000	
Kansas City		3			1	1	1	1	42,648	37,495	42,648	
KS City/St. Jos.		9			3				115,621	21,681	84,234	
Lafayette	17	7			2	2	61	3	8,420	8,420	61,110	
Lake Charles						1	4					0
Lansing		26					5	2	33,000	33,000	33,000	
Las Cruces					1	1		1	55,155	10,614	50,241	
LaCrosse	1	1			3	2	1		177,014	61,292	177,014	
Lincoln					2	1						
Little Rock					3	2		1		4,013		0
Los Angeles	76	24	968		8	10	10	2				0
Louisville	35	5	2	1	3	3	3		20,520	20,520	88,170	
Lubbock					1	1	9	1	30,099	11,303	18,796	
Madison					4	2	1					

305

TRIBUNAL STATISTICS SUMMARY FILE
LIST OF FIRST INSTANCE TRIBUNALS

Diocese	Privilege of Faith	Pauline Privilege	Second Instance	Third Instance	Full-Time Personnel Professional	Full-Time Personnel Secretarial	Part-Time Personnel Professional	Part-Time Personnel Secretarial	Total Revenue	Fees Collected	Total Expenditures	Notes
Manchester	7	4			2	3	2	2	73,000	40,000	113,000	
Marquette					1			1	33,674	6,380	33,674	
Memphis	1	1			1	1	5		31,260	4,050	31,260	
Metuchen	1				6	2	10		49,312	49,312	122,993	
Miami	1	2	1740		7	5	1	1				91
Milwaukee					5	4			221,824	129,086	239,608	
Mobile					3	2	3	1	84,000	23,800	84,000	
Monterey		5			2	1	1	1	59,133	59,133	58,016	
Nashville		5			3	1	8	2	124,543	5,580	117,027	
New Orleans	4	1			3	2	15		57,250	57,250	117,060	
New Ulm					2	1	8		38,200	4,200	38,200	
New York	6	5			12	20	22	5	545,000	250,000	545,000	
Newark	3	2			4	3	25	1	150,000	150,000	225,000	
Newton-Melkites							4	3		750		1
Norwich	1	1				2	4		36,958	30,993	36,958	
Oakland	6	5			4	3	5		93,366	93,907	188,807	
Ogdensburg	1				3	1						
Oklahoma City					2	1	1		32,000	32,000	60,000	
Omaha	20	2			2	2	4	1	21,000	21,000	85,000	
Orange	3	10	613		3	3	1	1	91,520	91,520	116,059	
Orlando				1	3	3			150,974	62,160	150,974	
Owensboro					3	1	7	1	30,687	13,250	51,178	
Palm Beach					2	1	2			29,454	73,708	
Parma							8					
Passaic (Byzantine)							5	1	10,625	1,625	9,000	
Paterson	1	3			3	3	4	1	110,000	60,000	110,000	
Pensacola		2			1	1	2	1	54,966	24,387	43,510	
Peoria	30	2			3	2	1	1	159,903	65,510	129,609	
Phila/Ukrainian							2	1	2,250	2,250		
Phoenix		4			4	4	10			62,791	159,020	

306

TRIBUNAL STATISTICS SUMMARY FILE
LIST OF FIRST INSTANCE TRIBUNALS

Diocese	Privilege of Faith	Pauline Privilege	Second Instance	Third Instance	Full-Time Personnel Professional	Full-Time Personnel Secretarial	Part-Time Personnel Professional	Part-Time Personnel Secretarial	Total Revenue	Fees Collected	Total Expenditures	Notes
Pittsburgh	2	5	646		3	4	1	1	160,538	160,538	202,957	
Portland ME	13	1			6	3	2	3	168,400	42,000	168,400	
Portland OR	1	11			2	2	10					
Providence	3	1			5	4	2	1	205,334	87,554	205,334	
Pueblo	5	2			1		15	10	23,011	3,675	23,011	
Raleigh		3			3	1	8		66,090	20,045	60,331	
Rapid City					1	1	4		5,938	2,745	12,454	
Reno-Las Vegas		7			5	2	4		98,000	20,000	98,000	
Richmond		1			4	3	3	2	197,313	58,725	197,313	
Rochester					2	1			62,103	60,505	62,103	
Rockford	5	3			2	4	6					0
Rockville Centre	2	2			10	8		1	240,959	240,959	312,586	
Sacramento	6	13			3	3	1	2	144,882	68,011	139,454	
Saginaw		2	149			1	4		93,800	48,520	76,330	
Salina							5	4	37,756	18,396	37,756	
Salt Lake City		4			1	1	2	1	7,570	7,570	35,998	
San Angelo		3			1	1	3		29,205	29,205	53,374	
San Antonio		2			2	4	28	2	165,200	92,000	165,200	
San Bernardino		2			1	2	5		55,584	30,654	55,584	
San Diego	8	11			2	2	7		31,612	50,316	81,928	
San Francisco			540				1	1				
Santa Fe	6				1	3	8			15,409		
Santa Rosa	1				1	1	1		67,000	2,000	60,000	
Savannah	1	1			1	2	1		65,000	65,000	250,000	
Scranton					3	4	22	3	93,300	85,000	159,237	
Seattle		5			4	2	1		72,041	20,000	72,000	
Shreveport		4			1	1	2	1	50,550	20,550	47,596	
Sioux City	3				2	2			65,540	10,430	54,801	
Sioux Falls					1	1	1	1				
Spokane		5				1	5		8,528		36,434	

307

TRIBUNAL STATISTICS SUMMARY FILE
LIST OF FIRST INSTANCE TRIBUNALS

Diocese	Privilege of Faith	Pauline Privilege	Second Instance	Third Instance	Full-Time Personnel Professional	Full-Time Personnel Secretarial	Part-Time Personnel Professional	Part-Time Personnel Secretarial	Total Revenue	Fees Collected	Total Expenditures	Notes
Springfield IL	10	3			6	3			41,542	41,615	83,157	
Springfield MA			454		3	4	5		42,931	42,931	132,500	
Springfield/Girar	7	1			1	1		1	54,600	6,425	48,436	
St. Augustine					2	2	5		48,307	54,756		
St. Cloud MN						1	17	3	34,682	34,271	35,208	
St. Maron							5	1	15,500	14,700	13,850	
St. Paul & Minn	16	2			3	4	4	2	226,625	130,000	226,625	
St. Petersburg					2	2	2	2				
Stamf/Ukrainians							2	2				
Steubenville OH												
Stockton		2				1	3		17,819	20,832	27,010	
Superior	2					1	1			12,827		0
Syracuse		3			1	2	20			90,000	110,000	
Toledo		3			6	3			97,231	77,878	150,202	
Trenton	2	1			2	3	2	2	50,000	50,000	130,000	
Tucson	1				4	3	3					0
Tulsa		4	154		1	3	3					
Van Nuys							3	1				
Venice/FL		2					5		520	520		
Washington	9	3			3	2	5	1	149,983	38,048	104,592	
Wichita	2	3			6	3	8	1	149,983	86,410	149,983	
Wilmington	1				2	1	4	1	63,522	57,472	63,522	
Winona	7				5	1	2	3				
Worcester		1			1	3	11		60,472	6,984	67,456	
Yakima					2	3	5	1	141,111	32,000	141,111	
Youngstown OH		2			1	1	5		30,000	8,000	36,500	
	7	6			2	5	3	1	117,100	17,900	135,000	

TRIBUNAL STATISTICS SUMMARY FILE
LIST OF SECOND INSTANCE TRIBUNALS

Court	Year	Cases Submitted	Cases Ratified	Cases Admitted to Hearing	Cases Decided	Decision Confirming First Instance	Simply Reversing First Instance	First-Instance Reversed; Retired as in First Instance	Cases Appealed to Third Instance	Appealed to Rota	Appealed to U.S. Third Instance
Atlanta	86	587	519	28	28	27	1				
Baltimore	86	1342	1342						2	2	
Boston	86	2712	2664	59	48	42	5	1			
Chicago	86	2508	2487	19	4	3	1				
Denver	86	263	219	6	6	6					
Diocese of Green Bay	86	580	577								
Grand Rapids	86	231	231								
Interdiocesan Omaha	86	370	335	32	32	4	32				
Kansas	86	637	629	4	4						
Los Angeles	86	973	945	23	23	21	1	1	1	1	
Milwaukee	86	801	797								
New Orleans	86	192	191	1		1					
New York	86	3521	3487	10		6	4				
Newark	86	1079	1068	10	10	5	5				
Ohio & Washington DC	86	2475	2377	7	7	3	4				
Oklahoma City	86	536	489								
Orange	86	607	587	14	14	10	3	1	1	1	
Prov/Louisville	86	834	832	4	4	2	2			1	
Province of Hartford	86	1114	1070	18	13	12	1				
Province of Iowa	86	8080	8080								
Region XII Seattle	86	1357	1323	9	8	8					
Saginaw	86	181	149								
St. Paul & Minneapolis	86	1563	1548	15		12		3			
Texas	86	2628	2627	19	19	15	4				

TRIBUNAL STATISTICS SUMMARY FILE
LIST OF SECOND INSTANCE TRIBUNALS

Court	Cases Received in Third Instance	Cases Decided in Third Instance	Full-Time Personnel Professional	Full-Time Personnel Secretarial	Part-Time Personnel Professional	Part-Time Personnel Secretarial	Total Revenue	Fees Collected	Total Expenditures	Notes
Atlanta			2		8	1	66,172	66,172	66,172	
Baltimore										
Boston			1			1			26,951	
Chicago			1	1	49	22	75,240	75,240	57,486	
Denver			1	1	19					
Diocese of Green Bay										
Grand Rapids									20,000	
Interdiocesan Omaha			1	1	8	2	12,800	12,800	7,378	
Kansas			11	1						
Los Angeles										
Milwaukee			1	1	5					
New Orleans										
New York										
Newark										
Ohio & Washington DC					1					
Oklahoma City						1				
Orange										
Prov/Louisville					1	1	11,062		11,062	
Province of Hartford										
Province of Iowa					1	1	27,445	24,445	25,699	
Region XII Seattle							4,751	6,561	11,313	
Saginaw					62					
St. Paul & Minneapolis			1	1	77	1		87,500	57,094	
Texas										

310

CANONICAL STANDARDS IN LABOR-MANAGEMENT RELATIONS:

A REPORT

Foreword

This report is the product of eight years of study and evaluation stemming from a resolution adopted in October 1979 at the forty-first Annual Meeting of the Canon Law Society of America. That original resolution called for the development of procedures to assist employees of the Church or of Church related institutions in the exercise of their natural right to collective bargaining.[1]

The committee named to implement the resolution, headed by Robert L. Kealy, reported at the following year's Annual Meeting that in the judgment of the committee it would be inappropriate to fulfill its charge exactly as it had been given.[2] Instead, the committee suggested a joint undertaking with the NCEA and other interested groups. The Society's membership, however, adopted a different course at that meeting. It resolved that the CLSA:

> develop and propose to the NCCB a set of canonical standards for labor and management and that the CLSA propose to collaborate with the NCCB and existing Catholic agencies concerned with collective bargaining for the purpose of providing canonical expertise in the promotion of fair practice policies.[3]

In 1981 the Board of Governors of the Society commissioned William V. Sullivan of Richmond, Virginia, to draft an initial report to implement the first part of this resolution. His report was later revised by Rosemary Smith, S.C., then a doctoral student at The Catholic University of America, in light of her licentiate dissertation, "The Right of Lay Employees to Form Labor Unions" (1982). Before that report could be submitted to the Society, the new code was promulgated and came into force. The Board later requested James H. Provost, Executive Coordinator of the Society, to update the report in light of the provisions of the new code. This revised version was submitted to the BOG in the Summer of 1986, and then to the members attending the 1986 CLSA convention in Denver where it was the topic of a special hearing.

An ad hoc committee composed of those involved in developing the various drafts of the report was constituted to conduct the hearing and to prepare a further revision of the report. The committee drew on the results of the hearing and on written observations submitted to it. It also took into consideration the resolution

---

[1] *CLSA Proceedings* 41 (1979) 157; resolution fourteen.
[2] See report in *CLSA Proceedings* 42 (1980) 199-204.
[3] Ibid., p. 244.

adopted at the 1986 convention to incorporate canonical principles for affirmative action in the report.

In November, 1986 the National Conference of Catholic Bishops adopted its pastoral letter *Economic Justice for All: Catholic Social Teaching and the U.S. Economy.* This letter has been taken into consideration in preparing this report so that it might properly be understood as responding to the bishops' invitation to "undertake research into many of the areas" their document "could not deal with in depth."[4]

The committee submitted its findings to the Board of Governors at the end of 1986. After careful consideration the Board now submits the following report to the CLSA membership for adoption at the 1987 Annual Meeting of the Society.

When adopted, this report is to be communicated to the appropriate officials of the NCCB, various Catholic organizations and movements, and made available for all other persons interested in labor and management relationships in the Catholic Church. At the same time, the CLSA Board of Governors is to begin the necessary steps to implement the second part of the 1980 mandate, namely "to propose to collaborate with the NCCB and existing Catholic agencies concerned with collective bargaining for the purpose of providing canonical expertise in the promotion of fair practice policies."[5]

Introduction

Current church law is based on the official teachings of the Church's magisterium and is expressed in the 1983 Code of Canon Law. The new code also draws on the Church's centuries-old canonical tradition. These sources contain substantive provisions which bear directly on the sensitive issue of labor-management relations in church institutions, agencies and offices.

Within a Roman Catholic context, the relationship between employers and employees is a moral question. This relationship has been the topic of formal attention by the Church's magisterium, including the teaching of all the popes in this century, the college of bishops at an ecumenical council, and bishops teaching in their own dioceses or gathered as a conference of bishops. The magisterium's teaching in this case is on a question of morals, and Catholics are conscious they must approach the issues involved in this relationship from this moral perspective, prior to financial, legal and other considerations.

However, questions of labor and management are not exhausted by examining their moral dimensions; there are also legal questions in both civil and canon law. The Church as an institution and individual Catholic institutions, agencies and programs are required to work within the framework of church law, as well

---

[4]NCCB, *Economic Justice for All: Catholic Social Teaching and the U.S. Economy*, November 13, 1986 (Washington: USCC, 1986), n. 362.
[5]*CLSA Proceedings* 42 (1980) 244.

as other sources, when searching for solutions. The purpose of this paper is to examine briefly those selections of church law which have bearing on the field of employer-employee relationships in order to extract general standards within the context of which more specific practices and procedures can be developed. Only when the legal issues are clearly differentiated from the economic constraints and the interpersonal relationships of any particular situation, will there be a possibility for morally acceptable, just and reasonable resolutions of difficult labor-management situations in the Church.

Implementation of general standards may vary somewhat from state to state, as the law of the several states varies: it may also vary with the type and condition of employment, as the diversity and complexity of the employment situation varies. Yet in all implementation, the law and teaching of the Church remain normative.

a. Definitions

In this report, the following terms are being used without prejudice to their meaning in other contexts. "Employer" is considered to be any physical or juridic person, agency or institution which retains the services of another for the purpose of carrying out its stated purpose, or for general services of benefit to the employer. An employer is considered to be church related, and therefore covered by the standards in this report, if the employer is acting officially in the name of the Church, is owned or operated by a public juridic person, or even calls itself "Catholic."

The word "employee" is considered to be any person whose services are retained by an employer, and earns a living in this manner. Employees here are considered in the broad sense, analogous to both the exempt and non-exempt categories in United States federal law. Employees are distinguished from volunteers who freely offer their services, but not as a means of making a living.[1]

Persons who voluntarily agree to contribute some of their services, but nevertheless make a living from employment, are considered to be "employees" and not "volunteers" for the purposes of this report.[2] Clergy and religious have a unique relationship with the Church; their livelihood is assured through incardination or membership in an institute of consecrated life. Normally they are not considered "employees," although there may be situations in which they are to be included as "employees" for the purpose of this report. Special consideration needs to be given permanent deacons who dedicate themselves completely to ecclesiastical ministry, particularly those who are married (c. 282, §3). The situation of each of these special classifications has to be evaluated on a particular basis and cannot be detailed here.

---

[1] NCCB, pastoral letter *Economic Justice for All: Catholic Social Teaching and the U.S. Economy,* November 13, 1986 (Washington: USCC, 1986), n. 352.

[2] For additional clarification about the employee who voluntarily contributes some service, see Robert L. Kealy, "The Just Wage and The Quasi-Volunteer," *America* 150/14 (April 14, 1984) 280.

Finally, this report addresses the relationship between labor and management in the traditional terms of "collective bargaining." This is not to imply, however, that this is the only approach to structuring such a relationship. Indeed, collaborative approaches such as "participative management," or "collegial management" may be more appropriate in the church context.[3] The standards expressed in this report are intended to apply to all approaches to labor management relations; appropriate adaptations will have to be made in practice according to the particular situation.

b. Canonization of Civil Law

A preliminary canonical question needs to be addressed, namely the relationship between canon law and civil law. While this is a major topic in itself, so much so that the Canon Law Society of America has established an on-going committee to research it, at least the following basic considerations are pertinent to this paper.

> Can. 22—Civil laws to which the law of the Church defers should be observed in canon law with the same effects, insofar as they are not contrary to divine law and unless it is provided otherwise in canon law.

Ladislas Orsy offers these comments on this canon:

> In some cases . . . canon law incorporates the norms of civil law into its own system, that is, making them equivalent to ecclesiastical norms. This is more than a mere recognition of civil law; it is civil law made into canon law. In fact, traditionally it is called the "canonization" of civil law.[4]

The extent to which the current law of the Church "canonizes" the civil law on labor-management relations, to that extent the norms from civil legislation have become Church legislation. There are differences of opinion among canon lawyers as to the extent of this canonization in labor-management relations. A narrow interpretation of the canon recognizes that at times the civil law exempts the Church from some of its provisions; respecting the mind of the civil legislator, this interpretation holds that canon 22 "canonizes" only those civil laws which the civil law itself intends to apply to the Church. A broad interpretation holds that all laws to which the canon law defers are intended by the church legislator to be "canonized," including those laws from which the Church has been exempted by the civil legislator. There has been no attempt in this report to resolve these differences.[5] The report has, however, followed the narrow interpretation

---

[3] See *Economic Justice for All,* n. 353: "In the light of new creative models of collaboration between labor and management described earlier in this letter, we challenge our church institutions to adopt new, fruitful modes of cooperation." See chapter 4 of the pastoral letter, "A New American Experiment: Partnership for the Public Good."

[4] *The Code of Canon Law: A Text and Commentary* (New York: Paulist Press, 1985), p. 38.

[5] For a fuller treatment of these issues from a health care perspective, but with wider possible applications, see Adam Maida, ed., *Issues in the Labor-Management Dialogue: Church Perspective* (St. Louis: CHA, 1982).

of canon 22 since it is accepted by both opinions as a binding interpretation of the law.

Grounding for a just policy in the labor-management field can be found in four general areas of the Church's law:

1. Law governing the employer-employee relationship;
2. Law on associations;
3. Law on contracts;
4. Law on other fundamental rights.

1. The Employer-Employee Relationship

The Church's law deals with the employer-employee relationship from two directions. The first is from the perspective of those who dedicate themselves as professionals in church services:

Can. 231—§1. Lay persons who devote themselves permanently or temporarily to some special service of the Church are obliged to acquire the appropriate formation which is required to fulfill their function properly and to carry it out conscientiously, zealously, and diligently.

§2. With due regard for can. 230, §1, they have a right to a decent remuneration suited to their condition; by such remuneration they should be able to provide decently for their own needs and for those of their family with due regard for the prescriptions of civil law; they likewise have a right that their pension, social security and health benefits be duly provided.[6]

The second perspective on the employer-employee relationship deals with those persons who are called administrators in the Church:

Can. 1286—Administrators of goods:

1⁰ are to observe meticulously the civil laws pertaining to labor and social policy according to church principles in the employment of workers;

2⁰ are to pay employees a just and decent wage so that they may provide appropriately for their needs and those of their family.

Included within these canons is the requirement to pay a just family wage, and also to observe laws regulating working conditions as at least the minimal stan-

---

[6]Translation of this canon and subsequent citations from the 1983 code are taken from *Code of Canon Law, Latin-English Edition* (Washington: CLSA, 1983). For commentary on this canon see: Giuseppe Dalla Torre in *Commento al Codice di Diritto Canonico*, ed. Pio V. Pinto (Rome: Urbaniana University, 1985), p. 137-139; Javier Hervada in *Codigo de Derecho Canonico, Edicion Anotada*, ed. Pedro Lombardia and Juan I. Arrieta (Pamplona: EUNSA, 1983), pp. 185-186; Julio Manzanares in *Codigo de Derecho Canonico, Edicion bilingue comentada* (Madrid: BAC, 5th ed. 1985), pp. 146; James H. Provost in *The Code of Canon Law: A Text and Commentary*, ed. James A. Coriden et al. (New York/Mahwah: Paulist, 1985), pp. 169-170; Heinrich Reinhardt in *Munsterischer Kommentar zum Codex Iuris Canonici* (Essen: Ludgerus, 1985), pp. 231/1-2.

dard enforceable within canon law.[7] For example, in the United States church employers are held to observe child labor laws, laws regulating health and safety standards, and laws regulating social security tax payments.

The canons enforce within the Church all the civil law obligations of employers except in cases where the intent of the civil legislation is to exempt churches or church institutions, and provided "they are not contrary to divine law and unless it is provided otherwise in canon law" (c. 22). For some church employers this has long been the case. For example, some church institutions which receive significant government funding are normally bound by labor law, including law affecting working conditions. Other institutions, such as health care facilities, which meet the "significant involvement in commerce" criteria, are subject to greater regulation in labor-management practices.

These canons are not new in the legal history of the Church. They are a significant continuation of canonical tradition and a practical application within the life of the Church of what the Church's own magisterium has proclaimed in terms of all employer-employee relations. It may help to understand their importance if we place them in this traditional context.

a. Canon Law Context

In the 1917 code, canon 1524 dealt directly with the employer-employee relationship within the Church.[8] As with the corresponding canon in the 1983 code, it was placed in the context of the norm that church employers were held to a standard of administration which has an ancient tradition. They are to be as conscientious as the head of the household, a wise and loving caretaker.[9] The 1917 canon had its roots in Leo XIII's 1891 encyclical *Rerum novarum*,[10] and the text of the canon closely resembled Pius X's 1903 motu proprio *Fin dalla prima* which dealt with the obligations of employers.[11]

The canon on employer-employee relationships in the 1917 code was directed not only to clergy, religious and lay people who are administrators of church property in the strict sense, but to all the baptized who are obliged to observe

---

[7]For commentary see: Lamberto de Echeverria in *Codigo de Derecho Canonico, Edicion bilingue comentada*, pp. 611-612; Mariano Lopez Alarcon in *Codigo de Derecho Canonico, Edicion Anotada*, pp. 769-770; John J. Myers in *The Code of Canon Law: A Text and Commentary*, pp. 876-877; Francesco Salerno in *Commento al Codice di Diritto Canonico*, p. 732.

[8]1917 code, c. 1524: "All, and especially clerics, religious and administrators of ecclesiastical goods must, in hiring workers, give them respectable and just compensation; employers must also see to it that they are free to perform their religious duties at a convenient hour; they shall make no arrangement that will interfere with the workers' duties to their families and practice of thrift, and shall not impose on them work which is heavier than their strength can bear, or which is not suited to their age or sex."

[9]"Diligentia boni patrisfamilias": 1983 code c. 1284; 1917 code c. 1253.

[10]Leo XIII, encyclical letter *Rerum novarum*, May 15, 1891: *ASS* 23 (1890-1891) 641-670. See especially nn. 53, 58 and 60; pp. 658, 660-661.

[11]Pius X, motu proprio *Fin dalla prima*, December 18, 1903: *AAS* 36 (1903-1904) 339-345, especially pp. 341-342.

the laws of the Church.[12] Although dealing with all employers the canon was included in the section of the code on church employers to emphasize for the Church's own members and institutions the doubly binding nature of the obligation it imposed.[13] The new code presents the broader responsibilities of all Catholics to promote social justice in the general canons on the rights and responsibilities of the faithful (c. 222, §2), and in the section on temporal goods applies these principles of social justice internally to the Church in terms of the relations between church employers and employees.[14]

Canon 1286 applies to all who employ workers in the Church,[15] and therefore applies also to work which has been subcontracted. In his 1981 encyclical *Laborem exercens,* John Paul II distinguished between the direct and the indirect employer. The direct employer "is the person or institution with whom the worker enters directly into a work contract in accordance with definite conditions," whereas the indirect employer includes many different factors (persons, institutions, legislation, etc.) "that exercise a determining influence on the shaping both of the work contact and, consequently, of just and unjust relationships in the field of human labor."[16] The pope asserted that both the direct and the indirect employers bear true responsibility in specific work contracts and in labor relations in general.[17] The responsibilities of the direct and indirect employers differ but are interdependent. The pope stated unequivocally: "When it is a question of establishing an *ethically correct labor policy,* all these influences must be kept in mind. A policy is correct when the objective rights of the worker are fully respected."[18]

In the context of the Church in the United States the local ordinary will sometimes be the direct employer, as in the case of some of the people who work in the chancery. More frequently he will be the indirect employer who oversees the administration of church related property, coordinates the work of the apostolate in the diocese, proclaims justice as a gospel value, and works to create

---

[12]Alberto Blat, *Commentarium Textus Codicis Iuris Canonici,* vol. 3 (Rome: Angelicum, 1938), p. 537; Eduardus F. Regatillo, *Institutiones Iuris Canonici,* vol. 2 (Santander: Sal Terrae, 1942), p. 140; Edward A. Reissner, *Canonical Employer-Employee Relationship: Canon 1524,* Canon Law Studies, 427 (Washington: Catholic University of America, 1964), p. 15; Stephanus Sipos, *Enchiridion Iuris Canonici* (Rome: Orbis Catholicae-Herder, 1954), p. 351.

[13]Blat, 3:537; Guidus Cocchi, *Commentarium in Codicem Iuris Canonici ad Usum Scholarum,* vol. 3 (Turin: Marietti, 1932), p. 317.

[14]For commentaries, see: Lamberto de Echeverria in *Codigo de Derecho Canonico, Edicion bilingue comentada,* pp. 611-612; Mariano Lopez Alarcon in *Codigo de Derecho Canonico, Edicion Anotada,* pp. 769-770; John J. Myers in *The Code of Canon Law: A Text and Commentary,* pp. 876-877; Francesco Salerno in *Commento al Codice di Diritto Canonico,* p. 732.

[15]This was even more directly stated in the 1917 code: "All . . . in hiring workers." Although the new code only addresses directly the administrators of ecclesiastical goods, in keeping with c. 21 the new code should be harmonized with the earlier one, particularly when it is clearly the intention of the magisterium, as will be evident from what follows.

[16]John Paul II, encyclical letter *Laborem exercens,* nn. 16 and 17, September 14, 1981: *AAS* 73 (1981) 618-620. Translation from David M. Byers, ed., *Justice in the Marketplace* (Washington: USSC, 1985), pp. 317-318.

[17]*Laborem exercens,* n. 17: *AAS* 73 (1981) 620.

[18]Ibid.; translation from *Justice in the Marketplace,* p. 318. Emphasis in the original Latin text.

a climate where justice for all is possible and expected. As the direct or indirect employer, the local ordinary has a responsibility, in varying degrees, for those employed in church related institutions, offices, programs and agencies.

Moreover, both codes place ultimate responsibility on the local ordinary to watch over the administration of church property, to issue instructions on its correct administration, and to enforce the law.[19] Even for church institutions which are not under his direct or indirect control, this vigilance function makes him responsible to see to the observance of the church's law on labor relations by any entity which would lay claim to being Catholic.

In addition to the obligation of providing a just wage, canon 1286 binds church employers to observe the standards set in civil law for working conditions.[20] This would include such considerations as working hours and scheduling, environmental factors, work load, and the suitability of various kinds of work for various people. Essentially, the Church is focusing on the dignity of the human person in the context of the common good as the foundation for determining justice in employer-employee relationships.

b. Context of the Magisterium

To focus on the dignity of the human person is in keeping with a tradition which has been expressed a number of times in this century. The dignity of the individual has been most clearly developed in terms of the just wage due a worker. In his 1931 encyclical *Quadragesimo anno* Pius XI called for a wage sufficient for the support of a worker and family because in an increasingly industrialized world, labor is often a person's only means of livelihood.[21] While an enterprise's economic condition must be taken into account, the pope explicitly stated that workers are not to be made to bear the effects of bad management, a lack of industriousness, or inefficiency.[22]

The well being of one segment of society cannot be pursued or achieved at the expense of another; they are integrally related to one another. The Second Vatican Council in its Pastoral Constitution on the Church in the Modern World *Gaudium et spes* discussed the question of wages in the larger employment relationship: the duty of individuals to work faithfully but also their right to obtain work; the duty of society to help people find work; and payment for work, which must be such that people "may be furnished the means to cultivate worthily their own material, social, cultural and spiritual lives and that of their

---

[19] 1983 code cc. 391-392, 1276; cf. 1917 code cc. 335, 1519. Vatican II emphasized this role of the diocesan bishop in *Lumen gentium*, 32-33: *AAS* 57 (1965) 38-39.

[20] The 1917 code had to spell a number of these out since in many countries the civil legislation on working conditions was far from adequate. The development of social legislation in most nations since the First World War makes it possible for the Church to refer to these standards in the 1983 code, rather than attempting to draw up a list of its own.

[21] Pius XI, encyclical *Quadragesimo anno*, nn. 59-75, May 15, 1931: *AAS* 23 (1931) 198-202.

[22] Ibid., n. 72, p. 201.

dependents." The council recognized this will vary according to "the functions and productiveness of each one, the conditions of the factory or workshop, and the common good."[23]

Subsistence level wages do not satisfy this concept of just wages. Each person is a complexus of many gifts and needs, all of which are conditioned by the particular historical moment in which the person lives. Individual human needs—social, cultural, spiritual—vary, but the opportunity to pursue full human development must be possible because the dignity of the person as well as the common good require it.[24]

The 1971 Synod of Bishops added a concrete and challenging dimension to this discussion. In its document *Justice in the World* the Synod called on the Church not only to preach justice, but to be just itself:

> While the Church is bound to give witness to justice, it recognizes that anyone who ventures to speak to people about justice must first be just in their eyes. Hence we must undertake an examination of the modes of acting and of the possessions and life style found within the Church itself. Within the Church rights must be preserved. No one should be deprived of ordinary rights because he or she is associated with the Church in one way or another. Those who serve the Church by their labor, including priests and religious, should receive a sufficient livelihood and enjoy that social security which is customary in their region. Lay people should be given fair wages and a system of promotion.[25]

John Paul II also addressed human dignity as the key to the issue of just wages, stating in *Laborem exercens* that the wage should be sufficient for an adult to establish and properly maintain a family, and provide some security for its future.[26] The pope even identified wages as the concrete means to verify the justice of a whole economic system.[27]

In their pastoral on the economy, the bishops of the United States reaffirmed this teaching of the magisterium, and applied it specifically within the Church:

> All the moral principles that govern the just operation of any economic endeavor apply to the Church and its agencies and institutions; indeed the Church should be exemplary. . . . We bishops commit ourselves to the prin-

---

[23]*Gaudium et spes*, n. 67: *AAS* 58 (1966) 1088-1089; translation from *Justice in the Marketplace*, p. 189.

[24]The "common good" is not just the good of each individual taken together—the "collective" good. Rather, the council described it as embracing "the sum of those conditions of social life by which individuals, families, and groups can achieve their own fulfillment in a relatively thorough and ready way"—*Gaudium et spes*, n. 74: *AAS* 58 (1966) 1096. Translation from *The Documents of Vatican II*, ed. Walter M. Abbott (New York: America, 1966), p. 284. Here the council is drawing on the description given by John XXIII, encyclical *Mater et magistra*, n. 65, May 15, 1961: *AAS* 53 (1961) 417.

[25]1971 Synod of Bishops, *De Iustitia in Mundo*, III, November 30, 1971: *AAS* 63 (1971) 933; translation from *Justice in the Marketplace*, p. 257.

[26]*Laborem exercens*, n. 19: *AAS* 73 (1981) 627.

[27]Ibid., p. 626.

ciple that those who serve the Church—laity, clergy and religious—should receive a sufficient livelihood and the social benefits provided by responsible employers in our nation.[28]

In light of this rich tradition of official Catholic social teaching, the importance of canons 231 and 1286 is all the more evident. Those who are engaged in professional service and those who are employed for wages are entitled to a just wage as the Church understands "just wage," a rich concept based on the dignity of the person in the context of the common good. In their working situation they are entitled to at least the minimum protection afforded in civil law. Moreover, the diocesan bishop is to see that administrators not only obey the civil law which applies to them, but also meet the standard of diligence appropriate to a good householder (c. 1284, §1). To determine an appropriate standard of diligence in regard to wages, benefits and working conditions the bishop can take into consideration even those civil laws from which the Church has been exempted, for they may provide helpful clarification on what is considered an appropriate standard of diligence in that place.

In summary, some general statements can be deduced from the above:
1. The dignity of the human person within the common good is the yardstick by which all considerations regarding the relationships between employers and employees are to be judges.
2. Out of the employer-employee relationship there arise both rights and duties for all parties involved. In the Church these rights and duties are not isolated claims and responsibilities, but are to be integrated in the overall communion of the life of the people of God.
3. The Church's teaching and law on employer-employee relationships applies to direct and indirect employers, including sub-contractors.
4. Provision is to be made for a just and equitable compensation so that workers may adequately provide for themselves, their families, and others who depend on them. Wages and benefits must at least be up to the standards set in the applicable civil laws.
5. Working conditions are to be assured which respect the dignity of the persons involved and must at least be up to the standards set in the applicable civil laws.
6. The local ordinary, and in particular the diocesan bishop, has a vigilance role over all church related activity in the diocese, including the observance of church law on employer-employee relationships.
7. Church administrators are bound by canon law to observe the standard of diligence of a good householder. In enforcing this norm, the diocesan bishop can determine more precisely what this standard entails, and in doing so may take into consideration even those civil laws from which the Church is exempt.

---

[28]*Economic Justice for All*, nn. 347, 351; the bishops observe that only if there is adequate monetary support to the Church by everyone in it will it be possible to live up to this commitment (n. 351).

2. The Right of Association

Official magisterial teaching, even prior to the 1917 code, explicitly acknowledged the right of association, and developed this acknowledgement specifically in the social encyclicals when dealing with workers' organizations. Leo XIII in *Rerum novarum* affirmed both the right to autonomous governance within them.[29] He based this right on the same natural right to associate which sustains the Church's more specifically religious organizations, such as religious institutes.[30] Forty years later Pius XI reaffirmed the natural right of all workers freely to associate.[31] John XXIII, writing another thirty years later, made numerous positive statements about workers' associations and the right to associate; in his encyclical *Mater et magistra* he even recommended associations to workers of every kind.[32] In *Pacem in terris* the same pope emphatically reaffirmed the natural right to associate:

> From the fact that human beings are by nature, social, there arises the right of assembly and association. They have also the right to give the societies of which they are members the form they consider most suitable for the aim they have in view, and to act within such societies on their own initiative and on their own responsibility in order to achieve their desired objectives.[33]

Drawing on this rich magisterial tradition, the Second Vatican Council affirmed in very direct words the right to form labor unions:

> Among the basic rights of the human person is to be numbered the right of freely founding unions for working people. These should be able truly to represent them and to contribute to organizing of economic life in the right way. Included is the right of freely taking part in the activity of these unions without risk of reprisal.[34]

The council also affirmed the right of lay persons to found, to direct, and to join associations in the Church.[35]

John Paul II, in an entire section of *Laborem exercens* devoted to the importance of unions, reaffirmed the right of association specifically in the context of the workplace, and again stated that this right belongs to all workers and is not limited to certain types of workers: "Obviously this does not mean that only in-

---

[29]*Rerum novarum*, nn. 69-78: *AAS* 23 (1890-1891) 664-667. "Although we have spoken of (associations of workers) more than once, it seems well to show in this place that they are highly opportune and are formed by their own right, and, likewise to show how they should be organized and what they should do" (n. 69, p. 664; translation from *Justice in the Marketplace*, p. 35).

[30]Ibid., n. 73, p. 666.

[31]*Quadragesimo anno*, nn. 31-37; *AAS* 23 (1931) 186-188.

[32]*Mater et magistra*, nn. 97-103: *AAS* 53 (1961) 425-426.

[33]John XXIII, encyclical *Pacem in terris*, n. 23, April 11, 1963: *AAS* 55 (1963) 262-263; translation from *Justice in the Marketplace*, p. 155.

[34]*Gaudium et spes*, n. 68: *AAS* 58 (1966) 1090; translation from *Justice in the Marketplace*, p. 190.

[35]*Apostolicam actuositatem*, nn. 19 and 24: *AAS* 58 (1966) 853-854, 856-857.

dustrial workers can set up associations of this type. Representatives of every profession can use them to ensure their own rights."[36]

Addressing specifically the exercise of this right by church employees, the bishops of the United States affirmed in their pastoral on the economy that "all church institutions must also fully recognize the rights of employees to organize and bargain collectively with the institution through whatever association or organization they freely choose."[37]

A correct understanding of the Church's law must take into consideration these expressions of the "mind of the Church," indeed, the "mind of the legislator." While the 1917 and 1983 codes have not dealt directly with the formation of labor unions by church employees, the new code quite explicitly takes over the social teaching of the Church on the formation of associations and applies it internally to the Church.[38] The purposes for such associations are not restricted to charitable and religious purposes, but also include "the promotion of the Christian vocation in the world" (c. 215), to "animate the temporal order with the Christian spirit" (c. 298, §1).[39]

Moreover, by neither code and at no point in the official statements of the magisterium since Leo XIII have the faithful been barred from labor unions or associations formed for the purpose of collective bargaining. The Church's law and teaching have not excluded the activities of these associations within church institutions themselves. Neither the Church's law nor its teaching require prior permission for members of the faithful to join such associations.

In addition to there being no ban on such activity, it could also be argued that the Church presents itself as ready to assure the freedom of such associations with regard to its own activities. The 1971 Synod of Bishops affirmed that "while the Church is bound to give witness to justice, it recognizes that anyone who ventures to speak to people about justice must first be just in their eyes."[40] Having proclaimed the right to form unions as a fundamental human right, and so a question of justice, the Church can hardly exclude this form of association from those which canon 298, §1 proposes as seeking "to animate the temporal order with the Christian spirit."

The formation of associations of church employees does not require prior approval of church authorities. Church authorities need intervene only if an associa-

---

[36]*Laborem exercens*, n. 20: *AAS* 73 (1981) 629; translation from *Justice in the Marketplace*, p. 324.

[37]*Economic Justice for All*, n. 353; the bishops cited *Laborem exercens*, n. 12 in support of this statement.

[38]This is perhaps most explicit when comparing c. 215 on the right to form associations and hold meetings, with John XXIII's statements in *Pacem in terris*, n. 23, cited above. Canon 215 states: "The Christian faithful are at liberty freely to found and to govern associations for charitable and religious purposes or for the promotion of the Christian vocation in the world; they are free to hold meetings to pursue these purposes in common."

[39]For commentaries, see: Dalla Torre, pp. 12-123, 172-193; de Echeverrea, pp. 177-190; Jose Luis Gutierrez in *Codigo de Derecho Canonico, Edicion anotada*, pp. 229-247; Hervada, p. 176; Ellsworth Kneal in *The Code of Canon Law: A Text and Commentary*, pp. 243-257; Manzanares, p. 139; Provost, pp. 149-150; Reinhardt, pp. 215/1-3.

[40]*Justice in the World*, III: *AAS* 63 (1971) 933; translation from *Justice in the Marketplace*, p. 257.

tion wishes to use the term "Catholic" in its title (c. 300). If the association wishes to be recognized in the Church, its statutes are to be submitted for review by competent ecclesiastical authority (c. 299, §3), but this does not limit the right of individuals to form and govern their own associations. They may do so without seeking recognition as a church association.

Competent ecclesiastical authority, such as the local ordinary, has the right to be vigilant over associations in their territory, but this is for the purpose of seeing "that integrity of faith and morals is preserved in them and to watch lest abuse creep into ecclesiastical discipline" (c. 305, §1). This is the same authority a bishop has over the faithful in the diocese committed to his care (c. 397). Even for associations which have sought recognition as a church association, vigilance does not give ecclesiastical authorities the right to interfere in the rightful autonomy an association is guaranteed to govern itself according to its own statutes (c. 321), provided these conform to the basic requirements of justice articulated in the code.

In effect, therefore, the Church's magisterium admits the right of church employees to organize into associations for the purposes of collective bargaining and other purposes associated with labor unions. The Church's law does not prohibit such organizing.

To summarize:
1. All persons have the natural right to assemble freely and to form associations for legitimate purposes. Church teaching recognizes that these purposes include those of collective bargaining and other activities proper to labor unions.
2. The Church's law recognizes the fundamental rights to assemble and to form associations, and affirms them within the Church itself.
3. Associations formed by the Christian faithful, while they are under the vigilance of church authorities, are governed by the members themselves in keeping with their statutes.
4. No types of work, no areas or segments of the workplace, are excluded a priori from the formation of labor unions or associations for collective bargaining, including diocesan offices and church related institutions, agencies and programs.

3. Contracts

A third source of legal grounding for church principles and practices in the labor-management field is the canon law on contracts. A contract is a legally binding agreement between two or more persons which effects or prevents some change between them.[41] Both the 1917 and the 1983 codes deal with contracts in the con-

---

[41] Sipos, p. 696; *Black's Law Dictionary,* s.v. "contract."

text of the Church's temporal goods.[42] Contracts can govern how property is acquired, administered and disposed of, as well as relationships between persons and conditions of employment. In this setting, the codes have "canonized" prevailing civil law within certain limits; the 1983 code expresses it this way:

> Can. 1290—Whatever general and specific regulations on contracts and payments are determined in civil law for a given territory are to be observed in canon law with the same effects in a matter which is subject to the governing power of the Church, unless the civil regulations are contrary to divine law or canon law makes some other provision, with due regard for the prescription of can. 1547.[43]

When the canon obliges the observance of civil law on contracts it applies not only to contracts in general, but also to specific kinds of contracts and their effects. The canon exempts from enforcement in canon law those provisions of civil law which are considered to be contrary to divine law, or in which canon law makes some other provision. In the United States there appears to be little in the field of labor-management relations which would fall under these exceptions. As the authority charged with enforcing canon law (c. 392), it pertains to the diocesan bishop to determine whether specific civil laws are not enforceable in the Church.

Employer-employee relations are often regulated by contracts. Leo XIII recognized such contracts as necessary, but also cautioned that natural justice requirements be met in making these agreements.[44] Pius XI reaffirmed the importance of such labor-contracts, and looked toward developing partnership-contracts.[45] This recognition of labor contracts by the magisterium clarifies that this type of contract also falls under what is an acceptable contract in the Church, and which in light of canon 1290 must conform to the civil law of the area.

Because of the intent of Congress or State legislatures, the Church or church employers in the United States may be exempted from enforcement in civil law of certain norms which otherwise apply to labor contracts, or from being forced to enter into certain contracts with various groups of employees. It is important to be careful lest this civil exemption lead to an attitude that the Church can ignore the standards set in civil law insofar as these may help to clarify the standard of diligence appropriate to a good householder.

For example, in a celebrated case a few years ago the United States Supreme Court ruled the National Labor Relations Board (NLRB) did not have jurisdiction to enforce the law with regard to teachers in Catholic high schools.[46] The teachers claimed they were the victims of unfair labor practices and appealed

---

[42]For commentaries, see: Echeverria, p. 613; Lopez Alarcon, p. 772; Myers, pp. 878-879; Salerno, p. 734.
[43]Canon 1547 permits the testimony of two witnesses to provide proof in church law, even if civil law in some places does not accept this for contractual matters.
[44]*Rerum novarum*, n. 61-64: *AAS* 23 (1890-1981) 661-662.
[45]*Quadragesimo anno*, nn. 64-65: *AAS* 23 (1931) 199.
[46]NLRB v. Catholic Bishop of Chicago, 400 U.S. 490 (1979).

to the NLRB. The Board asserted its jurisdiction. The local ordinary claimed immunity, stating that the schools were integrally connected with the mission of the Church and therefore were subject only to the internal governance of the Church. The first amendment right of free exercise of religion had been consistently interpreted in this manner. In deciding the case the Supreme Court avoided the constitutional issue, basing its decision on the intent of Congress.

While it is important to maintain the freedom of the Church to manage its own affairs, the legal future of such a precedent is dubious, especially if the Church as an institution were to fail to provide alternate and adequate avenues of recourse to its employees in labor disputes. Even though canon law does not require good faith bargaining and other elements of fair labor practices which the civil law may require of others, the moral values embodied in the civil law are binding within the Church,[47] and provide helpful indications of what the standard of diligence appropriate to a good householder might be in such circumstances.

Currently there are two systems for vindicating claims in church law. One is to appeal to a church court.[48] The other is to appeal to the hierarchical superior for enforcement of the law. Unfortunately, there are weaknesses in the current ability of either system to respond adequately in labor disputes. In some dioceses offices for "due process" have been established; however, their effectiveness varies and such procedures are not universally available to all church employees. The new code encourages the establishment of mediation services in each diocese (c. 1733, §2).[49]

From this brief look at the law on contracts, the following summary can be proposed:
1. Administrators in the Church are bound even by the law of the Church to observe the local civil law on labor contracts where applicable.
2. The presumption is that civil laws in the United States are generally in conformity with church teaching; the diocesan bishop is the competent authority to decide if a specific civil law is not to be observed because it is contrary to church teaching or to canon law.
3. Church administrators are bound by canon law to observe the standard of diligence of a good householder. In enforcing this norm, the diocesan bishop can determine more precisely what this standard entails, and in

---

[47] *Economic Justice for All,* n. 347.

[48] Canon 1400, §1 states that the object of a trial in a church court is "1°to prosecute or to vindicate the rights of physical or juridic persons, or to declare juridic facts; 2° to impose or declare the penalty for offenses." Cases involving failure to observe the civil law on contracts are "cases which concern administration" and can be brought "before the tribunal of the place where the administration was conducted" (c. 1413, 1°).

[49] In response to a resolution at its 1983 Annual Meeting, the CLSA is engaged in a complex study to explore ways to improve the ability of church structures to respond to the call for the protection and vindication of rights. See *CLSA Proceedings* 45 (1983) 329-330, resolution seven. A national survey has been conducted of due process experience in United States dioceses, the results of which are available from the office of the CLSA executive coordinator at Catholic University of America in Washington, DC.

doing so may take into consideration even those civil laws on contracts from which the Church is exempt.

4. Other Fundamental Rights

a. Equality

The Second Vatican Council made a direct affirmation of the basic equality of all persons, "since all possess a rational soul and are created in God's likeness, since they have the same nature and origin, have been redeemed by Christ, and enjoy the same divine calling and destiny."[50] The council went on to draw this conclusion from such equality:

> True, all are not alike from the point of view of varying physical power and the diversity of intellectual and moral resources. Nevertheless, with respect to the fundamental rights of the person, every type of discrimination, whether social or cultural, whether based on sex, race, color, social condition, language, or religion, is to be overcome and eradicated as contrary to God's intent.[51]

Recognizing the legitimate differences that do exist among persons, nevertheless the magisterium taught in this conciliar statement that "the equal dignity of persons demands that a more humane and just condition of life be brought about," and called on "human institutions, both private and public, . . . to minister to the dignity and purpose" of human persons.[52]

In their pastoral statement on the economy, the bishops of the United States applied this magisterial teaching to discrimination in regard to job opportunities, stating "it is a scandal that such discrimination continues in the United States today."[53] The bishops taught that in its own internal actions the Church must root out this kind of discrimination wherever it exists, whether it be based on race[54] or on sex.[55]

The new code reaffirms the magisterial teaching on the fundamental equality of the Christian faithful "with regard to dignity and the activity whereby all cooperate in the building up of the Body of Christ in accord with each one's own condition and function" (c. 208). It also affirms that "qualified lay persons are

---

[50]*Gaudium et spes*, n. 29: *AAS* 58 (1966) 1048; translation from Abbott, p. 227.
[51]Ibid., pp. 1048-1049; Abbott, pp. 227-228.
[52]Ibid., p. 1049; Abbott, p. 228.
[53]NCCB, *Economic Justice for All*, n. 73.
[54]NCCB, pastoral letter on racism "Brothers and Sisters to Us," November 14, 1979, nn. 44-54: *Pastoral Letters of the United States Bishops, Vol. IV 1975-1983* (Washington: USCC, 1984), pp. 352-354.
[55]NCCB, *Economic Justice for All*, n. 353: "In seeking greater justice in wages, we recognize the need to be particularly alert to the continuing discrimination against women throughout church and society, especially reflected in both the inequities of salaries between women and men and in the concentration of women in jobs at the lower end of the wage scale."

capable of assuming from their sacred pastors those ecclesiastical offices and functions which they are able to exercise in accord with the prescriptions of law" (c. 228, §1). Canonical tradition recognizes the principle of competence rather than personal influence as the chief criterion for appointment to office. Appointment to office requires that the candidate have those qualities required by law.[56] Discrimination on the basis of racial, sexual or social consideration which would exclude otherwise qualified persons from appointment to positions which the law permits them to exercise in the Church is contrary not only to the magisterium's moral teaching, but also to these canonical principles.

The code does not specify how discrimination in these matters is to be overcome; that is left to the responsible prudence of those in charge of particular churches, in keeping with the conditions of their time and place. The guidance provided by the bishops of particular churches fulfill this responsibility. In 1966 they recommended affirmative action as an expression of the open attitudes which "best express the Christian response to racial discrimination."[57] In 1978 they acknowledged that "discrimination in American society urgently demands our attention" and announced a set of guidelines for affirmative action to be published "for diocesan evaluation and implementation. Our own conference offices, in their hiring practices, are prepared to take leadership in the implementation of such guidelines."[58] The promised guidelines were issued in August, 1979.[59]

From a canonical perspective, these guidelines are not a form of particular law. They were adopted by the Administrative Committee of the NCCB as policy internal to the operations of the conference's offices, and were "offered to the dioceses as a positive witness of a commitment to social justice in policies and practices."[60] They have moral, not legal, force. However, the principle taught by the bishops in their 1986 pastoral letter on the economy must be recalled here: "all the moral principles that govern the just operation of any economic endeavor apply to the Church and its agencies and institutions; indeed, the Church should be exemplary."[61]

Affirmative action as presented by the bishops entails the following elements:
 a. A policy of non-discrimination.[62]
 b. A policy of equal employment opportunity.
 c. A policy of recruitment to solicit minority applicants.

---

[56]Under the 1917 code this applied to appointments made by "free conferral" (1917 code, c. 153, §1); under the new code it applies to any appointment to office (c. 149, §1).

[57]NCCB, "Pastoral Statement on Race Relations and Poverty," November 19, 1966: *Pastoral Letters of the United States Catholic Bishops, Vol. III 1962-1974* (Washington: USCC, 1983), p. 86.

[58]NCCB, statement "To Do the Work of Justice," May 4, 1978, n. 36: *Pastoral Letters of the United States Catholic Bishops, Vol. IV 1975-1983*, p. 252.

[59]"Affirmative Action Plan for National Bishops' Conference," *Origins* 9/11 (August 30, 1979) 161, 163.

[60]Ibid., p. 161.

[61]*Economic Justice for All*, n. 347.

[62]The NCCB excludes discrimination because of "race, color, sex, national origin, handicap or age. "Affirmative Action Plan," p. 163.

d. Procedures for redress of grievances under the policy, and for review of compliance with the policy.

b. Participation

Faced with the social problems of the modern era, the Church's magisterium has turned repeatedly to the principle of participation as a means of bringing the best efforts of employers and employees together. Pius XI made their mutual cooperation the chief element of his proposals for reforming the social order.[63] John XXIII addressed the need for active and positive participation of workers in the enterprise.[64] In *Gaudium et spes* the Second Vatican Council called for an active sharing by all (workers and employers) in the administration of enterprises, and saw unions as a means to achieve this end.[65] John Paul II sees these proposals as having a special significance in the Church's continued effort to build a just social order on the recognition of the human character of work, centered on the dignity of the human person who does the work.[66] In their pastoral on the economy, the American bishops reiterated the centrality of the principle of participation.[67]

The right to participate in the enterprise, that is in decisions which affect one's life, appears from this official teaching as a fundamental human right. While not directly expressed in the revised Code of Canon Law, respect for this right is implicit in the obligation of all the faithful "to promote social justice" (c. 222, §2).

The Church affirms the right to participate even in the inner life of the Church. All are called to share in the mission of the Church, promoting the sanctification of the Church (c. 210) and proclaiming the gospel (c. 211). Various structures of participation have been established, ranging from the formal participation in particular councils (c. 443), diocesan synods (c. 463), and diocesan and parish pastoral councils (cc. 512 and 536), to the inclusion of qualified members of the faithful in various offices and positions as experts (c. 228). If in its own inner workings the Church has sought to implement the social teaching on participation, less could hardly be expected of those activities in which persons are employed and therefore resemble more closely the socio-economic situations which the Church's social teaching has directly taught should implement this same principle.[68]

c. Expression of Opinion

The new code takes up the teaching of the magisterium on expressing one's opinion in the Church. In canon 212 dealing with fundamental duties and rights

---

[63]*Quadragesimo anno*, nn. 88-98: *AAS* 23 (1931) 202-209.
[64]*Mater et magistra*, nn. 91-96: *AAS* 53 (1961) 423-426.
[65]*Gaudium et spes*, n. 68: *AAS* 58 (1966) 1090.
[66]*Laborem exercens*, n. 14: *AAS* 73 (1981) 614-615.
[67]*Economic Justice for All*, n. 77: "Basic justice demands the establishment of minimum levels of participation in the life of the human community for all persons."
[68]Ibid., n. 353.

in the relationship between the hierarchy and the rest of the faithful, the code affirms the responsibility of all to obey what the hierarchy as representative of Christ teach or mandate for the Church.[69] On the other hand, "The Christian faithful are free to make known their needs, especially spiritual ones, and their desires to the pastors of the Church" (c. 212, §2).

The Second Vatican Council addressed this same concern in its Dogmatic Constitution on the Church *Lumen gentium*.[70] The Synod of Bishops in 1971 reaffirmed this teaching, putting it even more succinctly: "The Church recognizes everyone's right to suitable freedom of expression and thought. This includes the right of everyone to be heard in a spirit of dialogue which preserves a legitimate diversity within the Church."[71]

The Synod document makes two key points which help to clarify the implications of the canon. First, concomitant with the right to express one's needs and opinions is the right to be given a fair hearing. Second, there will be legitimate differences of opinion.

In addition to the right to dialogue with pastors, the Christian faithful have the right to develop public opinion. The code expresses this with the cautions appropriate to its own system of law:

> Can. 212—§3. In accord with the knowledge, competence and preeminence which they possess, they have the right and even at times a duty to manifest to the sacred pastors their opinion on matters which pertain to the good of the Church, and they have a right to make their opinion known to the other Christian faithful, with due regard for the integrity of faith and morals and reverence toward their pastors, and with consideration for the common good and the dignity of persons.[72]

The Second Vatican Council affirmed a general right of persons to have access to information and to form public opinion on issues which concern them.[73] In a subsequent pastoral instruction the right is stated even more directly:

> It is absolutely essential that there be freedom to express ideas and attitudes. In accordance with the express teaching of the Second Vatican Council it is necessary unequivocally to declare that freedom of speech for individuals and groups must be permitted so long as the common good and public

---

[69]For commentaries on c. 212, see: Dalla Torre, pp. 118-119; Hervada, p. 175; Manzanares, pp. 138-139; Provost, pp. 144-147; Reinhardt, pp. 212/1-3.

[70]"The laity have the right, as do all Christians, to receive in abundance from their sacred pastors the spiritual goods of the Church. . . . All laypersons should openly reveal to them their needs and desires.

"Let the sacred pastors recognize and promote the dignity as well as the responsibility of laypersons in the Church. Let them willingly make use of their prudent advice. Let them confidently assign duties to laypersons in the service of the Church, allowing them freedom and room for action," *Lumen gentium*, n. 37: *AAS* 57 (1965) 42-43; translation from Abbott, pp. 64-65.

[71]*Justice in the World*, III: *AAS* 63 (1971) 934; translation from *Justice in the Marketplace*, p. 257.

[72]See Provost, p. 147, for a discussion of the significance of the qualifiers used in this canon.

[73]Decree on the Instruments of Social Communication *Inter mirifica*, n. 5: *AAS* 56 (1964) 147.

morality be not endangered.[74]

The right to express opinions was applied specifically within the Church by the council in *Lumen gentium* (n. 37). It is this statement which forms the basis for the canon in the new code.

d. Reputation

A fundamental human right affirmed by the Church's magisterium is the right to a good reputation (*Gaudium et spes,* n. 26). The new code has included this in the fundamental rights of the Christian faithful: "No one is permitted to damage unlawfully the good reputation which another person enjoys" (c. 220). Even if the reputation is not warranted, that is no reason to damage it. Criminal action or other grave sin, admonition by church authorities, and obstinacy in the wrongful activity are required for someone to intervene actively with the purpose of damaging another's reputation.[75]

The dealings between employers and employees are interpersonal of their nature. A proper respect for the good reputation enjoyed by all parties must mark these dealings.

e. Privacy

Another fundamental human right affirmed by the Church's magisterium (*Gaudium et spes,* n. 26) is the right to privacy. The new code also recognizes this right in a canon designed to protect personal rights and the good reputation of the Christian faithful (c. 220). The code recognizes other implications of this right, such as access to certain files.[76]

f. Vindication of Rights and Settlement of Disputes

The Catholic Church has a long tradition of providing means for people to vindicate their rights and settle disputes peacefully. In addition to the traditional right to appeal to the Apostolic See, the responsibilities of bishops and other local officials has been to aid in resolving disputes and protecting the rights of persons in the Church. The Church's own tribunal system bears witness to this tradition even today, and the new code calls for renewed efforts to provide means of media-

---

[74]Pontifical Commission for the Social Communications Media, pastoral instruction *Communio et progressio,* n. 26, May 23, 1971: *AAS* 63 (1971) 604. English translation from Austin Flannery, ed., *Vatican Council II: The Conciliar and Post Conciliar Documents* (Northport, NY: Costello Publishing, 1975), p. 303.

[75]The Church's own penal law cautions that "care must be taken lest anyone's good name be endangered" by a preliminary investigation into wrongdoing (c. 1717, §2), and advises the bishop to use a variety of means to correct a wrongdoer before even entering into that preliminary investigation (c. 1341).

[76]In reference to the diocesan chancery, c. 487, §2 states: "It is the right of interested parties to obtain personally or through their proxy an authentic written copy or a photocopy of documents which are public by their nature and which pertain to the status of such persons." This is a new provision in canon law and it will take some time to clarify what is meant by "documents . . . public by their nature" and the precise meaning of "status of such persons" in this context. However, the canon does seem to include basic personnel records; if these must be made available from the chancery files, the same would seem to apply to files of other church agencies.

tion and reconciliation.

The fundamental right to vindicate and defend one's rights in the Church is affirmed in the new code (c. 221, §1). Although traditional church structures such as diocesan tribunals have not been utilized for this purpose in recent years, aside from sacramental questions, there is an obligation on the part of church officials to provide adequate channels through which persons can vindicate their rights and settle disputes within the Church. This applies as well to rights and disputes which may relate to employer-employee relationships in the Church.

What the Church has taught as applying to all of society, and which it applies even to its own inner workings, clearly applies as well to those church related enterprises which employ workers.

From the foregoing fundamental rights, the following can be drawn in way of a summary.

1. Persons have a right to be treated in keeping with their fundamental equality in dignity; discrimination to the contrary is to be eradicated by means of affirmative action.
2. Persons have a right to participate in coming to decisions which affect their lives.
3. They have a right to express their needs, and to participate in the formation of public opinion about matters in which they enjoy some competence or experience.
4. The have the right to enjoy their good reputation, and not to have it damaged unlawfully.
5. They have the right to privacy and to access to some files which concern their status as a person.
6. They have the right to vindicate their rights, and to the resolution of disputes in the Church.
7. What the Church has taught as applying to all of society, and which it applies even to its own inner workings, clearly applies as well to those church related enterprises which employ workers.
8. Associations for collective bargaining or labor unions have been proposed by the Church as appropriate means for persons to exercise similar rights in secular society.
9. These rights apply within the Church as well as in secular society; a fortiori, they apply to church related institutions, agencies and programs which employ persons in carrying out their activities.

Considerations Toward Practice

The above considerations provide only a skeletal framework for considering the relationship of labor and management in church related institutions, agencies and programs. Implementation is a more complex process, one which demands the exercise of prudence and a sense of the Church's role as both proclaiming and modelling the Kingdom of God in this world.

The preceding discussion has focused primarily on those who are considered "employees," or wage earners in the Church. They also apply, in light of canon 231, to those who are more frequently termed "non-ordained ministers" or professionals in the Church. It may also be argued that they apply analogously to some deacons and priests, and also to some religious who, though they live a life vowed to evangelical poverty, also have the responsibilities of their religious religious family for which they must provide. Diocesan law for deacons and priests, and the proper law of their institute for religious, will determine whether they may join associations for collective bargaining, or unions.[77]

In light of the four areas of principle studied above, five topics for reflection may assist in implementing the Church's teaching and law on justice in labor and management relations.

1. Information

Adequate and timely information is needed for both employer and employee to participate actively and fruitfully in their common enterprise. A periodic careful analysis of information systems and communication procedures is a fundamental requirement for developing and maintaining just relations between labor and management in church related institutions, agencies and programs.

2. Personnel Procedures

The development of systematic personnel procedures based on a respect for the dignity of persons, the needs of the enterprise, and the common good are legitimate concerns of both employer and employee. These procedures, which appropriately include requirements for equal employment opportunity and affirmative action, apply to both direct and indirect employers, and can be insisted on by church administrators in dealing with sub-contractors.[78]

3. Just Wage

Concern for a just wage is a cornerstone of Catholic social teaching. Applying this teaching within the Church may require a broader consideration thab the individual institution, agency or program, and should be taken into consideration

---

[77]Religious, and clergy other than permanent deacons, may not have a directive role in such associations without a determination by competent ecclesiastical authority (c. 287, §2) and, for religious, the permission of their legitimate religious superior (c. 671).

[78]There are a number of aids available to church officials in regard to personnel questions. The National Association of Church Personnel Administrators has developed extensive materials on personnel policies and procedures to assist dioceses and religious institutes; see especially their position paper, *Just Treatment for Those Who Work for the Church* (cincinnati: NACPA, 1986), as well as their publications *Clergy Personnel Policies* (compiled by Jane M. Gehring), *Lay Personnel Policies* (compiled by Barbara Garland), and *Personnel Policies: Congregations of Women Religious* (compiled by Jane M. Gehring). The National Catholic Education Association has developed similar aids for educational institutions, and the Catholic Health Association has materials to assist iunstitutions in the health care field.

in financial and pastoral planning in the Church. The legitimate role of volunteerism in church life must also be taken into account.

4. Contracts

In principle, contracts for ministry and employment pertain to the good functioning of the Church. They have been encouraged even with regard to religious[79] and ordained ministers, specifically deacons.[80] Their use will contribute greatly to better understanding of expectations and clarification of various issues affecting justice in the relationship of employers and employees.

Alternatives to contracts are sometimes termed "job descriptions" or other expressions of the expectations which pertain to a particular position. Instead of engaging in an individual contract, persons are employed in light of existing policy and practices clearly set forth in an employee's manual. This approach is acceptable provided adequate participation of all those affected is assured in the revision of such documents.

5. Collective Bargaining

Church teaching clearly supports collective bargaining, but also calls for a proper attitude toward this endeavor. An examination of one's own attitudes with regard to collective bargaining may be needed on the part of church officials, employers, and employees to bring about conformity with this teaching of the official magisterium.

Existing structures for collective bargaining deserve respect, both in light of church teaching and of the civil standards to which the church's law binds. These structures are more commonly found in health care institutions, schools, and similar institutions.

The development of new structures for collective bargaining is also possible. In addition to traditional associations formed for this purpose, church teaching has proposed structures of collaboration and participation which may prove effective in church related institutions, agencies and programs.

If collective bargaining is to be effective, means must be provided for enforcement, and for the settlement of grievances. In some situations secular agencies already provide this service. In other situations the Church is exempted from the jurisdiction of those agencies, and needs to develop its own alternatives. This will be a complex and demanding task, requiring the collective resources of the hierarchy, experts in civil and canon law, representatives of employers and employees, and other interested parties in the Church. It is a worthy task, one for which the Church in the United States is especially equipped in light of its

---

[79]Congregation for Religious and Secular Institutes and Congregation for Bishops, Directives for the Mutual Relations Between Bishops and Religious in the Church *Mutuae relationes*, n. 58, May 14, 1978: *AAS* 70 (1978) 502-503.

[80]See NCCB, *Permanent Deacons in the United States: Guidelines on Their Formation and Ministry*, 1984 Revision (Washington: USCC, 1985), n. 117, pp. 43-44.

tradition of concern for social justice and fair treatment of employees and employers.

Appendix: Summary of Canonical Standards

1. Out of the employer-employee relationship there arise both rights and duties for all parties involved. In the Church these rights and duties are not isolated claims and responsibilities, but are to be integrated in the overall communion of the life of the people of God. (Pages 315-320)
2. Provision is to be made for a just and equitable compensation so that workers may adequately provide for themselves, their families, and others who depend on them. Wages and benefits must at least be up to the standards set in the applicable civil laws. (Pages 315, 317-319)
3. Working conditions are to be assured which respect the dignity of the persons involved and must at least be up to the standards set in the applicable civil laws. (Pages 315, 317-319)
4. The Church's teaching and law on employer-employee relationships applies to direct and indirect employers, including sub-contractors. (Page 317)
5. The local ordinary, and in particular the diocesan bishop, has a vigilance role over all church related activity in the diocese, including the observance of church law on employer-employee relationships. (Pages 317-320)
6. The dignity of the human person within the common good is the yardstick by which all considerations regarding the relationships between employers and employees are to be judged. (Pages 318-320)
7. Church administrators are bound to observe the standard of diligence of a good householder. In enforcing this norm, the diocesan bishop can determine more precisely what this standard entails, and in doing so may take into consideration even those civil laws from which the Church is exempt. (Pages 319, 320, 325)
8. All persons have the natural right to assemble freely and to form associations for legitimate purposes. Church teaching recognizes that these purposes include those of collective bargaining and other activities proper to labor unions. (Pages 321-323)
9. The Church's law recognizes the fundamental rights to assemble and to form associations, and affirms them within the Church itself. (Pages 321-323)
10. Associations for collective bargaining or labor unions have been proposed by the Church as appropriate means for persons to exercise similar rights in secular society, and in the Church. (Pages 321-323)
11. No types of work, no areas or segments of the workplace, are excluded a priori from the formation of labor unions or associations for collective bargaining, including diocesan offices and church related institutions, agencies and programs. (Pages 321-323)
12. Associations formed by the Christian faithful, while they are under the

vigilance of church authorities, are governed by the members themselves in keeping with their statutes. (Pages 322-323)
13. The presumption is that civil laws in the United States are generally in conformity with church teaching; the diocesan bishop is the competent authority to decide if a specific civil law is not to be observed because it is contrary to church teaching or to canon law. (Page 324)
14. These fundamental rights apply within the Church as well as in secular society; a fortiori, they apply to church related institutions, agencies and programs which employ persons in carrying out their activities. (Pages 326-331)
15. In keeping with fundamental equality in human dignity, there is to be no discrimination on the basis of race, color, sex, national origin, handicap or age in employment by church agencies or institutions. Affirmative action is an appropriate means to overcome existing discrimination. (Pages 326-328)
16. Persons have a right to participate in coming to decisions which affect their lives. (Page 328)
17. They have a right to express their needs, and to participate in the formation of public opinion about matters in which they enjoy some competence or experience. (Pages 328-329)
18. They have the right to enjoy their good reputation, and not to have it damaged unlawfully. (Page 330)
19. They have the right to privacy and to access to some files which concern their status as a person. (Page 330)
20. They have the right to vindicate their rights, and to the resolution of disputes in the Church. (Pages 330-331)

OBSERVATIONS ON THE 1986 SCHEMA CODICIS IURIS CANONICI ORIENTALIS

INTRODUCTION

In October, 1986, the *Pontificia Commissio Codici Iuris Canonici Orientalis Recognoscendo* (PCCICOR) distributed to its members a complete draft of the *Codex Iuris Canonici Orientalis*.[1] The text is comprised of 1561 canons divided into thirty titles with six preliminary canons.

One of the responsibilities of the CLSA Committee on Eastern Canon Law and Interritual Matters is to keep the membership informed of the progress on the codification and revision of the future Eastern Code of Canon Law. The pages which follow are select observations made by the respective members of the Committee: Revs. John Sekellick, William Wolfe, and John Faris, Chairperson. It should be noted that Fathers Sekellick and Wolfe had access only to Title II of the *Schema*, "Autonomous Churches and Rites." For that reason, their comments are restricted to the canons of that title.

(Rev.) J.D. Faris
Chairperson,
CLSA Committee on Eastern
Law and Interritual Matters

OBSERVATIONS ON CICO TITLE II

John Sekellick

The theological principle of incorporation by baptism into the Church is a necessary part of canonical legislation. It is enunciated in *Lumen Gentium,* nn. 8 and 14. Baptism, then, incorporates a person into the membership of the church, but that membership itself is determined by association with a particular rite within the universal church. This is a principle enunciated in *Orientalium Ecclesiarum* n. 2. The formulation of canons 27 through 40 of Title II enflesh juridically the

---

[1] The cover letter, dated October 17, 1986, indicates that the members of the Commission were to present their comments and observations to the Secretariat before April 30, 1987. The Draft was accompanied by "Relazione circa lo Schema Codicis Iuris Canonici Orientalis" dated September 8, 1986, which describes a history of the project and the criteria for the final redaction of the text made by the Coetus de Coordinatione.

concepts embodied in paragraphs 3 through 6 of the same decree on the eastern churches.

While Canon 27 provides a succinct definition of "Ecclesia sui iuris," the placing of the qualification "in hoc Codice" seems superfluous since there is no other Code providing a definition of the term. The use of the designation "Ecclesia sui iuris" consistently in the canons clarifies the confusion of using the term "Particular Church" in previous revisions of this Schema since "particular church" in the Latin Code specifically designates a diocese (c. 368). Canon 1 of the Latin Code admits the existence of other churches like itself when it restricts that Code to "only the Latin Church." However, a later canon, 111, §1, calls other such churches "Ritual Churches." Canon 112, §1, 3⁰ speaks of "other Ritual Churches." Canons 111, §1 and 112, §§1 and 2 then contain a further qualification "Ritual Church sui iuris." Canon 27 of our latest Schema, then, keeps separate the concepts of "rite" and "Church." This represents a distinction not clearly drawn by the Council. Paragraph 2 of O.E. states, "It is the mind of the Catholic Church that each individual church *or rite* (my emphasis) retain its traditions whole and entire, while adjusting its way of life to various needs of time and place."

The Council document includes a statement (parag. 3) which is missing in the presentation of c. 27, §2, 2⁰; *the rites are of equal dignity.* This can easily be added by a simple relative clause to conclude 2⁰. The term "traditionibus" should be qualified with "apostolicis" to balance the constant use of "Sedes Apostolica" to refer to the Holy See as though it were the sole apostolic see. Designating the see of Rome as Apostolic flies in the face of the other also "apostolic" ancient sees and is ecumenically insensitive in the Eastern Code.

Canon 28, §1 eliminates the confusion of earlier schemas which had used "particular" to describe the Ecclesia sui iuris simply with the designation "Ecclesiae, cui pater ascriptus est" - a definite improvement.

The canons, however, do not address the circumstances of vagrants, lapsed and lax Catholics, that is, fringe elements of ecclesial society who present their children for baptism (and hence ascription) and who have very minimal claim to the designation "catholic." A complication arises more and more on a parochial level when non-practicing Catholics of another rite request baptism at a parish of an Eastern rite and the Pastor accedes to their wishes based on fragile hope that the parents will return to or become active again in the church. Perhaps a third s to C. 27 could address this issue by affirming the necessity of a faith-committment (Cf. *Lumen Gentium,* n. 14).

A more logical sequence in the presentation of the canons might be, using the present numbering: 28, 29, 31, 32, 33, then 30, 34, 35, etc. The progression in this fashion would be: the baptism of children of catholic parents (c. 28); the baptism of a child or person older than 14 (c. 29); the relationship between spouses of different Ecclesiae sui iuris (c. 31) and their children (c. 32), ascription of baptized non-Catholics (c. 33) and then the particular dynamics of effecting a transfer from one Ecclesia sui iuris to another (c. 30), the prohibition of proselytism (c. 34) and finally the effects of transfer (c. 35).

Canon 29 eliminates references in previous legislation (*Cleri sanctitati* c. 17) and previous schemas (c. 10 - *Nuntia* 1982) to the age of puberty. Age 14 is given for both male and female. Children under this age follow their parents in their proper rite (c. 32). When a child reaches age 15 (expleto decimo quarto aetatis anno), children may return to their original Ecclesia sui iuris.

Canon 33 makes it clear that baptized non-Catholics are expected to retain membership in their proper Ecclesia sui iuris when they enter into full communion with the Catholic Church. They no longer are permitted to embrace the rite which they prefer. Recourse to the Holy See for different determination is available in special cases for individuals, communities and regions. Canon 33 is consonant with paragraph 4 of O.E.

Transfer from one Ecclesia sui iuris to another requires, for it to be valid, authorization on the part of the Holy See (c. 30, §1). No mention, however, is made of previous legislation (*C.S.* c. 8, §1) stipulating that after legitimate transfer, the permission of the Holy See is again required to go back to the original rite.

Although non-Christians who come to the Catholic faith through the grace of preaching by Latin missionaries in Oriental territory are free in principle to choose the church to which they would appertain, practically the influence of those who shared their faith with them, almost inevitably causes them to choose the church of the missionaries. It certainly is ecumenically appropriate that such new Catholics be incorporated as members of their local oriental Catholic Church. Such new Christians should be exhorted to choose the Ecclesia sui iuris proper to their own culture and tradition.

In evaluation of Title II, two considerations seem germane. The first is that of religious liberty. The Second Vatican Council upholds the right of every individual to religious freedom and to worship in a manner congruent with his religious convictions (*Dignitatis humanae* n. 2). This is a reflection of concern about the religious freedom of the individual within the context of civil society. However, within the church itself, the same principle must be operative. A person has the inherent and inalienable right to worship in a manner most suited to his spiritual and cultural needs. An operative factor today is the ready influence of the communications media as well as the mobility of people affecting faith development and affiliation. It is not at all unusual for children to disassociate themselves from the values, traditions and convictions of older generations. Within the Catholic Church, such dynamics, especially in our pluralistic American context, must be respected.

The second principle that must be taken into account is the spiritual integrity of the family itself. The Second Vatican Council refers to the family as the domestic church (*Lumen Gentium* n. 11). If the members of one family belong to different Ecclesiae sui iuris, the life of worship within the family would be inhibited. It is imperative that the family share the same faith traditions.

A great measure of pastoral sensitivity, then, to ascription in an Ecclesia sui iuris is of crucial importance. The church to which a person is ascribed is not only a legal (canonical) issue. It is a question of fact as well. The immigration of the Ruthenian and Ukrainian people certainly have proved that within the past 100 years. Presently world circumstances involving other Eastern Catholics (among the Maronites from Lebanon, the Malabars in India, and various scattered Coptic, Albanian and other national groups) merit resolution of interritual concerns.

With adaptation, assimilation, intermarriage and other numerous variant factors constantly occurring, it is becoming increasingly difficult to discover the factual ascription of an individual. It is not uncommon that for various personal reasons, this fact is not revealed or even hidden from ecclesiastical authorities. Many "Christifideli" sometimes are offended and, perhaps not unjustly, feel themselves victimized by being forced to retain in their personal lives a kind of fictional link with the spiritual tradition or a national heritage for which they no longer feel any sympathy, or to which they honestly feel psychologically unable to conform.

The validity of certain acts that affect individual lives depends upon the observance of the laws governing ascription, particularly considering matrimonial issues. There is too the further consideration of how the laws of fast and abstinence bind individuals, which holy days are preceptive, and even the differing aspects of matrimonial impediments (e.g., spiritual relationship).

Where it definitely is possible for individuals to maintain the spirit and traditions of their proper ritual ascription, as is true for the most part here in this country, the injunction of O.E. n. 6 without exception should be heeded. Chapter II of Title II is a welcome and needed adjunct to our Oriental Code.

OBSERVATIONS ON CICO TITLE II

WILLIAM P. WOLFE

I have studied *De Ecclesiis sui juris et de ritibus* from the 1986 Schema.

I see a number of modifications that have worked their way into the latest draft. I am very pleased (of course, from a Latin background) with the latest canons. Actually I have a comment on only one canon, that is canon 33. The first part of this canon is almost verbatim from the Decree of the Second Vatican Council on Oriental Churches. Strangely, the Latin Code does not incorporate this quotation. I question the relevance of canon 33 with regard to Protestants. Practically speaking, it seems to me that as a consequence of canon 33 a Protestant in the United States who wishes to come into full communion with the Maronite Rite would have to approach the Holy See for permission to do so. I think it is arguable to take a position that Protestants have a heritage deriving from the Latin Rite. In my opinion a Protestant is a dissident who cannot claim any heritage with any ritual Church. At any rate, I see canon 33 as problematic.

Overall, I am favorably impressed notwithstanding the exception above.

OBSERVATIONS ON THE 1986 SCHEMA CODICIS IURIS CANONICI ORIENTALIS

JOHN D. FARIS

The observations which follow are not intended to provide even a cursory commentary on the canons of the 1986 Draft. Rather, the remarks are intended to address those aspects of the 1986 Draft which appear to be problematic in some way. Quite often the major point of the canon will be ignored while minor points will be addressed in the observations.

An overall appraisal of the 1986 Draft is quite positive. While being an authentic expression of the canonical tradition of the eastern catholic churches, it is appropriate to the pastoral needs of these churches today. It also seems to have found the delicate balance between what should be legislated in the common code and what should be left to the legislation of the autonomous churches.

OBSERVATIONS OF THE INDIVIDUAL CANONS

Canon 1

Canones huius Codicis omnes et solas Ecclesias orientales catholicas respiciunt, nisi, relationes cum Ecclesia latina quod attinet, expresse aliud statuitur.

This canon is an exclusionary clause delineating the scope of the authority of the Code. Apparently for the sake of precision, the canon indicates that the Latin Church is also affected by the provisions of the Code. (RCIC c. 1[2] makes no mention of the eastern catholic churches.) Every effort must be made not to give the impression that the Eastern Code is to be understood as supplementary to the Latin Code. Both Codes are complementary. Reference solely to the Latin Church might give this impression. Therefore, reference to any specific ecclesial communion should be omitted.

Prescinding from any claim to ecclesiastical authority over non-catholics, the Code should take into account that non-catholic churches, ecclesial communions (e.g., cc. 668, §§2-5; 682, §2; 699; 702, §2; 808-811) and even the non-baptized (e.g., cc. 583; 798, §1) are affected indirectly by the Code.

Proposed Text:

Canones huius Codicis omnes et solas Ecclesias orientales catholicas respiciunt, nisi, ex natura rei vel expresse aliud statuitur.

---

[2]Canones huius Codicis unam Ecclesiam latinam respiciunt.

Canon 6 1⁰ *et passim*

Codice vim obtinente:

1⁰ abrogatae sunt omnes leges iuris communis vel iuris particularis, quae sunt canonibus Codicis contrariae aut quae materiam respiciunt in Codice ex integro ordinatam;

The term "ius particulare" is employed in the Code to designate any legislation which is not common to all of the autonomous churches. No adequate distinction is made between the legislation of the synod enacted for the entire autonomous church, legislation enacted by the See of Rome for a certain group of eastern catholics, or the legislation of an eparchy.

The term "ius proprium" should be applied to legislation which binds all the members of a specific autonomous church.[3]

The term "ius particulare" should be applied to legislation which concerns any group of eastern catholics. This group could be a certain portion of an autonomous church (e.g., those residing within the territorial boundaries of the patriarchal church) or members of several autonomous churches residing in a certain territory (e.g., the eastern catholics residing in the United States).

The term "ius eparchiale" should be applied to any legislation of a specific eparchy.

Canon 27 §2

1⁰ ritus est patrimonium liturgicum, theologicum, spirituale et disciplinare culture ac rerum adiunctis historiae populorum distinctum, quod modo fidei vivendae uniuscuiusque Ecclesiae sui iuris proprio exprimitur;

2⁰ ritus, de quibus in Codice agitur, sunt, nisi aliud constat, illi, qui oriuntur ex traditionibus Alexandrina, Antiochena, Armena, Chaldaea et Constantinopolitana.

This canon does not have a counterpart in the Latin Code. Thus, it is the only opportunity to delineate in an official canonical text the major traditions of the Church, including that which originated in Rome. Mention of the Roman tradition would probably require the omission of the phrase "de quibus in Codice agitur." There is no need to abandon the alphabetical order since all traditions are equal.

Proposed text:

2⁰ ritus sunt illi qui oriuntur ex traditionibus Alexandrina, Antiochena, Armena, Chaldea, Constantinopolitana et Romana.

Canon 28 §1

Ipso baptismo quisquis ascribitur Ecclesiae, cui pater ascriptus est; si vero sola mater est catholica aut, si ambo parentes concordi voluntate petunt,

---

[3]This is the proposal made by Cardinal Coussa in *Epitome Praelectionum de Iure Ecclesiastico Orientali:* "Proprium dicimus ius quo regitur universa aliqua orientalis Communitas seu Ritus; *particulare,* quod viget pro aliquo coetu vel territorio certae Communitatis seu Ritus." I:8, n. 10.

ascribitur Ecclesiae, ad quam mater pertinet, salvo iure particulari a Sede Apostolica statuto.

Many might welcome the provision of this canon which affords parents the possibility of choosing the autonomous church of the father or the mother, but there are difficulties with this provision for several reasons:

—It will ultimately contribute to the diminution of membership in the eastern catholic churches. In some cases, parents will choose the eastern catholic church for the child, but, human nature being what it is, they will usually opt for the parish church which is usually geographically closer and more convenient. It is also important to consider that the canon is placing a burden on the parents to decide for (and logically, against) an autonomous church.

—It will create canonical doubts *(dubium facti)* in many cases. For example, a Maronite father and Latin mother want their child to be a member of the Maronite Church, but no Maronite parish is located near them. In order to have the child baptized, they take the child to the local Latin parish. If no notation is made in the parish record concerning their desire to have the child be a member of the Maronite Church, anyone who refers to the records later will presume that the child is a member of the Latin Church. The defect in the provision is that a determination of membership is made no longer in consideration of any objective fact (the membership of the father) but on the intentions of the parents, which cannot always be ascertained twenty years after the conferral of baptism when the question arises in arranging for a marraige.

—The creation of canonical doubts will eventually result in the fact that membership in an autonomous church will have little more significance than membership in a parish.

—If the canon permits parents to choose the autonomous church, the clause "salvo iure particulari a Sede Apostolica statuto" is an invitation for hierarchies of both the Latin and eastern churches to petition for a restriction of the provisions subsequent to the promulgation of the Code.

It would be advantageous to formulate the provisions of the canon in a strict manner and then expand the possibilities if the circumstances warrant such an action.

Proposed Text:

§1. Ipso baptismo quisquis ascribitur Ecclesiae, cui pater ascriptus est; si vero sola mater est catholica, adscribitur ad quam mater pertinet, salvo iure particulari a Sede Apostolica statuto.

Canon 30 §1

Nemo potest sine consensu Sedis Apostolicae ad aliam Ecclesiam sui iuris valide transire.

This paragraph is contradictory to c. 31, which allows for a person to transfer to the autonomous church of the spouse without the consent of the Apostolic See. (It does not seem to be appropriate to consider the provisions of c. 31 itself as an expression of consent of the Apostolic See.) Therefore, reference to the pro-

visions of c. 31 should be made in this canon.
Proposed Text:
Nemo potest sine consensu Sedis Apostolicae ad aliam Ecclesiam sui iuris valide transire, *salvo praescripto canonis 31.*

The canon does not clearly indicate what should be done if the bishops are not in agreement concerning the transfer. The following paragraph should be added:
Proposed Text:
§3. *Si Hierarchae loci dissentiant ad Apostolicam Sedem res devolvitur.*

Proposed Addition

Even though the matter is addressed in some way in c. 37, the text from RCIC c. 112, §2 should be included in the Code:

Mos, quamvis diuturnus, sacramenta secundum ritum alicuius Ecclesiae ritualis sui iuris recipiendi, non secumfert ascriptionem eidem Ecclesiae.

Canon 31

Integrum est coniugi ad Ecclesiam alterius coniugis transire in matrimonio celebrando vel eo durante, nisi ius particulare a Sede Apostolica statutum aliud fert; matrimonio autem soluto libere potest ad pristinam Ecclesiam redire.

As mentioned in the comments on c. 28, §1, it might be advantageous to make provisions of this canon restrictive and then allow for particular law to expand the possibilities if the circumstances warrant it. Thus, the canon should permit only the wife to transfer to the autonomous church of the husband. This is a case in which the provisions of the Latin Code (RCIC c. 112, §1 2º) should be modified.

In the Middle East, it would seem strange for the husband to transfer to the autonomous church of his wife.

Under the provisions of the legislation now in force, quite often a woman does not make a formal declaration of her desire to transfer to the autonomous church of her husband, but simply begins to attend his parish. *Cleri Sanctitati* c. 13 is rarely applied since many presume it to be applicable only in those cases wherein a rescript was granted by the Apostolic See. Thus, one is obliged to refer to the intentions of the individual in order to determine membership in an autonomous church. It would be advantageous if this canon made reference to the formalities of a transfer mentioned in c. 35.

Proposed Text:
§1. Integrum est *mulieris* ad Ecclesiam sui iuris viri transire in matrimonio celebrando vel eo durante . . .
§2. *De transitu ad aliam Ecclesiam sui iuris applicatur c. 35.*

Canon 33

Baptizati acatholici ad plenam communionem cum Ecclesia catholica convenientes proprium ubique terrarum retineant ritum eumque colant et pro viribus observent, proinde ascribantur Ecclesiae sui iuris eiusdem ritus salvo iure adeundi Sedem Apostolicam in casibus specialibus personarum, communitatum vel regionum.

There is no difficulty with the requirement that faithful of eastern non-catholic churches observe and retain their rite because there is a definite similarity of traditions between the catholic and non-catholic communities. However, the presumption that all Protestants have some kind of affiliation with the Roman tradition of the Latin Church is highly questionable. Therefore, these persons or communities should be free to select the autonomous church they want to enter when coming into full communion with the Catholic Church.

If a Protestant marries a Maronite Catholic and desires to become a Catholic, is it logical for the legal fiction to be created wherein the Protestant is received into the Latin Church and then transfers to the Maronite Church? It is important that the future Code resolve this question because in the United States, the Protestants constitute the majority and intermarriage is not rare.

Proposed Text:

§1. Baptizati acatholici *orientali* ad plenam communionem cum Ecclesia catholica . . .

§2. *Integrum est ceteri baptizati seligere quamcumque Ecclesiam sui iuris.*

Canon 36

Omnis ascriptio alicui Ecclesiae sui iuris vel transitus ad aliam Ecclesiam sui iuris in libro baptizatorum adnotetur; si vero fieri non potest, in alio documento in archivo paroeciali vel curiae eparchialis asservando.

This canon should include the stipulation that the transfer of membership should be recorded in the parish of baptism. Such an arrangement would facilitate location of the information in the future.

Proposed Text:

Omnis ascriptio alicui Ecclesiae sui iuris vel transitus ad aliam Ecclesiam sui iuris *adnotetur in libro baptizatorum paroeciae apud quem baptismus adnotatus est;* si vero . . .

Canon 47 *et passim*

Nomine Sedis Apostolicae vel Sanctae Sedis in hoc Codice veniunt non solum Romanus Pontifex, sed etiam, nisi ex rei natura vel sermonis contextu aliud apparet, Dicasteria aliaque Romanae Curiae instituta.

The See of Rome is not the only see which can bear the title "apostolic." Admittedly the term, "Apostolic See" or "Holy See" are technical terms employed not only in canon law but also in concordats, but a term should be found that is less offensive to the pride in apostolicity enjoyed by other autonomous churches. Preferable terms would be "Sede Romana" or "Prima Sede."

Canon 94 §2

Patriarcha curet, ut Episcopi eparchiales pastorali muneri fideliter satisfaciant et in eparchia, quam regunt, resideant; eorum zelum excitet; si in aliquo graviter offenderunt, eos consulta, nisi periculum in mora est, Synodo permanenti monere ne ommittat et, si monitiones optatum effectum non sortiuntur, rem ad Romanum Pontificem deferat.

Neglect or misconduct on the part of an eparchial bishop should not be immediately referred to the Roman Pontiff. Rather, the principle of subsidiarity should be applied whereby the case is referred to the synod of bishops which is the superior tribunal of the patriarchal church (cf. c. 1077, §1). There is always the possibility of recourse to the Roman Pontiff.

Proposed Text:

Patriarcha curet, ut Episcopi eparchiales pastorali muneri fideliter satisfaciant et in eparchia, quam regunt, resideant; eorum zelum excitet; si in aliquo graviter offenderunt, eos consulta, nisi periculum in mora est, Synodo permanenti monere ne ommittat et, si monitiones optatum effectum non sortiuntur, *ad Synodum Episcoporum rem deferat, salvo recursus Episcopi admoniti ad Romanum Pontificem cum effectu suspensivo.*

Canon 139

Episcopus eparchialis, qui extra fines territorii propriae Ecclesiae patriarchalis potestatem suam exercet et ad nullam provinciam pertinet, aliquem Metropolitam consulto Patriarcha et cum approbatione Sedis Apostolicae designet; huic Metropolitae competunt iura et obligationes, de quibus in can. 133, nn. 3-6.

With the exception of the Ukranian and Ruthenian jurisdictions, the current situation of eastern catholic hierarchies established outside the territorial boundaries of the patriarchal church does not lend itself to the metropolitan system: there are usually only one or two bishops of a certain autonomous church in a country. They would naturally be obliged to select a bishop of another autonomous church to be the metropolitan. To appoint a Latin bishop as metropolitan will cause confusion since the latin bishops are quite often not familiar with the circumstances, history, mentality, or traditions of the eastern churches.

Titulus IV
De Ecclesiis patriarchalibus

Caput VIII
De territorio Ecclesiae patriarchalis atque
de potestate Patriarchae et Synodorum extra hoc territorium

Canon 146

§1. Territorium Ecclesiae, cui Patriarcha pareest, ad illas regiones entenditur, in quibus ritus eidem Ecclesiae proprius servatur et Patriarcha ius legitime acquisitum habet provincias, eparchias necnon exarchias erigendi.

§2. Si quod dubium de finibus territorii Ecclesiae patriarchalis exoritur aut si de immutatione finium agitur, Synodi Episcoporum est rem investigare audita superiore auctoritate uniuscuiusque Ecclesiae sui iuris cuius interst, necnon re in eadem Synodo discussa petitionem apte instructam de dubio solvendo vel de finibus immutandis ad Romanum Pontificem porrigere, cuius solius est dubium authentice dirimere vel decretum de immutatione finium ferre.

Canon 147
Intra fines territorii Ecclesiae, cui praeest, potestas Patriarchae ac Synodorum exercetur non tantum in omnes christifideles eidem Ecclesiae ascriptos, sed etiam in ceteros, qui Episcopum eparchialem propriae Ecclesiae in eodem territorio constitutum non habent quique, etsi propriae Ecclesiae permanent ascripti, curae Hierarcharum loci eiusdem Ecclesiae patriarchalis committuntur firmo can. 912, §5.

Canon 148
§1. Patriarchae ius et obligatio est circa christifideles, qui extra fines territorii Ecclesiae, cui praeest, commorantur, opportunas informationes exquirendi etiam per Visitatorem a se de assensu Sedis Apostolicae missum.

§2. Visitator, antequam suum munus init, horum christifidelium Episcopum eparchialem adeat eique nominationis litteras exhibeat.

§3. Visitatione peracta Visitator ad Patriarcham relationem mittat, qui re in Synodo Episcoporum discussa Sedi Apostolicae opportuna media proponere potest, ut ubique terrarum tuitioni atque incremento boni spiritualis christifidelium Ecclesiae, cui praeest, etiam per constitutionem paroeciarum ac exarchiarum vel eparchiarum propriarum provideatur.

Canon 149
Candidatos, saltem tres, ad officium Episcopi eparchialis, Episcopi coadiutoris vel Episcopi auxiliaris extra fines territorii Ecclesiae patriarchalis implendum Synodus Episcoporum eiusdem Ecclesiae ad normam canonum de electionibus Episcoporum eligit et per Patriarcham Romano Pontifici ad nominationem proponit secreto servato ad omnibus, qui quomodolibet electionius exitum noverunt.

Canon 150
§1. Episcopi extra fines territorii Ecclesiae patriarchalis constituti habent omnia iura et obligationes synodalia ceterorum Episcoporum eiusdem Ecclesiae firmo can. 102, §2.

§2. Leges a Synodo Episcoporum latae et a Patriarcha promulgatae, si liturgicae sunt, ubique terrarum vigent; si vero disciplinares sunt vel si de ceteris decisionibus Synodi agitur, vim iuris habent intra fines territorii Ecclesiae patriarchalis.

§3. Velint Episcopi eparchiales extra territorium Ecclesiae patriarchalis constituti legibus disciplinaribus ceterisque decisionibus synodalibus, quae eorum competentiam non excedunt, in propriis eparchiis vim iuris tribuere; si vero hae leges vel decisiones a Sede Apostolica approbatae sunt, ubique terrarum vim iuris habent.

Perhaps the most difficult question facing the PCCICOR is the question of the authority of patriarchs and patriarchal synods beyond the territorial boundaries of the patriarchal church. After all of the consultation and criticism presented concerning the provisions of the 1984 *Schema Canonum de Constitutione Hierarchica Ecclesiarum Orientalium,* it is surprising that there is no substantial change in this area in the 1986 text.

There are a few factors which make it difficult to arrive at a solution to the problem which is satisfactory for everyone.

The first of these factors is that a Code, by its very nature, is intended to enjoy a certain permanence. The provisions which it makes are intended to remain in effect for a rather long period. It might be better for the PCCICOR to consider that the evolution which has taken place in the eastern catholic churches during the past twenty years is dramatic and all of the ramifications are not yet ascertained. Perhaps a definite, permanent canonical arrangement cannot be made at this time. The Code could feasibly make provisions concerning patriarchal/synodal jurisdiction with the understanding that these provisions will be evaluated and modified if deemed necessary after a certain period. Such an arrangement is admittedly not consistent with the canonical tradition of the Church, but it could alleviate many difficulties.

Secondly, it is the mandate of the PCCICOR to revise the Code of Eastern Canon Law in light of the Second Vatican Council. This mandate not only gives the PCCICOR a goal to reach, but also apparently places a restriction on the proposals which can be made: it seems that the proposals can go no further than those made by the Second Vatican Council. The Council already addressed the matter of the hierarchies established outside the patriarchal territories in *Orientalium Ecclesiarum* n. 7:

> Wherever a prelate of any rite is appointed outside the territory of his patriarchate, he remains attached to the hierarchy of his rite, in accordance with canon law.

Specific canonical arrangements were later formulated in a decree of the Cong. for the Eastern Churches on March 25, 1970.[4] The 1984 Draft and the 1986 Draft have simply codified the provisions of the conciliar and post-conciliar decrees.

It should be recalled that the PCCICOR is the only real forum where there can be any effective discussion concerning the relationship between the patriarchs/synods and the hierarchies established outside the land of origin.

---

[4] *AAS* 62 (1970):179. Translation in *CLD* 7:9.

The question of patriarchal/synodal authority beyond the historical boundaries of the patriarchal church requires a response which is established on sound ecclesiological and practical principles.

Certain ecclesiological principles must be taken into consideration:

1. *Authority of the Roman Pontiff*—By virtue of his Petrine Office, the Roman Pontiff enjoys supreme, full, immediate and universal power over the universal church. (c. 42) If the future Eastern Code grants to the patriarchs and synods the full jurisdiction over the clergy and faithful of their respective autonomous churches throughout the world, the Roman Pontiff still retains the doctrinal right to intervene in any matters he deems appropriate. (There are recent incidents of intervention in the affairs of the patriarchal churches even within the territory.) Therefore, the accordance of jurisdiction to patriarchs/synods over the entire autonomous church will not exclude the influence of the Roman Pontiff from the affairs of the eastern catholic churches.

2. *The Right of Self-Governance*—The authority of the patriarchs/synods should conform to the generic title of their churches which they govern: Accordance of the status of *sui iuris* should entail the recognition of the right of self-governance in all matters excepting those which necessarily are reserved to the Roman Pontiff and the ecumenical councils or to those specific cases wherein it is not feasible for the superior authorities of the autonomous church to exercise overall governance.

3. *Inherent Ecclesial Unity*—Membership in an autonomous church is not altered because of re-location. A member of the Maronite Catholic Church retains membership in that same church no matter where he/she resides. A person is to do all that is humanly possible to observe the rite of his/her church.[5] If a person retains membership in an autonomous church wherever he/she is in the world, why should the person leave the jurisdiction of the church when he/she crosses a line of demarcation? Has the Church adopted too broadly the civil notion of territoriality in the determination of jurisdiction? Should not a sense of "ecclesial communion" be permitted to surmount any geographical boundaries?

Ecclesiastical administration is not based solely on theoretical ecclesiological principles; certain pragmatic factors must also be taken into account. As will be seen, some of these factors do not favor an all-encompassing recognition of patriarchal/synodal authority. Certain restrictions will be required.

Some of the pragmatic considerations are as follows:

1. In the establishment of eastern catholic hierarchies outside the historical boundaries of the patriarchal churches, it is very important that the Roman Pontiff be directly involved since the process involves arrangements with the local Latin

---

[5] "Finally, each and every Catholic, as also the baptized members of any non-Catholic church or community who come to the fullness of Catholic communion, must retain each his own rite wherever he is, and follow it to the best of his ability. . ." *OE* n. 4. See also *Draft* c. 39.

hierarchy. The prestige and support of the Roman Pontiff is often required for the eastern catholic hierarch to obtain the cooperation that is required. The prestige and power of the See of Rome cannot be employed only at the convenience of the eastern catholic churches. These churches must defer to the authority of Rome when it is a matter of the common good.

2. The Church must be careful not to place an administrative burden on the patriarchs/synods which they are unable to bear due to a lack of personnel or means. Some of the patriarchal churches find themselves in circumstances which prevent rapid communication. In certain matters, it is not practical for the patriarchs to exercise authority over the hierarchy established outside the historical boundaries.

3. The local hierarchs must not be subject to undue interference. There is quite often a difference in mentalities and culture which make universal application of certain synodal legislation impossible. The Code must prevent abuse in this area. As mentioned above, there is always recourse to the Roman Pontiff.

4. The eastern catholic churches are at a crucial point in their history. In the homeland, they are beset with religious and political persecution. In the land of the emigration, they face many difficulties which oppose the preservation of their identity. If the Code effectively partitions these churches, history will be a harsh judge.

5. If certain fundamental modifications are not made, the provisions of the Code will be viewed as obnoxious by any non-catholic churches or communions which might consider communion with the Catholic Church. No religious authority will consider full communion with the See of Rome if they are obliged to submit to such a partition of authority.

In consideration of the above factors, I propose that the following approach be taken:

The future Code should recognize patriarchal/synodal jurisdiction over the clergy and faithful of the autonomous church throughout the world excepting in those matters determined by the canons or which the Roman Pontiff reserves to himself subsequent to the promulgation of the Code. This is precisely the opposite of the approach taken in the *Schema,* which restricts the authority of the patriarch within the historical boundaries except in those cases wherein the canons grant him the authority.

Further, if a patriarchal synod makes a decision which is within its competency, but which the hierarch established outside the historical boundaries finds impossible or impractical to implement, this same hierarch should at first state his objection to the synod and request an exemption. (The formal presentation of an objection should be required since exemption should be an exception to the rule rather than the rule.) If the synod rejects the request and the hierarch continues in his opposition, suspensive recourse can be made to the Roman Pontiff.

The proposal which is stated above requires a substantial modification of the canons. It will not be practical for me to attempt to indicate every canon wherein modification will be required.

One point should be reiterated: The proposed canonical relationship is admittedly not a perfect solution. Perhaps any solution should be considered as an *ad hoc* until we have a clearer understanding of the way things will develop.

Canon 198

Episcopi eparchialis est in tota eparchia sacras functiones celebrare, quae secundum praescripta librorum liturgicorum ab ipso omnibus insignibus pontificalibus induto sollemniter perficiendae sunt, non vero extra fines propriae eparchiae sine expresso vel saltem rationabiliter praesumpto Episcopi eparchialis consensu.

There is a problem with bishops coming into an eparchy, pontificating and collecting funds, and attempting to confer sacred orders without even notifying the local eparchial bishop of their presence. Sometimes this is done in local Latin parishes, thus avoiding the jurisdiction of the eparchial bishop. In order to address the matter, the phrase "vel saltem rationabiliter praesumpto" should be omitted.

Art. II
De iuribus et obligationibus Episcoporum eparchialium

Reference to the administration of temporal goods should be made somewhere in this section.

Canon 200

Episcopi eparchiales plurium Ecclesiarum sui iuris in eodem territorio potestatem suam exercentes curent, ut collatis consiliis in periodicis conventibus unitatem actionis foveant et viribus unitis communia adiuvent opera ad bonum religionis expeditius promovendum et ad cleru disciplinam efficacius tuendam.

The canon should not restrict itself to vigilance over the discipline of the clergy; the bishops should also oversee all ecclesiastical discipline:

Proposed Text:

Episcopi eparchiales plurium Ecclesiarum sui iuris in eodem territorio potestatem suam exercentes curent . . . ad bonum religionis expeditius promovendum et ad disciplinam *ecclesiasticam* efficacius tuendam.

Canon 204

§1. Episcopus eparchialis intra fines territorii Ecclesiae patriarchalis potestatem suam exercens tenetur singulis quinquenniis relationem Patriarchae facere circa statum eparchiae sibi concreditae secundum modum a Synodo Episcoporum statutum; exemplar relationis Episcopus quam primum ad Sedem Apostolicam mittat.

§2. Ceteri Episcopi eparchiales singulis quinquenniis eandem relationem Sedi Apostolicae facere debent et, si de Episcopis alicuius Ecclesiae patriarchalis vel Ecclesiae metropolitanae sui iuris agitur, exemplar relationis

Patriarchae vel Metropolitae quam primum mittant.

It would be better to have all of the eparchial bishops send a report in a form approved by Rome to the patriarch and the Apostolic See at the same time.

Proposed Text:

Episcopus eparchialis tenetur singulis quinquennis relationem Patriarchae et Sedi Apostolicae facere circa statum eparchiae sibi concreditae secundum modum a Synodi Episcoporum statutum et a Sede apostolica approbatum.

Canon 208 §1

Episcopus eparchialis, qui septuagesimum quintum annum aetatis explevit aut ob infirmam valetudinem aliave gravi de cause officio suo implendo minus aptus evasit, rogatur, ut renuntiationem ab officio exhibeat.

In its attempt to respect the dignity of the eparchial bishop, the phraseology in the canon is almost exhortative. It is better than the canon express in unequivocal terms the will of the legislator. There is always the possibility of not accepting the resignation if it is not deemed opportune; however, at the age of seventy-five a resignation should be submitted in order to evaluate the situation. This will result in unnecessary confusion and confrontations.

Proposed Text:

Episcopus eparchialis, qui septuagesimum quintum annum aetatis explevit aut ob infirmam valetudinem aliave gravi de cause officio suo implendo minus aptus evasit, *enixe* rogatur, ut renuntiationem ab officio exhibest.

Canon 209 §1

Episcopus eparchialis, cuius renuntiatio ab officio acceptata est, titulum Episcopi emeriti eparchiae, quam regebat, obtinet atque habitationis sedem in ipsa eparchia servare potest, nisi certis in casibus ob specialia adiuncta a Sede Apostolica vel, si de eparchia intra fines territorii Ecclesiae patriarchalis sita agitur, a Patriarcha de consensu Synodi Episcoporum aliter providetur.

A retired bishop should not be able to establish residence in another eparchy without the permission of the eparchial bishop of the place.

Canon 278 §1

Paroecia regulariter sit territorialis, quae scilicet omnes complectatur christifideles certi territorii; si vero de iudicio Episcopi eparchialis consulto consilio presbyterali id expedit, constituantur paroeciae personales ratione nationis, linguae, ascriptionis christifidelium alii Ecclesiae sui iuris immo vel alia definita ratione determinatae.

For the eastern catholic churches in the United States, parishes are usually established in consideration both of personal status (membership in an autonomous church) and in consideration of territory. Quite often the considerations of territory are not strictly applied, because the boundaries are difficult to determine.

This canon should not give priority to territoriality, but equate personality and territoriality as factors in the determination of a parish.

Proposed Text:

Paroecia est territorialis et personalis, scilicet complectatur christifidelium certi territorii ratione ascriptionis Ecclesiae sui iuris, nationis, linguae vel aliae definitionis.

Canon 282 §4

Parochus in suo officio stabilis est, quare ad tempus determinatum ne nominetur, nisi agitur de sodali insitituti vitae consecratae, de candidato, qui ad hoc scripto consensit, de casu speciali, quo in casu requiritur consensus collegii consultorum eparchialium, aut si ius particulare propriae Ecclesiae sui iuris id permittit.

While the *Praenotanda* of the 1984 *Schema Canonum de Constitutione Hierarchica Ecclesiarum Orientalium* indicated that the system of benefices was going to be abandoned or at least reformed (p. 18), the 1986 *Schema* still apparently presumes that pastors have a "right" to a parish. A priest has a right to support and a position in the Church (cf. c, 388, §1); he should not have a right to any specific parish. However, this canon indicates that the pastor is almost permanent in his office. Cc. 1411-1415 ("De modo procedendi in translatione parochorum") make it difficult to transfer a priest; cc. 1403-1410 make it very difficult to remove a pastor from office. Consequently, permanence and not simply stability are the effects of the provision.

While there must be a certain stability in the administration of a parish, the periodic transfer of pastors is beneficial for the priest, the pastor and the eparchy. Certain pastors desire to be transferred periodically; where will they go and who will replace them if the eparchial bishop is obliged to wait for a resignation or death? It should be lawful to appoint a pastor for a period of time. To do otherwise will inevitably create disputes and scandal in the Church.

Canon 293

In paroecia habeantur ad normam iuris particularis propriae Ecclesiae sui iuris opportuna consilia ad res pastorales et oeconomics tractandas.

The law regulating the parish council should not be articulated in the law of the autonomous church, but should be eparchial law. The situations in the various eparchies of an autonomous church can be quite different.

Proposed Text:

Curet episcopus eparchialis ut in paroecia habeantur ad normam iuris propriae eparchiae opportuna consilia ad res pastorales et oeconomicas tractandas.

Canon 320

§1. Patriarchae, Metropolitae Ecclesiarum metropolitanarum sui iuris, Episcopi eparchiales et, si statuta ita ferunt, etiam ceteri Hierarchae loci plurium Ecclesiarum sui iuris, etiam latinae, in eadem natione vel regione potestatem suam exercentes ad periodicos conventus statis temporibus convocandi sunt a Patriarcha aliave auctoritate a Sede Apostolica designata, ut communicatis prudentiae et experientiae luminibus et collatis consiliis sancta fiat ad commune Ecclesiarum bonum virium conspiratio, qua unitas actionis foveatur, communia opera iuventur, bonum religionis expenditius promoveatur atque disciplina ecclesiastica efficacius servetur.

§2. Decisiones huius conventus vim iuridice obligandi non habent, nisi de iis agitur, quae nulli possunt esse praeiudicio ritui uniuscuiusque Ecclesiae sui iuris vel potestati Patriarcharum, Synodorum, Metropolitarum atque Consiliorum Hierarcharum atque simul saltem per duas ex tribus partibus suffragiorum membrorum voto deliberativo fruentium latae necnon a Sede Apostolica approbatae sunt.

§3. Decisio, etsi unanimo suffragio facta, quae quomodocumque competentiam huius conventus excedit, omni vi caret, donec ab ipso Romano Pontifice approbata est.

§4. Unusquisque conventus Hierarcharum plurium Ecclesiarum sui iuris sua conficiat statuta, in quibus foveatur, quatenus fieri potest, etiam participatio Hierarcharum Ecclesia catholica; statuta, ut valeant, a Sede Apostolica approbari debent.

The canon seems to be creating the counterpart of the episcopal conferences in the Latin Code. However, it does not adequately address the situation of eastern catholic bishops established outside the territorial boundaries. It seems to address the situation of the localities where the eastern catholic bishops are the majority.

It should be recalled that the Latin Code (c. 450, §1) treats eastern catholic bishops as exceptions to the rule, asserting that they can be invited to attend with only a consultative vote unless the statutes stipulate otherwise.

On the other hand, they are excluded from participating in the conventions described in this canon since they do not exercise authority in the locale (cf. §1).

What is in mind of the legislator is this matter? Should the eastern catholic bishops enjoy a deliberative vote in the local episcopal conferences or does the future Code intend for the eastern catholic bishops to establish their own conventions, distinct from the episcopal conferences of the Latin Church?

Canon 324

Clerici in gradibus ordinis ipsa sacra ordinatione constituuntur; potestatem autem regiminis exercere non possunt nisi ad normam iuris.

The canon creates too much of a dichotomy between the *potestas ordinis* and the *potestas regiminis*. Since the phrase "potestatem autem regiminis exercere non possunt nisi ad normam iuris" was employed rather than "ad exercitium autem potestatis regiminis requiritur canonica provisio ad normam iuris,"[6] the

---

[6]*Nuntia* 20 (1985): 66.

canon can indicate that neither the *potestas ordinis* nor the *potestas regiminis* can be exercised except in accord with the norm of law.

Proposed Text:
Clerici in gradibus ordinis ipsa sacra ordinatione constituuntur; potestates autem *ordinis* et regiminis exercere non possunt nisi ad normam iuris.

Canon 371

Dum ubique permagni faciendus est clericorum caelibatus propter regnum coelorum delectus et sacerdotio tam congruus, prout fert universae Ecclesiae traditio, item status clericorum matrimonio iunctorum Ecclesiae primaevae et saeculari traditioni Ecclesiarum orientalium praxi sancitus in honore habendus est.

The inclusion of the phrase "item status clericorum iunctorum Ecclesiae primaevae et saeculari traditioni Ecclesiarum orientalium praxi sancitus in honore habendus est" has caused much discussion among the Latin and eastern bishops in the United States as to whether the December 23, 1929, prohibition[7] against married eastern catholic clergy serving in North, Central and South America, and Australia would be abrogated in virtue of c. 6 1° ("abrogatae sunt omnes leges iuris communis vel iuris particularis, quae sunt canonibus Codicis contrariae aut quae materiam respiciunt in Codice ex integro ordinatam").

It is my opinion that the current provisions of the *Draft* do not abrogate the provisions of the 1929 decree since the question of where married clergy can lawfully exercise their ministry is not one that is treated in the *Draft*. One can hardly conclude that the mere reference to the honor which is due to the state of married clergy completely regulates the matter of clerical celibacy.

To say that the provisions of the *Draft* do not abrogate the 1929 prohibition is not to say that it should not be abrogated. The Code should include the provision that the competent authority of the autonomous church is to determine if there is to be a married clergy and any restrictions which might be imposed concerning the exercise of their ministry.

Perhaps the most effective manner to support this proposal is to address the obstacles which stand in the way of the abrogation of the 1929 prohibition:

1. Some assert that a married priest would be the source of scandal to the clergy and faithful (especially those who are members of the Latin Church). When the prohibition was imposed, this was perhaps the case, but the experience of married deacons and the converted Anglican priests have acquainted the clergy and faithful with married men in the priesthood. If we are to take c. 371 at face value, that is, if we truly accept the assertion that the status of married clergy is to be honored, then the possibility of "scandal" is eradicated.

2. Some eastern catholic bishops do not want married priests serving in their eparchies because of the administrative difficulties which will arise as a conse-

---

[7] *AAS* 12 (1929) p. 9 ff.

quence. It must be admitted that certain problems will arise. Appointments and transfers of clergy are already the sources of considerable problems. Taking into account the needs of spouses and children will further complicate the process. However, the lifting of the prohibition will not require eparchial bishops to ordain married men or to permit them to exercise their ministry in their eparchies. It will be left to the discretion of the eparchial biship in a manner similar to determining the necessity of married deacons.

Certain eastern catholic bishops desperately need priests and are most willing to have married priests serve in their eparchies. To deprive communities of priests because of the celibacy requirement will be detrimental to the future of many eastern catholic churches in the United States.

3. Perhaps the greatest obstacle to the possibility of married priests serving in the United States are the difficulties such an arrangement would cause for the Latin Church, with its long-standing tradition of mandatory celibacy. From the various statements of the Roman Pontiff, it is apparent that this venerable tradition is to be upheld. Therefore, how can the Catholic Church deal with the situation of married (eastern catholic priests) and celibate (Latin catholic) priests exercising their ministry in the same territory? Will not the candidates who are subject to the Latin dioceses transfer membership to eastern catholic jurisdiction simply to be able to marry?

It is likely that certain individual cases will occur. However, the provisions of the future Code concerning transfers of membership (c. 30) will allow for the local hierarchies and the Apostolic See to address abuses and intervene when necessary. I also offer the conjecture that an abrogation of the 1929 prohibition will not result in an avalanche of requests for a transfer of membership. The institution of the married diaconate has existed in both the Latin and eastern churches in the United States for more than a decade and we do not suffer from a super-abundance of qualified candidates.

4. Some assert that some localities such as the United States are regions of the latin church, and, therefore, the eastern catholic clergy must observe the discipline of the Latin church. Beyond being offensive, such an assertion is incorrect in consideration of *PA* c. 303, §1 3º, whose provisions stipulate that the United States is an eastern territory since eastern catholic hierarchies are established.

Rome should refrain from maintaining the prohibition against married eastern catholic priests, because the existence of such a prohibition unjustly portrays the Roman See as a tyrannical authority which disregards the legitimate traditions and rights of eastern catholic churches. Such an image is detrimental to any ecumenical efforts.

Canon 602

Ad Episcopos praesertim in Synodis coadunatos, singulariter vero ad Sedem Apostolicam pertinet integritatem et unitatem fidei bonosque mores auctoritative promovere, custodire et religiose defendere, etiam reprobando, quatenus opus est, sententias, quae eisdem contrariae sunt, vel monendo de iis, quae eadem in discrimen ponere possunt.

Some of the autonomous churches do not have synods. Reference should be made to the council of hierarchs.

Proposed Text:

Ad Episcopos praesertim in Synodis *vel Consiliis* coadunatos, singulariter . . .

Canon 680

Filii, qui decimum quartum aetatis annum nondum es pleverunt, baptizari debent secundum praescripta liturgica Ecclesiae sui iuris, cui ad normam iuris ascribendi sunt.

All persons—not just persons under the age of fourteen—must be baptized according to the liturgical prescriptions of the autonomous church.

Proposed Text:

Baptismus celebratur secundum praescripta liturgica Ecclesiae sui iuris, cui ad normam iuris *baptizandus ascribendus est.*

Canon 691

Ex Ecclesiarum orientalium traditione chrismatio sancti myri sive coniunctim cum baptismo sive separatim ministratur a presbytero.

For the sake of precision, the canon should also include the bishop as an ordinary minister of chrismation.

Proposed Text:

Ex Ecclesiarum orientalium tradition . . . cum baptismo sive separatim ministratur *ab episcopo aut presbytero.*

Canon 704 §2

Iusta de causa remota tamen christifidelium admiratione alterius Ecclesiae sui iuris vestibus liturgicis et pane uti licet.

The provision of this canon allows for liturgical experimenation, syncretism, and even abuse. The canon should restrict wearing vestments or the use of haristic bread of another autonomous church to those cases of concelebration or when their own vestments or bread are unavailable.

Canon 744

In aliena eparchia Episcopus prohibetur sacram ordinationem celebrare sine licentia Episcopal eparchialis, nisi ius particulare alicuius Ecclesiae patriarchalis, ad Patriarcham quod attinet, aliud statuit.

There have been cases wherein an eastern catholic bishop has attempted to ordain someone to the priesthood in his own rite in a Latin church without the permission of the local eastern catholic bishop. The canon should clearly prohibit such abuses.

Proposed Text:

In aliena eparchia *etsi in locis alterius Ecclesiae sui iuris,* Episcopus prohibetur . . .

Canon 749
Sacram ordinationem valide suscipere potest solus vir baptizatus et sancto myro chrismatus.

Is it necessary to require chrismation under the pain of validity? RCIC c. 1033 requires confirmation only for the sake of lawfulness. Perhaps there are even doctrinal ramifications with this requirement.

Canon 750
Episcopus eparchialis et Superior maior nonnisi gravissima de causa, etsi occulta, possunt diacono sibi subdito ad presbyteratum destinato ascensum ad ipsum presbyteratum interdicere, salvo iure recirsus ad normam iuris.

It is appropriate that a man should not be ordained a deacon if there are doubts about his vocation or suitability for ministry. However, some problems appear only after a person is ordained a deacon and exercises the ministry. The phrase "nonnisi gravissima de causa" requires too much of an eparchial bishop who deems it necessary to refuse to advance someone to priesthood. This bishop should be able to act "gravi de cause." A mistake can have been made in ordaining the man to the diaconate, but the eparchial bishop should be free to remedy the situation.

Canon 775
In matrimonio ineundo interpartem catholicam et partem baptizatam acatholicam aut partem non baptizatam, quod attinet ad impedimenta, quae non sunt iuris divini, ius proprium utriusque partis servetur, nisi iuri divino contrarium est.

The canon fills a *lacuna* in canon law, insofar as it determines what laws must be observed in mixed marriages. However, the canon creates one difficulty which must be addressed by the Code. What if the laws governing both of the parties cannot be observed? For example, according to the law of the Coptic Orthodox and Ethiopian Orthodox Churches, a person who marries a member of these churches must become a member of the Coptic or Ethiopian Church. These churches do not permit their faithful to marry someone who is not a member of their church. Another case would be that according to Islamic law a Moslem woman can validly marry only a Moslem man.

The recognition of the laws of other communities is admirable, but a canonical solution should be provided in cases such as those mentioned.

Canon 801
Cum persona abducta vel saltem retenta intuitu matrimonii cum ea celebrandi matrimonium valide celebrari non potest, nisi postea illa ab abducente vel retinente separata et in loco tuto ac libero constituta matrimonium sua sponte

eligit.

The provisions of this canon seem to consider the possibility of a man being kidnapped or retained. This is not the case in RCIC c. 1089. Does the canon intend to introduce this innovation?

Canon 826 §2

Matrimonium coram sponsi parocho celebretur, nisi vel ius particulare aliud fert vel iusta causa excusat.

The phrase "vel iusta causa excusat" effectively takes all the strength out of the canon. If it is necessary, particular law can allow for the marriage to be celebrated in the parish of either the groom or the bride, but the common law should stipulate that the marriage is to be celebrated in the parish of the groom.

Canon 829

Dispensatio a forma iure praescripta reservatur Sedi Apostolicae vel Patriarchae, qui eam ne concedat nisi gravissima de cause.

Dispensation from canonical form in mixed marriages should not be restricted to the Apostolic See or the patriarch. While all of the eastern catholic faithful should be strongly urged to observe the eastern catholic form of marriage, situations in which this is pastorally difficult are not rare. Like the local Ordinary in the Latin Code (RCIC c. 1127, §2), the eparchial bishop should enjoy the power to grant a dispensation when necessary. The *Draft* already grants the eparchial bishop the power to grant a dispensation from canonical form in certain cases: cc. 844 and 848 allow for an eparchial bishop to grant a radical sanation in cases which are invalid due to a defect of form.

Proposed Text:

§1. Dispensatio a forma iure praescripta pro matrimonio duorum catholicorum Apostolicae Sedi vel Patriarchae reservatur, qui eam ne concedat nisi gravissima de cause.

§2. Si graves difficultates formae iure praescriptae servandae obstent, Episcopo eparchiale partis catholicae dispensandi ab eadem in singulis casibus competit, et salve ad validitatem aliqua publica forma celebrationis.

§3. Iure particulari uniuscuiusque Ecclesiae sui iuris statuatur normas, quibus praedicta dispensatio concordi ratione concedatur.

Canon 843 *et passim*

Matrimonium invalidum vel nullum ob defectum formae, ut validum fiat, celebrari denuo debet forma iure praescripta.

The phrase "matrimonium invalidum vel nullum" seems to be redundant. Is there a reason for such a distinction?

Canon 921 2º

Episcopi eparchialis est consulto collegio consultorum eparchialium illas personas iuridicas supprimere, quas ipse erexit, nisi ab auctoritate superiori approbatae sunt.

In consideration of the role given to the presbyteral councils and the eparchial consultors (cf. cc. 262-269), it would seem more appropriate that the presbyteral councils rather then the college of consultors be consulted.

Canon 1410 §2

Si vero de infirmo agitur, qui ex domo paroeciali sine incommodo non potest alio transferri, Episcipus eparchialis eidem relinquat eius usum, etiam exclusivum, eadem necessitate durante.

The provisions of this canon can cause grave difficulties in the administration of an eparchy: a priest can claim that he is ill and unable to move and, consequently, the eparchial bishop is obliged to allow him the use—even the exclusive use—of the rectory. Instead of allowing him the use of the rectory, the eparchial bishop should be obliged to provide him with a dignified residence and support. (Cf. c. 209 §2 for retired bishops.)

Canon 1411-1415

1411—Si bonum animarum vel Ecclesiae necessitas aut utilitas postulat, ut parochus a sua, quam utiliter regit, ad aliam paroeciam aut ad aliud officum transferatur, Episcopus eparchialis eidem translationem scripto proponat ac suadet, ut pro Dei atque animarum amore consentiat.

1412—Si parochus consilio ac suasionibus Episcopi eparchialis obsenqui non intendit, rationes scripto exponat.

1413—Episcopus eparchialis, si non obstantibus allatis rationibus iudicat a proposito non esse recedendum, cum duobus parochis ex coetu, de quo in can. 1405, §1, selectis rationes perpendat, quae translationi favent vel obstant; si vero exinde translationem peragendam censet, paternas exhortationes parocho iteret.

1414—§1. His peractis, si adhuc et parochus renuit et Episcopus eparchialis putat translationem esse faciendam, hic decretum translationis ferat statuens paroeciam elapso determinato die esse vacaturam.

§2. Hoc tempore inutiliter transacto Episcopus eparchialis paroeciam vacantem declaret.

1415—In casu translationis serventur can. 1410, iura quaesita et aequitas.

One must always recognize the dignity of the office of pastor, but the provisions of this article can create grave difficulties and scandals in the Church, especially the eastern catholic churches in this country. If the eparchial bishop is obliged to propose and persuade a pastor in writing (c. 1411), the unwilling pastor will immediately take the case to the faithful who will initiate a campaign against the bishop. Any action subsequent to that will be performed in an atmosphere of confrontation and polemic.

Any eparchial bishop should be free to appoint a pastor for a certain period of time (cf. above, c. 282, §4). This will eradicate any expectations of a permanence on the part of the pastor or the parochial community.

THE CANON LAW SOCIETY OF AMERICA
MINUTES OF THE FORTY-NINTH ANNUAL MEETING

October 12-15, 1987
Hyatt Regency Hotel
Nashville, Tennessee

Monday, October 12, 1987

Reception 3:30 p.m.-5:00 p.m.

New members and others interested in organizations in the Canon Law Society of America were welcomed by the President, Richard Cunningham, who introduced some of the CLSA officers and chairpersons of CLSA committees. The Vice-President, Leonard Scott, also welcomed the guests and invited everyone to become part of CLSA projects and committees.

Opening Prayer Session 5:00 p.m.

The CLSA Liturgy Committee planned and led the membership in an opening prayer session.

Opening General Session 5:30 p.m.

Stanley Teixeira, General Convention Chairperson, called the Convention to order and announced all the sessions and seminars at this year's Convention would be non-smoking. He then introduced President Richard Cunningham. President Cunningham welcomed the general membership to the first session of the Forty-Ninth Annual Meeting of the Canon Law Society of America. He introduced the Most Reverend James D. Niedergeses, Bishop of Nashville. Bishop Niedergeses opened the meeting with a prayer and welcomed the Convention to Nashville.

President Cunningham introduced the President of the Canadian Canon Law Society, Bernard Prince; the President of the Canon Law Society of Great Britain and Ireland, David Cousins; the Secretary of the Pontifical Commission for the Authetic Interpretation of the Code, Julian Herranz; and other dignitaries.

The President then presented the keynote speaker, Ann Rehrauer, of Green Bay, Wisconsin, who delivered the Keynote Address entitled, "Diocesan Synods."

Reception 7:00 p.m.

Hosted by The Canon Law Society of America.

Tuesday, October 13, 1987

Black/Hispanic Caucus   8:00 a.m.

Liturgy Opportunity   8:00 a.m.

Seminars   9:00 a.m.-10:30 a.m.

1. "Instituted Lay Ministry: The History and Future of Canon 230," presented by Thomas Richstatter.

2. "Ecumenical Questions in the New Code," presented by Royce R. Thomas.

3. "NCCB Implementation of the Code," presented by Donald E. Heintschel.

4. "Lay Persons in the Diocesan Curia: Legal Structures and Practical Issues," presented by Rosemary Smith, S.C.

5. "The Permanent Diaconate: A Commentary on Its Development from the End of the Second Vatican Council to the 1983 *Codex Iuris Canonici*," presented by Richard J. Lyons.

6. CLSA Scholarship Fund Hearing, reported by William Schumacher.

7. "Deference or Neutral Principles: The Dual Approach by Civil Courts to Ecclesiastical Disputes," presented by Peter M. Shannon, Jr.

8. "Canon 1098 of the Revised Code of Canon Law: Key Points and Questions in Its Historical Development and Interpretation," presented by Kevin W. Vann.

Liturgy Opportunity   11:00 a.m.

Women's Caucus   12:00 p.m.

Seminars   2:00 p.m.-3:30 p.m.

1. "Secular Institutes: Can They be Both Clerical and Lay?" presented by Sharon L. Holland, I.H.M.

2. "Issues in Sacred Orders," presented by David M. Hynous, O.P.

3. "Religious Issues of Dissolution, Mergers, Aggregation," presented by Ellen O'Hara, C.S.J.

4. "Civil and Canonical Liability for Lay Ministers," presented by Melanie DiPietro, S.C.

5. "The Economic Pastoral: Foundation in the Church's Mission; Challenges for the Church's Life," presented by the Most Reverend John J. Myers.

6. "Presbyteral Councils and Colleges of Consultors: Current Law and Some Diocesan Statutes," presented by James H. Provost.

7. "Synodal Governance in Eastern Catholic Churches," presented by J. D. Faris.

8. "Clerical Misconduct: Canonical and Practical Consequences," presented by John G. Proctor, Jr.

Open Hearing on the Budget and Resolutions 4:00 p.m.

Wednesday, October 14, 1987

Seminars 9:00 a.m.-10:30 a.m.

The topics listed for Tuesday morning were repeated by the same presenters except the CLSA Scholarship Fund Hearing was not repeated.

Annual Business Meeting 11:00 a.m.-1:00 p.m.

Richard Cunningham, President of the Canon Law Society of America, called the Business Meeting to order and led the members in prayer. President Cunningham explained the meeting would be conducted according to Robert's *Rules of Order,* with John Proctor of San Diego acting as parliamentarian during the first part of the discussion of the resolutions. During the rest of the discussion, Richard Cunningham would serve as parliamentarian. He pointed out the separate seatings for active and associate members. The President invited a motion to permit non-voting members the privilege of addressing the assembly. Dennis Burns of Boston so moved, and August Moretti of Los Angeles seconded the motion. It was passed unanimously.

President Cunningham announced the Business Meeting, as with all sessions of this General Convention, was non-smoking. He requested that individuals go to the microphone when they wished to address the assembly.

Announcements from the General Convention Chairperson

Stanley Teixeira, General Convention Chairperson, made the following requests of the membership: (1) Please turn in the Convention critique forms before leaving on Thursday; (2) All old and new members of the Board of Governors should see him at the end of this meeting; (3) The Judicial Vicars of the New York Province will meet for lunch later today at one of the hotel restaurants; (4) All newly-elected and continuing members of the Board of Governors, as well as all those involved in the liturgy, should meet at four o'clock this afternoon in the Ballroom; and (5) The Wednesday afternoon seminars begin at two-thirty and not two o'clock to allow for more time for lunch.

Minutes

The President indicated that the Minutes of the last Business Meeting would be read unless he heard a motion to accept the Minutes as published in the *Proceedings of the Forty-Eighth Annual Convention.* Several members moved to accept the Minutes as published and many seconded the motion; the motion passed.

Elections

President Cunningham called on Patricia McGreevy, Chairperson of the Committee on Membership and Nominations. Patricia referred the membership to the Committee's report in the Convention Booklet. She pointed out the forms in the convention packet on which to nominate individuals for committees and positions on the Board of Governors. Patricia presented the list of candidates for each position on the Board of Governors, asking each nominee to stand:

Office of Vice President
  Paul Golden of Chicago, Illinois
  Sidney Marceaux of Beaumont, Texas

Office of Secretary
  John Bell of Dallas, Texas
  Lynn Jarrell of Evansville, Indiana

Office of Treasurer
  Royce Thomas of Little Rock, Arkansas

Office of Consultor
  John Amos of Mobile, Alabama
  Raymond Burke of LaCrosse, Wisconsin
  J. James Cuneo of Bridgeport, Connecticut
  Barbara Ann Cusack of Skokie, Illinois
  Frank Wallace of Los Angeles, California
  Daniel Ward of Collegeville, Minnesota

President Cunningham opened the floor for further nominations for any of the positions on the Board of Governors. There were no further nominations and the nominations were closed. President Cunningham directed the membership which ballots to use at this time and the procedure on tie votes. The balloting began.

President's Report

President Cunningham referred the membership to the reports contained in the Convention Booklet from him, the Executive Coordinator and all the CLSA committees. He then called on the Treasurer for his report.

Treasurer's Report

Royce Thomas explained the "General Ledger Program" for the IBM/36 has been introduced into the CLSA computer and is functioning. As a result of the CLSA Investment Policy and the recommendations of the Board of Governors Budget Committee, the funds are in the process of being transferred from Merill Lynch to the Christian Brothers Investment Service.

The budget report is as it is usually reported, with a few changes. The category of "Receivable" is an addition to the CLSA budget. Under "Receivables," he had these comments. A large percentage of the membership has not paid dues as of this date. The Inventory is down. The Quasi-Endowment Fund has grown by $15,000 this past year. Under "liabilities," the Deferred Revenues refer to monies which the CLSA has collected in the past but cannot be used until this fiscal year, such as fees for pre-convention workshops and membership fees for this year. Under "Accounts Payable," the General Operations cover salaries to be paid out and bills yet to be paid on the *1986 Proceedings*. There is still a large amount of royalties being paid to the Vatican since many copies of the 1983 Code are being sold. The Scholarship Fund has grown significantly because of the fund-raising efforts, headed by William Schumacher, this past year.

Under "Income," the amount of Interest is down because it was applied to the Scholarship Fund since most of the money earning interest was from the Scholarship Fund. The amount of income from royalties is down since there has not been a best-seller. Under "Expenses," most of the line items are under the budgeted amount except for two categories. "Scholarship Maintenance" is over due to the Scholarship Fund-Raising Campaign to the membership this past February. "Membership Services" were over budget, especially because of an increased cost in printing and mailings to the membership.

Under "Conventions," an average expense is developing for the Annual Convention. It is not known yet what the cost will be for the Nashville Convention. Under "Workshops," the members were encouraged to consider sponsoring in their geographical regions the workshops which the CLSA already has packaged.

The report of the Treasurer was accepted by the membership and President Cunningham thanked him for his work.

Report on the Work of the Project Co-Directors of the Scholarship Fund

William Varvaro, one of the Co-Directors of the Scholarship Fund, briefly explained the present status of the work on the Scholarship Fund. He asked the membership to assist in providing: (1) Names of individuals who could give a large donation; (2) Names of individuals who would be willing to serve as area coordinators of this next phase of the fund-raising effort (asking major donors to contribute); and (3) A personal donation to the Scholarship Fund (even if previously donated). He recognized these individuals who have already agreed to serve as area coordinators:

> Vincent A. Tartarczuk of Falmouth, Maine
> David P. Bailey of Brighton, Massachusetts
> Anthony C. Diacetis of Albany, New York
> Michael C. Connolly of Wilmington, Delaware
> Cora Marie Billings of Richmond, Virginia
> Dennis C. Klemme of Venice, FLorida
> Rose McDermott of Philadelphia, Pennsylvania
> James L. Ruef of Columbus, Ohio
> Michael J. Rosswurm of Ft. Wayne, Indiana

John Quinn of Chicago, Illinois
Bobby D. Hajovsky of Austin, Texas
John J. Hedderman of Salt Lake City, Utah
Rita Jensen of Seattle, Washington
Harmon D. Skillin of Stockton, California

President Cunningham thanked the Project Co-Directors, William Varvaro and James Coriden, for their work and all those individuals willing to serve as area coordinators.

Resolutions

President Cunningham explained the procedure for introducing new resolutions. He then opened the floor for new resolutions. No new resolutions were submitted.

John Renken, Chairperson of the Resolution Committee, presented the following resolutions to the membership.

Resolution One

The following revisions in the original Resolution were introduced by the Resolution Committee in light of the discussion at the Hearing on Tuesday:
1. Item #2 under the first "Be it resolved" as added.
2. Item #3 under the first "Be it resolved" was previously Item #2 in the original Resolution.
3. Item #4 under the first "Be it resolved" was previously Item #3 in the original Resolution.

John Huels of Chicago asked for the reason for the above changes in the Resolution. John Renken explained the revisions resulted from the consensus of the discussion at the Hearing. A vote was taken and the revisions were accepted by over two-thirds of the membership.

The following Resolution was then moved by the Resolution Committee:
Be it resolved that:
   Article III of the present CLSA Constitution be revised to read:
   Members are those who have currently paid their annual dues or are not more than two years in arrears.

   1. Without prejudice to the status of persons who are members at the time of the adoption of this article ACTIVE membership is open to those who have earned at least a licentiate in Canon Law.

   2. Active membership is also open in the future to other practitioners in Canon Law who demonstrate a broadly based competence in canonical issues, and who have fulfilled the stipulated requirements established by the Board of Governors as enumerated in the By-Laws.

   3. ASSOCIATE members are any others who wish to associate themselves with the purposes of the Society.

   4. HONORARY members are:

       a. *ex officio* all the Most Reverend Bishops of the United States, and

       b. those persons by reason of outstanding contributions in the field of Canon Law or in support of the Society, are proposed for this distinction of honorary membership by the Board of Governors and accepted by a majority vote of the active members at a General Meeting. Such elected honorary members shall be considered active members in good standing but shall not be required to pay annual dues.

Be it further resolved that:

    The following revisions be made to reflect the change in Article III:
- 1,c. Committee on Nominations
- 2,d. Committee on Nominations
- 5. Committee on Nominations
- 5.b. To propose for approval of the Board of Governors applicants for active membership under Article III, No. 2, of this Constitution, and to propose for honorary membership in the Society those who, in its opinion, qualify according to Article III.

The Resolutions presented by the Committee do not need a second.

William Varvaro of Brooklyn spoke in favor of the Resolution. President Cunningham called for the vote, explaining a two-thirds majority vote was necessary on a Constitutional Amendment.

The Resolution was passed by the necessary two-thirds vote of the membership with some negative votes and some abstentions. President Cunningham explained the Resolution would become part of the CLSA Constitution at the close of the Forty-Ninth Annual Convention.

Resolution Two

    The following Resolution was moved by the Resolution Committee:
    Be it resolved that:

        The BOG present a By-Law regarding the stipulated requirements for active membership for approval by the membership of the CLSA in 1988.

William Varvaro of Brooklyn spoke in favor of the Resolution. John Alesandro of Rockville Center suggested the following possibilities for the criteria called for in the Resolution: (1) Other ecclesiastical degrees or other degrees parallel to or complementary to a J.C.L.; (2) Publication in the field of Canon Law but not holding a canonical degree; (3) Considerable experience (of at least five years) in the field of Canon Law; (4) Associate members for a period of time and contributions to the CLSA through workshops and other ways; (5) Other ways of distinction in some recognizable form.

The Resolution was passed by a majority vote of the membership with some negative votes and abstentions.

Resolution Three

The following Resolution was moved by the Resolution Committee:
Whereas:
The CLSA has initiated and effected a Scholarship Fund; and
Whereas:
The membership of the CLSA has ordered the BOG to establish a Board of Trustees to administer the Scholarship Fund (Resolution 6 of the 1985 Convention);
Be it resolved that:
The BOG establish a Board of Trustees to administer the Scholarship Fund of the Society;
Be it further resolved that:
The make-up of the Board of Trustees consist of five (5) individuals, three (3) of whom must be active members of the CLSA; that care should be taken that any members of the Board of Trustees who are not members of the CLSA be drawn from a broad geographic base or from corporate and public service areas of the community; and that the project director(s) of the Scholarship Fund shall always be non-voting member(s) of the Board of Trustees, in addition to the five (5) appointed members.
Be it further resolved that:
The CLSA President appoint the Board of Trustees in accordance with the above criteria in varying terms, of one, or two, or three years initially, the terms of office thereafter to be for three years.
Be it further resolved that:
The function and basic responsibilities of the Board of Trustees are to conserve, invest and disperse the monies of the Scholarship Fund.

John Folmer, of San Francisco and member of the Board of Governors Committee which submitted the Resolution, spoke in favor of the Resolution and explained the Resolution no longer contains the idea of incorporation, as originally presented at the Hearing on Tuesday. James Provost of Washington, D.C., questioned the meaning of the term Project Directors and their role. Leonard Scott of Camden explained the Project Director(s) are to try to solicit donations from major donors. James Provost then asked if the Board of Trustees will select the scholarship recipients. Leonard Scott answered the Board of Trustees will authorize the disbursement of the money. As a result of this explanation, James Provost proposed an amendment of the last "Be it further resolved" by adding this phrase after the last word in the sentence: "according to the criteria established by the Society." John Folmer seconded the amendment.

Barbara Ann Cusack of Chicago and Milwaukee asked how this amendment fits in with the Scholarship Selection Committee proposed by the Criteria Committee under Resolution Five. William Schumacher of Chicago replied to the question by saying it has not been determined who will do the selecting of recipients.

James Coriden of Washington, D.C., asked for clarification on whether the amendment means the Board of Trustees will do the selecting. James Provost answered in the negative, saying the amendment means the Board of Trustees will be bound by the criteria established by the Society but not will necessarily do the selecting itself. The amendment passed.

John Alesandro of Rockville Center proposed an amendment in the first "Be it resolved" clause as follows: change "Board of Trustees" to "Committee." It was seconded. Thomas Malloy of Rockville Center agreed with the amendment. Robert Becker of Chicago asked if the amendment would leave the Board of Governors the option to choose to name the committee a Board of Trustees. John Alesandro answered affirmatively. The amendment was passed.

The vote then was taken on the amended Resolution and the Resolution passed almost unanimously.

Resolution Four

The following resolution was moved by the Resolution Committee:
Whereas:
The CLSA has recommended to diocesan bishops and to major religious superiors that they encourage, sponsor, and support suitable Black and Hispanic Catholics to study canon law for an academic degree (Resolution 6 of the 1984 Convention); and
Whereas:
The CLSA has gone on record as supporting affirmative action programs which promote equal opportunity for Asians, Blacks, Hispanics, Native Americans, and women and has included the principles for affirmative action in the report on "Canonical Standards in Labor-management Relations" (Resolution 12 of the 1986 Convention); and
Whereas
The CLSA is presently determining the criteria for receiving a CLSA scholarship;
Be it resolved that:
The BOG see to it that affirmative action, as supported by the CLSA Resolution 12 of the 1986 Convention, be included in the criteria for receiving CLSA scholarships; and
Be it further resolved that:
The Affirmative Action Plan of the NCCB, as outlined in the CLSA's "Report on Canonical Standards in Labor-Management Relations" be applied to the granting of CLSA scholarships.

Dennis Burns of Boston reminded the membership that the original idea for the Scholarship Fund was to aid blacks, Hispanics, women, or any lay person who is not able to obtain funding. This is as opposed to those individuals being sent from dioceses experiencing financial difficulties.

The Resolution was passed almost unanimously.

Report on Elections

Before beginning discussion on Resolution Five, the tellers had completed counting the ballots. Patricia McGreevy, Chairperson of the Committee on Membership and Nominations, reported 137 ballots were needed to be elected. The results of the balloting were as follows:

Office of Vice President
   271 ballots were cast.
   164 Paul Golden (elected)
   106 Sidney Marceaux
     1 Abstention

Office of Secretary
   272 ballots were cast.
    92 John Bell
   180 Lynn Jarrell (elected)

Office of Treasurer
   272 ballots were cast.
   262 Royce Thomas (elected)
     9 abstentions
     1 invalid

Office of Consultor
   273 ballots were cast. There was one blank ballot.
   113 John Amos
   132 Raymond Burke
   187 James Cuneo (elected)
   163 Barbara Cusack (elected)
    78 Frances Wallace
   127 Daniel Ward

For the third Consultor, a run-off vote took place between Raymond Burke and Daniel Ward, the two with the highest number of votes who has not received an absolute majority on the first ballot. Patricia McGreevy returned after Resolution Eight was passed with the results of the run-off.

Office of Consultor
   256 ballots were cast. There was one blank ballot.
   124 Raymond Burke
   132 Danial Ward (elected)

This completed the elections and President Cunningham thanked the members of the Committee on Membership and Nominations for their work.

Resolution Five

The following Resolution was moved by the Resolution Committee:
Whereas:
   The Canon Law Society of America has committed itself to establish a scholarship fund to assist in the canonical training of those who are

needy; and
Whereas:
Funds have already been collected; and
Whereas:
Criteria for the dispersement of these funds are needed;
Be it resolved that:
The report of the Committee on Scholarship Criteria be adopted as the policy of the CLSA.

Paul Golden, Chairperson of the Scholarship Criteria Committee, pointed out changes which were made in the Committee's report in the Convention Booklet after the discussion at the Hearing on the Resolutions on Tuesday. Otto Garcia of Brooklyn asked for clarification in the proposed criteria on what canonical status means. Sharon Holland of Washington, D.C., explained the intent of the two sub-points was to prevent any distinction between clerical and law. She did express her concern that the expansion of the criteria to include doctoral students get started. James Provost of Washington, D.C., made a friendly amendment in #2 of the Committee's proposed criteria, changing "Board of Trustees" to the "Committee responsible for the Scholarship Fund." The friendly amendment was accepted.

The Resolution was passed almost unanimously.

Resolution Six

The following Resolution was moved by the Resolution Committee:
Whereas:
The CLSA Task Force to Survey Due Process Experience, mandated by the Board of Governors in keeping with a resolution from the 1983 CLSA Annual Meeting, has completed its work and published the results (see *Due Process in Dioceses in the United States 1970-1985* [Washington: CLSA, 1987]); and
Whereas:
The Task Force, in collaboration with experienced personnel from various Due Process Offices around the country, has dveloped a series of recommendations as a result of its work (see "Recommendations" in Final Report contained in the Committee Reports for 1987 Annual Meeting);
Be it resolved that:
The Canon Law Society of America receives and accepts the recommendations from its Task Force to Survey Due Process Experience; and
Be it further resolved that:
The Board of Governors shall see to the implementation of these recommendations.

James Provost of Washington, D.C., urged implementation of the recommendations of the report. The Resolution was passed almost unanimously.

Resolution Seven

The following Resolution was moved by the Resolution Committee:
Whereas:
> The members of the Symposium on the Laity mandated by the Board of Governors has been held and has published the results of its work in *The Jurist* (47 [1987] 1); and

Whereas:
> The members of the Symposium, after careful research and consideration, have submitted recommendations to the CLSA for further research (no. 18 in the final statement of the Symposium, "Laity in the Renewing Church: Vision and Opportunities");

Be it resolved that:
> The CLSA receives and accepts the recommendations to the CLSA from its Symposium on the Laity; and

Be it further resolved that:
> The Board of Governors shall see that the research identified in these recommendations be pursued, and shall report annually to the Society on the progress of this research.

James Provost of Washington, D.C., pointed out the Resolution calls for implementation of the recommendations of the of the Committee's report. The recommendations to the Synod on the Laity have already been conveyed to some of the participants in the Synod. The Resolution was passed almost unanimously.

Resolution Eight

The following Resolution was moved by the Resolution Committee:
Whereas:
> The severe shortage of priestly vocations is causing critical problems in our Church's ministry, despite the admirable efforts of myriad lay ministers; and

Whereas:
Approximately twenty-five married men have been ordained to the presbyterate in our country within the past few years; and
Whereas:
> The expansion of this policy of ordaining those who are already married may be one important element in solving the current crisis in ministry,

Be it resolved that:
> The Board of Governors commission a modest study of the present practice of ordaining married men, including the norms which have been issued by the Holy See, their implementation in the United States, the acceptance of the ministry of these married presbyters, and some suggestions as to how this practice might be reasonably extended; the Board

shall see to it that the study shall be completed within one year and its results communicated to the membership of the CLSA.

James Coriden of Washington, D.C., made an editorial change in the Resolution by adding the phrase, "to the Presbyterate" in the second line of the "Be it resolved" after "ordaining married men." John Faris of Brooklyn urged the study since such an inquiry is already taking place concerning the ordination of married men for certain Eastern Rite churches. He requested a change in the approach in the "Whereas" clauses of the Resolution to reflect how the ordination of married men has long been a part of the Catholic Church's tradition rather than to speak of ordaining married men since there is currently a shortage of priests.

William Stetson of Chicago spoke against the Resolution since the CLSA will be entering into a study of celibacy which has been forbidden. John Myers of Peoria spoke against the Resolution for these reasons: the content of the "Whereas" clauses is questionable; the study could present an air of dissension between the CLSA and the hierarchy of the Church; and the study has the possibility of invading the privacy of those individuals who are married clergy.

Frederick McManus of Washington, D.C., was in favor of the Resolution since it is a modest study and addresses an issue which did surface at the Synod of the Bishops. Patrick Cogan of New York City felt the issue had ecumenical ramifications and the study would be of value to the priority set by the CLSA to focus on ecumenism.

Thomas Malloy of Rockville Center spoke against the study because it is a way of looking for exceptions from the practice of the Latin Rite Church on celibacy when, at the same time, the Eastern Rite churches are forbidden to practice their tradition of having married clergy.

Dennis Burns of Boston reminded the assembly there have been many studies commissioned by the Society and none of these studies has bound the membership to abide by any unacceptable positions taken in the studies. Harmon Skillin of Stockton was in favor of the Resolution since the Resolution calls for a study which is the type of work a professional society should undertake. He went on to say it does not indicate arrogance or disrespect to undertake such a study.

Bennett Constantine of Lansing was against the Resolution since it uses the cover of a modest study to question celibacy being required for priesthood.

John Faris of Brooklyn proposed the deletion of the phrase "and some suggestions as to how this practice might be reasonably extended" from the "Be it resolved." The amendment was seconded. James Coriden of Washington, D.C., spoke against the amendment since it will inhibit the study. A vote by division was taken. The results were:

128 in favor of the amendment
78 against the amendment
30 abstentions

Joseph Zube of Peoria asked what modest means. James Coriden explained "quick and easy."

A vote was taken on the entire Resolution and the Resolution passed by a majority vote.

Resolution Nine

The following Resolution was moved by the Resolution Committee:
Whereas:
> The Board of Governors has submitted the report "Canonical Standards in Labor-Management Relations" in keeping with the mandate of the Forty-Second Annual Meeting of the CLSA in 1980,

Be it resolved that:
> The CLSA receive and adopt the report, "Canonical Standards in Labor-Management Relations;" and

Be it further resolved that:
> The report be communicated to the appropriate officials of the NCCB, various Catholic organizations and movements, and be made available for all other persons interested in labor and management relationships in the Catholic Church; and

Be it further resolved that:
> The Board of Governors begin the necessary steps to implement the second part of the 1980 mandate, namely "to propose to collaborate with the NCCB and existing Catholic agencies concerned with collective bargaining for the purpose of providing canonical expertise in the promotion of fair practice policies."

James Provost of Washington, D.C., requested a closing quotation be added after the end of the second "Be it further resolved." The Resolution was passed almost unanimously.

President Cunningham thanked the Resolution Committee for its work.

Old Business/New Business

President Cunningham reported on the progress by the CLSA to take control of the publication of the *Canon Law Digest* and to publish the next volume in the near future. President Cunningham then called for the adjournment of the Business Meeting and closed with prayer.

Seminars 2:30 p.m.-4:00 p.m.

The topics listed for Tuesday afternoon were repeated by the same presenters.

All-Convention Eucharistic Liturgy 4:30 p.m.

Principal Celebrant and Homilist: The Reverend Richard Cunningham, President, CLSA. The Officers of the Board of Governors were installed preceding the homily.

Reception 6:30 p.m.-7:30 p.m.

Host: The Most Reverend James D. Niedergeses, Bishop of Nashville, Tennessee.

Dinner 7:30 p.m.

President Cunningham thanked the outgoing members of the Board of Governors for their service and welcomed the newly-elected members. He also thanked those individuals who ran for office but were not elected and all those who served on CLSA committees and projects this past year.

Then the Vice-President, Leonard Scott, was called upon to speak. He praised the work done by President Cunningham and expressed his own readiness to serve as President of the Society in the upcoming year.

President Cunningham introduced James Coriden, the recipient of the "Role of Law Award." James Coriden presented three challenges to the CLSA in serving the American Church.

Thursday, October 15, 1987

Prayer Service 9:00 a.m.

Prepared and directed by the CLSA Liturgy Committee.

Closing General Session 9:30 a.m.

The Reverend Monsignor Julian Herranz, Secretary of the Pontifical Commission for the Authentic Interpretation of the Code, spoke on "The Personal Power of Governance of the Diocesan Bishop."

Lynn Jarrell, O.S.U.
Secretary

CITATION FOR THE ROLE OF LAW AWARD

RICHARD G. CUNNINGHAM

Each year, among its other responsibilities, the Board of Governors is charged with the pleasant duty of determining the recipient of our annual Canon Law Society of America Role of Law Award.

It is my privilege to announce that this year's recipient is Father James A. Coriden.

A priest of the Diocese of Gary, Indiana, Father Coriden attended St. Meinard's Seminary, received a Licentiate in Sacred Theology and a Doctorate in Canon Law from the Gregorian University, and a Doctor of Laws from The Catholic University's School of Law.

He has been admitted to practice before the bar of the Supreme Court of the State of Indiana, the Court of Appeals and the United States District Court of the District of Columbia, and the United States Court of Appeals of the District of Columbia Circuit.

Presently he serves as Academic Dean, Vice-President for Academic Affairs and Professor of Church Law at the Washington Theological Union.

Among the criteria of the By-laws of our Constitution for the Role of Law Award, a commitment to research and study by the recipient is to be evident.

In addition to teaching Canon Law courses in the Department of Canon Law and the Department of Religious Education at Catholic University, Jim has served also as Chairman of the Department of Theology and an associate professor in Catholic University's School of Theology. Among his many research and study contributions to the Canon Law Society of America, he has served as a member of our Committee for the Study of the Internal Forum and he has chaired and coordinated seven interdisciplinary symposia.

Another criterion for the Award requires that the recipient has faciliated dialogue and interchange of ideas within our Society and with other groups.

Jim has served as consultant to the United States Catholic Conference/National Conference of Catholic Bishops for their committees on a National Pastoral Council and Dialogue with the Women's Ordination Conference. As a member of the Canon Law Society for 26 years, he has served as Secretary/Treasurer and a member of the Board of Governors of our Society. He has presented seminars at our national conventions, keynoted the Regional Midwest Convention, offered workshops on the 1983 Code for diocesan officials and for bishops. He has given many talks to diocesan priests and religious men and women and a number of national professional organizations.

He has further facilitated dialogue and the interchange of ideas through his 20 year membership in the Canadian Canon Law Society, where he has presented a major paper; his 18 years as a member of the Catholic Theological Society of America, where he has chaired a committee and presented a workshop; his participation in 10 accreditation visits for the Association of Theological Schools of the United States and Canada; together with his membership in the International Association for the Promotion of the Study of Canon Lw, the Executive Committee of the Washington Theological Consortium and membership in a half dozen other professional societies.

A third criterion is that the recipient has participated in the Revision of Law. Jim has co-chaired our Task Force in the Revision of the Code, worked in the area of constitutional government for the Church, coordinated the English translation of the 1983 Code, co-edited the *Canon Law Society of America's Text and Commentary on the Code*, and authored the section on Book III, "The Teaching Office of the Church," an appropriate monument to his long, on-going interest, involvement and concern for education and the Church's teaching ministry in colleges and, especially, in theological education.

It is with the other two criteria, however, that Jim probably feels more at home, and, indeed, it is how we have come to know the authentic quality of the man. Those criteria are the recipient's practical response and assistance to the needs of other persons and his embodiment of pastoral attitude.

So many of us first met Jim Coriden because of his always generous response to our requests for his help. He has never hesitated to share with us his gifts, talents and expertise. His pastoral works in Gary, Indiana, included the parish, chancery, tribunal, Confraternity of Christian Doctrine and programs of Adult Education, together with liturgical, ecumenical and civic interests and efforts, and his work with the Indiana Catholic Conference.

We know and have been blessed by his strong pastoral sense. It is manifested in so many ways, as for example, in some of the titles of his over 40 publications: *The Primacy of the Person in the Church*, *We, the People of God*, *Human Rights in the Church; the Case for Freedom*, *Co-Responsibility*, and *Law in Service to the People of God*.

In so many areas and in so many ways, Jim has narrowed the gap between the abstractions of the law and the needs of persons. His pastoral and prophetic stands has both engaged us and outraged us. His ideas have ignited fires, illuminating for some, scorching for others. His tongue and his mind have kept him and us in motion, but always ultimately in the service of the Body of Christ, the Church. Jim is an individual; one who can never be taken for granted and a grateful Canon Law Society of America has no intention of doing that.

With much respect, admiration and appreciation, it is my honor to present, in the name of the members, the 1987 Role of Law Award from the Canon Law Society of America to Father James A. Coriden.

RESPONSE TO THE ROLE OF LAW AWARD

JAMES A. CORIDEN

The presentation of this award to me is vivid testimony that the Board of Governors has a sense of humor! The other lesson to be learned from it is that if you stay around long enough and persist in coming to the conventions, eventually they will give you a prize!

I am very grateful for this award, and I am deeply honored to accept it.

I would like to begin with two very personal and heartfelt remarks. First, I want to say thanks to you, my sisters and brothers of the Society, for all that you have done for me and meant to me over the years. Your trust and encouragement, your cooperation and collaboration have literally given me life. You invited me in on many projects, you tested and stretched and challenged me, and in doing so you have sustained and renewed me. It is no exaggeration to say that you have enlivened me over and over again. For all that I am more grateful than I can say.

I also want to apologize. I want to express my sincere regret to you, my brothers and sisters of the Society, whom I have offended over the years. My abrasive interventions and activist antics, amusing to some, have been offensive to others. I publicly beg your pardon.

On the occasion of the presentation of this award, we long-suffering conventiongoers have a right to expect an inspirational message, some carefully crafted poetic or philosophic discourse, something profound. I am sorry to disappoint, but what I have to present instead is an action agenda.

I suggest three items for that action agenda, for each of you personally and for the Society, as we enter into the celebration of our fiftieth year. I judge these three to be matters of urgency. I earnestly exhort you to *do* something about them. They are concerned with:

   1) due process in the local church,
   2) legitimate diversity of opinion,
   3) the structure of ministry.

1) *Due Process.* The report on due process which has been presented to the Society is in two parts. A set of more theoretical papers were published as the first issue of *The Jurist* for 1986. The second is now available from the office of the Executive Coordinator, *Due Process in Dioceses in the United States, 1970-1985* (edited by James H. Provost, 1987). I urge you to obtain and read a copy of this survey. It contains a wealth of information about the experiences with due process in dioceses and in religious communities. We adopted the recommendations from the report in this morning's business meeting, and we asked the Board of Governors to take action on them.

But the findings of the survey are truly shocking. The only fair conclusion to draw from the study is that due process does not exist in our church! As an available, operative reality it simply is not there. It really has not been tried.

The report finds that over 50% of the 185 dioceses in the U.S. have taken some action, have had some experience with due process. About 40% of them have processed at least one case in the fifteen year period covered by the report. But only twelve dioceses have averaged one or more cases per year! Six dioceses (St. Paul/Minneapolis, Cleveland, Seattle, Detroit, Rockville Centre, and Milwaukee) account for fully two-thirds of all cases (632 out of a total of 939). Only in those six jurisdictions does there appear to be a realistic possibility for conflict resolution or a suitable grievance procedure. The report also states that the most common obstacle to the effective utilization of due process is that the people don't know about it.

Coming as it does nearly twenty years after the Society's splendid work on the original *Due Process* report, which is still described as "state of the art" by practitioners, this survey report is sad and sobering.

I beg you to do something about it, to put it in place, to let our people know about it, to give it a chance to work.

Due process in in profound harmony with our tradition:

—Paul demanded of the church of Corinth, "Can it be that there is no one among you wise enough to settle a case between one member of the church and another?" (I Cor. 6, 5).

—The "due process" described in the Matthean church is another example: "If your brother or sister should commit some wrong against you, go and point out the fault, but keep it between the two of you . . . If he or she does not listen to you, summon another . . . If he or she ignores them, refer it to the church." (Mt. 18, 15-17.)

—A large part of the episcopal role, from the early fourth century on, was the peaceful reconciliation of disputes. The *audientia episcopalis* was very often spent trying to settle conflicts between parties (e.g., P. Brown, *Augustine of Hippo,* pp. 195, 226).

—All of the canonical collections, from the sixth century right up to the present day, include sections on the settlement of disputes through arbitration or other non-judicial means.

The revised Code of 1983 contains at least three explicit invitations to install and use "due process" mechanisms for the resolution of disputes and settlement of grievances, namely, canons 221 and 1446, 1713-1716, and 1733.

"Alternative Dispute Resolution," that is, the settlement of disputes through such means as negotiation, conciliation, mediation or arbitration, is coloring the legal landscape of our country like the changing leave of autumn. The applications of these procedures proliferate up and down the land. Two most recent examples are the provisions for arbitration in the proposed trade agreement between Canada and the U.S., and the attempt to settle the National Football League players' strike by means of arbitration.

The reasons for the acceptance and popularity of these procedures are many, e.g., they are cheaper and faster than court cases, more personal, less formal, and with results better adapted to the individual dispute, but the main reason is that they *work!* They really do settle disputes.

Peter Shannon reminded us, in the paper he presented at this convention, of another very persuasive reason for establishing and carefully following such procedures for resolving conflicts in the church: our civil courts will very often dismiss suits if the church has followed its own fair processes in dealing with complaints. Today, as in St. Paul's day, we are better off staying out of court!

(Resources: "Alternative Dispute Resolution in the Church," Coriden and Dye, *Canon Law Society Proceedings,* 1986, pp. 61-82; *Alternative Dispute Resolution: An ADR Primer* (American Bar Association, 1987); Bureau of National Affairs' *Alternative Dispute Resolution Report:* Washington, D.C. 20037.)

2) *Legitimate Diversity of Opinion.* The cold winds of repression are rising in our church. The pressures to conform are intensifying. The permissible scope of expression of diverse opinions—in matters which are not defined, not *de fide divina et catholica*—is being narrowed, straightened. The chilling effects of this trend are felt everywhere, from the groves of academe to the parish communion rail.

Pope John Paul stated a very rigorous position in his address to the American bishops in Los Angeles last month: "It is sometimes claimed that dissent from the magisterium is totally compatible with being a "good Catholic" and poses no obstacle to the reception of the sacraments. This is a grave error that challenges the teaching office of the bishops of the United States and elsewhere." (*Origins* 17:16, Oct. 1, 1987, p. 261.)

The inference seems to be that any dissent from the magisterium precludes one from being a "good Catholic" and sets up an obstacle to the reception of the sacraments. A position such as that, with no distinctions about the quality of the doctrine or the nature of the dissent, means that absolute conformity of views is necessary for full communion within our church. If that is the intended meaning, then the position is a dangerous innovation.

Our tradition permits diverse views. Historically, as Pope John XXIII frequently repeated, we ask for unity in essentials, but allow freedom in doubtful matters. The freedom of the act of faith, the primacy of conscience, and the powerful presence of the Holy Spirit in the community of the faithful—all these are basic to our beliefs. For that reason, over the centuries, we have developed a hierarchy of truths, a gradation of "theological notes" to indicate the relative importance or cenrality of the various doctrines of our faith. Any attempt to equate or homogenize all teachings into one, undifferentiated body of doctrine which must be accepted without qualification is simply wrong. It distorts our theological tradition.

These are disciplinary matters as well as doctrinal. The pope spoke not only of dissent, but also of the reception of the sacraments. We canonists need to attend to this issue. The Society, together with the Catholic Theological Society of America, in 1982 published a fine study, *Cooperation Between Theologians and the Ecclesiastical Magisterium* (ed., L. O'Donovan), and this November a set of procedures, from the same source, to resolve disputes between bishops and theologians is on the agenda of the NCCB.

More needs to be done. We must retrieve and maintain the best of our long tradition, canonical as well as theological, on legitimate disagreement and on access to the sacraments. The whole question of allowable diversity of views and the process of discernment in disputed cases needs more study and public discussion. I urge that we attend to this task together.

3) *The Structures of Ministry.* The eucharistic life of our people is being threatened by the dearth of priestly vocations and our refusal to do anything about it. Some are not even willing to speak openly about the real parameters of the problem and its perfectly possible solutions.

The Most Holy Eucharist is central to the faith and worship of Roman Catholic communities everywhere.

> The renewal in the Eucharist of the convenant between the Lord and humankind draws the faithful into the compelling love of Christ and sets them afire. From the liturgy, therefore, and especially from the Eucharist, as from a fountain, grace is channeled to us; and the sanctification of humankind in Christ and the glorification of God, to which all other activities of the Church are directed as toward their goal, are most powerfully achieved. (Second Vatican Council, *Const. on Sacred Liturgy,* par. 10.)

This vital eucharistic life of our people is being sacrificed on the altar of an exclusively male and celibate priesthood. There is an obvious and urgent need to respond to the present critical situation, yet we remain intransigent when it comes to considering changes in the qualifications for ordination to the priesthood. Celibacy is an excellent charism, a precious gift. But to continue to limit eucharistic leadership to celibate males when the charism is in persistently short supply, is to turn the church on its head. It risks distorting the worship of our communities. It puts the Christian life of the people at the service of ministerial structures, rather than the other way around. Ministry must be returned to the service of the people.

Pope John Paul, in a recent address, gave guidelines for Sunday celebrations without a priest—a situation faced by thousands of Catholic communities around the world every weekend. He spoke of a service of the Word followed by a distribution of Holy Communion reserved from previous eucharistic celebrations. Such pastoral accomodations are required, but it is also necessary to address the roots of the problem.

The qualifications for ordination are matters of ecclesiastical law, not of divine law. For example, the ordination of married men is our most ancient tradition, it has always been honored in the Eastern Church, and it has frequently been permitted for a variety of pastoral reasons in recent times in the Western Church. A return to that practice deserves most serious consideration.

We are canonical professionals who care desperately about the health and future of our church. We can and must search for, study out, propose and press for reasonable solutions to this critical problem of ministry and Eucharist. It is within our purview and it is our responsibility.

Those are the three items on my action agenda. They are complex and serious issues. I harbor no illusions about "quick fixes" or easy consensus. I hope, for the good of the church, that we can work on them together.

Thank you very much for this award.

HOMILY

October 14, 1987

RICHARD G. CUNNINGHAM

Luke 11:42-46

Considering the occasion for this Eucharistic celebration and the distinguished community gathered here, I can not imagine a more inappropriate Gospel reading than this one called for in the *Ordo*.

The Pharisees were a religious party whose members, because of their thorough knowledge and observance of the letter of the law, claimed superiority over the poor and the uneducated. Beyond themselves they believed Judaism could have no further development.

The lawyers mentioned in this Gospel were the Scribes, the legal scholars. The majority of them belonged to the Pharisee party. We have learned that many of them were vain and self-righteous, hostile to Jesus; and with the priests (the Sadducees, who were even more hostile) they plotted the death of Jesus because he was a threat to the integrity of the law, which they held to be the heart of Judaism.

Neither the *New Testament* nor the *Talmud* have much that is flattering to say about these Scribes, and especially about the Pharisees. And I have never heard a homily that has said anything good about them either. That, however, is not fair, nor just, nor merciful.

Among the lawyers, there was at least one who offered to follow Jesus, "wherever you go." Jesus approved the insight of another Scribe who asked, "Which is the first of all the commandments?" and Jesus told that lawyer he was not far from the kingdom of God. Those Scribes who were learned about God's kingdom were praised by Jesus, and some of the Scribes in turn praised Jesus for correcting the Pharisees. Other Scribes defended Paul. Obviously, then, there were some good ones.

The Pharisees, too. They were lovers of tradition, placing the same stress on its importance as we do. They also believed in the resurrection of the dead, unlike the priests who did not. After the Roman destruction of Jerusalem, it was the Pharisees who alone were responsible for the preservation of Judaism. Nicodemus, the Pharisee, was one of the few of Jesus' male followers to assist in the preparation of his body for burial. The Pharisee, Gamaliel, saved the apostles from being put to death. And Paul, of course, boasted that he was a Pharisee.

Clearly there were some Scribes and Pharisees you might have had to think twice about taking to lunch during Brotherhood Week, just as there were some you might have wanted to number among your friends. But maybe we are missing the point . . .

Considering the occasion for this Eucharistic celebration and the distinguished community gathered here, perhaps this is a most appropriate Gospel.

Jesus' words are addressed to all those who neglect justice, probably because they lack mercy and thus are failing in their love for God. I believe this to be the case because Jesus warned his followers, "You cannot even enter the kingdom of God unless your justice exceeds that of the Pharisees."

Apparently the Scribes and Pharisees should have known better. The Law and the Prophets were their inheritance, as well as the justice and mercy characteristic of them. Just as we should know better. The Gospel and Tradition are our inheritance, as well as the justice and mercy manifested by Jesus, in whose life justice and mercy are perfectly balanced.

Jesus calls us to be just and merciful by recognizing in ourselves and others our oneness as human persons; our common blood line as children of God; our solidarity in sinfulness, and thus the need each one of us has for forgiveness and healing, for justice and mercy.

It is our glory as human persons to be called to understand and appreciate this . . . and our gift as Christ-followers and Canon Lawyers to be given the vocation and opportunity to live it.

CONTRIBUTORS TO *PROCEEDINGS*

James A. Coriden, S.T.L., J.C.D., J.D., is Vice President for Academic Affairs, Academic Dean and professor of canon law at the Washington Theological Union, Washington, D.C.

Richard G. Cunningham, J.C.D., is professor of canon law at Saint John's Seminary, Brighton, Massachusetts and at Pope John XXIII National Seminary, Weston, Massachusetts. He is President of the Canon Law Society of America.

Melanie DiPietro, S.C., J.C.L., J.D. is associated with the firm of Mansmann, Cindrich and Titus, Pittsburgh, Pennsylvania.

John D. Faris, J.C.O.D., is chancellor of the Diocese of Saint Maron, Brooklyn, New York and adjunct professor of Eastern Canon Law at The Catholic University of America, Washington, D.C.

Donald E. Heintschel, J.C.D., is associate general secretary of the National Conference of Catholic Bishops and the United States Catholic Conference, Washington, D.C.

Julian Herranz, J.C.D., is secretary of the Pontifical Commission for the Authentic Interpretation of the Code of Canon Law, Rome, Italy.

Sharon Holland, I.H.M., J.C.D., is assistant professor of canon law at The Catholic University of America, Washington, D.C.

David M. Hynous, O.P., J.C.D., is vice-chancellor of the Archdiocese of Chicago.

Richard J. Lyons, J.C.L., is pastor of Saint John the Evangelist Parish, Dunellen, New Jersey and associate judicial vicar of the Tribunal of the Diocese of Metuchen.

John J. Myers, D.D., S.T.L., J.C.D., is coadjutor bishop of the Diocese of Peoria.

Ellen O'Hara, C.S.J., J.C.L., is director of the Tribunal of the Diocese of Boise.

Edward G. Pfnausch, J.C.L., is Executive Coordinator of the Canon Law Society of America, Washington, D.C.

John G. Proctor, J.C.L., is pastor of Corpus Christi Catholic Parish, Bonita, California.

James J. Provost, J.C.D., is assistant professor of canon law at The Catholic University, Washington, D.C.

Ann F. Rehrauer, O.S.F., J.C.L., is chancellor of the Diocese of Green Bay.

Thomas Richstatter, O.F.M., D.T.S., is associate professor of sacramental and liturgical theology at St. Meinrad Seminary, St. Meinrad, Indiana.

Peter M. Shannon, Jr., J.D., J.C.L., S.T.L., is a partner with Keck, Mahin and Cate, Chicago, Illinois.

Rosemary Smith, S.C., J.C.D., is assistant to the General Superior, Sisters of Charity of Saint Elizabeth, Convent Station, New Jersey.

Royce R. Thomas, J.C.L., is vicar general and judicial vicar of the Diocese of Little Rock and Treasurer of the Canon Law Society of America.

Kevin W. Vann, J.C.D., is parochial vicar of Blessed Sacrament Parish, Springfield, Illinois and judge and defender of the bond of the Diocese of Springfield.

Institute for Justice and Peace
Walsh College Canton, Oh 44720